Legal Writing

Legal Writing
Process, Analysis, and Organization

LINDA HOLDEMAN EDWARDS

Professor of Law
Director of Legal Writing
Mercer University

 ASPEN LAW & BUSINESS
Aspen Publishers, Inc.

Library of Congress Catalog Card No. 95-81927
ISBN 0-316-21240-7

Third Printing

MV-NY

Published by Aspen Law & Business
Formerly published by Little, Brown & Company

Printed in the United States of America

TO DAN

Words fail.

Summary of Contents

┌─────┐
│ I │   *The Process of Writing Predictively: The Office Memo*
└─────┘

II *The Process of Writing Persuasively: The Brief*

Contents

The Process of Writing Predictively: The Office Memo

II   *The Process of Writing Persuasively: The Brief*

Acknowledgments

No book is the product of the author alone; certainly this one is not. All of my Mercer colleagues have encouraged and supported this book from its inception. Their belief in the importance of legal writing has made all the difference. Mercer legal writing faculty, Kathy Sampson, Kevin Shelley, Greg Spicer, Stasia Williams, Lenora Ledwon, Gus Lehouck, David Walter, and Jim Hunt, have taught me much and have made the learning fun. Three deans, Phil Shelton, Dick Creswell, and Larry Dessem, have paved the way. Suzanne Cassidy, Sarah McPherson, Cary Gonzalez, Michelle Davis, and Jane Burns have served faithfully and without glory. Special thanks to Jack Sammons for bold ideas, to Hal Lewis and Reynold Kosek for wise counsel, and to Sidney Watson and Joe Claxton for their faith in the project.

Like all teachers of legal writing, I am blessed by being part of the national legal writing community. No list could identify all of the colleagues who have shared generously of their vision, enthusiasm, wisdom, and experience. I am especially indebted to Deirdre Alfred, Jan Armon, Mary Beth Beazley, David Drueding, Alice Dueker, K.K. Duvivier, Neal Feigenson, Dennis Hynes, Steve Jamar, Katie McManus, Phil Meyer, Teresa Phelps, Leslie Reed, and the anonymous Little, Brown reviewers who made such perceptive comments on earlier drafts. Particular thanks to Mary Lawrence, Richard Neumann, and Marilyn Walter for their steadfast support of their legal writing colleagues, including me.

I gratefully acknowledge my debt to Emilie and Katie Edwards for their forbearance; to Cathi Reinfelder for redeeming the text from many errors; to Carol McGeehan for nurturing and enlarging my vision of the book; and to Little, Brown and Company for its long-standing commitment to the teaching of legal writing.

And finally, heartfelt thanks to Professor Anthony G. Amsterdam, whose example has inspired a generation of lawyers and law teachers.

I would also like to thank the following copyright holder for permission to reprint the map of the federal judicial circuits:

1996 Judicial Staff Directory 537 (Ann L. Brownson ed., 10th ed. 1996). Copyright © 1996 by Staff Directories, Ltd. Phone: (703) 739-0900; W³ address: http://www.staffdirectories.com.

Introduction

Writing is a crucial lawyering skill, and one that many lawyers find difficult. This book aims to give you a plan, a writing process that can help you master each writing task. It also aims to give you the most help in the shortest number of pages. It is a basic, no-frills instruction manual for developing and organizing your legal analysis, communicating that analysis to a law-trained reader, and persuading a judge that your analysis is correct.

Another goal of the book is to teach you how to teach yourself. Your legal writing teacher will be your coach as you begin your study, but your teacher won't be with you on your first summer clerkship or after you graduate. As you practice using the tools the text introduces you will become your own teacher, and your writing will get better and better each year of your legal practice.

 ## LEGAL WRITING AS A PROCESS

Legal writing is a process with distinct stages and distinct goals at each stage. Each stage serves an important function as you work toward the goal of a finished document. This text identifies the four main stages of a writing task and invites you to use each stage, consciously and fully, as your writing tool. As the following paragraphs describe each stage, refer to the table of contents to identify the chapters that fall within each.

Your first job as a writer is working out your analysis of the issue, so the first two writing stages (Chapters 2 through 10) create a "working draft." Your primary purpose in writing a working draft is to use the writing process as your own analytical tool. Dean and former Judge Donald Burnett put it this way:

> Clear expression, then, is not merely a linguistic art. It is the testing ground for ideas. Through the discipline of putting an argument into words, we find out whether the argument is worth making. . . . The secret . . . is to start verbalizing early—while there is still time to learn from the discipline of forming ideas into words. You must begin by identifying your client's goal and the issues to be resolved. Each issue is defined by a cluster of facts and governing legal

principle. If you cannot articulate this nexus of law and fact, you do not yet have a grasp of the case.[1]

Your working draft is nothing less than "grasping the case." It guides, deepens, and tests your analysis in a number of ways, but its most important role is in forming your ideas into the kind of rule-based reasoning that lawyers must master. Rule-based reasoning applies the relevant legal rules to the client's facts. This kind of reasoning is not our culture's dominant mode of thought or expression. Many of us come to law school without much prior experience in this sort of reasoning. The discipline of the working draft will help you develop this vital lawyering skill.

After your analysis is solid, stage three converts that analysis into a document designed for your reader. The text first introduces the study of law-trained readers, a study you should pursue during your entire legal career. Then the text shows you how to select an organizational plan that will meet your reader's needs and achieve the document's goal. The third stage is completed by adding the other components of the document, including a statement of the relevant facts about your client's situation. In the fact statement you will use narrative techniques to tell your client's story. Effective and strategic narration requires skills different from the rule-based reasoning process you will be practicing when you write the legal analysis sections of your documents. The text will introduce you to the storytelling skills you'll need for good legal writing.

The final stage turns your attention to the fine points of writing, calling for decisions about style, tone, level of formality, and strategic word choice. It is also the stage for editing to achieve clarity and strength, correct citation form, punctuation, and grammar. These matters may seem like technicalities compared to the importance of accurate analysis, but grammar, style, and citation form are the most easily visible criteria for judging writing. Readers will notice these areas first and draw from them conclusions about the skill and care of the writer. A sloppy document invites a reader to doubt the document's substantive accuracy.

The book takes you through each of these four stages, and it introduces, in each stage, the information you'll need for that stage. Here are several hints for using this writing process to its greatest advantage:

First, be alert for signs that you need to revisit earlier stages. While the completed document should take the reader on a linear journey toward the document's conclusion, you will find that the *process* of creating the document is far from linear. Rather, the process is recursive; it requires you to circle back to earlier stages again and again as you understand more about your legal issue, your client's facts and goals, and the available legal strategies. The dynamic nature of this process is what makes it alive, challenging, and fun. Your willingness to construct, disassemble, and reconstruct your document will be crucial to achieving a good written product.

Second, compose with a word processor. Word processors make major structural revisions easier, less painful, and less time consuming. Don't expect good thinking and writing to come easily. They won't. But if you use a computer

---

1. Donald Burnett, *The Discipline of Clear Expression,* 32 The Advocate 8 (June 1989).

you will spend more of your time and energy doing the things that really count—improving your analysis, organization, and style—because the ease of manipulating your text gives you the freedom to take your text much farther along the road to good thinking and writing.

Third, experiment with different writing strategies and observe your own writing process. What works well for you at each stage and what doesn't? Do you work better if you dictate a draft first? Does free-writing help you? How about charts or colored pens? Each writer's creative and analytical processes are unique. Part of your goal in your first few years of legal writing should be to observe as much as you can about your own process so that you can adopt writing strategies that work for you.

Fourth, be patient. On your first few writing assignments, take each stage in its turn without trying to combine or compress them. Your goal on these first assignments is to let each stage of the writing process *teach* you some critical skills. Soon you will have developed those skills well enough to speed up each stage. For instance, you may find that you can accomplish the goals of the working draft stage with some other quicker form of prewriting, like a detailed and annotated outline. You will learn to customize each stage to fit your own skill level, the complexity of the assignment, and your own unique creative processes.

Finally, master the general principles before you decide to try something new. Learning legal writing is a little like learning music theory. In college, music students take many courses in music theory and composition. In these courses, they first learn the "rules"—the principles most composers use in most situations. Then after they understand those principles, they learn when and how to depart from them.

This is an introductory course on legal writing, so it teaches the basic substantive and organizational principles that operate in most situations. Following these organizational principles in your first legal writing assignments will teach you important information about law study and about legal writing. First master the basic substantive and organizational principles covered in this course. Soon you will develop the judgment to know when and how you can depart from them.

II TWO CAVEATS

First, in keeping with this book's straightforward goals, the text is written in an informal style. It uses contractions, speaks in the second person, uses images and analogies freely, tells stories, and occasionally attempts some humor. This conversational style would be inappropriate for court documents and other formal legal writing. However, this book is not written for judges or senior partners. It is written for new law students who must read and digest complex new material described in unfamiliar terms. The book's informality is designed to make its material as accessible as possible at a time when accessibility is at a premium.

Second, the book uses both feminine and masculine forms for general reference. Again, the reason relates to the book's goals. The book is designed for new law students, most of whom are encountering the study of law for the first time. For centuries the legal world was entirely male. Our "default" image of a lawyer is of a man. Today's practice of avoiding gender references, commendable as it is, does nothing to change that default image. It does nothing to remind us that lawyers come in both genders. It does nothing to welcome women to the study of law.

Because this book seeks to welcome both women and men to the study of law, it intentionally makes gender references. And to counteract the "default" image of a lawyer as male, it uses more feminine than masculine forms for general reference. Practitioner writing, however, has other goals. In practitioner writing, gender-neutral references are the appropriate choice. Chapter 15 will explain this concept and provide techniques for implementing it.

 III   **LAW STUDY AND IDENTITY**

As you have just learned, the practice of law will require skill in both rule-based reasoning and narrative reasoning. Rule-based reasoning values rational, analytical thought, while narrative reasoning values creative, intuitive thought. The best lawyers learn to integrate rule-based reasoning and narrative reasoning so they can harness the power of each.

Because narrative reasoning is more dominant in our culture than rule-based reasoning, however, the traditional law school curriculum concentrates on rule-based reasoning to the seeming exclusion of narrative. And because thought process is so fundamental to identity, law school's emphasis on rule-based thinking can be disturbing. During the first year of law study, many law students wonder whether they are losing vital parts of themselves. It seems as if the ways they have always thought and reacted are not valued in the law and indeed that law study is requiring them to become different people.

If this sounds like your experience, do not be discouraged. Not only will these other parts of yourself survive law school, but they will be vital to practicing law. They will deepen your analysis and strengthen your persuasion. They will serve you in other important lawyering tasks too, such as counseling clients, working with witnesses and other third parties, presenting oral arguments to judges and juries, putting together business transactions, and resolving disputes outside the courtroom.

Perhaps this analogy will help: A tennis player needs both a good forehand and a good backhand. For most beginning players, the backhand stroke feels awkward and weak. It is hard to control and nearly impossible to accomplish with any real power. The stroke feels awkward because it requires a movement not common to the player's pre-tennis way of moving. The only solution is practice, especially concentrated backhand practice. A partner or coach hits to the player's backhand over and over. Surely a beginning player could begin to wonder whether tennis is the sport for her, especially if she had to hit almost entirely with her backhand for months and months.

Law school is a little like that tennis player's experience. Because its primary task is teaching the skills required for basic competence in legal analysis, much of what you do will focus on linear, rule-based thinking. If you have not already developed your skills in that mode, you sometimes may feel as if you are hitting backhand shots day in and day out. You may wonder whether the law is for you. Try to remember that real lawyering will require skill in both the linear and the narrative modes. That way you can practice the one without fear of losing the other.

Legal Writing

First Things First

Before you begin to draft your first legal writing assignment, take a moment to consider yourself, your role and professional responsibilities, and the nature of the authorities you will be working with.

 ## I WHO ME? A WRITER?

Most students entering law school would not call themselves writers; nor would they say that in three years they plan to take a job as a professional writer, earning a significant part of their income by writing documents that will be published in one form or another. Yet, that is precisely what lawyers do. Most lawyers write and publish more pages than most novelists, and with greater consequences hanging in the balance.

It is important to realize now that you are preparing to be a professional writer, even if you don't think your skills yet justify the title. Why does this realization matter and matter now? It has to do with the way you approach law school and especially your legal writing courses. If you think of yourself as a writer working on ways to improve your own craft, you will find it much easier to internalize and retain the skills you're learning. You'll find yourself noticing good and bad writing everywhere you look, and imagining ways to improve it. You'll take the time to look up a pesky grammar rule in a grammar handbook, and you'll probably incorporate that rule into your writing from then on. You'll be more willing to revise and edit.

In other words, good writing will be important to you and you'll believe that it is within your grasp. In the long run, your determination to write well will make more difference in the quality of your writing than will your entry-level writing skills.

◆ II ◆ PREDICTING VERSUS PERSUADING — UNDERSTANDING YOUR ROLE

A lawyer's writing differs significantly depending on the kind of document the lawyer is writing. So we need to distinguish between two of a lawyer's roles and between the two most common documents the lawyer writes while performing those roles.

Imagine that Paula Johnson has ordered a photocopier for her business. The copier has arrived and Johnson is dissatisfied with its performance. She has refused to pay for the copier, arguing that it does not perform in the way the sales agent promised it would. The copier company has sued Johnson's business to collect the price of the copier, and Johnson has asked Griffin Walters, one of the lawyers in your firm, to represent her.

When Johnson first brings this problem to Walters, both Johnson and Walters will want to know how likely it is that Johnson will win the lawsuit. In other words, will the judge rule that Johnson must pay for this copier despite her dissatisfaction with it? Walters may ask you to research the law and predict the judge's ruling. If so, your task would be to analyze the relevant law *objectively*, as the judge will do, and explain to Walters the most likely ruling. The document you would write is called an "office memorandum" or, more informally, office memo. It would be addressed to Walters, and it would *predict* what the judge will decide. Your task is to predict as accurately as you can by objectively weighing the strengths and weaknesses of the possible arguments. Your answer may not be the answer Johnson wants to hear, but if Johnson is likely to lose, both she and Walters need to know that now rather than at the end of the case.

Now imagine that you have written an office memo predicting that Johnson probably will lose because she used the copier too long before she made any complaint to the seller. You have analyzed the legal authorities that describe how long is too long. The authorities do not give a clear answer, but you predict that the odds are greatest that the judge will decide that Johnson waited too long.

Johnson and Walters try to settle the case, but the seller refuses to agree to a reasonable settlement. So, your firm continues to defend the suit, hoping to persuade the judge that Johnson did not wait too long after all. In other words, you are trying to beat the odds you predicted in your earlier office memo. The document you would write to persuade the judge that Johnson did not wait too long is called a "brief" or a "memorandum of law." Your reader will be the judge rather than Walters, and your task will be to *persuade* rather than to predict.

The first half of this book will take you through the process of analyzing predictively (objectively) and then writing an office memo. The second half will take you through the process of analyzing for persuasion and writing a brief. The book will tackle prediction and persuasion separately because this course will be your first experience with each. However, on a fundamental level, objective analysis and persuasive analysis cannot be separated. To predict a result, a writer must understand the arguments each side would present. To persuade, a writer must understand how the argument will strike an objective reader. Thus, as you work on improving your objective analysis, you will be strengthening your skills at persuasive analysis as well, and vice versa.

Before you go on, turn to Appendix A, which contains a sample office memo, and to Appendices B and C, which contain sample briefs. We will study the parts of each document in more detail later. Your goal at this point is simply to understand the function of each kind of document and get a sense of what the end products will look like before beginning the process of creating them.

 ANALYSIS AND PLIABLE AUTHORITY

It is common to arrive at law school expecting that learning the law will be like learning the rules of Monopoly. As a player of Monopoly, you rarely have to wonder whether a certain rule applies to you. When you land on unimproved Park Place, you know that you must pay $350 in rent. When you draw the dreaded yellow card, you do what it says to do—you go to jail; you do not pass "Go"; you do not collect $200. You do not have to wonder whether either rule applies to you. You know that it does because you know that you have landed on Park Place or drawn the yellow card. Every player can see that. The rule does not have to try to identify you with a subjective description such as "a player who has acted negligently" or "a player who has landed on an up-scale property."

You also do not have to wonder about the meaning of the rule's consequence. The rent on Park Place is $350, not "rent in a reasonable amount." The instruction on the yellow card tells you to go to jail; there is only one such place on the board and it is clearly labeled. The rules unambiguously set out how you can get out of jail. Your release does not depend on convincing the other players of your good conduct as a prisoner. You know that you can leave jail only by paying $50, using a "get out of jail free" card, or rolling doubles.

Further, there is only one statement of the rules. The game does not contain several different statements of the rule about landing on Park Place, but only one. The game's rule booklet does not add commentary by other Monopoly officials about what the Park Place rule means and when it applies.

Finally, the rule about Park Place is thoroughly thought out and well drafted. The rule-makers thought through the way the Park Place rule would operate in the context of all of the other Monopoly rules. The writer of the rule focused on the task of drafting a clear, unambiguous rule to be applied to all future Monopoly players. Doubtless other writers proofread the draft of the rule carefully. Perhaps the rules were tested during games by novice players to see if the rules were stated clearly and unambiguously. Certainly the rules have been used by generations of Monopoly players, and the rule-writer has had the opportunity to clarify any ambiguity in succeeding editions of the game.

The law is not quite like Monopoly. First, many legal rules are "written" as part of a series of judicial opinions. Thus, the researcher of the law usually will find a number of versions of the rule written by different judicial writers. Second, these opinions are written by judges whose primary task is to dispose of the case presently before them rather than to legislate for all possible future situations. Third, some of these judicial writers are not particularly talented writers, or perhaps they are too overwhelmed with heavy caseloads to take the care necessary to think and write as clearly as they would like. Fourth, even rules written by a legislature (statutes) have probably been the subject of comment and explanation in case-by-case fashion by these same judicial writers.

Further, the law must use a general verbal description to identify the person to whom the rule applies. It cannot rely simply on identification by drawing a card. Nor can the descriptions always be as concrete as "a player who lands on Park Place." In the task of regulating our relationships with others, the law often must rely on such indefinite standards as "reasonable care" or "best interests of the child."

Understanding the law is actually more like a detective's task than a Monopoly game. A lawyer must engage in an interpretive process, finding clues from the language and decisions of a number of courts, legislatures, agencies; evaluating the meaning and significance of each; and combining the clues to reach an answer that makes sense of those clues. Thus, understanding the law is a constructive act by a lawyer.

This text will help you recognize and work with these legal "clues" so that your legal analysis will be more accurate and thorough. Even so, adjusting to the uncertainty of the law and the pliability of authorities can be unsettling when you are looking for firm ground on which to stand. Just recognize that this sort of anxiety and frustration is part and parcel of beginning law study. Soon you'll be used to the uncertainty, and you'll even come to like the opportunities it provides to influence the law's development.

IV ◇ HOW LAWYERS REASON

Lawyers and judges use several methods of reasoning to argue and decide cases; mastering these methods is one of the most important goals of a law school education. The most important of these methods of reasoning are:

(1) rule-based reasoning, (2) analogical reasoning, (3) policy-based reasoning, and (4) narrative reasoning. *Rule-based reasoning* reaches an answer by establishing and applying a rule of law. It asserts, "*X* is the answer because *the principle of law* articulated by the governing authorities mandates it."

RULE-BASED REASONING

Harold Collier should not be bound by the contract he signed because he is only sixteen and *A v. B* establishes that minors do not have the capacity to execute binding contracts.

Analogical reasoning reaches an answer by showing *direct factual similarities* between governing case law and the client's facts. It asserts, "*X* is the answer because the facts of this case are just like the facts of *A v. B* and *X* was the result there."

ANALOGICAL REASONING

Harold Collier should not be bound by the contract he signed because, like the defendant in *A v. B*, he is only sixteen, and in *A v. B* the defendant was not bound by the contract she signed.

Policy-based reasoning reaches an answer by analyzing which answer would be the best for the society at large. It asserts, "*X* is the answer because that answer will encourage desirable results for our society and discourage undesirable results."

POLICY-BASED REASONING

Harold Collier should not be bound by the contract he signed because he is only sixteen, and people that young should be protected from the consequences of making decisions before they are mature enough to consider all the options.

Narrative reasoning reaches an answer by telling a story that calls forth that result. It asserts, "*X* is the answer because that is how this story should end."

> ### NARRATIVE REASONING
>
> Harold Collier should not be bound by the contract he signed because he is only sixteen; he has never before shopped for a car; he was pressured by a sophisticated sales agent; he did not have the benefit of advice from any advisor; and the car purchase will exhaust the funds he has saved for college.

Each method of reasoning has persuasive power, and each has particular functions in written legal analysis. Rule-based reasoning establishes the structure of the discussion of the authorities (Chapters 2 through 6, 17 and 18). Within that structure, a complete analysis includes reasoning based on rules, analogies, policy, and narrative (Chapters 7 through 10, 18). In addition to its role in the discussion of authorities (Chapter 8), narrative reasoning is paramount in fact statements (Chapter 21).

Begin to notice the kinds of reasoning you find in the cases you read, the arguments you hear your classmates make, and your own analysis of hypothetical questions. Much of the first year of law school works on rule-based reasoning, analogical reasoning, and policy-based reasoning; by next year at this time your skills in these areas will have increased dramatically. Narrative reasoning is a true art, and law school can only introduce it. Mastery of the use of narrative will take a lifetime of reading, hearing, and telling stories—the stories of your clients and of the many real and fictional characters you encounter throughout your life.

 **ETHICS**

Your legal practice, including your legal writing, will be governed by the ethical standards your jurisdiction has adopted for lawyers. Most jurisdictions have adopted a version of either the American Bar Association's Model Rules of Professional Conduct or the earlier Model Code of Professional Responsibility.[1] Sanctions for violation of these rules range from private censure to disbarment.

No matter what the specifics of your jurisdiction's ethical rules, your legal writing must meet at least the following professional obligations:

   1. *Competency.* A lawyer must provide competent representation, including legal knowledge, skill, thoroughness and preparation.[2]

---

   1. The ethical rules in most jurisdictions are supplemented by opinions from the jurisdiction's highest court and also by opinions from a bar ethics committee.
   2. Model Rules of Professional Conduct Rule 1.1 (1994); Model Code of Professional Responsibility DR 6-101(A) (1980).

2. *Diligence.* A lawyer's representation must be diligent.[3]
3. *Promptness.* A lawyer must do the client's work promptly.[4]
4. *Confidentiality.* A lawyer must not reveal a client's confidences except with the client's permission.[5]
5. *All lawyers are bound by the rules of ethics.* Every lawyer is bound by the rules of professional conduct, no matter whether that lawyer is in charge of the case or working under the direction of another lawyer.[6]

In addition to these general standards, your *objective* legal writing must meet at least the following ethical standards dealing with giving advice:[7]

6. *Loyalty.* A lawyer's advice must be candid and unbiased. The advice must not be adversely influenced by conflicting loyalties to another client, to a third party, or to the lawyer's own interests.[8]
7. *Moral, economic and political factors.* While a lawyer's advice must provide an accurate assessment of the law, it may refer also to moral, economic, social, and political factors relevant to the client's situation.[9] However, the lawyer's representation of a client does not constitute a personal endorsement of the client's activities or views.[10]
8. *Criminal or fraudulent activity.* A lawyer must not advise or assist a client to commit a crime or a fraud.[11] When the client expects unethical assistance, the lawyer must explain to the client the ethical limitations on the lawyer's conduct.[12]

These ethical standards will apply to your legal writing after you are a lawyer. They will also apply, directly or indirectly, to the legal writing you do as a law clerk before you are admitted to the bar. They will be among the standards by which your legal writing teacher evaluates your law school writing. Be sure that every document you write meets these standards of professional responsibility.

---

3. Model Rules of Professional Conduct Rule 1.3 (1994); Model Code of Professional Responsibility DR 6-101(A)(3) and DR 7-101(A) (1980).
4. Model Rules of Professional Conduct Rule 1.3 (1994); Model Code of Professional Responsibility DR 6-101(A)(3) and DR 7-101(A) (1980).
5. Model Rules of Professional Conduct Rule 1.6 (1994); Model Code of Professional Responsibility 4-101 (1980).
6. Model Rules of Professional Conduct Rule 5.2 (1994).
7. The ethical rules governing *persuasive* legal writing are covered in Chapter 16.
8. Model Rules of Professional Conduct Rule 1.7 (1994); Model Code of Professional Responsibility DR 5-101 and DR 5-105 (1980).
9. Model Rules of Professional Conduct Rule 2.1 (1994); Model Code of Professional Responsibility DR 5-107(B) (1980).
10. Model Rules of Professional Conduct Rule 1.2(b) (1994).
11. Model Rules of Professional Conduct Rule 1.2(d) (1994); Model Code of Professional Responsibility DR 7-102(A)(7) (1980).
12. Model Rules of Professional Conduct Rule 1.2(e) (1994); Model Code of Professional Responsibility DR 2-110(C)(1)(c) (1980).

PLAGIARISM

Plagiarism is the act of presenting as one's own, words or ideas taken from another source. Most of us first encountered the concept of plagiarism in an academic environment. In academe plagiarism occurs primarily in one or both of these two situations: (1) failure to attribute an idea to the source from which it was drawn; or (2) failure to use quotation marks to show that the words themselves, not just the idea, came from another source. In an academic setting, authoring a document constitutes a representation that the author is the source of all ideas and words not otherwise attributed. Thus, in an academic setting, failure to attribute borrowed words or ideas constitutes plagiarism. It is both a lie and a theft.

However, in law practice, the concept of plagiarism can be confusing. Lawyers and judges often adapt and use, without attribution or quotation marks, language and ideas drawn from other lawyers' work. Firms keep form files and brief banks so documents prepared by one lawyer can be "recycled" by another. Law clerks write opinions to be signed by their judges. Judges incorporate into their opinions sections of briefs filed by the parties' lawyers. Associates write briefs to be signed by partners. Law publishers publish books of pleadings and other forms.

Some question whether the concept of plagiarism applies at all in a practice setting. They argue that writing in law practice does not carry a representation that the author is the source of all unattributed ideas and words. In legal practice, the writer's goal is not to take personal credit for originating everything in the document, but, rather, to serve the client. Serving the client makes the identity of the writer irrelevant. Instead, it requires presenting the most effective material in the most effective manner for the least cost. Thus, they assert, a lawyer's signature on a document constitutes only the lawyer's representation (1) that the document is not being presented for any improper purpose, including the purpose of causing needless increase in the cost of litigation; (2) that the legal contentions are not frivolous; and (3) that any factual contentions or denials will be reasonably supported by the evidence.[13]

The application of the concept of plagiarism is currently a topic of hot debate. No matter what standards may apply to *law practice*, however, remember that your law school writing is being done in an academic environment where the writing assignment has pedagogical goals rather than goals of efficiency and economy. The law school project focuses on enabling the writer *to learn* and the teacher *to evaluate* that learning. Thus, you need to generate ideas and text on your own to learn how it's done, and your teacher needs to be able to identify your ideas and text to be able to evaluate them.

Your school's honor code probably prohibits plagiarism, which it may define to include conduct resulting either from an intent to deceive or from "mere" carelessness. Being charged with an honor code violation is serious business for any student, but especially serious for law students. In a couple of years

13. Fed. R. Civ. P. 11(b).

you will be applying for admission to the bar, and most "character and fitness" committees ask questions designed to discover whether you have violated your school's honor code. Any prosecution for an honor code violation brings a risk that the proceeding will have to be reported to the character and fitness committee, that you will have to appear personally to explain the proceeding, and that your bar admission will be delayed or denied as a result.

So, carefully follow your teacher's instructions about using material from another source or working with another student. Be precise in your note-taking so you can tell where ideas came from and distinguish between para-phrases and quotes. *Unless you have explicit instructions to the contrary, do not use the words or ideas of another without proper attribution and, where appropriate, quotation marks.*[14]

Now that you have in mind your own status as a professional writer, your role, the professional and ethical standards that govern your writing, and the nature of the authorities you will be working with, it's time to begin working out your analysis of the legal issue you have been assigned.

---

14. *See* pp. 209-211 for a discussion of when quotation marks are appropriate.

I

THE PROCESS OF WRITING PREDICTIVELY: THE OFFICE MEMO

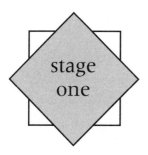

stage one

STRUCTURING FOR ANALYSIS: OUTLINING THE WORKING DRAFT

Outlining a Rule of Law

The first stage in the writing process is formulating and outlining the applicable legal rule. This outline will become the outline of your analysis and of the discussion that communicates it. Ultimately the draft of your legal analysis will take the form of a document designed to communicate with your reader, but first it will go through several stages, and perhaps multiple drafts in each stage. Do not worry yet about creating a document for your reader. First concentrate on working out your own analysis. Your goals in the early stages are to complete and test your answer to the question you have been asked.

 I OUTLINING A RULE OF LAW: OVERVIEW

The foundation of any legal analysis is the relevant rule of law. By *rule of law* we mean a statement that explains how the law tells us to decide the particular legal issue.[1] Begin working out your analysis by finding the rule that will govern your issue and outlining it.

This chapter introduces this idea of outlining a legal rule by first outlining a rule in the abstract, that is, without reference to a particular set of facts or a particular legal question. This is how you will outline rules for a "course

---

1. Often it is possible to express a rule in a number of ways. In Chapters 5 and 17 we will explore further the flexibility inherent in articulating rules of law. In the meantime, try to resist the temptation to invest the written "description" of a rule with more certainty than it merits.

outline," in preparation for a final exam. For a course outline, you'll need to outline rules in the abstract because you will not yet know the questions that will appear on the examination.

For the purposes of this chapter, omit roman numerals; we'll add those in Chapter 3. Otherwise, however, the outline should appear in traditional outline form, using large case letters, arabic numerals, and small case letters, as necessary:

> A. ....
>   1. ....
>   a. ....
>   (1) ....

For example, imagine that you are working on a course outline for a course in criminal law. You are about to outline the rule that defines burglary. Assume that you have learned that the rule is this:

> Burglary is the breaking and entering of the dwelling of another in the nighttime with the intent to commit a felony therein.

Now, how might you "outline" this rule—that is, write it out in a way that makes its structure visible? As you can see, this rule contains a number of elements, and *each* must be established before a set of facts can constitute burglary. Here is an outline of this rule:

> To establish a burglary, the state must prove *all* of the following elements:
>
> A. breaking
> B. entering
> C. dwelling
> D. of another
> E. in the nighttime
> F. intent to commit felony therein

This outline of the relevant rule will allow you to focus your analysis on each element in an orderly way, not forgetting any element and not confusing your analysis of any one element with any other element.

II **COMMON RULE STRUCTURES**

As you gain experience in outlining legal rules you will notice certain common rule structures. Becoming familiar with these common structures early in your legal training will help you to recognize them quickly and thus to outline the rule and your legal analysis more easily. We'll introduce them here. Then, as you encounter rules of law later in this book or in your other law school courses, develop the habit of noticing the rule structure. Learning to recognize rule structures will be fundamental to your legal analysis in all settings—legal writing assignments, course outlines, and examinations.

1. A rule that sets out a test with mandatory elements. This kind of rule identifies elements and requires that each be present. The burglary rule above is an example of this "mandatory elements" structure.

2. A rule that sets out an "either/or" test. This kind of rule sets out two or more subparts, and establishes a certain result if the facts fall within any *one* subpart. Here is such an "either/or" rule:

A lawyer shall not collect a contingent fee in a criminal matter or a divorce.

Placed in outline form, the rule would look like this:

> A lawyer shall not collect a contingent fee in either of the following kinds of cases:
>
> A. a criminal matter
> B. a divorce

3. A rule that sets out a flexible standard guided by certain criteria or factors. Some rules condition the legal result on a more or less objective standard. The burglary statute, for instance, defines burglary using a number of fairly objective criteria. Was it a dwelling? Did it belong to another? Did the defendant enter it? However, some rules condition the legal result on a much more flexible standard, giving more leeway or discretion to the decision-maker. To keep judges from being totally arbitrary and to help them exercise their discretion wisely and uniformly, rules using flexible standards often prescribe factors or criteria to guide the decision-maker. Here is an example of such a rule:

Child custody shall be decided in accordance with the best interests of the child. Factors to consider in deciding the best interests of the child are: the fitness of each possible custodian; the appropriateness for parenting of the lifestyle of each possible custodian; the relationship between the child and each possible custodian; the placement of the child's siblings, if any; living accommodations; the district lines of the child's school; the proximity of extended family and friends; religious issues; any other factors relevant to the child's best interests.

Placed in outline form, the rule would look like this:

Child custody shall be decided in accordance with the best interests of the child. Factors to consider in deciding the best interests of the child are:

A. the fitness of each possible custodian
B. the appropriateness for parenting of the lifestyle of each possible custodian
C. the relationship between the child and each possible custodian
D. the placement of the child's siblings, if any
E. living accommodations
F. the district lines of the child's school
G. the proximity of extended family and friends
H. religious issues
I . any other factors relevant to the child's best interests

4.   A rule that sets out a balancing test, balancing countervailing considerations against each other.   A rule setting out a balancing test is also inherently flexible, so such a rule also often includes factors or guidelines to assist the decision-maker in weighing each side of the balance.

For example, consider this dispute over legal procedure. Prior to trial, parties in civil litigation try to obtain information from each other by using *interrogatories* (written questions directed to another party and calling for answers under oath). Sometimes the party receiving a set of interrogatories will object to certain interrogatories, arguing that answering would be "unduly burdensome." To decide whether the party must answer the interrogatories, the judge applies the following rule:

A party must respond to properly propounded interrogatories unless the burden of responding substantially outweighs the questioning party's legitimate need for the information.

To measure "burden," the judge might consider a number of factors, such as the time and effort necessary to answer; the cost of compiling the information; any privacy concerns of the objecting party; and any other circumstances particular to the objecting party's situation. To measure "legitimate need," the judge might consider a number of other factors, such as how important the information would be to the issues of the trial; whether the information would be available from some other source or in some other form; whether the party seeking the information could bear some of the burden of compiling the information; and any other circumstances relating to the party's need for the information. Placed in outline form, the rule would look like this:

A party must respond to properly propounded interrogatories unless the burden of responding substantially outweighs the questioning party's legitimate need for the information.

A.   The burden of answering is measured by:
   1.   the time and effort necessary to answer
   2.   the cost of compiling the information
   3.   any privacy concerns of the objecting party
   4.   any other circumstances raised by that particular party's situation
B.   The questioning party's need for the information is measured by:
   1.   how important the information would be to the issues of the trial
   2.   whether the information would be available from some other source or in some other form
   3.   whether the party seeking the information could bear some of the burden of compiling the answers
   4.   any other circumstances relating to the party's need for the information

5.   A rule with one or more exception(s).   Any of these rule structures also may include exceptions. Here is an example of a rule with an exception:

A lawyer shall not prepare any document giving the lawyer a gift from a client except where the gift is insubstantial or where the client is related to the lawyer.

Placed in outline form, the rule would look like this:

A lawyer shall not prepare any document giving the lawyer a gift from a client except:

A.   where the gift is insubstantial, or
B.   where the client is related to the lawyer.

6.   A rule with no elements, factors, or other subparts.   Sometimes the rule you are dealing with will be a simple declarative statement with no subparts and no factors or criteria for applying the rule. For instance, if you are analyzing the validity of an unsigned will, you might be dealing with a rule like this:

> To be valid, a will must be signed.

If you have looked carefully and find no subparts, factors, or other criteria for applying the rule, you can assume that your rule is a simple declarative rule. In such a case, your structure will be a simple one-point structure. However, take care to assure yourself that your rule has no lurking elements or other subparts. Missing elements or other subparts is a common mistake for beginning legal writers.

 ## RULES COMBINING SEVERAL STRUCTURES

You'll notice that some rules reflect more than one rule structure. Such a rule will use a larger structure like one of the examples set out here. However, one of the rule's subparts will use another rule structure. For instance, consider this rule applying to criminal defendants who take the stand:[2]

> Evidence that the accused has been convicted of a prior crime shall be admitted only if the crime (1) was punishable by death or imprisonment in excess of one year under the law under which he was convicted, and the court determines that the probative value of admitting this evidence outweighs its prejudicial effect to the defendant, or (2) involved dishonesty or false statement, regardless of the punishment.[3]

This rule uses the "either/or" structure for its larger structure, like so:

> Evidence of a prior conviction may be admitted if it falls within *either* of the following categories:
>
> A. if it was punishable by death or imprisonment in excess of one year, and its probative value outweighs its prejudicial effect; or
> B. if it involved dishonesty or false statement, regardless of the punishment.

---

2. At a trial, the judge decides what testimony or documents can be "admitted" into evidence by applying the rules of evidence in effect for that court. If the judge refuses to admit into evidence a document or certain testimony, that information cannot be considered when deciding the case.

3. *See* Fed. R. Evid. 609(a)

Notice, however, that subpart *A* sets out a two-part "and" test. Further, one of these "and" prongs uses a balancing test (probative value versus prejudicial effect). What's more, the cases interpreting this rule probably describe the factors to be considered in gauging "probative value" and "prejudicial effect." Thus, a more detailed outline of the rule would look like this:

Evidence of a prior conviction may be admitted if it meets the criteria of either A or B.

A.   The evidence can be admitted if both 1 and 2 are true:
  1.   the prior conviction was punishable by:
    a.   death, or
    b.   imprisonment in excess of one year
  2.   its probative value outweighs its prejudicial effect;
    a.   probative value is gauged by:
      [list factors]
    b.   prejudicial effect is gauged by:
      [list factors]
B.   The evidence can be admitted if it involved either of the following:
  1.   dishonesty or
  2.   false statement

THE IMPORTANCE OF RELATIONSHIPS AMONG SUBPARTS

Always clarify your understanding of the relationships among any subparts of the rule—that is, how they function in relation to each other. This piece of advice can dramatically deepen your understanding of the rule and your legal analysis of it. For instance, when you have a rule that sets out a test with several subparts, like structures one and two on page 16, be sure you know whether the rule requires that all subparts be established or whether one would do.

What if you are dealing with factors guiding the decision-maker in deciding a subjective test, such as in structure three or four on pages 17-19? Again you must ask yourself how the factors interrelate. Do they function simply as a checklist and thus all count equally? Or are several more important than the others—perhaps because of their inherent importance or perhaps because of facts particular to this case—and therefore these factors weigh more heavily? Or can a heavy dose of one make up for a scarcity of another? This sort of understanding about the subparts of a rule will deepen your legal analysis dramatically. You will find clues to these questions in the cases that apply the rule, and you also can use your own common sense. The point here is simply to remember to ask yourself these questions as you formulate the rule of law.

◆ V ◆ A FEW HINTS ABOUT OUTLINING RULES

Outlining a rule of law will prompt you to ask important questions. By looking for the answers you will develop a deeper, clearer, and more thorough understanding of the rule. This is the primary point of outlining a rule (or a course). Outlining is really a tool for careful, critical reading—perhaps the most important of all lawyering skills. Here are a few pointers for outlining rules:

1. Follow traditional principles of outlining. Two of the principles of outlining apply especially to outlining legal rules. First, each subdivision must have at least two parts. Second, each subpart should constitute the whole analysis of that point and nothing more. For instance, in the burglary rule, notice that each subpart covers one element and only one element.

2. Read word-by-word and phrase-by-phrase, noticing signals of important structural information. Words like "and," "or," "unless," "except," and "include" will give you much of the structural information you need. Pay particular attention to these signals.

SOME WORDS THAT SIGNAL STRUCTURAL INFORMATION			
and	include	unless	other
or	limited to	outweighs	shall
either	except	all	may

3. Be sure to notice whether the list of elements or factors is meant to be exclusive. The rule may tell you expressly whether the list is exclusive, using such language as the phrase "any other factors relevant to the child's best interests" in the rule governing child custody on page 18. Or the rule may merely imply whether the list is exclusive, such as by introducing the list with the word "including," which would indicate there may be other factors in addition to those listed. Sometimes the language of the rule will not even hint at whether the list is exclusive, but you will be able to tell by reading other authorities or simply by using your common sense.

4.   Except for the key terms in the rule, use your own words when you outline the rule.   Restating the rule in your own words is an effective learning tool, and you can often state the rule more simply and clearly than its original writer did. Watch out for two things, however. First, do not rephrase the *key terms* of the statute. Those terms will be defined and explained by the authorities; thus, they will have developed their own meaning, and that meaning is the critical question of the analysis. Second, take care that your rephrasing is an accurate translation of the rule's original language and structure.

5.   If you are having difficulty identifying the parts of the rule, ask yourself what a party would have to prove to show that the requirements of the rule are or are not met.   For example, consider a rule providing that a speaker's words will be considered an offer if the hearer had a reasonable belief that the speaker intended by the words to make an offer. The words "reasonable belief" would require the hearer to prove two things: (1) that she believed that the speaker intended to make an offer, and (2) that her belief was reasonable.

6.   If the statute or case from which you take the rule uses numbers and letters for subparts, you do not *have* to use the same numbering and lettering scheme in *your* outline of the rule.   You may be able to organize the rule more simply and clearly than its original writer did. However, depart from the drafter's lettering and numbering only if (1) your version will be easier to understand; (2) your version is still accurate; and (3) the rule-drafter's structure is not so well known and commonly accepted that the authorities interpreting it will all use that structure in discussing the rule. Since a major part of your analysis will be explaining how the authorities interpret the rule, your explanation will be clearer if your structure matches the explanation in the authorities.

7.   Convert layered negatives to affirmative statements when you can do so without changing the meaning of the rule.   Layered negatives most often occur in rules with exceptions, that is, rules where the main clause says that something is *not* permitted *unless* certain facts are true. For instance, notice the layered negatives in the example from page 19:

> A lawyer shall *not* prepare any document giving the lawyer a gift from a client *except*:
>
> A.   where the gift is insubstantial, or
> B.   where the client is related to the lawyer.

Layered negatives are hard to understand. They make the rule structure more complex, often needlessly. Get rid of them when you can.

> A lawyer *can* prepare a document giving the lawyer a gift from a client *only if*:
>
> A. the gift is insubstantial, or
> B. the client is related to the lawyer.

 ## VI EXERCISES IN FORMULATING A RULE

For each of the following exercises, outline the rule. Your outline should resemble the outlines used as examples in the preceding pages. These exercises begin easy and increase in difficulty. Some are statutes already in a format resembling an outline, so you should find it relatively easy to create your own outline of them. Remember, though, to break out separate elements even where the statute drafter has not already done so. Also, remember that you do not *have* to use the same subsections that the drafter used. Finally, remember that often you can characterize a rule's structure in several ways. What matters in these exercises is to characterize the rule's structure accurately, regardless of whether your structure is the same as that of your classmates.

 ### EXERCISE 1

ABA MODEL RULES OF PROFESSIONAL CONDUCT—RULE 1.5(a)

(a) A lawyer's fee shall be reasonable. The factors to be considered in determining the reasonableness of a fee include the following:

(1) the time and labor required, the novelty and difficulty of the questions involved, and the skill requisite to perform the legal service properly;

(2) the likelihood, if apparent to the client, that the acceptance of the particular employment will preclude other employment by the lawyer;

(3) the fee customarily charged in the locality for similar legal services;

(4) the amount involved and the results obtained;

(5) the time limitations imposed by the client or by the circumstances;

(6) the nature and length of the professional relationship with the client;

(7) the experience, reputation, and ability of the lawyer or lawyers performing the services; and

(8) whether the fee is fixed or contingent.

EXERCISE 2

ABA MODEL RULES OF PROFESSIONAL CONDUCT—RULE 1.6(b)

(b) A lawyer may reveal [information relating to the representation of a client] to the extent the lawyer reasonably believes necessary:

(1) to prevent the client from committing a criminal act that the lawyer believes is likely to result in imminent death or substantial bodily harm; or

(2) to establish a claim or defense on behalf of the lawyer in a controversy between the lawyer and the client, to establish a defense to a criminal charge or civil claim against the lawyer based upon conduct in which the client was involved, or to respond to allegations in any proceeding concerning the lawyer's representation of the client.

EXERCISE 3

ABA MODEL RULES OF PROFESSIONAL CONDUCT—RULE 1.5(c)

(c) . . . A contingent fee agreement shall . . . state the method by which the fee is to be determined, including the percentage or percentages that shall accrue to the lawyer in the event of settlement, trial or appeal, litigation and other expenses to be deducted from the recovery, and whether such expenses are to be deducted before or after the contingent fee is calculated. . . .

EXERCISE 4

29 U.S.C. § 623(a)(1), (2)—PROHIBITION OF AGE DISCRIMINATION

It shall be unlawful for an employer

(1) to fail or refuse to hire or to discharge any individual or otherwise discriminate against any individual with respect to his compensation, terms, conditions, or privileges of employment, because of such individual's age;

(2) to limit, segregate, or classify his employees in any way which would deprive or tend to deprive any individual of employment opportunities or otherwise adversely affect his status as an employee, because of such individual's age;

EXERCISE 5

ABA MODEL RULES OF PROFESSIONAL CONDUCT—RULE 1.9(a)

(a) A lawyer who has formerly represented a client in a matter shall not thereafter represent another person in the same or a substantially related matter in which that person's interests are materially adverse to the interests of the former client unless the former client consents after consultation.

Outlining a Rule to Organize Your Analysis of a Legal Issue

Chapter 2 introduced the concept of outlining a rule of law. Now we turn to the task of outlining a rule in order to organize the working draft of a legal analysis.

I THE WORKING DRAFT OF YOUR LEGAL ANALYSIS

The first step toward creating your working draft is creating its organization or outline. The outline of the working draft serves two functions: First, it is an essential part of the process of legal analysis. It helps the writer complete and check her own analysis. Chapter 2 demonstrated how outlining serves these functions.

Second, the working draft's outline is the starting point for organizing the draft that ultimately will go to the reader. Remember the example of the Johnson case from Chapter 1. When Mr. Walters reads your office memo in the Johnson case, he will expect to see a clear outline of the law and its application to Ms. Johnson's facts. He will be relying on you not only to *do* the analysis necessary to answer the question, but also to provide him with the framework for his *own* analysis. Chapter 12 discusses how you will revise the working draft's outline to form the organization of the document for your reader; but no matter what editing decisions you make at that stage, a weak working draft outline will result in a weak final draft.

So how shall you outline your legal analysis? The most important principle for organizing the working draft is this:

Use an outline of the rule of law to form the outline of the analysis.

For a simple example, assume that you are working in a prosecutor's office. The police have charged Gerald Shaffer with criminal assault on his wife. Because Mr. Shaffer forcibly entered his estranged wife's house, the police want to know whether they can also charge Mr. Shaffer with burglary—in other words, whether Mr. Shaffer's conduct falls within the definition of burglary.

Here your legal *issue* might be stated: "Did Mr. Shaffer's acts constitute burglary?" Assume that you have located and outlined this rule as we did in Chapter 2:

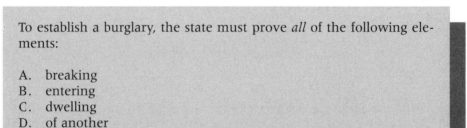

To establish a burglary, the state must prove *all* of the following elements:

A. breaking
B. entering
C. dwelling
D. of another
E. in the nighttime
F. intent to commit felony therein

Notice how the rule's outline will order your legal analysis. Using this outline as a guide, your analysis of the Shaffer question would discuss each element separately, completing the discussion of one element before proceeding to the next.

II   USING THE RULE TO STRUCTURE A WORKING ANALYSIS

Outlining a rule to answer a legal question is virtually the same as outlining a rule in the abstract. Here are the few differences and a couple of hints that will make the process easier:

1. Begin with a roman numeral devoted to the question you have been asked. Generally in predictive legal writing you will be responding to one or more question(s) from another lawyer. The roman numerals of the working draft should be reserved for these questions. For example, for the Shaffer question, the roman numeral would be:

I. Did Mr. Shaffer's acts constitute burglary?

If you have been asked to answer several questions, use a roman numeral for each. If you have been asked only one question, use a roman numeral "I" for that question, and do not be concerned that you will not have more than one roman numeral. Let the use of the roman numeral assure you (and later your reader) that this is the issue you were given and, therefore, that this is the point of connection between the question and your own analysis.

2. Immediately after the question, state the rule. For instance, in the burglary example the sentence would be:

I. Did Mr. Shaffer's acts constitute burglary?

To establish a burglary, the state must prove that the defendant broke and entered the dwelling of another in the nighttime with the intent to commit a felony therein.

3. Add the subparts from the rule. They will become the headings and subheadings of the corresponding parts of your analysis. Headings will provide a thinking and writing discipline important to the accuracy of your analysis. They will help you stay oriented during the process of writing, rather than wandering off track. Without these visible reminders, writers are more apt to mix the discussions of separate issues, and thus to end up with both fuzzy thinking and fuzzy writing. Here is the Shaffer outline with subparts:

I. Did Mr. Shaffer's acts constitute burglary?

To establish a burglary, the state must prove that the defendant broke and entered the dwelling of another in the nighttime with the intent to commit a felony therein.

A. breaking
B. entering
C. dwelling
D. of another
E. in the nighttime
F. intent to commit felony therein

4.   Be sure that the outline answers the question you have been asked.   When you have been asked to apply the rule to a particular set of facts and to answer a particular question, your outline should directly answer the question you have been asked. Two examples will help explain this point.

Assume that this is your outline of the ethical rule governing will-drafting:

A lawyer shall not prepare a will for a client if:

A.   the will gives the lawyer a bequest from the client;
B.   the bequest is substantial; and
C.   the client is not related to the lawyer.

Now assume that you are given the following facts and asked the following question:

Facts: Eilene Flynt, a client, has asked Alice Crews, a lawyer and close friend of Flynt's, to prepare a will in which Flynt will bequeath a parcel of real property to Crews.

Question: May Crews prepare the will?

Conveniently, the rule is already phrased to answer the question you have been asked. The question is whether the lawyer can prepare the will. The rule begins "A lawyer shall not prepare a will for a client if: . . ."

But sometimes the rule will not be phrased so conveniently for your particular question. For instance, assume that two lawyers from different firms, Janice Colby and James Kraft, are married to each other. Colby represents the owner of a parcel of real property listed for sale. Prospective buyers of the real property ask Kraft to represent them in negotiating a better purchase price. Kraft wants to know if he must tell the prospective buyers about his relationship to the lawyer for the owners. Here is the rule, phrased as you find it in the applicable code:

A lawyer related to another lawyer as parent, child, sibling, or spouse shall not represent a client in a representation directly adverse to a person who the lawyer knows is represented by the other lawyer except upon the consent by the client after consultation regarding the relationship.

You could outline this rule, phrased just as you found it, like this:

A.   A lawyer may not represent a client if *all* of the following are true:

1. the lawyer is related to another lawyer as one of the folowing:
   a. parent
   b. child
   c. sibling, or
   d. spouse
2. the lawyer's relative represents another party to the legal matter
3. the interests of the two clients are directly adverse
B. Despite section A, the lawyer may represent the client if both of the following requirements are met:
   1. the lawyer discloses to the client the relationship with the opposing lawyer, and
   2. the client consents

However, this outline does not *directly* answer the question you were asked. You were asked "Must Kraft tell the prospective buyers about his relationship to the lawyer for the owners?" The direct question this rule answers is "Under what circumstances can the lawyer represent the client who is adverse to the relative's client?" When the rule is not phrased to answer directly the question you were asked, reorganize your outline to answer the question you were asked.

I. Must Kraft disclose to the prospective buyers his relationship to Colby?

A lawyer must disclose to his client his relationship to another lawyer if (a) the lawyer is related to the other lawyer as parent, child, sibling, or spouse; (b) if the lawyer's relative represents another party to the same legal matter; and (c) if the interests of the two clients are directly adverse.

A. the lawyer is related to the other lawyer as one of the following:
   1. parent
   2. child
   3. sibling, or
   4. spouse
B. the lawyer's relative represents another party to the same legal matter
C. the interests of the two clients are directly adverse

Now the outline of the rule is phrased to answer the question you have been asked. The question is "Must the lawyer tell his client about his relationship to the lawyer for the owners?" The rule begins, "A lawyer must disclose to his client his relationship to another lawyer if . . ." The outline of the rule still accurately communicates the rule's meaning, but its subparts are rearranged to answer directly the question posed.

5.   Personalize your outline.   The rules you will be working with are written to apply to citizens at large. They do not refer to individual names or facts. If you are outlining the rule as part of a course outline for law school, this generalized version of the rule is sufficient. However, when you are using the rule to work out your answer to a particular legal question (such as on the course examination, on a legal writing assignment, or in a summer clerking job) personalize the outline by substituting the names and key facts from the fact scenario.

Back to Kraft and Colby for an example. Personalize the outline by using the appropriate names and facts, like so:

I.   Must Kraft disclose to the prospective buyers his relationship to Colby?

Kraft must disclose his relationship to Colby if (a) Kraft is related to Colby as parent, child, sibling, or spouse; (b) Colby represents another party to the same legal matter; and (c) the interests of the two clients are directly adverse.

A.   Kraft is related to Colby as one of the following:
   1.   parent
   2.   child
   3.   sibling, or
   4.   spouse
B.   Colby represents another party to the same legal matter
C.   the interests of the two clients are directly adverse

This outline of the rule has rearranged the rule's content to answer the question you have been asked, and it has personalized the rule to the particular factual situation. Notice how much clearer and easier to work with this outline will be than the abstract outline on page 31.

6.   Phrase the subheadings as questions.   The outline will be easier to use as a guide and your task will be clearer if you phrase the subheadings as questions.

I.   Must Kraft disclose to the prospective buyers his relationship to Colby?

Kraft must disclose his relationship to Colby if (a) Kraft is related to Colby as parent, child, sibling, or spouse; (b) Colby represents another party to the same legal matter; and (c) the interests of the two clients are directly adverse.

A.   Is Kraft related to Colby as one of the following?
1.   parent
2.   child
3.   sibling, or
4.   spouse
B.   Does Colby represent another party to the same legal matter?
C.   Are the interests of the two clients directly adverse?

Phrasing the subheadings as questions will remind you to stay objective as you work out the analysis. In other words, it will help you avoid slipping into advocating for your preliminary conclusions.

7. Don't be too quick to leave out part of the rule. If you are outlining the rule because you have been asked to apply it to a particular fact scenario, you may be tempted to leave out part of the outline (an element or a factor perhaps) because it appears that those parts are not applicable to your facts or because the application of those parts appears obvious.

For instance, assume that you have been given a fact scenario involving a lawyer preparing a will in which the client bequeaths a parcel of real property to the lawyer. Assume that the rule of law is:

A lawyer shall not prepare a will for a client if:

A.   the will gives the lawyer a bequest;
B.   the bequest is substantial; and
C.   the client is not related to the lawyer.

You may be tempted to assume that a parcel of real property is a bequest of substantial value and thus omit *B* from your outline because you are taking it as "given." The reasoning behind this decision would be that, since *B* seems obviously true on these facts, there is no point in discussing *B*. The only points at issue seem to be *A* and *C*.

However, don't be so ready to make assumptions about particular elements or factors just yet. While you are first outlining the rule, let the outlining process teach you about how the rule works. When you have its structure clearly in mind, you'll need to find out what the authorities say about the rule's meaning. The authorities will teach you the meaning of the key terms as well as the way the rule would be applied to particular situations.

You'll also need to verify that you've been given all of the relevant facts. For instance, in the will-drafting example, the facts say nothing about how big the parcel of real property is, about its value, or about the relative wealth of the lawyer. Maybe the property is only ten square feet in a location of virtually no value. Maybe the property even carries with it significant liabilities, thus rendering it valueless. Maybe the "substantiality" of the gift is measured, in part, by reference to how wealthy the lawyer is (and therefore, how "substantial" the gift would be *to this particular lawyer*). Only after you have researched both law and facts will you be ready to predict how the rule will apply to your client. Only then will you know whether you can treat any parts of the rule as "given."

 ## III ▸ EXERCISES IN OUTLINING A RULE

These exercises revisit four of the legal rules from the exercises at the end of Chapter 2. Now, however, we add facts and a question. For each exercise, outline a legal discussion of the question, using an outline of the rule as this chapter has explained. In other words, (1) draft the question designated by the roman numeral; (2) draft the sentence stating the rule; (3) add the outline of the rule's subparts; (4) be sure that the outline directly answers the question; (5) personalize the outline; and (6) refrain from omitting any relevant subparts. Do not try to *answer* the legal issue. Just draft the *outline*.[1]

 ### EXERCISE 1

Wallace Luttrell, a lawyer, is considering raising his customary fees. He wants to know whether charging a fee of $4,000 for an uncontested divorce would be unethical. You researched the governing ethical rules and found the following:

ABA MODEL RULES OF PROFESSIONAL CONDUCT—RULE 1.5(a)

(a) A lawyer's fee shall be reasonable. The factors to be considered in determining the reasonableness of a fee include the following:
(1) the time and labor required, the novelty and difficulty of the questions involved, and the skill requisite to perform the legal service properly;
(2) the likelihood, if apparent to the client, that the acceptance of the particular employment will preclude other employment by the lawyer;
(3) the fee customarily charged in the locality for similar legal services;
(4) the amount involved and the results obtained;

---

1. These exercises deal with a few of the ethical issues lawyers face. Rules and duties other than the rules set out here also may be implicated, depending on additional facts.

(5) the time limitations imposed by the client or by the circumstances;

(6) the nature and length of the professional relationship with the client;

(7) the experience, reputation, and ability of the lawyer or lawyers performing the services; and

(8) whether the fee is fixed or contingent.

 **EXERCISE 2**

Janice Tobin represents Victor Carletta in a divorce. While discussing the property issues of the divorce, Carletta told Tobin that he does not wish to disclose certain financial accounts to his wife's attorney because he does not plan to report the income from those accounts on his income tax filings. Intentionally not reporting income is a crime. Tobin is not comfortable with knowing and not disclosing to someone Carletta's plans, although she is not sure to whom she would like to disclose Carletta's plans. May Tobin ethically reveal her client's plans? You researched the issue and found the following rule:

ABA MODEL RULES OF PROFESSIONAL CONDUCT—RULE 1.6(b)

(b) A lawyer may reveal [information relating to the representation of a client] to the extent the lawyer reasonably believes necessary:

(1) to prevent the client from committing a criminal act that the lawyer believes is likely to result in imminent death or substantial bodily harm; or

(2) to establish a claim or defense on behalf of the lawyer in a controversy between the lawyer and the client, to establish a defense to a criminal charge or civil claim against the lawyer based upon conduct in which the client was involved, or to respond to allegations in any proceeding concerning the lawyer's representation of the client.

Note: This rule covers only the question of whether Tobin ethically can *reveal confidential information*. Other rules govern whether Tobin can *continue to represent* Carletta in spite of his plans. The general rule here would be that she cannot continue to represent him if he persists in his plans.

 **EXERCISE 3**

Matthew Willett has agreed to represent Juanita Bautista in a civil claim against another driver in a car accident. The fee will be a *contingent fee,* that is, a percentage of the recovery in the case. Willett has drafted a letter to Bautista describing the fee arrangement. He wants to know if his letter complies with ethical requirements by sufficiently describing the fee agreement. You have researched the applicable ethical rules and found the following:

ABA MODEL RULES OF PROFESSIONAL CONDUCT—RULE 1.5(c)

(c) . . . A contingent fee agreement shall state the method by which the fee is to be determined, including the percentage or percentages that shall accrue to the lawyer in the event of settlement, trial or appeal, litigation and other expenses to be deducted from the recovery, and whether such expenses are to be deducted before or after the contingent fee is calculated. . . .

 **EXERCISE 4**

Several years ago Clifford Foodman defended Carson on hit-and-run charges. Now a new client, Janoff, has asked Foodman to defend her on a contract dispute. Carson is the plaintiff in the case.

Foodman wants to know whether he must obtain Carson's consent to represent Janoff in the case of Carson v. Janoff after formerly representing Carson on the hit-and-run charges.

ABA MODEL RULES OF PROFESSIONAL CONDUCT—RULE 1.9(a)

(a) A lawyer who has formerly represented a client in a matter shall not thereafter represent another person in the same or a substantially related matter in which that person's interests are materially adverse to the interests of the former client unless the former client consents after consultation.

Formulating a Rule from a Case Opinion

Now that you are familiar with rule structures and you have had some practice outlining rules, we'll turn our attention to formulating and outlining rules from a case opinion.

 ## THE SLIPPERY TASK OF FORMULATING A RULE FROM A CASE OPINION

As you know by now, lawyers and judges formulate legal rules from primary legal authorities such as cases and statutes. Formulating and outlining a rule from a statute is not always straightforward, but at least the drafter of the statute was engaged in that same task. The statute-drafter's sole objective, at least theoretically, was to write out the whole rule, in one spot, using a rule structure. Also, the language of a statute usually goes through a process of examination by a number of critics. This legislative process is never as good as high school civics texts contemplate, but at least the drafter's language is scrutinized by a number of critical outside readers.

Not so with case opinions. On the whole, judges do a good job of writing opinions, especially considering the handicaps of too few law clerks, too many cases, and too little time in which to decide them. But these handicaps cannot be overcome completely, even by perfect people, and judges are not perfect. They are human, just like the rest of us. Some of them are not superlative legal writers, and even the best legal writers sometimes write unclearly.

Perhaps more important, the opinion writer's primary objective is to resolve the disputes of a particular set of parties.[1] While it is customary to discuss principles of law in the process of explaining the resolution of a particular dispute, the opinion writer does not have to use a certain format or comply with any particular level of thoroughness or clarity. Also, the author is writing in prose rather than in legislative format, a literary genre much more conducive to precision. Even if the opinion writer tries to write with legislative precision, the writer seldom has the benefit of feedback from a group of other critical readers.

Finally, when dealing with a statute, a lawyer has only one authoritative source for the rule. There will be only one version of the statute, not twenty. Even if a number of case opinions interpret the statute's language, the statute creates the authoritative language. For rules primarily articulated by case law, however, a researcher may find many case opinions with each author restating what that author thinks the rule is. These opinions often use different language. Sometimes the variations in language will be slight and sometimes dramatic. The task of formulating and outlining a rule from these differing authorities can be challenging.

In the final analysis, a legal "rule" is simply an idea in the mind of the rule-maker. The written version of that idea is merely the rule-maker's attempt to describe the idea in words. The rule-maker may not have done a particularly good job of describing the idea. Or perhaps the rule-maker described the rule in one way, but could just as easily have described it in another way without changing its meaning.

When you formulate a rule from an opinion, you are trying to get inside the mind of the opinion's author. You want to determine what principles the author applied to reach the opinion's result, and how the author intended that these principles would function in the future. If you find the task of formulating a rule from an opinion difficult, you have good reason. But the material in this book and in your legal research text, as well as the practice you are getting in all your law school classes, will give you the skills you'll need for the task.

II   THE INHERITED RULE AND THE PROCESSED RULE

Usually an opinion will begin its legal analysis by stating a rule from earlier cases or from a statute. The opinion then applies the rule to the facts before the court and reaches a result. When we recognize that result and understand how the court got there, we should know more about the rule and what it means than we did before the court issued the opinion. The combination of

---

1. Although case opinions deal with disputes between individuals, case opinions also create law applicable to future litigants. This is so because the same rules of law that governed the litigants in the case opinion should govern all other litigants from that jurisdiction who are in similar situations. This principle is called "stare decisis."

the pre-existing rule and the new information we glean about it from the opinion constitutes the complete rule from that opinion.

Notice that we are using the word "rule" to refer both to the rule of law the opinion inherits from prior authorities and the complete rule as it appears when the opinion concludes. You might think of these as "the inherited rule" and "the processed rule." The opinion usually inherits a rule from earlier authorities and processes it by applying it to a particular fact situation. When the opinion applies the inherited rule, it may change the rule, so that the rule coming out of the case is different in some way. Or the opinion may simply add more information about the inherited rule, so that the rule coming out of the case is the same rule but accompanied by new information about what it means. In either event, the rule you are primarily interested in is the processed rule.

Also notice that we are using the word "rule" to refer to any statement of the law. In Chapter 2's example of the burglary statute, we spoke of the entire statute (listing all elements) as a rule, and so it is. But if we make a statement of law about any one of the elements, that statement is a rule as well. So, all the following statements are rules of law:

- A burglary is the breaking and entering of the dwelling of another in the nighttime with the intent to commit a felony therein.
- A burglary requires a "breaking."
- A burglary requires intent to commit a felony inside the dwelling.
- A burglary requires that the breaking and entering be done in the nighttime.
- The definition of "nighttime" is the time between thirty minutes after sunset and thirty minutes before sunrise.

The first rule is the rule defining all of the elements of burglary. In a discussion of this rule, the second, third, and fourth rules would be structured as subrules beneath the rule setting out all of the elements. The last rule is the rule defining one of the elements and would be structured as part of the discussion of the nighttime element. However, all of these statements of law are "rules" even though some are parts of a larger rule.

To formulate a rule from a case, start by identifying (1) the inherited rule that governs the legal issue; (2) the facts relevant to that rule of law; (3) the new information the opinion gives us about the rule; and (4) the court's decision about the rule's application to the parties before it.

The *inherited rule* is the legal principle the court gleans from prior authorities. For a contracts case dealing with whether a certain communication was a valid offer, the inherited rule might be the rule that an effective offer must include all the essential terms. Or consider a torts case where the defendant's negligence caused a building to burn and the plaintiff was injured when he entered that burning building. If the issue is whether the plaintiff's entry into the burning building constituted assumption of the risk, the inherited rule of law might be that assumption of the risk requires a voluntary choice.

The *facts relevant to the rule of law* are the facts the court used to decide how to apply the inherited rule in that case. For the contracts case, a relevant fact might be that this particular offer did not include a statement of price and that the parties had no prior course of dealing or other standard that would determine price. For the torts case, the facts might be that the plaintiff entered the burning building to save his child.

The *new information about the rule* is anything we learn about the rule from the case. The court might change the rule, add an exception, or give us new information about what the rule means or how it is to be applied. In the contracts case, the court might tell us that price is an essential term. In the torts case, the court might tell us that a choice is not "voluntary" where a father must choose between entering the burning building and allowing his child to remain in danger.

The court's *decision about how the rule applies to these facts* is the result the court reached when the court applied the inherited rule and the new information to the litigants' situation. For the contracts case, the decision might be that the plaintiff had not made an effective offer. For the torts case the decision might be that the plaintiff had not assumed the risk of injury.

The inherited rule modified or supplemented by the new information about the rule is the *processed rule*. Your notes distilling these parts of the opinion might look like this:

CONTRACTS CASE	
Inherited rule	An effective offer must include all of the essential terms of proposed contract.
Relevant facts	The plaintiff's communication did not include a price, and the parties had no prior course of dealing or other standard that would determine price.
New information	Price is an essential term of a valid contract. The term must be stated expressly or it must be discernible from the past dealings of the parties or from some other accepted standard.
Decision	The plaintiff did not make an effective offer.

TORTS CASE	
Inherited rule	Assumption of the risk requires a voluntary choice.
Relevant facts	The plaintiff entered the burning building to save his child.
New information	A choice is not "voluntary" where a father must choose between entering the burning building and failing to save his child.
Decision	The plaintiff did not assume the risk of injury.

So you can formulate the processed rule of the contracts case like this:

> An effective offer must include all essential terms. Price is an essential term of a valid contract. The price must be stated expressly, or it must be discernible from the past dealings of the parties or from some other accepted standard.

Before you continue reading, formulate the processed rule from the torts case.

III   TOOLS FOR FINDING NEW INFORMATION ABOUT THE RULE

When you are looking for the new information a case gives you about a rule, your primary tools are (1) noticing what the court *said* about the rule; (2) noticing how the court *applied* the rule; (3) noticing how the court did *not* apply the rule; (4) noticing the *facts* the court emphasized; (5) reading what leading commentators have said about the case; and (6) noticing the *policy* considerations the court described.

1. Notice what the court said about the rule.   In most opinions, the author gives the reader some explanation of the rule before applying it to the facts of that particular case. Here the author's primary goal is to tell the reader about the rule. Begin with this part of the opinion. The *court's* explicit explanation of the rule gives you the most basic new information from the case.

2. Notice how the court applied the rule.   After you have examined carefully what the court *said* about the rule, look at how the court *applied* the rule to the facts before it. You might expect an opinion to state and explain a rule of law and then to apply that rule of law exactly as the opinion just explained it. Often that is exactly what happens. But sometimes the court's *application* of the rule differs from the court's explanation of it. So, one of the best ways to understand the rule is to observe how the court applied it. A court "holds" what it *does*, not what it *says*.

3. Notice how the court did *not* apply the rule.   After you have observed how the court applied the rule, ask yourself how the court did *not* apply it. A court's unexplained silence rarely can be characterized as a binding rule of law. However, judicial silence can have persuasive value if the most likely reason for the silence is that the ignored topic is not a part of the relevant legal analysis.

After all, your goal here is to figure out what rule was governing the judge when deciding the case and how that rule would apply to your client's facts. If you are wondering whether a certain fact true of your client's situation would affect the outcome, ask yourself whether that kind of fact seemed to affect the judge's ruling in the earlier case.

4.   Notice any facts the court emphasized.   When a court sets out the facts or applies the law, it sometimes will emphasize a particular fact. Usually, the court's explanation of the law will tell you why the court found that fact important. However, sometimes a court will emphasize a fact without explicitly explaining the fact's significance. Even if the court did not directly explain whether or why that fact was important, the opinion's emphasis on it implies that the judge found it legally significant.

Your task is to figure out why the court chose to emphasize that fact. Think about what else the opinion tells you and use your common sense. You may be able to develop a theory about the legal significance of the fact. Perhaps that fact actually played a part in the judge's legal analysis, even though the opinion does not say so explicitly.

5.   Find out what leading commentators have said about the case.   Case opinions actually make law, but a wealth of secondary authorities exist. *Secondary authorities* are explanations of the law written by legal commentators. Secondary authorities have persuasive value, depending on factors such as the reputation of the author(s) and the publication, the level of detail of the discussion, and the recency of the writing. If you are working with a well-known and influential case, commentators may have discussed it. Finding secondary authority can help you understand the case and formulate a rule from it.

6.   Look for any policy considerations that underlie the rule. Sometimes the authorities will explain *why* this particular rule is better than other possible ways to decide this issue. Perhaps the reasons include a lofty constitutional concern for a citizen's civil rights. Perhaps the reasons are utterly pragmatic, such as a recognition that a different rule would not work because of some facet of human nature or some business custom. These reasons are called "policies." When the court discusses the underlying policies, we learn more about what the court meant by the rule and how the rule would function in other kinds of situations.

The opinion may set out explicitly what the policies teach us about the rule. The opinion may simply explain the policies without telling us more; but even then we can surmise information about the rule from understanding policy. Perhaps we can theorize that a court might not apply that rule to a somewhat different set of facts if those facts would not raise the same policy concerns. Perhaps the rule's policies help us evaluate the relative importance of the rule's elements. *What* we can learn about a rule by understanding its policy foundation will vary from situation to situation; but the rule's policy always yields clues to *some* important information about the rule.

You can learn about the rule's underlying policies even if the opinion is silent about policy. Look for policy discussions in a treatise or law review article. You also can use your common sense. What mischief is the rule designed to prevent? What social good is the rule designed to further? Even if you have no proof that this policy was part of the intent of the rule-maker, you can deepen your understanding of a rule by thinking about the policies it implicates.

IV DECIDING THE BREADTH OF THE RULE YOU FORMULATE

Remember from this and earlier chapters that rules can be formulated in different ways. One of the ways that rule formulations can differ is in breadth. For instance, in the torts opinion above (let's call it *Cantwell v. Denton*) you might have formulated a rule that looks something like this:

> Assumption of the risk requires a voluntary choice. A father's choice to enter a burning building is not voluntary if he must choose between entering the building and failing to save his child.

This rule formulation describes the situations to which the rule would apply, and the description is narrow. It says that this rule applies to fathers who are choosing between a burning building and the lives of their children. It tells us nothing about whether the rule would apply to persons other than fathers, to situations other than burning buildings, or to saving people other than children. It certainly tells us nothing about whether the rule would include saving property rather than lives.

But you may need to predict how a court would rule in one of those situations. For instance, assume that Mr. and Mrs. Gregory have asked your firm to represent them in litigation against Jerico Autoworks, an auto repair business. Jerico advertised oil changes completed in twenty minutes "while you wait." On the fateful day, the Gregorys put a turkey in their oven, set the oven on 325 degrees, and left for town to have Jerico change the oil in their car. Jerico completed the job and turned the car back over to the Gregorys. The Gregorys paid Jerico and began driving the rural road toward their home.

They were only half way home when they noticed the internal engine heat beginning to climb. They realized that they were running low on oil and surmised, correctly, that Jerico had not sufficiently tightened the oil plug. But they also realized that the turkey in their oven was nearly done. They knew that this rural road was traveled so infrequently that the odds were small that they would be able to flag another driver and get home before the burning turkey might cause a fire in their kitchen.

They decided to drive on in the hope that they could make it home before their kitchen (and perhaps their house) burned. The Gregorys got close enough to walk the rest of the way and so saved their kitchen, but at the cost of serious engine damage. Jerico refuses to pay for the damage because the Gregorys continued driving after noticing the engine temperature.

As part of deciding whether to accept the case, an attorney in your firm has asked you to predict whether the decision to continue driving would be considered an assumption of the risk. If so, Jerico would be able to raise the defense of assumption of the risk, and recovery would be jeopardized. Assume that your only authority is *Cantwell v. Denton*. Suppose you stated the rule of *Cantwell* as we did above, that is:

> Assumption of the risk requires a voluntary choice. A father's choice to enter a burning building is not voluntary where he must choose between entering the building and failing to save his child.

This rule would not tell you much about whether the Gregorys' decision would constitute assumption of the risk. But what if you could state the rule more broadly? Perhaps a judge ruling on the Gregory case might agree that *Cantwell* created a rule that was broader than just fathers, burning buildings, and children.

Whether you will be able to formulate a broader rule will depend on what the court in *Cantwell* seems to have intended. Most opinions will contain at least several paragraphs explaining the court's decision. The language the court used is your main evidence of the court's intent, but also consider how the court actually applied its rule and what authorities the court cited for support. Consider these versions of the relevant part of the *Cantwell* opinion:

Version 1

A father's choice to enter a burning building is not voluntary where he must choose between entering the building and failing to save his child. The bond between a parent and a child is the strongest human bond. In situations that otherwise would constitute assumption of the risk, the law should not penalize a plaintiff for fulfilling the duties of a parent to a child.

Version 2

A father's choice to enter a burning building is not voluntary where he must choose between entering the building and failing to save his child. Our law places the highest value on human life, and the highest form of courage is to risk one's own life in an attempt to save the life of another. The doctrine of assumption of the risk was not designed to penalize one who demonstrates this kind of courage.

Version 3

A father's choice to enter a burning building is not voluntary where he must choose between entering the building and failing to save his child. We must remember, after all, that it was the defendant's negligence that placed the plaintiff in the position of having to choose between the threatened harm and an equal or greater harm. A defendant cannot subject the plaintiff to such a Hobson's choice and then defend against his own negligence by pointing to the plaintiff's response.

What broader rule might you formulate if *Cantwell*'s discussion reads like version 1? What about version 2? Version 3? Which version would allow you to formulate a rule that will accommodate the Gregorys' concern about their kitchen?

Version 1 grounds the rule in the particular obligations of a parent to a child. In version 1, you can formulate a rule that applies to parents, not just fathers; you might even be able to formulate a rule that would apply to

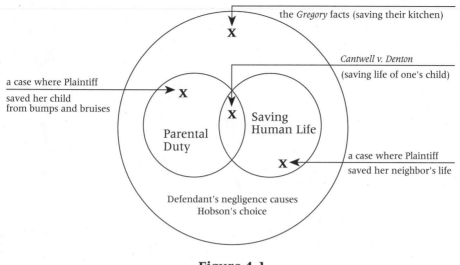

the *Gregory* facts (saving their kitchen)

Cantwell v. Denton
(saving life of one's child)

a case where Plaintiff saved her child from bumps and bruises

Parental Duty

Saving Human Life

a case where Plaintiff saved her neighbor's life

Defendant's negligence causes Hobson's choice

Figure 4-1
Situations Covered by Each Rule Formulation

property damage as long as protection of the property was a clear parental duty. But the Gregorys' dilemma did not involve parental duty, so the rule you formulate from version 1 will not tell the Gregorys much. Version 2 grounds the rule in the special value we place on trying to save human life. In version 2 your rule would not have to be limited to a parental obligation, but it still might not cover property damage as opposed to human life.

Version 3, however, grounds the rule in the observation that it is the defendant's negligence that has caused the necessity to choose between two bad options. Version 3 describes the characteristics that call for this rule as those where the defendant's negligence has forced the plaintiff to choose between the threatened harm and an equal or greater harm. Version 3 would allow you to formulate a rule like this:

> Assumption of the risk requires a voluntary choice. When the defendant's negligence forces the plaintiff to choose between the threatened harm and another equal or greater harm, the plaintiff's choice is not voluntary.

Figure 4-1 demonstrates how this broader formulation of the rule would allow the Gregorys to argue that they did not assume the risk of damage to their car by continuing to drive it.

V HOLDING VERSUS DICTA

You'll need to understand one more concept before you tackle rule formulation from a case opinion: the difference between *holding* and *dicta*.[2] The distinction

---

2. The full term is *obiter dictum*, literally meaning "a remark made in passing."

between holding and dicta is important because only a holding is binding on future courts. If the language you are interested in is dictum,[3] a judge in a future case may *choose* to follow it, but is not *bound* to do so. Therefore, when you are formulating the rule that you predict a future court will follow, you need to consider whether the language in your authority is holding or dictum.

Statements of law necessary to the result the court reached are part of the holding. However, the court might make other statements about the law—statements other than those necessary to the decision. Such statements of law not essential to the outcome of that particular case are called "dicta."[4]

Recall, for instance, the contracts opinion dealing with whether a communication that did not include a price could be a valid offer. In that opinion, the court might have made some other statements about other rules of law. The judge might have observed, for example, that a valid contract requires an offer, acceptance, and consideration. However, the judge did not decide that particular case by considering whether there had been a valid acceptance or sufficient consideration. Therefore, any statements the judge might have made about acceptance or consideration would be dicta.

Notice whether the language you are interested in is part of the opinion's holding or dictum. If it is part of the holding, you can use it to formulate a rule of law without wondering whether it is binding in future cases. If it is dictum and if it is the only authority you can find, you can still use it to formulate a rule. While dicta is not binding, a lower court will often give the dicta of the higher court great deference. Since the lower court's task is to determine and apply the law as the higher court would, dictum is persuasive evidence of what the higher court would hold. Take care, however, not to mislead the court or another lawyer by presenting your formulation of the rule as if it were part of the holding.

While the distinction between holding and dicta is sometimes clear, as in the contracts example above, it is often debatable. You will not always know for sure whether a certain statement of law was necessary to the court's decision. For instance, consider once again *Cantwell v. Denton*, our hypothetical case about assumption of the risk. What if the *Cantwell* opinion included all three versions we discussed in the preceding section. Assume that the opinion reads like this:

> A father's choice to enter a burning building is not voluntary where he must choose between entering the building and failing to save his child. The bond between a parent and a child is the strongest human bond. In situations that otherwise would constitute assumption of the risk, the law should not penalize a plaintiff for fulfilling the duties of a parent to a child.
>
> Further, our law places the highest value on human life, and the highest form of courage is to risk one's own life in an attempt to save the life of another.

---

3. "Dictum" is singular; "dicta" is plural.
4. Do not confuse dicta with the "inherited rule." Inherited rules can be dicta or they can be part of the holding, depending entirely on whether the inherited rule is part of the law necessary to the court's result. If the court describes an inherited rule and relies on it to reach the result, the inherited rule is part of the holding. If the court describes an inherited rule but the inherited rule is not a necessary component of the court's reasoning in reaching the case's result, the inherited rule is dicta.

The doctrine of assumption of the risk was not designed to penalize one who demonstrates this kind of courage.

We must remember, after all, that it was the defendant's negligence that placed the plaintiff in the position of having to choose between the threatened harm and an option of equal or greater evil. A defendant cannot subject the plaintiff to such a Hobson's choice and then defend against his own negligence by pointing to the plaintiff's decision.

Imagine that you are trying to persuade the judge that the Gregorys did not assume the risk of injury to their engine. No doubt you will argue that the rule drawn from the statements in the third paragraph constitutes *Cantwell's* holding. However, if you represent Jerico, no doubt you will argue that the statements in the third paragraph are dicta. You will argue that the narrower statements of law in the first and second paragraphs were all that were necessary to decide *Cantwell,* and therefore that the broad statements in the third paragraph are "mere dicta."

If you are writing an office memo predicting the judge's decision on the Gregory facts, your task will include predicting whether the judge would agree with the Gregory or the Jerico argument here. So the distinctions between holding and dicta can be important whether you are predicting the result most likely or advocating for the result most favorable to your client.

FORMULATING A MORE COMPLEX RULE

Thus far we have worked with two examples, the contracts opinion and the torts opinion, and both of them have yielded simple declarative rules. But many of the opinions you will read will set out more complex rules—rules with subparts, factors, or exceptions; rules that require a balancing test; or rules that have several of these characteristics. Let's look now at an example of an opinion that requires formulation of a more complex rule.

Assume that your firm represents Sharon Watson, a sales employee of Carrolton Company, headquartered in Atlanta, Georgia. Watson had sold Carrolton to its present owners. She remained employed by Carrolton and signed a covenant-not-to-compete, an agreement promising not to compete with Carrolton in certain ways for a certain period of time after the termination of her employment. Watson is considering leaving Carrolton to form a new business that would compete with Carrolton. She needs to know whether Carrolton would be able to enforce the covenant against her. You must write an office memo predicting how a court would answer this question.

First you research the issue, looking for any statutes that would govern the enforceability of covenants-not-to-compete or for case opinions that have decided similar questions in the past. You find *Coffee System of Atlanta v. Fox,* a Georgia case dealing with enforcement of covenants-not-to-compete. *Fox* appears in Appendix D. Take a moment to read it.

A beginning legal writer, finding the *Fox* case, might write out a legal discussion structured more or less like this:

- Description of the facts in *Fox* and statement of the court's conclusion that the covenant was enforceable.
- Comparison of those facts to Watson's facts.
- Conclusion about whether the Watson covenant is enforceable, based on the similarity or dissimilarity of the Watson facts to the *Fox* facts.

This legal writer has organized the analysis around the *facts* of the case authority rather than organizing based on a legal *rule*. The problem with this approach is that without identifying the legal rule the court was applying, neither the writer nor the reader can determine which of these factual similarities or differences have any legal significance—that is, which make any difference to the outcome. For instance, in *Fox*, the plaintiff was in the business of selling coffee systems. Did that fact affect the court's decision? Would it matter if the next litigants were disputing a covenant that prevented the defendant from manufacturing shoes? Without identifying a rule of law, we cannot tell. In legal analysis, the rule of law is the bridge between the facts of the case law and the facts of the present situation with which the lawyer is concerned.

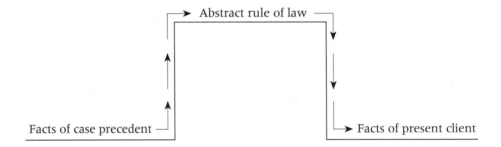

Thus, in order to use a case opinion as authority, the lawyer must articulate a *rule of law* from that opinion and then apply that *rule* to the client's facts.

This is not to say that a good legal writer will ignore the comparison between the facts of the present case and *Fox*. Reasoning by analogy to a similar case is an important tool of legal reasoning; indeed, when the facts of the two cases are strikingly similar, the analogy is probably the most powerful analytical tool of all. However, the writer still should articulate a rule of law connecting the two cases. The analogy can then show that the rule of law from *Fox* would apply to the present case in the same way the court applied it to the facts in *Fox* and should yield the same result.

So rather than organizing by factual comparisons, organize by the outline of the legal rule from the *Fox* opinion. For our purposes here, let's say that you have read *Fox* and formulated its rule like this:[5]

---

5.   You could formulate other versions of the rule from *Fox*, as we shall see in Chapters 5 and 17.

> A covenant is enforceable if all of the following elements are reasonable:
>
> 1. the kind of activity that is restrained;
> 2. the geographical area where it is restrained; and
> 3. the time period of the restraint.

Do you recognize the structure of that rule? It fits structure number one on page 17, a rule that sets out a test with elements, all of which must be met. Now, use it to draft the outline of your analysis of the Watson question, like so:

> I.   Is the Watson/Carrolton covenant-not-to-compete enforceable?
>
> The covenant is enforceable if the activity restrained, the geographic area of the restraint, and the time period of the restraint are all reasonable.
>
> A.   Is the kind of activity restrained reasonable?
> B.   Is the geographical area of the restraint reasonable?
> C.   Is the time period of the restraint reasonable?

EXERCISE 1.   Formulating and Outlining a Rule from an Opinion

For Exercises 1 and 2, formulate the rule of law from the opinion and use it to create an outline for the working draft discussion of the question you have been asked, just as you did for the exercises at the end of Chapter 3 and just as this chapter did for the Watson question. Do not write out the discussion or try to answer the legal issue. Simply create the *outline* for the analysis of the issue.

Remember that often you can characterize a rule's structure in several different ways. What matters in these exercises is to characterize the rule's structure in a way that you can justify as accurate, regardless of whether your answer is the same as those of your classmates.

Facts

Brenda Zenger has come to your firm to seek advice. She is the owner of the Westpark Veterinary Clinic. George Rafter, a newly licensed veterinarian, had interviewed for a job at the clinic. He told Zenger that he wanted to settle in your town, and that he thought the job at the clinic was just right for him. Zenger told him that she would think about his application and let him know something shortly. Last week Zenger offered Rafter the job at the clinic, and Rafter told her that he would give her an answer within a week. There was no discussion about the length of the employment.

Two days after making the job offer, Zenger learned that about a year ago Rafter had pleaded guilty to possession of cocaine with intent to sell. She immediately reconsidered and called Zenger to withdraw the job offer. Zenger was furious. He told her that he had just bought a brand new Porshe in reliance on the job offer—a Porshe that he could not even make the first payment on now that he was unemployed. He said that he knew he couldn't force her to give him the job, but that she would have to pay the car payments until he could sell the car, as well as pay the difference between the Porshe's purchase price and whatever he could get from its sale. Zenger is outraged. She wants to know if Rafter can make her pay.

Assume that in your jurisdiction, either an employer or an employee can terminate the employment at any time and without a reason (unless the parties have entered into a contract for employment for a set period of time). Assume that *Wheeler v. White* is your only authority. The relevant parts of the opinion are found in Appendix D, beginning on page 395.

  EXERCISE 2.   Formulating and Outlining a Rule from an Opinion

Facts

Attorney Karen Berry provided her client with $50,000 in financing for a business undertaking. In exchange for the funds, Berry received a security interest in several of the assets of the business and assumed partnership status. The relationship between Berry and her client went bad, and the client has reported Berry to attorney disciplinary authorities, alleging that Berry unethically took advantage of the lawyer-client relationship in the transaction. The lawyer who is investigating the complaint has asked you to determine whether Berry complied with the ethical duties that apply to business transactions with a client.

Assume that *Goldman v. Kane* is your only authority. The relevant parts of the opinion are found in Appendix D, beginning on page 391.

EXERCISE 3.   Distinguishing Holding from Dicta

Based on what you learned about *Goldman v. Kane* in Exercise 2, which of the following are part of the holding and which are dicta?

1. The court's statements about the requirement that the attorney refrain from misrepresenting or concealing any material fact.

2. The court's statements about the requirement that any advice the attorney gives the client must be the same advice that the attorney would be expected to give if the transaction were between the client and a stranger.

3. The court's statements about the requirement that the client be fully informed of the nature and effect of the transaction.

4. The court's statements about the requirement that the transaction not be fundamentally unfair or egregiously overreaching.

Formulating a Rule from Multiple Authorities

I THE CONTINUING SEARCH FOR A RULE

Sometimes a case or a statute will set out the rule in a clear and well-organized manner. No other statute or case law will create confusion about formulating the rule of law. When that is true, be grateful, formulate the rule, use it to organize your analysis and start to write. Often, though, the rule is not so clear. Perhaps you will find several cases that use differing words for the rule, or that even seem to articulate different rules for the same issue. The large-scale organization of your working draft may show you that you need to return to the cases to get a clearer understanding of the rule. To demonstrate why, let's return to Ms. Watson's covenant-not-to-compete.

Assume that while you were researching Georgia law on the Watson issue, you found not only *Fox,* but also *Clein v. Kapiloff. Clein* appears in Appendix D. Stop now and read it.

You could formulate several slightly different rules from *Clein.* Let's assume that you have formulated this one:

To be enforceable, a covenant-not-to-compete:

1. must be supported by sufficient consideration, and
2. must be reasonable. The test for determining reasonableness is:
   a. whether the covenant is reasonably necessary to protect the interests of the party who benefits by it;
   b. whether it unduly prejudices the interests of the public; and
   c. whether it imposes greater restrictions than are necessary.

But recall that in Chapter 4 we formulated this rule from *Fox*:

A covenant is enforceable if all of the following elements are reasonable:

1. the kind of activity that is restrained;
2. the geographical area where it is restrained; and
3. the time period of the restraint.

Fox and *Clein* seem to lay out different rules. You know that you need to organize according to the structure of the legal rule, but here you seem to have two different legal rules.

Novice legal writers will be tempted to organize the discussion of the law applicable to the Watson case by describing and applying, one at a time, the "rules" set out in *Fox* and in *Clein*. The discussion would first give a sort of a "case brief" of one of the cases, *Fox* perhaps, describing the facts of that case and the rule of law set out by that court. The discussion would then apply the rule from *Fox* to the Watson facts. Then, the discussion would do the same thing with *Clein*, setting out the rule of law from that case and applying that rule to the Watson facts. The organizational structure would look something like this:

I. Is the Watson covenant-not-to compete enforceable?

    A. the rule in the *Fox* case

        The covenant is enforceable if the activity restrained, the geographical area of the restraint, and the time period of the restraint are all reasonable.

        1. Is the kind of activity restrained reasonable?
        2. Is the geographical area of the restraint reasonable?
        3. Is the duration of the restraint reasonable?

B. the rule in the *Clein* case

The covenant is enforceable if it is supported by sufficient consideration and its terms are reasonable.

1. Is the covenant supported by sufficient consideration?
2. Are its terms reasonable? Reasonableness is judged by the following criteria:
   a. Is the covenant reasonably necessary to protect Carrolton's interests?
   b. Does the covenant unduly prejudice the interests of the public?
   c. Does the covenant impose greater restrictions than are necessary?

There is a problem with this approach, however. The reader needs to know the state of *Georgia's* rule of law on enforcing covenants-not-to-compete. Determining Georgia's rule is the writer's most important analytical task. Organizing by the separate cases here would give the reader two possible rules and two possible outcomes. Yet our legal system contemplates that a jurisdiction ordinarily will have only one rule of law on a particular issue so that people can know what the law is and how it will apply to their conduct.[1] What is Georgia's rule here? Is it one of the rules set out in these opinions? If the Georgia rule is a combination of the rules set out in these opinions, how are they combined?

The legal writer who organizes around separate cases rather than by a single rule of law has not completed the task of legal analysis. Remember this point. It is one of the ways your organizational process can serve as a signal for a potential problem in your analysis. Here, you must wrestle with these two opinions until you can predict the rule a Georgia court would apply.

When you are confronted with seemingly inconsistent authorities, your two main methods of resolving the apparent conflict are (1) comparing the relative precedential value of each authority, and (2) studying the authorities to see if you can reconcile or distinguish the opinions.

COMPARING THE PRECEDENTIAL VALUE OF EACH AUTHORITY

Cases serve as precedent for the legal rules they articulate. This status as precedent underlies the claim that the case is an authority binding on a future

---

1. Occasionally a jurisdiction genuinely may have, simultaneously, two different and unreconciled rules of law on a certain issue. This sort of situation is not common, and is, one hopes, temporary.

court. However, not all cases carry the same degree of precedential value. The degree of deference a court will give to any particular case will depend on a number of factors.

Because your task is to predict what a court will do, you must always be sensitive to the relative precedential values of the authorities you find. However, when you find seemingly inconsistent authorities, the relative precedential weight of each becomes particularly significant. To measure the relative precedential values of the authorities you are working with, ask the following questions for each authority:

A. PRIMARY AUTHORITY: IS THIS AUTHORITY REALLY "LAW"?

Some authorities are "law," and some are simply commentary on the law or suggestions about what the law ought to be. Authorities that are actually law are called "primary authorities." Authorities that are explanation or commentary on primary authorities are called "secondary authorities."

Primary authority is created by an entity that has the legal power to create law, and it is in one of the forms used to create law. In addition to federal and state constitutions, three basic kinds of law exist: (1) case law created by courts, (2) statutory law created by legislatures, and (3) administrative law created by governmental agencies. All three of these kinds of authorities are "law." Situations governed by Michigan law are governed by the Michigan Constitution and by the statutes the Michigan legislature creates. They are governed by the case law the Michigan courts create. They are governed by the administrative law the Michigan state agencies create. They are also governed by applicable federal case law, statutes, and administrative law. All of these sources are primary authority.

Secondary authority comes in many forms. You may already be familiar with some secondary sources such as treatises or hornbooks on particular subject areas, legal encyclopedias, or law review articles. These sources are created by private individuals or businesses. They may help you locate primary law or understand it better once you have found it. For some, respect for the author or for the drafting process will cause judges to pay deference to the source's content, but those private individuals or businesses do not have the authority to create law. So generally, when a secondary source conflicts with a primary source from that jurisdiction, the primary source controls.

B. MANDATORY AUTHORITY: IS THIS AUTHORITY BINDING?

Not all primary authorities will be binding on the Georgia court that will ultimately decide Watson's question. For instance, an Iowa statute or case opinion would not bind the Georgia court. The Georgia court may find the Iowa opinion persuasive, perhaps because of the strength of its reasoning or because it represents the rule in a majority of jurisdictions or because the judge who wrote the opinion is particularly well respected; but the Georgia court would not be *required* to follow it. The Iowa court will be explaining Iowa law, and Georgia is not bound to follow Iowa law. Thus the Iowa opinion would be *persuasive* authority, not *mandatory* authority.

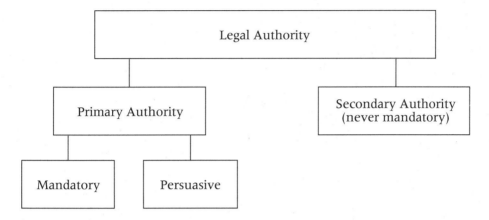

Probably you have already learned about the structure of court systems from your legal research text. Here is a summary of the way this structure affects the determination of whether a primary authority is mandatory or persuasive.

Each state has two court systems—a state system and a federal system. Each of those systems has a trial-level court and at least one appellate-level court. The federal court system is the same for each state. It is structured like this:

United States Supreme Court	Highest appellate court
United States Court of Appeals (for that circuit)	Intermediate appellate court
United States District Court (for that district)	Trial-level court

A case is filed in the trial court, here the District Court. Subsequently, it may be appealed to the intermediate appellate court, the Court of Appeals for that circuit. Finally, under certain circumstances it may be appealed to the Supreme Court, the highest appellate court in the federal system.

State court systems follow a similar pattern, though the courts may have different names. Cases are filed first in the trial court and then may be appealed to an intermediate appellate court (if one exists) and ultimately to that state's highest appellate court. For example, the state court system for Idaho is:

Idaho Supreme Court	Highest appellate court
Idaho Court of Appeals	Intermediate appellate court
Idaho District Court	Trial-level court

On issues of state law, the decisions of a state's highest court are mandatory authority for all other courts of that state, as well as for all federal courts applying that state's law. The state's highest court is not bound by its own decisions. Its role as a developer of the law requires it to be free to overrule itself. However, reluctance to change the law without compelling reason causes even the highest court to pay great deference to its own prior holdings.

Decisions of intermediate appellate courts are binding on trial courts within the geographic boundaries of the intermediate appellate court's jurisdiction. Decisions of courts from other states or of federal courts, including the United States Supreme Court, are persuasive but not mandatory.

On issues of federal law, decisions of the United States Supreme Court are binding on all federal and state courts in the country. Decisions of the intermediate-level federal appellate court (the United States Court of Appeals for that particular circuit) are binding on all federal district courts in that circuit. Figure 5-1 shows the geographic jurisdictions of the federal circuit courts of appeal.

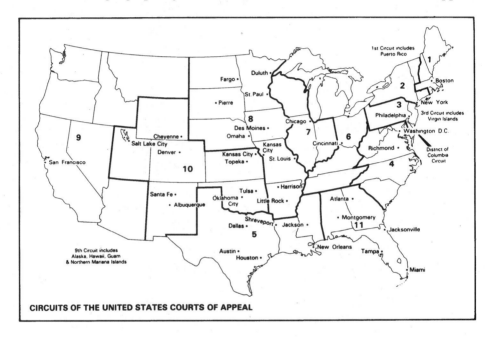

CIRCUITS OF THE UNITED STATES COURTS OF APPEAL

Figure 5-1
The federal judicial circuits, as shown in **1996 Judicial Staff Directory 537 (Ann L. Brownson ed., 10th ed. 1996).**

Decisions of federal intermediate appellate courts and federal trial courts on issues of federal law are not mandatory authority for state courts. However, as a practical matter, state courts generally give the opinions of those courts significant weight. This is particularly true of state courts within the geographical boundaries of the particular federal court.

C.   SUBSEQUENT TREATMENT: IS THIS AUTHORITY STILL "GOOD LAW"?

Before relying on any authority, you must update it to find out whether it is still valid authority, still "good law." A case opinion can be reversed by a higher court or overruled (expressly or implicitly) by a later opinion in a different case.[2] A statute can be repealed or amended by a later statute. The effect of a statute may be limited or even expanded by a later court ruling interpreting the statute. A court may have nullified the statute on constitutional grounds. Your research text will explain how to update your sources. Never rely on any authority you have not updated.

D. WHAT OTHER CHARACTERISTICS MAY AFFECT THE PERSUASIVE VALUE?

Mandatory authority is, of course, binding. However, occasionally you may find two conflicting sources of mandatory authority. For instance, you may find a statute and a conflicting case opinion from the jurisdiction's highest court. If the legislature has enacted a statute governing a particular issue, a court is bound by it. So, the first thing to do is to compare the dates of the statute and the opinion. If the opinion predates the statute, the statute takes precedence. The opinion is binding only as to issues not addressed by the subsequent statute.

Once the statute is enacted, however, courts are bound by the statute. A court can declare a statute invalid if the statute suffers from some constitutional infirmity; but if the statute is valid, the court is bound by it. However, courts often interpret statutes—they tell us what the statute means. If the subsequent opinion interpreted the statute in a particular way, the opinion's interpretation of the statute takes precedence over any other interpretation. In that sense, the opinion controls the statute.

For nonbinding case law, precedential value can be affected by a number of other factors, including the following:

1. The relative level of the issuing court.   The more prestigious the court, the more persuasive its opinions. For instance, a decision of the United States Supreme Court is powerful persuasive authority, even when it is not mandatory.

2. The date of the opinion.   All other things being equal, more recent opinions carry more persuasive value.

3. The comparison between what the opinion says and what the court actually does.   Remember that a court holds what it does and not what it says. The greater the consistency between the rule the opinion announces and the rule it actually applies, the greater the precedential value.

---

2.   An opinion is reversed when that *same* case is appealed to a higher court and that court reverses the opinion of the court below. Once a case has completed the litigation process and is closed, it cannot be reversed except by reopening proceedings in that same case. However, the opinion in that case can be overruled. An opinion is overruled if, in a later opinion in a *different* case, the issuing court or a higher court recants the law set out in the earlier opinion.

4.   The strength of the opinion's reasoning.   A well-reasoned opinion is more persuasive than a poorly reasoned opinion. An opinion that includes a thorough discussion of policy[3] is more persuasive than an opinion that simply applies existing legal authorities without exploration of the policy rational for the rule.

5.   The subsequent treatment of the opinion by other authorities.   Later authorities, both primary and secondary, may comment on your authority. For instance, later case opinions may discuss and rely on the case you are evaluating. Conversely, a later opinion may question or reject the reasoning of the earlier case. Legal writers may comment on the case in treatises or law review articles. An opinion that has received favorable notice usually will carry greater persuasive weight than an opinion that has received no notice or critical notice.

6.   Whether the court's statements about your issue are part of the holding or dicta.   Statements that are not part of the holding are dicta, and are not as persuasive as statements that are part of the holding.[4]

7.   How factually similar the opinion is to the facts of the present situation.   A judge will want to be sure that the writer of an earlier opinion meant that the rule of law articulated there should also apply to factual situations like the one the judge is now deciding. The more similar the facts of the two situations, the more sure the judge can be that the authority was meant to apply to situations like the present one.

8.   The number of subscribing judges.   Most federal intermediate-level appellate cases are decided by a panel of the court, usually three judges. Far less frequently a case will be decided by all judges of that court (the court sitting *en banc*). En banc opinions are binding on future panels of the same court. They are generally more persuasive to other courts than are panel decisions. Unanimous opinions are more persuasive than split decisions. Majority opinions are more persuasive than closely split decisions. A majority opinion generally is more persuasive than a concurring opinion, which is in turn more persuasive than a dissenting opinion.

Be careful with concurring or dissenting opinions. Look to see if the statement of law you are interested in is part of the disagreement between the concurring or dissenting opinion and the majority opinion. If so, the statement in the concurring or dissenting opinion may actually establish that what it says is *not* the law, since the opinion is disagreeing with the majority opinion on that point, and since the majority opinion is the one that establishes the law.

---

3.   A rule is supported by "policy" when the opinion explains not only *what* the law is, but also why that particular rule is the best choice.

4.   *See* pp. 45-47.

En banc opinion	An opinion issued in a case heard by all of the judges of that particular court.
Majority opinion	An opinion subscribed to by a majority of the judges who heard the case.
Concurring opinion	An opinion that agrees with the result reached by the majority opinion but for reasons different from those of the majority opinion.
Dissenting opinion	An opinion that disagrees with the result reached by the majority opinion.

9. The format of the opinion. Some opinions explain fully the facts of the case, the rule governing the issues, the policy supporting the rule, and the application of that law to the facts of that case. Some opinions barely report any facts, skim over a statement of law, announce a holding, and stop there. Of course, there are many possibilities between these two extremes. Generally, a full and careful discussion carries more persuasive value than a cryptic discussion.

10. Whether the opinion is published. If the opinion does not appear in an official collection of published opinions (an official case reporter), it is not "published." In most jurisdictions, an unpublished opinion has no precedential value, and many courts have local rules that prohibit citing or relying on an unpublished opinion. However, some courts will give some credence to an unpublished opinion on the theory that stare decisis should still operate, even with regard to unpublished opinions. Even if the court declines to give the unpublished opinion any precedential weight, an unpublished opinion may still help you predict how that same court would approach a similar situation.

11. The reputation of the particular judge writing the case opinion. Some judges have earned particular respect separate from the position they hold. The opinions of those judges may have added persuasive value.

12. Trends in the law. If you can discern a trend among other courts in the nation or in your state, opinions consistent with that trend may have greater precedential value than inconsistent opinions. For instance, if, over the past several years your state's highest court has been extending the liability of manufacturers in various situations, a case opinion consistent with that trend may have more precedential weight than an opinion that questions that trend.

 **RECONCILING THE AUTHORITIES**

Your second method for dealing with inconsistent cases is to reconcile the cases. You may be able to combine the language in the cases into one rule of law. This process is called "synthesizing" or "harmonizing" opinions. Often you will discover that a more careful reading of the court's language can resolve the apparent conflict. Perhaps you initially misread one opinion. Perhaps one opinion uses careless language. If so, the way the court *applied* the rule it articulated may help you see what the court really meant. Or the rule in one case may actually be a more complete explanation of one of the elements of the rule from the other case.

If you conclude that the language from the opinions really does set out different rules, ask yourself whether these seemingly inconsistent legal rules are meant to apply to different situations. Analysis that leads to a conclusion that the rules in two opinions apply to different situations often is called "distinguishing" cases. As you reexamine the cases, you may find factual or procedural differences that lead you to realize that the rules articulated in the cases are meant to apply to different kinds of situations. For example, one rule may apply when a business is a "lending institution" and the other rule may apply to other kinds of businesses. Perhaps one rule is meant to be an exception to the other. If the rules are meant to apply to different situations, then the rule in one of the cases will apply to your client's case while the other will not.

In attempting to reconcile cases, you will be looking for clues to tell you whether one of these resolutions is possible. You must reread carefully all of the language in the seemingly conflicting opinions. You must look for later cases that may resolve the seeming inconsistency. Even if the later cases do not mention the inconsistency, these later cases will probably articulate and apply a rule. As you study the way these later cases articulate and apply the law, you may find clues about whether one of these reconciliations is possible.

Finally, you may find that both rules are potentially applicable to your client's situation and that they are not reconcilable. As you have already learned, lawmakers seldom *mean* to maintain two inconsistent rules in a single jurisdiction. Yet, such a situation is possible. Two courts of equal rank may adopt differing rules until a higher court resolves the difference of opinion. Or perhaps in an area of constitutional analysis, the Supreme Court may apply different tests, particularly while the members of the Court are trying to reach consensus on the issue. If the clues you have found lead you to believe that both rules cover your issue, your task is to predict which rule the judge is more likely to apply. You may consider such factors as the direction in which the court seems to be moving, which rule is better reasoned, and which rule produces a more reasonable result under the facts of your case.[5]

No matter which resolution you reach, remember that if you are struggling with the large-scale organization of your first draft, you are struggling with formulating the rule. If you are struggling with formulating the rule, you have not yet mastered the authorities. When you are sitting in front of the computer keyboard or holding a dictaphone, you will be on your own. No teacher will be there to offer advice about how to get past a thinking or writing roadblock. Your first draft structure can offer important counsel. Don't forget to listen to it.

Back to the question of what to do with *Fox* and *Clein*. First, gauge the precedential value of each authority. You find that both opinions are mandatory au-

5.   Chapter 6 will explain how to organize your discussion when you must decide which of two potentially applicable rules will apply to your client's situation.

thorities, and both were issued by the highest court in the state. Both are factually similar to Watson's case. However, *Fox* is more recent, and it does not mention *Clein* at all. This may be particularly significant since *Fox* does cite several other earlier cases as support for its own articulation of the rule.

Further, *Fox* lays out a test in tabulated form, which seems to indicate that the court was intentionally announcing a rule. Compare this tabulation with the more rambling discussion that forms the basis for the rule formulation in *Clein*. The *Clein* court even drops factual conclusions about time and territory into the middle of this rambling discussion—a discussion that does not otherwise mention these aspects of the covenant as part of the test.

Finally, one of the differences between the rules the two opinions seem to lay out, *Clein*'s statement that the covenant must be supported by sufficient consideration, is dictum. Thus, it appears that the precedential value of *Fox* outweighs *Clein*, especially with regard to the part of the *Clein* rule that is dictum.

Next, try to distinguish the two opinions. You only find one potentially significant distinction—the covenant in *Fox* was part of an employment contract and the covenant in *Clein* (like the Watson facts) was part of the sale of a business. However, *Clein* explains that the effect of this distinction is simply that more latitude is allowed a covenant arising as part of the sale of a business. Neither opinion indicates that the test for determining reasonableness (the rule) would be different based on this distinction.

Trying to harmonize the opinions causes you to wonder whether perhaps *Clein* implies two of the three *Fox* elements, time and territory. After all, those two aspects of the covenant are mentioned in the court's discussion of the *Clein* facts. Although the *Clein* opinion does not include "time and territory" as part of the rule it seems to announce, *Clein*'s factual conclusions on those two aspects of the covenant do seem to recognize that they are legally significant.

Trying to harmonize the opinions also leads you to notice that, while *Fox* does not specifically mention adequacy of consideration (a *Clein* element), *Fox* does state that "the contract [must] be valid in other essentials," citing to two earlier cases. You know from your study of contracts law that one of the essential elements of a valid contract is adequacy of consideration, so it seems that *Fox* is not inconsistent with the first element of the rule you formulated from *Clein*. As a matter of fact, it appears that *Fox* supports an element that would incorporate all essential elements of a contract, not just sufficient consideration.

So, you use the results of your comparison of the two cases to try to formulate the most likely rule. Since you have noticed that the first element from your *Clein* rule is actually part of an additional element announced in *Fox*, one you had originally missed, you can include that additional element. The second half of your *Clein* rule seems to conflict with *Fox*, and no distinguishing feature of *Clein* seems to imply that the *Clein* rule rather than the *Fox* rule would apply to the Watson facts. Therefore, the apparent greater precedential value of *Fox* seems to trump the second half of the *Clein* rule. You decide that this is the Georgia rule on enforcing covenants-not-to-compete:[6]

---

6.   Several reconciliations of *Fox* and *Clein* are possible. As a matter of fact, in Chapter 17 we'll revisit these two cases, exploring a way to salvage some additional precedential value from *Clein*.

I. Is the Watson covenant-not-to-compete enforceable?

The covenant is enforceable if the contract is valid in all other essentials and if the activity restrained, the geographical area of the restraint, and the time period of the restraint are all reasonable.

A. Is the contract valid in all other essentials, including sufficiency of consideration?
    [Discuss any relevant cases pertaining to contract essentials including *Fox* and *Clein*.]

B. Is the kind of activity restrained reasonable?
    [Discuss any relevant cases pertaining to the nature of the restrained activity, including *Fox* and *Clein*.]

C. Is the geographical scope reasonable?
    [Discuss any relevant cases pertaining to the geographical limits of a restrained activity, including *Fox* and *Clein*.]

D. Is the duration of the restraint reasonable?
    [Discuss any relevant cases pertaining to the duration of a restraint, including *Fox* and *Clein*.]

Under each element, you'll discuss each case that tells you something important about that element. Notice that cases should appear under more than one element when those cases contribute to the analysis of more than one element. For instance, under element *C* you'll discuss what *Fox* tells you about how to decide whether the duration of the restraint is reasonable. You'll also discuss what *Clein* said about the duration element as well.

This organization serves the dual functions of a working draft. It helps you analyze, and it serves as the starting point for the organization of your later drafts. Although the idea of using the rule to organize your discussion sounds simple, you may be surprised at how easy it will be to stray away from this method of organizing a legal discussion. You will need to watch your drafts carefully until you develop writing habits that make this way of structuring the analysis second nature to you.

◆ IV ◆ EXERCISES

◆ EXERCISE 1. Gauging the Relative Weights of Authority

Your firm represents Kay Lang, who sold a piece of commercial property located in Los Angeles to Adam Kornfeld. Kornfeld claims that Lang failed to disclose to him the true condition of the property, and he has filed suit against her for damages in the state trial court. You are researching whether, under California law, a seller of real property has a duty to disclose to the buyer the condition of the property.

You have found the following authorities. (1) Which are primary authorities? (2) For each primary authority, describe the precedential value it likely will carry for the dispute between Kornfeld and Lang.

a. An opinion of the California Supreme Court deciding the duty of a seller to disclose to the buyer the condition of the property

b. An article in the University of California at Los Angeles (UCLA) Law Review discussing the applicable California rule on the seller's duty to disclose to the buyer the condition of the property

c. An opinion of the United States Court of Appeals for the Ninth Circuit applying the applicable California rule on the duty of a seller to disclose to a buyer the condition of the property

d. A California statute on the duty of a seller to disclose to a buyer the condition of the property

e. An unpublished opinion of another California state trial court applying the California rule on the duty of a seller to disclose to a buyer the condition of the property

f. A section from a California legal encyclopedia explaining the applicable California rule on the duty of a seller to disclose to a buyer the condition of the property

g. An opinion of the United States Supreme Court applying the California rule on the duty of a seller to disclose to a buyer the condition of the property

EXERCISE 2.   Gauging the Relative Weights of Authority

Your firm represents Marietta Jones, a plaintiff in an employment discrimination action. You have filed suit on her behalf against Treemart, your client's former employer, alleging that Treemart selected Jones for layoff because of her race. The suit is filed in the United States District Court for the Southern District of New York. The complaint alleges violations of the Civil Rights Act of 1964, 42 U.S.C. § 2000e-17, a federal statute that prohibits employment discrimination based on certain protected characteristics including race.

However, before Jones can bring suit in a court, the federal statute requires that she first file a charge with the applicable administrative agency. Her charge must be filed within 300 days of the allegedly discriminatory act.

On January 3, Treemart had notified Jones that she had been selected for layoff. The layoff was to be effective on February 3. Treemart has filed a motion to dismiss the Jones complaint, arguing that Jones did not file the agency charge within 300 days after January 3, the date that Treemart notified Jones of her selection for layoff. Jones argues that she filed suit within 300 days after February 3, the date her layoff became effective. The legal issue is whether the federal statute's time period began to run when Jones was notified of her selection or when the layoff actually became effective.

You research the issue and find the following authorities. (1) Which are primary authorities? (2) For each primary authority, describe how much precedential value it likely will carry in *Jones v. Treemart.*

    a. An explanation of the rule on when the time period begins to run found in the leading treatise on the Civil Rights Act of 1964

    b. An opinion of the United States Court of Appeals for the second Circuit discussing whether the time period begins to run from the notification date or the effective date of an employment decision

    c. An opinion of the United States Court of Appeals for the fifth Circuit discussing whether the time period begins to run from the notification date or the effective date of an employment decision

    d. An opinion of the New York Court of Appeals (the highest state court for New York) applying the Civil Rights Act of 1964 and deciding whether the time period begins to run from the notification date or the effective date of the employment decision

    e. An opinion of the New York Court of Appeals applying the comparable provision of the New York statute that also prohibits employment discrimination.

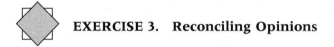 **EXERCISE 3.   Reconciling Opinions**

Remember that often you can formulate different rules from the same set of authorities. In the following exercise, you may find that your answers differ from those of your classmates. Part of the benefit (and fun) of these exercises is to compare these differing answers and to identify those that are most accurate and complete.

Reconcile the following four summaries of case opinions setting out the requirements for recovery under the attractive nuisance doctrine. Use them to formulate one rule of law, if possible. For each part of the rule you formulate, identify the case(s) you would cite for support of that part of the rule.

Use the rule you have formulated to create an outline of a working draft analyzing whether a hypothetical set of facts would allow recovery under the doctrine of attractive nuisance.

Bell v. Grackin (state's highest appellate court, 1959)

Facts: A piece of wire was lying in a neighbor's yard. A child walking by saw the wire and went into the yard to get it. As he was playing with the wire, the child bent it and then let it go. The wire recoiled, hitting the child in the eye. The child sought recovery from the neighbor based on the doctrine of attractive nuisance. The court denied recovery, stating:

    The doctrine underlying the "attractive nuisance" cases applies only where the instrument or artificial condition is within itself inherently dangerous even while being used properly, such as weapons, explosives, or power tools. It would be extending the doctrine entirely too far to apply it to such commonplace objects as a piece of wire, a pencil, a coat hanger, or a hammer, all objects so commonplace as to be found around any house or yard, but not dangerous in themselves, although they might be attractive to children and capable of inflicting injury if misused.

Andersonville v. Goodden (state's intermediate-level appellate court, 1961)

Facts: A neighbor's pickup truck was parked unattended in the neighbor's yard. A child came into the yard to sell the neighbor candy bars for a school fund-raising project. The child saw the truck, climbed on it, fell, and impaled himself on a hook on the end of a chain dangling from the rear of the truck. The child sought recovery from the neighbor based on the doctrine of attractive nuisance. The court denied recovery, stating:

> The attractive nuisance doctrine was developed for the benefit of children coming upon property even though trespassing. However, the courts of this state have been reluctant to extend the doctrine beyond its restricted application to situations in which the dangerous instrument is found to be one of actual and compelling attraction for children. The courts have not expanded the doctrine to cases where the instrument or artificial condition did not actually draw the children onto the property.

Newcomb v. Roberts (state's highest appellate court, 1982)

Facts: A swimming pool was located in a backyard with no fence, unshielded from view. A child visiting next door and playing hide-and-seek came into the backyard seeking a hiding place. She hid behind a utility shack for a while, but began to wonder whether her friends were still looking for her. She decided to go investigate the status of the game. As she was leaving the backyard, walking alongside the pool, she accidentally fell into the pool and suffered serious injury. She brought suit against the property owner under the doctrine of attractive nuisance. The court allowed recovery, stating:

> A landowner is liable for physical harm to trespassing children by an artificial condition if the place where the condition exists is one upon which the possessor knows or has reason to know that children are likely to trespass; if the risk posed by the condition is one that children, because of their youth, will not realize; and if the landowner fails to exercise reasonable care to eliminate the danger or otherwise to protect the children. This landowner should have known that neighborhood children were likely to trespass and that such children would not appreciate the risks posed by a swimming pool. The landowner did not enclose the pool in a fence or take any steps to shield the pool from view. Thus, the landowner is liable for the injuries to the child.

McDaniels v. Lanier (state's highest appellate court, 1987)

Facts: A natural pond lay behind a house located on two acres of property. The pond was visible to passersby, and no fence prevented access. A child saw the pool and decided to swim in the pool. The child suffered abdominal cramps and drowned. The court denied recovery, stating:

> An owner who has reason to know that children are likely to trespass is liable, under the doctrine of attractive nuisance, for injuries sustained by a child if the risk is one that children will not appreciate and if the owner has failed to exercise reasonable care to protect the child [cite to *Newcomb*]. However, here the condition that caused the injury was a naturally occurring condition rather than an artificial condition. While landowners have a duty to protect trespassing children from artificially created conditions on their property, they do not have the duty to protect trespassing children from naturally occurring conditions. Such a duty would often require landowners to take unreasonable or impossible actions such as fencing off huge tracts of land. Thus, the owner is not liable for the injuries to the trespassing child.

6 · Using a Rule to Form the Structure: Special Circumstances

As we have seen, the first step in the writing process is to formulate the rule of law and use its structure as the outline of your legal analysis. Chapters 2 through 4 set out this basic principle and explained how to find and structure a rule from a single authority. Chapter 5 tackled rule formulation from multiple authorities. This chapter clarifies several potential areas of confusion you may encounter in structuring-by-rule.

I   RULES WITHIN A RULE

Every time you analyze a rule of law that has elements within it, you are actually working with more than one substantive rule. For instance, in the Shaffer burglary example on page 28, the rule setting out the elements of burglary was a rule of law. Then, in each subsection, the analysis of that particular element required you to work with the rule of law that defines that particular element. The rule that defines the "nighttime" element, for example, might be "a time between thirty minutes after sunset and thirty minutes before sunrise." Thus, working with rules within a larger rule is quite common. We might call the larger rule, the one that establishes the relationships among the subrules, the "umbrella" rule.[1]

When you are working with an umbrella rule containing elements, each of which has its own subrule, the umbrella rule provides your structure. Look

1.   Richard K. Neumann, Jr., *Legal Reasoning and Legal Writing: Structure, Strategy, and Style* (2d ed. 1994).

back at the rule outlines in Chapters 2 through 4; notice how the umbrella rules create the relationships among the subrules.

Sometimes you will find the subrules in the same opinion or statute that establishes the umbrella rule. All of the rules in Chapters 2 through 4 are examples of such rules. But sometimes you will have to look in other cases or other statutes for the subrules. Let's look at an example of an umbrella rule that requires you to look elsewhere for its subrules.

Suppose that you are researching the enforceability of an oral promise to sell several sections of large concrete drainpipe. On May 15, the sales manager of Harper Building Supply orally promised to sell one section of concrete pipe to Raymond Garcia for the price of $400, delivery to occur on June 1. Also on May 15, this same sales manager orally promised to sell another section of concrete pipe to Garcia for the price of $400, delivery to occur on July 1. Each section of pipe weighs 1,500 pounds. The pipe was to come from Harper's existing stock in its yard. Neither of the parties created any documents showing that they made a contract.

When you research the law, you discover that your jurisdiction's version of § 2-201(1) of the Uniform Commercial Code (U.C.C.) provides that "a contract for the sale of goods for the price of $500 or more is not enforceable . . . unless there is some writing sufficient to indicate that a contract for sale has been made."

The outline of a legal analysis applying this rule might be:

> I.   Is Harper Building Supply's oral promise to sell concrete pipe enforceable?
>
> An oral contract is not enforceable if it is a contract for the sale of goods and the price is $500 or more.
>
>> A.   Is this a contract for the sale of goods?
>> B.   Is the price $500 or more?

Now you need to know whether there are subrules for each of the elements of your umbrella rule. First, is concrete pipe a kind of "goods"? Is there a rule of law that defines the term "goods"? You look for definitions in the U.C.C., and you find that the U.C.C. defines "goods" in another section, § 2-105(1), as "all things . . . movable at the time of identification to the contract for sale." Outline this definitional rule, placing it under *A* in your umbrella rule. Now your rule looks like this:

> I.   Is Harper Building Supply's oral promise to sell concrete pipe enforceable?
>
> An oral contract is not enforceable if it is a contract for the sale of goods and the price is $500 or more.

> A. Is this a contract for the sale of goods?
>
> Items are "goods" if they are movable at the time of identification to the contract.
>
>   1. When was the concrete pipe "identified"?
>   2. Was the concrete pipe "movable" at that time?
>
> B. Is the price $500 or more?

Now ask yourself whether subelements 1 and 2 require application of any rules. Is there a code provision or case law that defines "identification"? Is there a code provision or case law that defines "movable"? These questions send you back to your copy of the U.C.C. and to the case reporters.

Assume that you find no code provision defining "movable," but you find several case opinions holding that items are "movable," even when they are too heavy to be moved in ordinary ways. For instance, you found a case holding that a 10,000-pound fuel tank is "movable" and another holding that a 10,000-gallon water tank is "movable." In your discussion under subelement 1, then, you will state and apply this rule to the Harper transaction.

When you search the code for a definition of "identification to the contract," you find your jurisdiction's version of § 2-501. That U.C.C. code section provides that for goods already existing, "identification" occurs immediately upon the making of the contract. Now add the rules for subelements 1 and 2 to your outline:

> I. Is Harper Building Supply's oral promise to sell concrete pipe enforceable?
>
> An oral contract is not enforceable if it is a contract for the sale of goods and the price is $500 or more.
>
> A. Is this a contract for the sale of goods?
>
> Items are "goods" if they are movable at the time of identification to the contract.
>
>   1. When was the concrete pipe "identified"?
>
>   For goods already existing, "identification" occurs immediately upon the making of the contract.
>
>   2. Was the concrete pipe "movable" at that time?
>
>   Items far larger than the drainage pipe can be "movable" even though they are too heavy to be moved in ordinary ways.
>
> B. Is the price $500 or more?

Now what about the second element of the umbrella rule, the "$500 or more" element? The conduct of your buyer and seller may constitute two contracts, each for $400, or one contract for $800. You will need to search for a rule that determines whether you are dealing with one contract or two. Assume that you look through the rest of the U.C.C. and you do not find a rule that governs this question. However, you do find a case opinion dealing with similar facts. The case opinion tells you that the answer depends on the intent of the parties. The opinion also gives you some factors that might help you discern the intent of the parties, such as whether the two promises were made at the same time; whether the course of dealing between the parties established a custom of contracting for only one delivery per contract; whether the negotiations for the two transactions covered different topics; whether the items were going to be used on different construction jobs; and any other facts that would provide a clue about the parties' intent.

Next, outline this subrule with its factors, and place it under *B* of the umbrella rule. Now you have completed the structure for your analysis. It should look like this:

I. Is Harper Building Supply's oral promise to sell concrete pipe enforceable?

    An oral contract is not enforceable if it is a contract for the sale of goods and the price is $500 or more.

    A. Is this a contract for the sale of goods?

        Items are "goods" if they are movable at the time of identification to the contract.

        1. When was the concrete pipe "identified"?

            For goods already existing, "identification" occurs immediately upon the making of the contract.

        2. Was the concrete pipe "movable" at that time?

            Items far larger than the drainpipe can be "movable" even though they are too heavy to be moved in ordinary ways.

    B. Is the price $500 or more?

        The parties' intent governs the question of whether these facts establish two contracts or one. A court can consider the following factors in deciding intent:

        1. Were the two promises made at the same time?
        2. Was there a course of dealing between the parties establishing a custom of contracting for only one delivery per contract?
        3. Did the negotiations for the two transactions cover different topics?
        4. Were the items to be used on different construction jobs?
        5. Are there any other facts that would provide clues about the parties' intent?

You see that the subrules for § 2-201(1) (the umbrella rule) were located outside § 2-201(1) itself. They were located in other parts of the U.C.C. and in case law. However, the umbrella rule had established the relationships of the subrules to each other and to the umbrella rule. Thus, the umbrella rule provides the structure—the outline—for your working analysis.

 # SEVERAL SEPARATE RULES WITH NO UMBRELLA RULE

Suppose you find yourself working with several rules, and no umbrella rule has already set out the relationships among these rules. How will you organize these rules in relation to each other? Here is an example:

Assume that your firm represents Fairly Reliable Used Cars, Inc. as well as one of Fairly Reliable's sales agents, Tina Foster. Foster took her own car onto Fairly Reliable's lot and sold it to an individual who came to the lot looking for a good used car. As it turns out, the car was not even "fairly" reliable, and the buyer wants to get his money back. The requesting attorney has asked you to research the question of whether the law imposes a warranty on this sort of a sale. If your jurisdiction has adopted a version of the U.C.C., the answer to the question may be different depending on whether the U.C.C. warranty provisions apply to this transaction. Therefore, your analysis of the issue will need to include an answer to whether the U.C.C. applies to this situation. If the applicability is unclear, you will need to analyze the issue in two ways—under the U.C.C. and under non-U.C.C. contract law.

So, you find that you are working with three rules of law: (1) the rule of law that governs *whether* the U.C.C. applies; (2) the U.C.C. rule of law that will govern the issue if the U.C.C. *does* apply; and (3) the non-U.C.C. rule of law that will govern the issue if the U.C.C. does *not* apply.

Which rule of law will form your working draft structure? All three of them. Each will form the structure of a separate section of the analysis. Since you have no umbrella rule that already establishes the relationships between these rules, you will need to create the umbrella structure yourself. Your understanding of the rules and the question you are answering, combined with common sense, will give you the umbrella structure. Here, the rule of law governing the applicability of the U.C.C. will form the structure of one of the subheadings. The U.C.C.'s rule of law that would govern the warranty issue, assuming that the U.C.C. applies, will form the structure of another subheading. The non-U.C.C. rule that would govern the warranty issue if the U.C.C. does not apply will form the structure of a third subheading:

I.   Does the law impose a warranty on this sale?

A.   Do U.C.C. warranty provisions govern this transaction?

[Structure subsections according to the rule governing whether U.C.C. warranty provisions apply to this transaction.]

B. If U.C.C. warranty provisions govern this transaction, what warranties apply?

[Structure subsections according to the U.C.C. rule governing warranties.]

C. If non-U.C.C. law governs this transaction, what warranties apply?

[Structure subsections according to the non-U.C.C. rule governing warranties.]

Thus, when you are working with several rules that are not already placed in relationship by an umbrella rule, simply use each to organize a subsection of the analysis, and create the umbrella structure yourself, ordering the subsections in a manner that makes sense for the analysis.

III TWO RULES: ONE SUBSTANTIVE AND ONE PROCEDURAL

Sometimes you will be working simultaneously with a rule governing the substantive issue and a rule governing the procedural posture of the issue. For example, in the Fairly Reliable litigation, substantive rules will tell you whether the buyer can get his money back, but a procedural rule may tell you what standards he must meet in order to prevail *at this particular stage* of the litigation. In such a case, which rule will you use as the basis for your organization?

Use whichever rule tells you which *facts* have legal significance. If the substantive rule defines what facts are relevant and the procedural rule tells the judge only the *standard* for analyzing those facts, then the procedural rule really functions only as a gloss on the substantive rule. In such a case, use the substantive rule as your overall structure, simply phrasing the issue with reference to the standard imposed by the procedural rule.

Back to the Watson covenant-not-to-compete from Chapter 4 for an example. Assume that the Carrolton Company has sued Watson for violation of the covenant. At trial, the substantive rule of law will set out what Carrolton must prove to enforce the covenant-not-to-compete. Assume that you have concluded that all essentials of a contract are present and that the substantive rule governing whether the covenant will be enforced is:

A covenant is enforceable if all of the following are reasonable:

A. the kind of activity restrained
B. the geographical area of the restraint
C. the time period of the restraint

Now, suppose that the company thinks that the facts establishing the reasonableness of these three terms are so strong that a jury trial would be a waste of time and an unnecessary expense. Rule 56 of the applicable rules of civil procedure allows summary judgment (judgment without a trial) if the undisputed facts are so convincing that no reasonable judge or jury could decide that the terms are unreasonable. If the company can convince the judge that the facts are *this* clear, then the company can win *now* rather than going through a trial.

Notice that the procedural rule governing summary judgment doesn't make any facts relevant *other than* the facts that were already relevant to the covenant-not-to-compete. The procedural rule only tells the judge how to look at the facts that were already relevant. The judge will have to decide not just whether *the judge* thinks that the terms were reasonable, but whether no reasonable judge or jury could think otherwise. So, the substantive rule is the one that tells you what facts are relevant, and thus it will structure your analysis. Simply phrase the substantive rule with reference to the standards of proof required by the procedural rule, like so:

> I.   Can Carrolton obtain summary judgment?
>
> To obtain summary judgment Carrolton must show that, on the undisputed facts, no reasonable judge or jury could conclude that the nature of the restraint, the scope of the restraint, or the duration of the restraint is unreasonable.
>
> A.   Do the undisputed facts show that kind of activity restrained is reasonable?
>
> B.   Do the undisputed facts show that the geographical area of the restraint is reasonable?
>
> C.   Do the undisputed facts show that the time period of the restraint is reasonable?

The summary judgment rule is an example of a rule that does not define what facts are relevant. Some procedural rules, however, do more than govern the manner or standard by which the judge must view the facts made relevant by the substantive rule. Some procedural rules make some *additional* facts relevant before the party can get relief. In such a case, the *procedural* rule identifies the relevant facts, and it will form the structure of the analysis.

For instance, in the Watson case, the company might ask the judge for a preliminary injunction, an order prohibiting Watson from continuing to compete during the time between the beginning of the litigation and the trial. Assume that this is the procedural rule governing whether a preliminary injunction will be issued:

To obtain a preliminary injunction, Carrolton must show all of the following:
  A.   that Carrolton is likely to succeed at trial;
  B.   that Carrolton will suffer irreparable harm if Watson continues to compete while awaiting trial; and

    C. that the equities favor the issuance of the preliminary injunction protecting Carrolton's interests prior to trial.

This procedural rule does much more than tell the judge how to look at the facts that will be relevant to deciding the enforceability of the covenant-not-to-compete. Only one of the three elements (the first one) pertains to the facts of the covenant at all. The other two elements tell you that some additional facts (facts other than those the plaintiff must prove to prevail at trial) are relevant to whether to grant this type of pretrial order.

In this preliminary injunction situation, the rule that identifies which facts are relevant for this particular motion is the procedural rule; therefore, the procedural rule should form the umbrella structure of the legal discussion. The substantive rule will structure the argument under the first point heading, "likelihood of success at trial."

I.   Can Carrolton obtain a preliminary injunction?

    To obtain a preliminary injunction, Carrolton must show that it is likely to succeed at trial; that it will suffer irreparable harm before a trial can occur; and that the equities favor issuing an injunction.

    A. Is Carrolton likely to succeed at trial?

        To succeed at trial, Carrolton must show that all of the following terms are reasonable:

        1. Is the activity restrained reasonable?
        2. Is the geographic area reasonable?
        3. Is the time period reasonable?

    B. Will Carrolton suffer irreparable harm prior to trial?

    C. Do the equities favor the issuance of the preliminary injunction?

 PERSUADING THE JUDGE TO ADOPT A NEW RULE

Occasionally you will find that your jurisdiction has not yet adopted a rule governing your particular issue. Or perhaps your jurisdiction's rule reflects an unwise approach to the issue, and your client's interests would be served best by the adoption of a new and different rule. These situations will require you to predict what rule the court probably would adopt. Then, you can analyze the disposition of your client's particular issue assuming that your prediction is correct. You may also need to analyze the result if the decision-maker adopts the other rule. Your working draft outline might look like this:

A. If the court adopts rule *A*, what will be the result?

B. If the court adopts rule *B*, what will be the result?

C. Which rule is the court most likely to adopt?

When your uncertainty about the applicable rule is prompted by uncertainty about what rule your jurisdiction will adopt, your search for the rule will be guided primarily by the weight of authority supporting each possible rule and by policy analysis—that is, by discussion about what the rule *should* be and why. In either case, however, the principles guiding the *structure* of your working draft will be the same.

You have now taken your first run at *organizing* your working draft. Your next task is to *write* the working draft. The following chapters tell you how to organize your discussion of each part of your working draft outline. But remember that if you find yourself struggling with which authorities go where, you need to return to those authorities and revisit your organization. Especially as you are learning how to do legal analysis, you may find that you must rethink the tasks of Chapters 2 through 10 several times before your analysis is accurate and complete.

V. EXERCISES IN FORMULATING A RULE FROM MULTIPLE AUTHORITIES

This chapter describes occasions when the analysis must cover multiple rules, such as rules within a rule, several rules with no umbrella rule, or a substantive rule and a procedural rule. For each of the following exercises, identify the variety of multiple-rule discussion called for, and draft an outline for a working draft. Assume that the "rules" set out below are the rules you have formulated from the applicable authority.

EXERCISE 1

Facts

Amy Pyle owned a horse stable and occasionally bought horses from other stables. She bought a certain horse from Robert Coverdale after Coverdale had told her that the horse was in good health. Two weeks later the horse fell ill and died. Pyle has learned that the horse died of a congenital heart defect and that Coverdale knew of the defect when he sold her the horse. Pyle has brought suit against Coverdale for misrepresentation. Coverdale's attorney needs to know whether the complaint could be dismissed for failure to state a claim.

Rules

- A court can dismiss a complaint for "failure to state a claim" if all of the facts and inferences alleged, even if true, still would not constitute a claim on which relief can be granted. (For instance, if the complaint fails to allege one of the elements necessary for a cause of action the court might dismiss the complaint for failure to state a claim.)
- A person is liable for misrepresentation who has, with the intent to induce reliance, made a statement that was untrue, with knowledge of the statement's falsity (or with reckless indifference to the truth), where the plaintiff has justifiably relied and suffered damage therefrom.

 **EXERCISE 2**

Facts

Joe Barrymore and Reynold Manitoba, fans of different hockey teams, came to blows in a discussion of the relative merits of their teams. Barrymore came out the loser (with four broken ribs) and has come to your firm to find out whether he can sue Manitoba for battery.

Rules

- Battery is the intentional infliction of a harmful or offensive bodily contact.
- A contact is harmful if it causes pain or bodily damage.
- A contact is offensive if it would be damaging to a reasonable sense of dignity.
- To meet the requirement of intent for a battery claim, the defendant need only have intended to make the contact; intent to harm is not necessary.

EXERCISE 3

Facts

Dell has sued Canter for breach of contract. Canter believes that the contract is not enforceable because it was an oral contract for the sale of goods for more than $500. (See p. 71.) Canter was served with the summons and complaint, but failed to file a timely answer or other appearance. Dell has sought and been awarded a default judgment against Canter.

A default judgment is entered when the defendant has been served with the summons and complaint and has failed to file a timely answer or other appearance. A default judgment establishes liability and allows the plaintiff to proceed with collecting the amount awarded. If the defendant wants to defend against liability, the defendant must ask the court to set aside the default judgment.

Can Canter successfully move to have the default judgment set aside so that she can defend against Dell's claims?

Rules

- A contract for the sale of goods for the price of $500 or more is not enforceable . . . unless there is some writing sufficient to indicate that a contract for sale has been made.
- To prevail on a motion to set aside a default judgment the defendant must show that the failure to appear was due to mistake or excusable neglect and that an arguable defense to the plaintiff's claims exists.

 **EXERCISE 4**

Facts

Upon her graduation from Kelly Technical College, Shakira Turner began looking for a job in computer repair. She used the services of Grisham Employment Services. Turner, an African-American woman, has begun to suspect that Grisham has known of employment opportunities in her field and has not disclosed those opportunities to her. She has come to your law office to learn if the law gives her any recourse. You have researched Title VII of the Civil Rights Act of 1964 and found the following provisions:

Rules

- The term "employment agency" means any person regularly undertaking with or without compensation to procure employees for an employer or to procure for employees opportunities to work for an employer and includes an agent of such a person. 42 U.S.C. § 2000e(c).
- It shall be an unlawful employment practice for an employment agency to fail or refuse to refer for employment, or otherwise to discriminate against, an individual because of his race, color, religion, sex, or national origin. . . . 42 U.S.C. § 2000e-2(b).

DRAFTING FOR ANALYSIS: WRITING THE WORKING DRAFT

7

Writing the Analysis of a Single Issue: Rule Explanation

After you have created the large-scale structure, the next step is to write out the analysis, putting flesh to the bones of the structure. This task requires a solid understanding of the paradigm for legal analysis and the use of authorities as part of that analysis.

We will begin with a single-issue analysis using only one case. This chapter covers the first half of the paradigm—rule explanation. The following chapter covers the second half of the paradigm—rule application. After you understand these basic concepts, Chapter 9 will explain how to organize multiple authorities in the analysis of a single issue. It will cover both the use of multiple cases and the use of sources for interpreting a statute. Chapter 10 will explain how to organize an analysis of multiple issues.

One suggestion before we continue: You may find that writing out a working draft of the facts before you begin writing the rule explanation section will help you understand both the law and the facts better and earlier. You also may find that writing a draft of the fact statement will help overcome "writer's block." If you choose this approach, write out a draft of the legally significant facts now, before you begin writing the analysis of the law. This working draft of the facts need not follow any particular format. However, if you want to see what the fact statement will ultimately look like, review the fact statement in Appendix A, beginning on page 365. You can also refer to section IV of Chapter 13 (beginning on p. 183) for a description of this section of a completed memo.

HOW TO IDENTIFY A SINGLE-ISSUE DISCUSSION

First, we need to clarify what we mean by a "single-issue discussion." As you worked through the preceding chapters, you outlined the rule and used it to organize your legal discussion. Now distinguish between the parts of the rule that must be considered together and the parts of the rule that can be decided separately. The parts of the rule that must be considered together are all part of the same issue. The parts of the rule that can be decided separately constitute separate issues. Just as we can have rules within a larger umbrella rule,[1] we also can have issues within a larger umbrella issue. You may call these smaller issues "subissues," but they are separate issues nonetheless, and each requires its own separate paradigm. Let's look at some examples. Look back at the common rule structures we identified on pages 16-20 in Chapter 2.

In the first rule structure, the burglary rule (p. 16), which of the rule's six subparts can be decided separately and which must be decided together? Each subpart can be decided separately. None must be decided in conjunction with any other. This umbrella rule would contain six separate issues, and the organizational paradigm described in this chapter and the next would be written out separately for each of them.

Likewise the second rule prohibiting contingent fees in certain kinds of cases (p. 17). Each of the two subparts can be decided separately, so this rule would have two separate issues. The organizational paradigm described in this chapter and the next would be written out separately for each of them.

But the third rule (pp. 17-18) is different. It has nine subparts, but they are all factors to be considered only as *part* of deciding the best interests of the child. None has any legal effect other than as part of the mix of factors determining the child's best interests. So the third rule would have only one separate issue. You would write out only one paradigm, and it would cover all of the subsections of the rule. The subsections will not disappear, however; they will help you organize your discussion, as you will see below.

Now, how many separate issues do the last three rules (pp. 18-20) have? Check your answer against the answers in the footnote below.[2]

EXERCISE 1.   Identifying Single Issues

Smith has filed an action against Jones, but has not sued Bradley. If Bradley cannot be joined as a party, Jones wants the court to dismiss the action. Rule

---

1.   *See* Chapter 6, p. 69.

2.   The fourth rule has one separate issue since it is a balancing test and all of the factors must be weighed together. The fifth rule would raise two issues—whether the item is "a substantial gift" and whether the client is "related to" the lawyer. (Generally if the lawyer is preparing documents for someone, there will be no dispute about

19 of the Federal Rules of Civil Procedure governs this question. Here is the outline you have created for the analysis. Photocopy the outline and, on the copy, circle each part of the outline that constitutes a single issue. When you are finished, each circle should identify the part(s) of the outline that you would cover in a separate paradigmed discussion, and you should have a circle representing every paradigmed discussion you would write.

I. Will the court dismiss *Smith v. Jones* if Bradley cannot be joined as a party?

The court will dismiss the case if both *A* and *B* are met.

A. Either 1 or 2 must be true:
   1. that in Bradley's absence complete relief cannot be accorded among those already parties; or
   2. that both *a* and *b* are true:
      a. Bradley claims an interest relating to the subject of the action, and
      b. Bradley is so situated that the disposition of the action in her absence may:
         (1) as a practical matter impair or impede her ability to protect that interest, or
         (2) leave any of the persons already parties subject to a substantial risk of incurring inconsistent obligations by reason of the claimed interest.
B. In equity and good conscience, the action should not proceed without Bradley. Factors to be considered include:
   1. to what extent a judgment rendered in Bradley's absence might be prejudicial to Bradley or to those persons already parties to the litigation;
   2. the extent to which the prejudice can be lessened or avoided;
   3. whether a judgment rendered in Bradley's absence will be adequate;
   4. whether the plaintiff will have an adequate remedy if the action is dismissed.

THE WORKING DRAFT ORGANIZATION OF A SINGLE ISSUE: AN OVERVIEW OF THE PARADIGM FOR LEGAL ANALYSIS

II

Legal issues are decided by first figuring out what the rule of law is and then applying that rule to a particular set of facts. So first you must *explain* the rule that will govern the question; then you must *apply* that rule to the facts.

---

whether that person is a client.) The sixth rule has only one potential issue—what constitutes "signing" a will.

You may have heard this format described generally as IRAC (Issue, Rule, Application, Conclusion).

In the rule explanation half of the paradigm, you state the issue, state the rule you believe will govern it, and explain the rule. In the rule application half of the paradigm you apply the rule to your client's facts. This rule application leads directly to the conclusion—your answer to the question you were asked. Here is an overview of the basic paradigm:

PARADIGM FOR A WORKING DRAFT

Rule explanation

1. State the issue.
2. State the applicable rule of law.
3. Explain where the rule comes from and what it means.

Rule application

4. Explain the rule's application to your client's facts.
5. State your conclusion.

This reasoning process uses both inductive and deductive reasoning. In the first half of the process, a lawyer figures out what the rule is by looking at how earlier cases were decided and then using the results in those cases to formulate a general rule covering those sorts of situations. This is *inductive reasoning*—reasoning from the specific to the general.

EXAMPLE OF INDUCTIVE REASONING

In the *Fox* opinion, the court decided the enforceability of the covenant-not-to-compete by evaluating the reasonableness of the duration, the geographical scope, and the nature of the activity restrained. Therefore covenants-not-to-compete are enforceable if these three terms are reasonable.

In the second half of the process, the lawyer applies that general rule to the client's facts using *deductive reasoning*—reasoning from the general to the specific.

> **EXAMPLE OF DEDUCTIVE REASONING**
>
> Covenants-not-to-compete are enforceable if the duration, the geographical scope, and the nature of the activity restrained are reasonable. These three terms of the Watson/Carrolton covenant are reasonable. Therefore the Watson/Carrolton covenant is enforceable.

The interplay of these two kinds of reasoning should remind you of the ladder of abstraction illustration in Chapter 4 (p. 48).

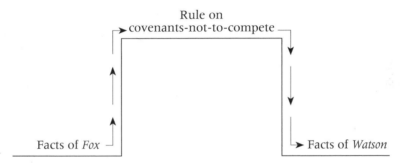

Rule on covenants-not-to-compete

Facts of *Fox*   Facts of *Watson*

If you keep this illustration in mind as you write out an analysis, it will operate as a map, helping you remember where you are in the organizational paradigm. It will be especially helpful in reminding you not to allow discussion of your client's facts (the second half of the paradigm) to slip into the first half of the paradigm—your explanation of the rule itself.

Keeping rule explanation and rule application distinct is important for several reasons. Some relate to the needs of law-trained readers, so we will cover those in Stage Three, where we turn our attention to creating a document designed for a reader. Keeping the two halves of the paradigm distinct is important in the working draft stage as well. The distinction will help you work out a better analysis in two ways.

Most new legal writers find that achieving sufficient depth and breadth of rule explanation is one of the most difficult challenges in legal analysis. Part of the difficulty is learning the linear, rule-based reasoning patterns lawyers use. You will find that keeping rule explanation and rule application distinct as you write your way through the paradigm will take you a long way toward learning this important reasoning pattern.

Another difficulty in attaining sufficient depth and breadth of rule explanation is learning to recognize rule explanation—learning what it is and the kind of information that it covers. For many writers, mixing explanation and application contributes to the confusion about what a thorough analysis covers. Learning what rule explanation is *not* (and moving that material out of the spot reserved for rule explanation) is vital to learning what rule explanation *is* (and to clearing space to insert it).

Mixing explanation and application is a roadblock to the writer's ability to evaluate the depth and breadth of his or her own analysis as well. Yet without evaluation the writer cannot know what needs improving. If rule explanation and application are intermixed, evaluating the depth and breadth of rule explanation is nearly impossible. Commonly, a writer states the rule and then proceeds to write several pages about the rule and how it applies to the facts. It "feels" like a thorough analysis, but how can the writer tell? An accurate self-evaluation requires checking the depth and breadth of both halves of the reasoning process, and that is difficult to do when they are intermixed.

Keeping the halves distinct means that you should not discuss client's facts in the rule explanation half. However, it does not mean that you will not discuss legal authorities in the rule application phase. As we shall see in Chapter 8, applying the law to the facts requires making the connections between the authorities and the client's facts. However, the connections are much clearer and come more easily, both to you and later to your reader, if you have first done a sufficient rule explanation.

Keeping the halves distinct also does not mean that while you are engaged in the process of writing the paradigm you must complete rule explanation before you attempt to write any rule application. For early versions of the working draft you can write more freely. Many writers find this unstructured prewriting helpful. Employing the paradigm simply means that at the conclusion of your writing process, the working draft should reflect distinct sections for rule explanation and rule application.

Before you read the following sections describing how to write the first half of the paradigm, take a moment to examine section B of the office memo in Appendix A, pages 368-369. Notice the parts of the paradigm and how they fit together, leading to the writer's conclusion.

EXERCISE 2.   Identifying and Labeling the Parts of the Paradigm

Read the "Facts" section of the office memo in Appendix A, beginning on page 365. Then read and photocopy section A (pp. 366-368) of the office memo (a single-issue discussion). In the margins of the photocopy, identify and label each part of the paradigm for a single-issue discussion.

III ⟩ STATING THE ISSUE AND STATING THE RULE OF LAW

Now that you have an overview of the paradigm in mind, it is time to examine each part more closely. In the next few sections we'll work through the first half of the paradigm. We'll use examples based on the following situation:

Linda Pyle is the owner of a commercial horse stable. The stable had formerly been located on land Pyle leased, but last year she bought several acres, relocated the stable there, and built her home next to it. Howard Gavin was Pyle's lawyer in the land purchase transaction. He is a skilled and well-respected partner in a medium-sized general practice firm. He has been in practice for seventeen years, but all of his previous practice involved litigation. Pyle's land purchase was Gavin's first venture into real property transactions. Gavin tried to handle Pyle's purchase carefully because he was nervous about working outside his usual practice area.

One of the questions Pyle raised with Gavin as part of his representation was whether there would be any problem with using this land as a stable. Gavin carefully checked the zoning regulations and assured Pyle that the land could be used as a stable without any problem. However, Gavin had not thought to check the title for possible easements.

The transaction was completed and Pyle began the construction of the house and new stable. About three months after she and the horses moved in, huge gravel trucks from the quarry on the other side of the hill began to rumble through her property and out to the county road. They quickly wore a rutted path right through Pyle's front yard and close beside the stable. The horses become upset each time a truck goes by, and several times horses and riders entering or leaving the stable have nearly been hit.

Pyle contacted the quarry owners and discovered that they own an easement across her property. They had purchased the easement some years ago, knowing that when their operations moved to the south side of the quarry site, they would need to transport the gravel out around the other side of the hill. The quarry operations have now moved to the south side of the quarry and are expected to continue for about eight years.

Pyle has come to a partner in your firm to find out what she can do. The partner has concluded that the easement is unassailable and that the sellers did not make any misrepresentation to Pyle about the property. Therefore, she has asked you to research the possibility of a claim against Gavin. Specifically, you are to research the issue of whether Gavin's failure to check the title for possible easements constituted legal malpractice.

Assume that you have researched the issue and found only one case, *Jacobson v. Kamerinsky*, an opinion from the highest appellate court in your jurisdiction. The opinion appears on page 398 in Appendix D. Stop now and read it.

As Chapters 3 through 6 described, state the issue you will analyze, designating it with a roman numeral. Later, when you convert your working draft to a document designed for a reader, you may choose to begin with a statement of your conclusion (your answer to the issue) rather than with a statement of the issue itself. For now, though, begin with stating the issue and let the process of writing your working draft help you reach the best conclusion.

I.   Did Howard Gavin commit legal malpractice in his representation
     of Linda Pyle?

Next, state your formulation of the rule that will govern the issue you have
just stated. Follow it with citations to the primary source(s) for the rule.
Remember that you will be completing and refining your understanding of
this rule as you write out the rest of the discussion. Don't be surprised if you
need to return several times to your statement of the rule, revising it to comply
with the analysis you are working out as you write. Here is a rule statement
for our example:

I.   Did Howard Gavin commit legal malpractice in his representation
     of Linda Pyle?

   A lawyer has a duty to provide a client with representation that
meets or exceeds the standard of professional skill and diligence commonly possessed and exercised by a reasonably prudent lawyer in this
jurisdiction. *Jacobson v. Kamerinsky* [citation].

Usually the statement of the rule should go in the first paragraph under
the heading stating the issue. Occasionally, however, the issue is complex
enough to require a little context or clarification. If so, *briefly* set out the
necessary context or clarification, but even in these unusual cases, be sure to
get to the rule statement as quickly as you can. The discipline of concisely
stating the rule within the first paragraph is an important part of your analytical
process. It forces you to articulate the focal point of the first half of the analysis,
and it focuses your attention on the rule you are about to explain.

After you have typed your statement of the rule, identify for yourself the
key term or standard. Just for the working draft, you may even want to use
italics for those words so that you can easily refocus your attention on them.
Your rule explanation will define that term or standard. Stop to look back at
the rule statement in our example. Can you identify the key term or standard
there? What is the term or standard the analysis must define and apply?
Check your answer against the answer in the footnote.[3]

---

3.   The heart of this standard is "commonly possessed and exercised by a reasonably
prudent lawyer in this jurisdiction."

GENERAL PRINCIPLES OF RULE EXPLANATION

The third step in the analysis of a single issue is explaining the source of the rule and what it means. You can think of this as using the available authorities to "prove"[4] to yourself (and later to your reader) that the rule is what you think it is and means what you think it means. The primary modes of reasoning for the rule explanation half of the paradigm are rule-based reasoning and policy-based reasoning.

When you are dealing with a rule based primarily on a case, your most important tools for "proving" the rule are (1) describing what the court said about the rule; (2) describing how the court applied the rule; (3) pointing out any relevant information about how the court did *not* apply the rule; (4) pointing out any relevant facts the courts emphasized; and (5) describing the policy considerations that support the rule. The value in each of these tools is not simply in reporting them, but rather in using them to make a point about the rule.

Writing the working draft of this section is more than just a rough draft of what ultimately will become a document for a reader; writing the working draft of the rule explanation helps you work out and deepen your own understanding of the rule. It also helps you double-check your answers to some critical questions: How binding on my court is information from this source? Did the source really *say* what I think it said? When the source said that, did it really *mean* what I think it meant?

Here are some general principles to follow when you write the rule explanation section:

1. Use all relevant tools of case law analysis. Reread the case several times, using each tool of analysis described in Chapter 4. Supplement your notes on the case to be sure that you have written down all relevant information that the tools helped you locate. For each piece of information you located, ask yourself what it tells you about the rule.

2. Cite to the relevant authorities when you make a point about the law, the reasoning behind the law, or the facts of a particular case. This is one of your opportunities to check the precedential value of each source and to assure yourself (and later your reader) that the source actually said what you think it said. Citing the source also insures that you will be able to relocate the material you are relying on. Chapter 14 will explain the details of proper citation form. For now, just be sure to identify the authorities in whatever way will allow you to relocate that source.

---

4. Richard K. Neumann, Jr., *Legal Reasoning and Legal Writing: Structure, Strategy, and Style* (2d ed. 1994).

3.   Keep your focus on the term or standard your analysis will define.   Most legal analysis is an exercise in defining terms, so keeping your focus on the key terms will keep you focused on the heart of your issue.

4.   Limit your explanation to those topics that will be relevant to the way the rule will apply to your client's facts.   When you explain what the authorities mean by the rule, don't include everything one might ever want to know about the rule. Include only the information that may pertain to your client's situation. This focus will save you writing time, and later it will save your reader's time and patience.

In your first draft of the rule explanation section, keeping your focus on the aspects of the rule that will apply to your client's facts may be tricky. Since you have not yet written the section *applying* the rule to your client's facts, you will have to anticipate the application you have not yet written. Then, when you write the application section, you will be refining your understanding of how the rule applies to your client's situation. You may need to return to the rule explanation section to add or delete topics of rule explanation. Your goal is to match the coverage of the explanation section to the coverage of the application section, thoroughly explaining what will be relevant to the application, but not more.

5.   Use only very short quotes of key language.   Your teacher may even instruct you not to quote at all. If so, your teacher's instruction does not reflect an arbitrary rule against quotations in legal writing; it is an effort to help you capitalize on the working draft's full potential for working out your own analysis. If you force yourself to use your own words for the information you find in the sources, you will understand that information better.

Also, your teacher's instruction is intended to help you avoid a common trap for beginning legal writers. Remember that this section must do more than simply quote a rule from an authority; it must explain what the authorities *mean* by the rule. If you quote freely, you may fill up several pages with nothing but quotations and your introductions to them. But merely retyping material from the sources is not analysis. While the sources must be your starting point, analysis begins only when you draw conclusions from the material in the sources and explain the reasoning that supports your conclusion. Quotation-filled pages may confuse you into thinking that what you have written is an "analysis."

6.   Use proper paragraphing techniques.   As you probably remember from earlier writing experiences, a paragraph should have a topic or a thesis sentence, which generally appears as the first or second sentence of the paragraph. The paragraph should be limited to information about that topic or thesis, and it should fit smoothly and logically between its neighbors. These principles are more than just principles of writing style—they are important to the substance of your analysis. Paying careful attention to proper paragraphing at the working draft stage will improve the substance of your analysis by helping you flesh out and order your thoughts, make appropriate decisions about the depth of your analysis for each point, and think of new points you want to include.

7. Use thesis sentences rather than topic sentences when you can.   For writing a legal analysis, we need to add one paragraphing principle that may be new to you: Prefer thesis sentences to topic sentences. A topic sentence identifies the topic the paragraph will discuss, but that's all it does. A paragraph centered on a topic sentence is better than a paragraph without either kind of lead sentence, but it is vulnerable to the trap of discussing the topic without ever making a point.

A thesis sentence, however, asserts a position on that topic. A paragraph centered on a thesis sentence will support or explain this thesis. The content of the paragraph will focus on the material that "proves" the assertion in the thesis sentence. Often the thesis is the rule itself, a part of the rule, or a point about how the rule functions. Compare the following paragraphs. Which has a thesis sentence? Identify it. Notice how it has forced the writer to articulate the paragraph's point. Notice how its discipline has led the writer to analyze rather than merely report on the authorities.

Cantwell v. Denton [citation] dealt with the issue of when a choice is sufficiently voluntary to constitute assumption of the risk. In that case, the defendant negligently caused a fire in an apartment building, and a father entered the burning building to save his child. The court held that the father's action was not sufficiently voluntary to constitute assumption of the risk. [citation]

A choice is not sufficiently voluntary to constitute assumption of the risk if the defendant's negligence has forced the plaintiff to choose between the threatened harm and another equal or greater harm. *Cantwell v. Denton* [citation]. In *Cantwell,* the defendant had negligently caused a fire in an apartment building. A father had to choose between entering the burning building and standing by while his child's life was in danger. The court held that standing by while the child was in danger would have been an equal or greater harm. [citation] Under such circumstances, the court held, the choice to subject one's self to danger is not "voluntary" in the sense necessary to constitute assumption of the risk. [citation]

As you clarify for yourself the point of the paragraph, you will often realize that the *topic* contains several different *theses,* each deserving its own supporting material from the authorities. Thus, the discipline of using thesis sentences leads you to a more thorough and complete analysis because it helps you notice additional points you had not yet seen.

Finally, limiting the paragraph's content to information about the paragraph's thesis will help you find the gaps in your reasoning and in the "proof" you have found in the authorities. If you take care to limit the paragraph to material that supports the thesis you have articulated, you will certainly notice if you have little or no support for that thesis. You will be able to gauge the strength of that support, and you will know when you need to go back to the authorities in search of stronger support.

Thesis sentences and proper paragraphing can make a major substantive difference in your analysis. If you implement those principles in your first draft, you will save yourself several revisions. However, if you cannot concentrate on the material and on paragraphing at the same time, simply write your initial draft in your normal way, and then turn your attention to thesis sentences and paragraphs in your first revision.

8.   Use a transitional word, phrase, or sentence each time you move on to a new point.   Being explicit about the relationships between the theses of succeeding paragraphs will help you insure that your reasoning is logical and complete. Here is a list of commonly used transitions:

TRANSITIONS[5]

Addition

also	in addition	not only
and	in fact	then
furthermore	moreover	

Sequence

first	next	finally
second		

Comparison

both	likewise	in comparison

Contrast

but	despite	nevertheless
while	still	however
instead	even though	notwithstanding
on the other hand	even so	
in contrast	though	

5.   Adapted from David Angell & Brent Heslop, *The Elements of E-Mail Style* 62-64 (1994).

Concession

although	even though	though

Illustration

for instance	in particular	specifically
to illustrate	for example	

Result

accordingly	consequently	as a result
therefore	for	since
because	thus	

Summary

accordingly	thus	therefore
in summary		

Emphasis

above all	more important	chiefly

9. Keep your paragraphs moderately short—a maximum length of roughly half of a double-spaced page. Keeping your paragraph short will help keep you focused on the thesis of that paragraph. When a paragraph gets long, often it has developed one of these two problems: (1) the paragraph has begun to wander from its thesis; or (2) the thesis of the paragraph is too big to be covered without dividing it into subpoints. Not dividing a large thesis into subpoints generally results in a large paragraph that mixes information about the subpoints more or less randomly. It also results in a discussion that is not sufficiently fleshed out. The best way to avoid these two problems is to keep your paragraph lengths at or below a half-page, double-spaced.

ORDERING RULE EXPLANATION USING A SINGLE CASE

No generic format for the discussion of a case opinion will fit each situation. However, here is an approach that will serve as a starting point for your writing decisions. As you read this section, refer to the sample rule explanation on pages 97-99 for an example of this approach.

Start organizing the rule explanation section by making a list of the points you have learned about the rule. Organize the points into categories starting with general information and proceeding to more specific information. For example, here are three common categories: (1) what you have learned about how the rule functions generally; (2) what you have learned about each identified subpart (factor or guideline), if any; and (3) any information about how the rule functions in particular situations.

Once you have organized the points into these categories, use the categories as your basic order for the explanation, beginning with how the rule functions *generally.* You have already stated the rule and cited the case, so now set out the facts and the part of the holding that establishes the rule. Use the tools for case law analysis to explain further the rule's general functioning. Include any relevant policy rationale that you find in the authorities or that your own common sense supplies.

Next, if your rule has identified factors or guidelines, take each relevant factor or guideline, one at a time, and follow the same procedure: (1) state each point you have learned about how that factor or guideline functions; (2) state the facts and holding relevant to *that* point; and (3) use any other tools for case law analysis to explain further your point about the factor or guideline.

Finally, state and explain each point you have learned about how the rule functions in particular situations. Follow the same procedure for each of these points. Include any policy rationale that applies especially to that particular situation.

This approach should operate as a starting point for your writing. As you write you will probably think of additional points. Simply add them to the appropriate category. Don't be concerned if you do not have information in one of the categories; simply omit that category. For instance, your rule might not have factors or guidelines, so you would not have a second category. Sometimes the case authority does not tell you any relevant information about how the rule is applied in particular situations, so you may not have a third category. However, intentionally looking for information in each category will help you find information you otherwise would have missed; and if you find it, this format will help you know where to place it in the analysis.

 VI **COUNTER-ANALYSIS**

If there is another reasonable interpretation of the rule, use your working draft to deepen and double-check your analysis of the strength of its support. Also, when you convert your analysis to a document for a reader, that reader will want to know whether another reasonable interpretation exists and what analysis supports it. This explanation of other possible interpretations is called "counter-analysis."

Your choice of a large-scale organization may have already provided a place for discussing the counter-analysis;[6] or your explanation of the rule may already have sufficiently covered the other possible interpretation. But if your explanation of the rule did not already set out the other reasonable interpretation and explain the rationale supporting it, you can place the counter-analysis here in the rule explanation section, following the explanation of the interpretation you think more likely.

Match the depth of your discussion to your assessment of the strength of the other interpretation. If it is possible but unlikely that a court would adopt it, cover it briefly. Summarize the rationale behind it enough to focus your mind (and later your reader's) on the extent of the interpretation's support, but not more than that. However, if the choice between the interpretations is a closer call, discuss the counter-analysis in more detail so that your exploration of it will assure you that you have not underestimated its support. Either way, conclude your counter-analysis with your reasons for believing that the interpretation you predicted is more likely.

Milk the authority for all you can learn about the rule; include in your rule explanation the parts that will be relevant to your client's facts. Remember that the rule explanation section explains *only* the rule itself—not how the rule applies to the facts of your client's situation. The application section comes next. *Do not include rule application in the rule explanation section.* As a discipline, draw a line between rule explanation and rule application on your working draft, to remind yourself to keep your discussion of your client's facts below the line.

Here is an example of rule explanation for the Pyle/Gavin issue.

A WORKING DRAFT OF RULE EXPLANATION

I.   Did Howard Gavin commit legal malpractice in his representation of Linda Pyle? | **ISSUE**

A lawyer has a duty to provide a client with representation that meets or exceeds the standard of professional skill and diligence *commonly possessed and exercised by a reasonably prudent lawyer in this jurisdiction. Jacobson v. Kamerinsky* [citation]. | **RULE**

| **RULE EXPLANATION**
| **Key facts**

In *Jacobson*, the lawyer failed to file a timely claim before the medical malpractice screening panel. By statute, a medical malpractice claim cannot be pursued unless it has been filed before the screening panel within the applicable time limit. [citation] Therefore the client's claim was

---

6. *See,* for example, the large-scale organization of the warranty issue on pp. 73-74.

barred. Because a reasonably prudent lawyer would research and comply with the statutory requirements for bringing a particular kind of claim, the court held that the lawyer was liable to his client for the losses that resulted from the failure to file the claim. [citation]

Holding

One signal for applying the prudent lawyer standard is whether the task is something general practitioners are familiar with doing. In *Jacobson*, the court had pointed out that the enactment of the screening panel requirement had been widely publicized in newspapers, electronic media, and the state bar journal. However, the court explained that even without publicity, a prudent lawyer would comply with filing requirements because filing lawsuits is something general practitioners are familiar with doing. [citation] Therefore if the task is familiar to general practitioners, the court need not ask whether the particular lawyer should have been aware of the particular requirement.

Thesis sentence (a characteristic the court found significant)
Key facts

Court's statement about those facts

How court's statement supports thesis

Another signal for applying the prudent lawyer standard is whether the error could have been prevented by research. In *Jacobson*, the court observed that an "error in judgment" does not constitute malpractice. [citation] While *Jacobson* did not expressly define the difference between an error in judgment and a breach of the prudent lawyer standard, the court distinguished the *Jacobson* facts from an "error in judgment" by pointing out that in *Jacobson* the correct answer would have been apparent had the lawyer done the necessary research. [citation] Therefore, although a prudent lawyer can make an error in judgment, a prudent lawyer does not make errors preventable by proper research.

Thesis sentence (another significant characteristic)

Disclosure that thesis is an inference

Reasoning from the court's observation about the facts

The "prudent lawyer" standard is not reduced for lawyers operating outside their area of special knowledge. In *Jacobson*, the lawyer-defendant had been in practice only ten weeks when he accepted the medical malpractice case. The court held that the lawyer's lack of experience did not excuse his failure. [citation] Clients should be entitled to at least the minimum standard of skill and diligence,

Thesis sentence (how rule applies to a particular situation)
Relevant facts

Holding on this point

Court's two policy reasons

according to the court. [citation] Also, a contrary rule would offer no incentive to lawyers to gain necessary knowledge or experience. [citation]

The standard probably would not be affected by facts indicating that the lawyer intended to be particularly careful, or that he was otherwise skilled and diligent, or that he was a well-respected partner of a well-respected firm. Although no facts like these were present in *Jacobson*, the court's language and policy statement explained in the previous paragraph would seem to apply to this question as well.

Thesis sentence anticipating an issue raised by Gavin's facts

Disclosure of lack of facts

Reasoning from policy

It is unclear whether the court would rely on expert testimony or would make its own judgment about what a prudent lawyer would do in a particular set of circumstances. This question was not at issue in *Jacobson*. However, the opinion does not mention the testimony of any expert witness, and the court's statements that a prudent lawyer would research the requirements for bringing a claim seemed to be statements of the court's own opinion rather than statements based on someone's testimony. The court's repeated references to the standard as "the minimum" that "any client should be entitled to expect" [citations] seem to indicate that the court considered itself competent to decide the standard.

Thesis sentence; kind of evidence necessary

Disclosure key to evaluating strength of thesis

Inferring a point from the court's language

Thus, whether certain conduct falls short of the "prudent lawyer" standard appears to be determined on case-by-case basis, by what the judge thinks a prudent lawyer would do. However, two signals for whether the failure will constitute malpractice are (1) whether the task is something general practitioners are familiar with doing; and (2) whether the problem could have been prevented by doing proper research.

Summary of points made in rule explanation

◇ Checklist for Rule Explanation Half of Paradigm

STATE THE ISSUE

- Place it in the heading with the roman numeral.

STATE THE APPLICABLE RULE OF LAW

- Place it within the first paragraph.
- Highlight the key terms.

EXPLAIN WHERE THE RULE COMES FROM AND WHAT IT MEANS

TOOLS FOR USING CASE AUTHORITY

- Set out the facts of the case.
- Explain what the court held about the rule.
- Explain any important *dicta*.
- Explaining how the court applied the rule.
- Where appropriate, explain how the court did *not* apply the rule.
- Point out any facts the court emphasized.
- Explain what legal commentators have said about the case or the rule.
- Explain the policies that underlie the rule.

GENERAL PRINCIPLES

- Cite a source for each statement of a rule, a holding, the court's reasoning, or facts from a case.
- Do not discuss your client's facts in this section.
- Where possible, use thesis sentences.
- Limit paragraphs to one topic or thesis.
- Connect each topic or thesis to the prior material.
- Check for excessive paragraph length (yardstick: 1/2 a double-spaced page).
- Include counter-analysis if necessary and not already covered.
- Conclude counter-analysis by explaining reasons that the predicted interpretation is more likely.

OVERALL EVALUATION

- Have you cited a source for each statement of a rule, a holding, the court's reasoning, or the facts of a case?
- Have you used thesis sentences where possible?
- Have you limited each paragraph to a single thesis or topic?
- Have you signaled each transition to a new thesis or topic?
- Have you kept paragraphs to a length of approximately half of a double-spaced page?
- In each section, have you read all of the thesis sentences in order to check for logical internal organization and to spot any gaps in reasoning?
- Have you remained as objective as possible?

EXERCISE 3. Writing the Rule Explanation

Write out the rule explanation section for the following memo assignment, using *Lucy v. Zehmer*[7] as your only authority. One of the most difficult parts of legal writing for new writers is learning how to explain a rule, and one of the most common errors in legal writing is rushing into rule application before writing a sufficiently thorough rule explanation. This exercise, which requires you to write the rule explanation section only, is good practice in learning how to write a thorough rule explanation section.

Facts

Virginia Ryan is the owner of an antique shop. She has come to your firm, relating the following story and asking your firm to advise her.

Ryan is acquainted with Stewart Kaplan and his older sister, Julia Kaplan. Stewart and Julia are not on good terms. Their mother recently died, bequeathing to Stewart an old quilt and to Julia their deceased father's World War II medals. During the settling of the estate, relations between Stewart and Julia became even more strained when Julia gave the medals to a local historical organization without offering them first to Stewart. Stewart had a strong sentimental attachment to the medals because his father used to let him play "war" with them as a child, and he believes that Julia gave them away on purpose to spite him.

Ryan knew the facts of the dispute about the war medals, and she knew that the relationship between Stewart and Julia was strained. Ryan did not get along well with Julia either, and she and Stewart felt a common bond in this respect.

Several weeks after learning of Julia's disposition of the medals, both Stewart and Julia happened to attend a community carnival. Stewart saw Ryan there, and said to her, "Let's have a little fun." Ryan said, "OK. What do you have in mind?" Stewart said, "Follow me. We'll give my dear sister a scare." He took Ryan by the arm and led her to within earshot of Julia. Stewart winked at Ryan and, in a stage voice, offered to sell her the old quilt. Ryan said she was interested and asked what price Stewart had in mind. Stewart said, "How about $150?" Ryan said, "That's pretty steep for an old quilt. How about $25?"

Both Stewart and Ryan could tell that Julia had heard the conversation from the beginning. However, Ryan believed that Stewart was serious about selling the quilt. Stewart and Ryan continued negotiating the price, through several offers and counter-offers, finally settling on a price of $75. "Done!" said Stewart, winking at Ryan. He said, "Let's do this right. Here, let me write out the terms." He wrote, "Stewart Kaplan hereby sells to Virginia Ryan the

7.   196 Va. 493, 84 S.E.2d 516 (1954). Opinion printed at pp. 400-402.

old quilt he inherited from his mother for the price of $75." They both signed it. Still enjoying the game, Stewart said, "Wait, we need today's date and the date I'll deliver the quilt to you." He inserted the date and added, "Delivery to occur next Wednesday." He also wrote, "Thanks for playing along. This was fun." Both parties initialed the additional writing, and Ryan put it in her pocket. She told Stewart that it was great doing business with him, that she had to get home to make supper, and she left.

The following Wednesday Ryan called Stewart to tell him that she had the check ready and to ask when he planned to deliver her quilt. Stewart stuttered that he had never actually intended to sell the quilt. Ryan said, "I thought that you wanted to get revenge on Julia." "Yes," said Stewart, "but just by letting her know how it feels to be ignored." "Well, that's not what I thought. I thought you wanted to get revenge by selling the quilt. I want that quilt, Stewart. It is an antique and $75 is a fair price. Besides I already promised it to one of my customers."

Ryan wants to know whether she can enforce what she thought was Stewart's agreement to sell the quilt. An attorney in the firm has asked you to analyze Ryan's question. The attorney has instructed you to assume that a judge would find that Ryan genuinely believed that Kaplan was serious.

Issue

Can Ryan enforce a contract for the sale of the quilt?

8 Writing the Analysis of a Single Issue: Rule Application

Now that you have explained the rule and what it means, you are ready to apply it to your client's facts. Remember that this half of the paradigm relies on deductive, syllogistic reasoning—that is, applying a general, often abstract principle to a particular situation and arriving at a result.

General principle	Covenants-not-to-compete are enforceable if the duration, the geographical scope, and the nature of the activity restrained are reasonable.
Application to particular facts	These three terms of the Watson/Carrolton covenant are reasonable.
Result	Therefore the Watson/Carrolton covenant is enforceable.

While rule-based reasoning is still important in the second half of the paradigm, analogical, narrative, and policy-based reasoning are at least as important to the analysis.

 I TWO APPROACHES TO WRITING THE APPLICATION SECTION

Since the point of the paradigm is to apply the rule you have just explained, the rule application section should track the rule explanation section. Each aspect of the rule you described in the rule explanation section should now be applied to your client's facts. Thus, some writers use the rule explanation section as the outline for the rule application section. If you use this approach, simply work your way through the application section by applying each point you discussed in the explanation section. This way you are sure to apply the rule you just explained instead of allowing your application section to wander.

You may find, however, that a slightly different approach works better for you. While legal arguments ultimately should be framed in tightly reasoned logic, legal arguments also should embrace a flowing narrative. Further, plugging into the narrative can give you insights about the authorities that rule-based reasoning misses.

Therefore, some writers find it more natural and more effective to begin writing rule application by focusing on the narrative (the facts), without looking back to the rule explanation section. As they write the first draft of the application section, they have the rule explanation in mind, but more impressionistically so. This strategy frees them to think like a storyteller thinks, and thus be more tuned-in to the particular facts that will be significant in that particular case.

If you choose this approach, revise your initial draft of each section so the rule explained in the first half matches the rule applied in the second half. You may need to add application of a point you discussed in rule explanation but forgot to apply in the application section. However, just as often, you will need to return to the explanation section to add or edit the discussion of a point you had not noticed until you began to write about your client's facts. No matter which way you approach the writing process, the end result should be the same—a logical analysis embracing your client's narrative.

II CONTENT OF THE RULE APPLICATION HALF OF THE PARADIGM

While the organization of each rule application section will be unique to the rule and facts involved, here are some general principles to keep in mind:

1. For each point you made about the rule in the explanation section, *write a thesis sentence stating how you think that point will apply to your client's facts.*

2. In one or more paragraphs following the thesis sentence, *use your client's facts to explain why your thesis sentence is probably an accurate prediction of how the rule you described would apply to your client's situation.* Explain the inferences and factual conclusions you think a judge or jury would draw from these facts. Work directly with your client's facts and with the inferences that one might draw from them, and use your common sense. Imagine the situation your client has described to you. What

would it have looked like? Seemed like? What other things might have been true if these are the facts? What additional unconfirmed facts might you be assuming? How might the scenario look to a judge or a jury? What facts would be important to a judge or a jury? Could someone else take the same facts and characterize them differently—that is, paint a different picture using the same facts?

3. *Where possible, support your thesis with direct fact-to-fact comparisons.* Identify the factual similarities between your client's situation and the case opinion, and explain how these similarities demonstrate your prediction of the rule's application to your client's facts. Also, identify any significant factual *differences,* and explain how these differences demonstrate your prediction. These direct factual comparisons constitute analogical reasoning. For an example, read the paragraph marked "analogy" at the top of page 109. Often such analogies are the most important part of the rule application section. Exercise 1 on page 106 will give you some practice in this important skill.

4. *Apply the rule's underlying policies to your client's situation.* Your client's facts may raise precisely the concerns that the rule was designed to address. If so, a court will be more likely to apply the rule strictly to your client's situation. A court will be less likely to limit the rule or to apply an exception. A court will be more likely to resolve doubts of application in favor of achieving the policy results the rule seeks.

    If your client's facts do not raise the policy concerns that the rule was designed to address, note this in your discussion. A well-settled rule with a relatively clear scope probably will govern your client's situation anyway. The rule is still the rule, after all. But if the rule leaves doubt about whether it would apply to facts like those of your client, then a court may be more likely to limit the rule, or to apply an exception for your client's circumstances, or to resolve doubts of fact application in a way that allows the court to avoid applying the rule to your client's facts.

5. *Include any necessary counter-analysis.* Just as you may need to discuss other reasonable interpretations of the rule, you may need to discuss other possible interpretations of the facts. Match the depth of your discussion to your assessment of the strength of the other interpretation. If it is possible but unlikely that a judge or jury would see the facts that way, cover it briefly. However, if the choice between the interpretations is a closer call, discuss the counter-analysis in more detail. Either way, conclude your counter-analysis with your reasons for believing that the interpretation you predicted is more likely.

6. In the draft of an office memo, *identify any unknown facts that would be important to a resolution of the legal issue.* Your analysis will not be complete without noting such important missing information.

7. *State your conclusion.* After you have worked through your explanation of how the rule applies to your client's facts, you will have reached your conclusion. State the conclusion at the end of the rule application section. If the analysis has been long or complex, summarize the key reasons supporting your conclusion.

EXERCISE 1.   Analogical Reasoning

Read the Zenger facts on pages 49-50. Then read *Wheeler v. White* on pages 395-397. Identify the legally relevant similarities and differences between the Zenger facts and the *Wheeler* facts. Based on these similarities and differences, would you say that a court would reach the same result on Zenger's facts? Write a discussion of several paragraphs explaining your answer.

III   COMMON TROUBLE SPOTS IN RULE APPLICATION SECTIONS

The three most common weaknesses in rule application sections are (1) failing to apply the rule as the first half of the paradigm explained it; (2) asserting the predicted outcome without sufficiently explaining the reasoning that supports the prediction; and (3) failing to realize the diverse possible interpretations of the facts. Understanding these three weaknesses will help you avoid falling victim to them in your own analysis.

We have already discussed in some detail the first common weakness: failing to apply the rule as it was explained. Yet this is such a common difficulty that it merits a reminder. Be sure to complete the rule application section by matching its coverage and approach to the explanation section. Equally important, be sure to revise the rule explanation section to reflect deepened and sharpened rule understanding gained by writing out the factual analysis. This double-checking of rule-based and narrative reasoning against each other is a perfect example of why both are critical to good legal writing.

The second common weakness may result from carelessness, but more often it results from a belief that the application of the rule to the client's facts is so obvious that no explanation of the supporting reasoning is necessary. Nearly always this belief is erroneous. Explaining the supporting reasoning is particularly important since it is this process that best helps the writer realize that the application may not be as obvious as it first appeared. Even in those cases where the application is clear, *some* explanation of the supporting reasoning is necessary.

The third common weakness is failing to realize the diverse possible interpretations of the facts. Sometimes this weakness results from forgetting to think independently and realistically about the facts. Many writers new to law study fall into the trap of assuming the infallibility of the inferences that someone else—like the client or the requesting attorney—has drawn from the facts. Yet, rare is the set of facts that does not support diverse inferences and interpretations.

Another and more insidious cause of this weakness is the difficulty of imagining multiple interpretations simultaneously. Perhaps an analogy will demonstrate how hard this can be. Look at Figure 8-1. You may have seen a graphic like this before. Do you see the old woman in this graphic? Do you see a young woman as well? Your brain can organize the black and white shapes of the graphic into a picture of either, but most of us can only see one at a time. More pointed for our purposes, once your brain has organized the sections to display one figure, it is difficult to find the other figure at all. Imagining diverse interpretations of facts is just as hard as imagining diverse interpretations of these black and white shapes.

Not "seeing" these diverse interpretations of the facts is the most difficult weakness for a writer working alone to diagnose and cure. If your assignment permits, ask the advice of others to help you imagine possible interpretations of the facts. Present a friend or colleague with a simple chronology or other sanitized version of the facts rather than with your written description of them.[1] Your goal is to see what story someone else might see in the facts, especially someone who has not first seen the story through your eyes.

Figure 8-1
How Old Is This Woman?

---

1. Take care not to breach client confidentiality. *See* Rule 1.6 of the Model Rules of Professional Conduct (1994).

However, if you are working alone, you must think both critically and creatively about the facts. Try to imagine how the various other parties to the situation would describe it. Imagine how you would describe it if you were representing those parties. Imagine how the facts might appear to someone who disliked your client and was therefore looking for an interpretation different from your client's position. This task will never be easy, and it will be particularly difficult in your early years of law study and practice. However, each year of law practice will improve your ability to see diverse interpretations of a set of facts. Take the opportunity presented by your first few writing assignments to begin practicing the skill of interpreting facts.

Here is an example of rule application for the Pyle/Gavin issue.

PYLE/GAVIN EXAMPLE—RULE APPLICATION ADDED

I. Did Howard Gavin commit legal malpractice in his representation of Linda Pyle?	**ISSUE**
A lawyer has a duty to provide a client with representation that meets or exceeds the standard of professional skill and diligence *commonly possessed and exercised by a reasonably prudent lawyer in this jurisdiction. Jacobson v. Kamerinsky* [citation].	**RULE**
[See pp. 97-99 for rule explanation.]	**RULE EXPLANATION**
	RULE APPLICATION
A judge would probably find that a reasonably prudent lawyer representing any purchaser in a real estate transaction would check the title to the property for easements. Receipt of title is, after all, the heart of the transaction, and carefully checking the title would be critical to evaluating the title the purchaser would receive from the seller.	**Thesis sentence stating general conclusion** **Reasoning from general facts**
The duty to check the title carefully would be particularly clear in a situation like Gavin's where the client has asked specifically whether there would be any problem with using the land for a particular purpose. A prudent lawyer would know that the use of real property can be limited either by law (such as by a zoning regulation) or by private agreement (such as an easement or a restrictive covenant recorded against the title). The client's specific question should have flagged	**Thesis sentence applying Gavin's particular facts** **Reasoning from facts**

the issue for Gavin, making Gavin's error even less excusable than the error in *Jacobson*. In *Jacobson*, the client did not ask a question that should have reminded the lawyer of the possible problem; yet the lawyer's error constituted professional malpractice anyway. [citation]

Comparing facts (analogy)

Further, both of the *Jacobson* signals are present in *Gavin's* facts. Representing a party to a real estate transaction probably falls within the group of tasks a general practitioner is familiar with doing. Basic real estate transactions are as common in the general practice of law as filing lawsuits. Nor was Gavin's omission a mere error in the exercise of professional judgment. The need to look for an easement would have been apparent if Gavin had done adequate *legal* research, and the easement itself would have been apparent if he had done adequate *factual* research. Just as in *Jacobson*, Gavin's error could have been prevented by proper research.

Thesis sentence applying an aspect of rule explanation
Applying 1st "signal"
Comparing facts
Applying 2nd "signal"
Reasoning from facts
Comparing facts

Since the standard is not reduced by virtue of facts particular to the lawyer's experience, Gavin's long absence from law school and his practice limitation will not affect the legal result. Nor will his status in the bar or his usual skill and diligence. However, these facts do add to the equities of his case, especially since a judge in this jurisdiction would probably be aware of them. While those facts should not change the ultimate result, they probably mean that the judge will not be happy about having to rule against Gavin. The evidence at trial will have to establish the cause of action clearly.

Thesis sentences dealing with another aspect of facts
Flagging the human impact

Finally, this evaluation that Gavin's representation fell below the prudent lawyer standard is based on an assumption that the standard can be judged without expert testimony. Additional research would be necessary to check this assumption. If the standard must be evaluated by reference to expert testimony, it will be necessary to consult with an expert.

Pointing out a necessary qualification.

The claim that Gavin breached the applicable standard of care is strong. The subject matter of

CONCLUSION
Statement

the representation is common to general practitioners. The problem could have been prevented with proper research. If Pyle is interested in pursuing the matter further, our next step should be the completion of our research on the need for expert testimony.

Summary of most important points

◇IV◇ CHECKING YOUR DRAFT

Once you have completed a working draft, reread the draft to evaluate it. If possible, put it away for a day or two first to let your mind clear. Then go through this procedure:

1. Check the paradigm.   Mark off and label each part of the paradigm. Check to be sure that each part is there and in its proper order. Be sure that rule explanation and rule application are not intermixed.

2. Evaluate the depth of rule explanation.   Ask yourself how well settled the rule is and how much explanation is necessary to clarify the rule's meaning.

3. Evaluate the depth of rule application.   Have you written out a complete discussion of how the rule would apply to your client's facts and what inferences a judge or jury might draw from them? Watch particularly for rules that include an element pertaining to someone's state of mind or rules that set out a flexible standard (such as "a reasonable person" or "the best interests of the child"). When such a rule governs your client's issue, you probably will need to do significant factual analysis in the application section.

Underestimating the factual analysis necessary to a legal question is one of the most common problems for people new to the study of law. If you take particular care to scrutinize your thinking and writing for appropriate depth in factual analysis, you can strengthen your legal writing skills dramatically.

4. Evaluate the content and internal organization of rule explanation and rule application.   First, confirm that the rule you explained is the rule you applied. Now, examine each section in smaller chunks. Identify the blocks of text devoted to particular substantive points, using labels in the side margin as the sample working drafts on pages 97-99 and 108-110 do. Is your organization logical? Does it communicate good ideas clearly?

5. Check your thesis sentences and paragraphs. For each paragraph, first ask yourself what your point is. Identify your thesis sentence, and underline it on your draft. Then identify the paragraph(s) that support that thesis, and be sure that you know how all of the other material in that paragraph pertains to that point. Now evaluate the strength of your analysis of that point by evaluating the strength of the supporting paragraph(s). This kind of point-by-point evaluation of the building blocks can dramatically improve your analysis. It helps you identify weak spots, leaps of logic, and misuse of sources.

6. Check paragraph length. Use the yardstick of a maximum length of about one-half of a double-spaced page. For those paragraphs that run longer, ask yourself whether the paragraph's thesis has subpoints that you can separate and address in two separate paragraphs. Often as you separate these subpoints of the analysis and treat them in separate paragraphs, you will find that the subpoints deserve more analysis than you had originally thought. As a matter of fact, sometimes you will find whole new issues that you had overlooked.

7. Check your transitions. Identify each transition to a new point and ask yourself how the new point is connected to the former point. Be sure that each transition is clearly communicated.

8. Read all of the underlined thesis sentences in order. They should provide a logically ordered summary of your reasoning, point by point.

9. Check your perspective. Remember the difference between predicting and persuading. Maintaining an objective perspective throughout the writing process is difficult. Many writers find themselves slipping into advocating their prediction rather than objectively evaluating it. After you have written your working draft, set it aside for a while and then reread it to be sure that you have not begun inadvertently to write as an advocate.

 Checklist for Rule Appplication Half of Paradigm²

APPLY THE RULE TO YOUR CLIENT'S FACTS

- Be sure that the content of the rule explanation and rule application sections are consistent and that you applied the rule you explained.
- Compare the key facts from the case authorities to the key facts of your client's situation, noting the legally significant similarities and differences.
- Explain the inferences and factual conclusions that a judge or jury could draw from your client's facts.

2. *See* p. 100 for checklist for the rule explanation half of the paradigm.

- In the draft of an office memo, identify any unknown facts that would be important to a resolution of the legal issue.
- Evaluate the appropriateness of the factual discussion's depth.

STATE YOUR CONCLUSION

- If the analysis has been long and complex, include a brief summary of the primary reasons supporting the conclusion.

———————————

OVERALL EVALUATION

- Have you cited a source for each statement of a rule, a holding, the court's reasoning, or the facts of a case?
- Have you used thesis sentences where possible?
- Have you limited each paragraph to a single thesis or topic?
- Have you signaled each transition to a new thesis or topic?
- Have you kept paragraphs to a length of approximately half of a double-spaced page?
- In each section, have you read all of the thesis sentences in order to check for logical internal organization and to spot any gaps in reasoning?
- Have you remained as objective as possible?

EXERCISE 2.   Writing the Rule Application

Write a working draft of your analysis of the issue set out in Exercise 3 on pages 101-102. If you wrote out an answer for Exercise 3 in Chapter 7, simply complete the working draft by adding the rule application half of the paradigm.

Writing the Analysis of a Single Issue: Organizing the Discussion of Multiple Authorities

Chapters 7 and 8 explained the organizational paradigm for legal analysis and how to use a case within that organization; but rarely will your analysis use only one case. The next step in understanding how to organize and write a legal analysis is learning how to order and work with multiple authorities. When you have a number of cases or other sources, which should come first and where should the others go? This chapter first covers organizing multiple authorities for an analysis governed primarily by case law; then it covers organizing tools and sources for an analysis primarily requiring statutory construction.

 ## I. ORGANIZING MULTIPLE AUTHORITIES FOR AN ANALYSIS PRIMARILY GOVERNED BY CASE LAW

Organizing the discussion of multiple authorities can be a challenge. Usually the key to a clear and orderly discussion of multiple authorities is the order of the rule explanation section of the paradigm. That section is key because most of the discussion of the authorities will be located there and because the rule application section usually follows the organization of the rule explanation section. The following sections explain how to organize the discussion of the authorities in the rule explanation section.

A.   ORGANIZATIONAL INVESTIGATION

Selecting an order for the authorities begins with an investigation to gather necessary information. The investigation should include (1) tracking the historical development of the rule; (2) identifying the factual situations represented in the authorities; (3) identifying the authorities that deal with separate aspects of the rule; and (4) evaluating the precedential value of the authorities. Like nearly every other writing task, this investigation will further deepen your understanding of the rule. Here is an example of how the investigation can help with the analysis:

Assume that Larry Jenkins, a summer associate, is analyzing whether a lawyer can draft a will when the client wishes to bequeath to the lawyer a $10,000 investment account. The current rule in the jurisdiction is:

> A lawyer not related to the client shall not prepare a document giving the lawyer any substantial gift from that client.

Notice that the key issue in applying this rule will probably be what constitutes a "substantial" gift.

As Jenkins researched the case law, he found a number of opinions dealing with similar situations. In two of the opinions, the lawyer had drafted a will or other document giving the lawyer a gift. In one, the lawyer had drafted a deed giving the lawyer a piece of real property worth in excess of $100,000. In another, the lawyer had drafted a will bequeathing to the lawyer an oil painting worth $22,000. In each case, the lawyer had produced convincing evidence that he had fully disclosed the potential conflict of interest and that the client had consented to the lawyer's continued representation. In both cases, the court approved the lawyer's conduct as ethical, explaining that the client's consent cured the ethical problem.

At that point, it appeared to Jenkins that he had learned two significant pieces of information. First, the cases seemed to amend the rule by holding that client consent obviates the ethical issue. Second, it appeared that the $10,000 investment account is not valuable enough to concern the courts, at least if the client has consented to the conflict of interest. The account's value is smaller than the value of the oil painting or the real property, and those gifts did not prompt the court to discuss the size of the transfer. This second conclusion seemed strange to Jenkins's common sense, but he had found no other explanation for the absence of judicial discussion of the gift's size.

Jenkins turned his attention to writing out the rule explanation section for his working draft. To prepare for selecting an order for the authorities, Jenkins went back to the authorities to track the historical development of the jurisdiction's law on this issue. When he did, he found that a different rule had been in effect at the time these two opinions were issued. The former version of the rule did not specifically deal with drafting documents, and it covered possible personal conflicts of interest simply by requiring the lawyer to secure the client's consent:

> Except with the consent of the client after full disclosure, a lawyer shall not accept employment if the exercise of his or her professional judgment on behalf of the client reasonably may be affected by the lawyer's own interests.

This former version of the rule made no distinction based on whether a gift was "substantial"; rather, the critical issue in the former rule was whether the client had consented after full disclosure.

Jenkins's organizational investigation gave him a more accurate understanding of the authorities, and it kept him from making a major error in the analysis. It explained the inconsistency among the authorities, kept him from devoting unwarranted attention to cases issued prior to the current rule, and allowed him to identify the parts of earlier cases that still might have relevance.

Here is how to conduct the organizational investigation:

1.   Track the rule's historical development.   Make a list arranging the authorities in chronological order. Use the list to understand the historical development of the rule, doing any additional research that your chronology requires. How has the rule evolved over time? What changes or refinements do you see? Sketch out notes comprising a history of the rule.

2.   Identify the factual situations represented in the authorities.   Make another list of the cases based on their facts. Look for factual categories, focusing on different kinds of factual situations in which the rule is commonly applied. Perhaps one group of cases involves one common kind of situation arising under the rule and another group involves a different kind of situation. For instance, in the "competent representation" example in Chapters 7 and 8, the reported cases would probably fall into some categories relating to the kind of lawyer conduct being questioned. Some might involve lawyers who missed the filing deadline for an appeal of an adverse trial court judgment. Some might involve lawyers who did not conduct thorough research. Others might involve lawyers who made substantive errors in drafting documents like wills or contracts.

Make a list of the factual categories you identify and note the authorities that fall into each. Ask yourself whether the rule seems to be applied differently depending on the kind of factual situation involved. Whether or not you see differences, can you discern patterns or signals for predicting how the rule is applied in these different scenarios? Look especially for the factual categories most similar to your client's facts. Even if you cannot discern any particular factual categories, make a list of cases in the order of their similarity to your client's facts, placing the most similar case at the top of the list and ordering the remainder by degree of similarity.

3.   Identify the authorities that deal with separate aspects of the rule.   Make a list of the cases by reference to the particular legal points each makes. Do some of the cases discuss the rule in general while some discuss different legal aspects of the rule? For rules with permissive subparts (like factors or guidelines), pay particular attention to whether the cases fall into categories dealing primarily with particular subparts.

Cases applying other kinds of rules can fall into topical categories as well. For instance in our "competent representation" example, some of the cases might give you a generalized description of what a client has a right to expect from a lawyer. Other cases might tell you whether the lawyer's representation must meet the standard created by a generalist or by a specialist in that area of law. Others might tell you whether the standard is different depending on whether the client was a paying client or a pro bono client.[1]

If you find that the authorities naturally fall into separate topical (nonfactual) categories of some kind, make a list of these categories and note each authority that deals with each particular topical category. Include "discussion of the rule in general" as one of the categories. If some authorities deal with more than one topic, be sure to list each authority under each topic that authority covers.

4. Evaluate the precedential value. Finally, make a list ordering the case authorities by their precedential value, considering the hierarchy of their issuing courts, the dates of the opinions, the thoroughness of their discussions, and other factors contributing to the precedential value of a case.[2] Do you see significant differences? Perhaps you have several opinions from the highest appellate court in your jurisdiction, several opinions from the intermediate level appellate court, and the rest are opinions from another jurisdiction. List the authorities in that order.

B.   ORGANIZATIONAL OPTIONS FOR RULE EXPLANATION

Now you have the information necessary to help you select an order for the authorities you will discuss. *The order you select for discussing the authorities should help you make one or more substantive points.* Examine what you have learned by making your four lists and the notes that accompany them. Which set of notes teaches important substantive point(s)? Do you see one or more significant historical turning points? Do you see several discrete topics of legal information about the rule? Do you see several kinds of situations governed by the rule, one or two of which are more like your client's facts than the others? Do you see an important difference between the precedential value of the authority?

Next, compare your notes to the most common organizational approaches: (1) the importance-to-analysis approach, (2) the topical approach, (3) the historical development approach, and (4) a combination of more than one approach. Here are descriptions of each of these approaches.

1.   *Importance-to-Analysis Approach*

This organizational choice (or a variation on it) is the workhorse of legal analysis; think of it as your default choice. Case authorities are important to an analysis primarily by virtue of their precedential value generally or by the similarity of their particular facts to your client's facts. The importance-to-analysis approach covers authorities important in either of these ways, and

---

1.   The full phrase is *pro bono publico,* literally meaning "for the public good." In common usage, the phrase refers to representing a client without charging a fee. The standard of competent representation is the same whether the client is paying a fee or not.

2.   *See* Chapter 5. Consider criteria other than factual similarity here, since factual similarity is already accounted for on the second list.

thus it uses the information from the lists organized by precedential value and by factual similarity.

Usually this approach begins with *general* rule explanation and then proceeds to an explanation of how the rule applies in situations factually similar to your client's. In each phase, order the authorities by their importance. Begin with *general* rule explanation. As Chapter 7 described, state the rule and cite to the primary source for the rule. If the rule comes from a statute, cite the statute, set out any helpful contextual information about the statute, and then move to the most important case discussing the rule *generally.* Usually this will be the case highest on your list ordered by precedential value. Summarize the facts and explain what the court held. Note, too, any important dicta included in the opinion.

Then return to your list ordered by precedential value to decide whether you have other important cases that explain the rule generally. If so, order them by their importance and discuss them here, just as you discussed the first case. Include only cases that add something to the general understanding of the rule. Limit your general discussion of the rule to a maximum of two or three cases. Conclude the general explanation with any relevant general information from a secondary source or any policies applying to the rule generally.

Now that you have provided a general description of the rule, it is time to explain how the courts have applied the rule *in situations resembling your client's.* Focus on the cases with facts most similar to your client's, but *don't mention your client's facts yet.* You'll get to them in the next part of the paradigm—rule application. In rule explanation, limit your discussion to setting out the information you have learned about the authorities themselves.

Order your discussion of the remaining authorities by their similarity to your client's facts, using the information you learned and recorded on your list of factual categories. A rough maximum number of cases to discuss in this phase of rule explanation is about three to four; often you will not have that many factually similar cases.

When you discuss the cases that are similar factually, *try to discern and articulate any standards, guidelines, or signals that seem to be operating when the courts apply the rule to these kinds of situations.* Sometimes such information will be described explicitly by the court; sometimes you will have to infer it from other comments the court made or from the way the court applied the rule. Note especially the kinds of facts the court seemed to find significant in that kind of fact scenario.

After you have finished discussing the cases in the factual categories closest to your client's facts, discuss cases from any dissimilar factual categories, again referring to your list of factual categories. Include only cases that add something instructive to your understanding of how the rule would apply to your client's facts. For instance, a case might apply the rule to a scenario different from your client's facts; however, the opinion might include dicta asserting that the result would have been different if the facts had been thus-and-so (a scenario more like your client's). A rough maximum number of cases to discuss in this third section of rule explanation is about two to three; usually you will not have this many.

Conclude your discussion of the rule's meaning in factually similar situations with any relevant information from a secondary source about these factually similar cases or with any policies relevant to the rule's meaning in factual scenarios like your client's.

Of course, you will need to adjust this organizational pattern depending on the authorities you have to work with. For instance, you may not have many cases to use in a particular section, but (assuming you have done thorough research) that is not your fault. Just use the most important cases you have in each category, and don't worry if you don't have as many as you'd like. Or you may find that some of your cases fall into more than one category. Perhaps one of your cases is both an important general explanation of the rule and also a case close to your client's facts. Simply use the case twice, first in the generalized explanation and then in the more specialized section. Use this organizational pattern as a guide, adjusting it in any way necessary to fit your issue and authorities.

You'll notice that this organizational approach contemplates a rough maximum of ten or so authorities. Often your research will not reveal this many important authorities.[3] Do not use unimportant authorities just to fill up space or to prove that you have read many authorities. Rather, demonstrate that you have the lawyerly skill of identifying the *key* authorities and analyzing them thoroughly.

Summary of Importance-to-Analysis Approach

- State the rule, citing to the statutory source (if any) and explain any relevant information about the statute.

GENERAL RULE EXPLANATION

- Cite to and discuss the most important case explaining the rule *generally.* Summarize the facts; explain the holding and any important dicta.
- Discuss one or two other important cases dealing with the rule *generally* (if you found any). Discuss in the same manner as the prior case.
- Discuss any relevant secondary authorities or policies bearing on the rule generally.

EXPLANATION OF RULE IN FACTUALLY SIMILAR SITUATIONS

- Discuss the case that applies the rule to facts most similar to your client's facts. To the extent you haven't already, summarize the facts; explain the holding and any important dicta. Explain any other relevant information you can learn by using the tools of case law analysis. Articulate any standards or guidelines that seem to operate in factual scenarios like this.

3.   Occasionally, if you are analyzing a large and complex issue, you may need to use more authorities; for instance some moot court competition problems require discussion of many authorities. However, most of the memos or briefs you will write in practice should stay below ten authorities.

- Discuss any other cases applying the rule to similar facts. Discuss these cases in the same manner as the discussion of the prior case.
- Discuss any relevant secondary authorities or policies bearing on how the rule will apply to fact scenarios like your client's.
- Discuss any factually dissimilar cases, limiting the discussion to cases that add something to your understanding of how the rule would apply to your client's facts.

2. *Topical Approach*

Another common organizational approach is the topical approach. This approach uses information from the list identifying legal topics and orders authorities by reference to those topical categories. The categories may be permissive subparts of the rule (such as factors or guidelines)[4] or other discrete points of information about the way the rule functions.[5]

Like the importance-to-analysis approach, the topical approach begins with an explanation of the rule *in general.* Use the most important authorities to state and explain the rule in general, just as described above. Then discuss each relevant separate legal topic. Order the topics by importance to the analysis, and discuss the most important authorities that establish the law on that legal topic. Finally, if the rule explanation section has been long and the legal topics numerous, consider adding a short summary (one paragraph or so) of the general rule and the particular legal points you have discussed.

◇ Summary of Topical Approach

- State the rule.
- Cite to the statutory source (if any) and explain any relevant information about the statute.

GENERAL RULE EXPLANATION

- Discuss the most important case explaining the rule *generally.* Summarize the facts; explain the holding and any important dicta.
- Discuss one or two other important cases dealing with the rule *generally* (if you found any). Discuss in the same manner as the prior case.
- Discuss any relevant secondary authorities or policies bearing on the rule generally.

4.   Remember the difference between permissive subparts (like factors) and separate elements. Each separate element constitutes a different legal issue, and therefore it will be the subject of its own separate discussion. While some situations may call for combining the discussions of several elements in the final draft, do not combine them for your working draft. Let the working draft help you learn the information that will allow you to decide whether to combine the discussions in later drafts.
5.   *See* the examples identified on pp. 115-116.

EXPLANATION OF PARTICULAR LEGAL TOPICS

- Discuss each relevant legal topic established by the authorities. Order them logically, usually by reference to their importance to the analysis. For each point, discuss the most important authorities establishing the point, setting out the facts, holding, and dicta that establish and explain the point. Include any relevant secondary authorities or policies bearing on that point.
- If the rule explanation section is long and the legal topics numerous, summarize the general rule and the particular points you have discussed before going on to rule application.

3. *Historical Development Approach*

The historical development approach is less common, but it is the best choice when (1) the rule's development is important for understanding the rule's current form and the authorities that articulate it; or (2) when the rule's current form does not decisively answer the legal question you have been asked, but the rule's historical development establishes a trend that can help predict the answer.

The historical development approach is less susceptible to a general format than are the first two approaches. Its order will vary by virtue of the rule's particular history, the reasons that an understanding of the rule's development is helpful for understanding its current form, and the particular part of the analysis that the rule's history helps explain. However, two examples of an historical development approach will demonstrate how this approach can be organized.

First, an example of the historical development approach where the rule's development is important for understanding the rule's current form and the line of authority dealing with it. The will-drafting example on pages 114-115 is such a situation. There, some earlier case law seemed inconsistent with the current version of the rule found in the relevant code. An explanation of the historical development of the rule was necessary to understand these earlier cases and to evaluate their current impact on the analysis of the legal question. The relevant historical development could be a statutory change (as in the will-drafting example) or it could be a subtle but significant change in the approach of the courts to the particular question. Here is an example of how the historical development approach might work in that situation:

Summary of One Format for the Historical Development Approach

- State and explain the current version of the rule just as in the importance-to-analysis approach. Use the parts of the authorities that retain important *current* precedential value.

- Set out the earlier phases of the rule's historical development and explain why the older authorities (or certain parts of them) do not retain precedential value.

A different historical development format would be appropriate when the rule's current form does not answer the legal question you have been asked but the rule's historical development establishes a trend that can help predict the answer. The historical development can be the rule's development inside the relevant jurisdiction or its development on a national level. If the trend helps predict the answer to a question your jurisdiction has not yet answered, consider this format:

 Summary of a Second Format for the Historical Development Approach

- State and explain the rule in its current form. Use the current authorities to set out whatever parts of the legal question the current rule *does* answer.
- Identify and explain the parts of the legal question that the current rule and its establishing authorities do not answer.
- Trace the historical development (inside or outside the jurisdiction, or both) to explain the trend of the rule's development.
- Explain your prediction for the unanswered parts of the legal question.

The point you wish to make from the rule's history will differ from situation to situation. Organize by the logical steps to the point you wish to make.

4. Combination Approach

Recall that the order of the authorities should help you make one or more substantive points. As you examined what you learned by making your four lists and the notes that accompany them, you may have noticed several kinds of important information—perhaps a case remarkably on point factually, an important historical turning point, and several relevant discrete topics of legal information. In such a situation, select a combination of the three approaches for ordering your discussion of the authorities.

A combination approach can combine any or all of the other approaches. While the combination approach defies reduction to a standard format, two principles usually apply: (1) Begin with a general explanation of the current rule and the several most important authorities establishing it. (2) Discuss all authorities significant for a particular point together. Here is an example of a format for a combined approach:

 **Summary of a Combination Approach**

GENERAL RULE EXPLANATION

- Discuss the rule and the most important authorities *generally* (statute, cases, secondary authority).

EXPLANATION OF PARTICULAR LEGAL TOPICS

- Discuss each relevant discrete legal point relating to how the rule functions. Order them logically, usually by reference to their importance to the analysis. If one of the discrete legal points has gone through a relevant historical development, set out the current law on that point and explain the historical development and its significance.

EXPLANATION OF RULE IN FACTUALLY SIMILAR SITUATIONS

- Discuss the authorities applying the rule to facts most similar to your client's facts.
- Discuss any factually dissimilar cases, limiting the discussion to cases that add something to your understanding of how the rule would apply to your client's facts.

SUMMARY (IF NECESSARY)

 # ORDERING AUTHORITIES FOR AN ANALYSIS PRIMARILY REQUIRING STATUTORY CONSTRUCTION

Earlier chapters have explained the tools for analysis of an issue primarily governed by case law. However, you will need some additional information when your analysis requires the interpretation of a statute.

A. ANALYTICAL TOOLS FOR STATUTORY INTERPRETATION

You have already learned that statutes are construed by case opinions. If case authority has already told you what the statute means, then you can rely on the case law to the extent of its precedential value. But what should you do if no binding case law has construed this statute, at least not with regard to your particular question? You will have to predict how a court would construe it.

When no binding case authority has construed a statute, judges decide what the statute means primarily by considering (in rough order of importance): (1) the text itself; (2) the intent of the legislature; (3) the policies implicated by the possible interpretations; (4) the interpretation of any governmental agencies charged with enforcement of the statute; and (5) the opinions of other courts and of respected commentators.

1. The Text Itself

The most important inquiry is the "plain meaning" of the text itself. When the plain meaning is unambiguous, a court generally will give effect to the plain meaning unless the result would be absurd. Look first at the plain meaning of the statute's words. Also look for other parts of the statute or act that may tell you more about the language you are concerned with, such as the section explaining the act's purpose. Many acts contain separate definition sections. Even when your term is not defined, other parts of the statute may give you clues about what the term means.

2. The Legislature's Intent

Often, the text of the statute will be unclear. In such a case, most courts will try to decide what the legislature intended by the text's language. This search for the legislature's intent is problematic at best. The statute was probably enacted by a large group of elected officials who were serving in that office some years ago. The particular language you are concerned with may have been the result of political compromise, and various factions of the legislature may have had vastly different intentions surrounding that language. Quite possibly, your question never occurred to them at all. How can one decide the intent of the legislature, as if the legislature were an entity with one mind? Yet, when a statute's language is unclear, a court that must apply the statute will have to have some basis for a decision. In such a circumstance, the court usually will try to discern the legislature's intent.

Many courts are willing to consider the legislative history of the statute as evidence of legislative intent. Legislative history consists primarily of the documents or other records generated by the legislative body during its deliberations about the bill that ultimately became the statute. Legislative history comes in many forms, such as committee reports, speeches, witness testimony, or studies introduced into the record. Your research text will tell you more about legislative history and how to find it.[6]

---

6. Generally, legislative history is much more helpful in analyzing a federal statute than a state statute because few states record legislative histories.

3.   Canons of Construction

In addition to legislative history, courts may look to a number of other clues to decide plain meaning and legislative intent. Some are maxims known as "canons" stating customary ways of interpreting statutes. Some are simply common sources for guidance. Here are some of the most generally applicable:

* Read the statute as a whole.
* Give effect to rules of grammar and punctuation.
* Construe technical terms technically and ordinary terms in their ordinary sense.
* When the same language is used in various parts of an act, the language is presumed to have the same meaning throughout.
* Where general words (such as "and any other") follow a list, the general words should be construed to refer to things similar to the items in the list.
* Modifying words or phrases modify the prior word closest to the modifier.
* Specific description of one or more situations in the text of a statute implies the exclusion of other kinds of situations not mentioned.
* Statutes should be read in the context of other related statutes, especially where the legislature intended to create a consistent statutory scheme.
* While not technically part of the statute's text, titles, preambles, and section headings are persuasive evidence of legislative intent.
* Sometimes courts will have construed the language of a statute in a particular way. Subsequently the legislature may amend the statute in ways that change or clarify other issues but do not address the issue the courts have interpreted. A later court may conclude that the legislature's lack of action to change the judicial construction is evidence of the legislature's approval of the court's construction.

These maxims are actually rules of law in and of themselves, so when you rely on one of them as part of the analysis of a rule, cite to a persuasive case opinion that adopts that maxim, if you can. However, even if you cannot find case authority adopting the maxim, a court will still be willing to consider the maxim's logic.

None of these guidelines for interpreting statutes will provide a certain answer. As a matter of fact, when applied to your legal issue they may support contradictory results.[7] However, they are customary ways that courts decide what statutes mean, and they will help you predict what a court would decide about your particular issue.

4.   Policy

The fourth tool for statutory interpretation is analysis of the policy concerns implicated by the statute. Like case law, statutes may be based on lofty constitu-

7.   Karl N. Llewellyn, Remarks on the Theory of Appellate Decision and Rules or Canons About How Statutes Are to Be Construed, 3 Vand. L. Rev. 395 (1950).

tional concerns for a citizen's civil rights or on simple pragmatic considerations of human nature. Whatever the policy foundation for the statute, it will play a part in a court's interpretation of the statute.

In addition to the policies specifically applicable to a certain statute, some *kinds* of statutes carry a general policy leaning applicable to all statutes of that particular kind. These policies call for either a strict or a liberal construction of that kind of statute. The most common of these general policies are:

- Statutes in derogation of the common law should be strictly construed.[8]
- Remedial statutes should be liberally construed to accomplish their remedial purpose.[9]
- Penal statutes should be narrowly construed, out of concern for the rights of the citizen-accused.

Finally, courts are guided by the general policy that the meaning of a statute should be construed in a way that will render the statute constitutional, if possible.

5. Agency Interpretation

When enforcement of a statute is assigned to a particular government agency, the agency must decide what the statute means in order to enforce it. Courts often look to this agency as the entity with the most expertise in the relevant issues, and thus may give deference to the agency's interpretation. The court also may consider the interpretation of an agency that has no authority to enforce the statute but nonetheless works with the statute routinely. Look for agency interpretations in the agency's regulations, in the agency's decisions, and in case law.

6. Commentators and Other Courts

Finally, courts may recognize persuasive value attaching to the opinions of other courts and of respected commentators. The persuasive value of another court's opinion depends on the factors indentified in Chapter 5. The persuasive value of a commentator's opinion depends on the reputation of the commentator and on the opinion's well-reasoned reliance on the other tools of construction.

———————————

All of these tools are available to a court when interpreting a statute, and thus all are available to you when you must predict how a court would interpret the statute. Your analysis should consider all of the tools that apply to your statute and your client's situation. Since the tools will sometimes

———————————

8. A statute is strictly construed when it is read narrowly, so that it changes as little as possible.

9. A statute is liberally construed when it is read broadly, so that it includes within its scope more kinds of situations than a narrow reading would allow.

support different results and since individual judges disagree about the relative importance they are willing to place on these tools, you will not be able to predict the court's interpretation with certainty. Unless you know the particular judicial philosophy of the judge who will decide your issue or of the judiciary in your jurisdiction, your best approach may be to analyze the statute using all of these tools and then to ask yourself what interpretation would persuade you if you were the judge.

B.   ORDERING STATUTORY TOOLS AND SOURCES

Now you know the available tools for statutory interpretation, but when you begin to write the rule explanation section of your discussion, how will you order them? Use these two principles as your guide: (1) *Group the authorities by type,* and (2) *order the groups by their importance to the analysis.* Begin with the group that contains the most important tools and place the least important group last. Since the relative importance of the tools will vary from issue to issue, no one order will fit all legal issues. However, here is a starting point for your own decision-making:

1. Always begin by quoting the specific statutory language in question. The discipline of identifying and setting out the key words in question is vital to your working analysis.
2. If you think that the language is "plain," explain why. If not, identify the particular ambiguities in order to focus the remainder of your discussion on those particular ambiguities.
3. If you have found binding or extremely persuasive case law interpreting the particular ambiguity at issue, discuss all the case authority next. Begin with the strongest case authority and conclude the case law discussion with a more curtailed discussion of the weaker authorities (to whatever extent you plan to include them at all). Generally it is better to place all case law discussions on a certain point together, even if some of the other kinds of authorities might carry more precedential value than the weaker case opinions. Include those weaker cases at the end of the case law discussion, and match the detail of your discussion of them to your estimate of their importance.
4. If you have found any legislative history of the provision, discuss it next. Even if the legislative history does not address your particular ambiguity, it probably describes the legislature's intent in enacting the statute as a whole. This intent will often be phrased as a policy statement. This generalized intent should give you a clue about the meaning the legislature might have intended for the particular ambiguity.
5. If the available case authority is only moderately persuasive on your issue (rather than binding or extremely persuasive), place the case law discussion here rather than earlier.
6. Next discuss interpretations of the particular ambiguity by any governmental agencies that enforce or otherwise routinely work with the provision.

7. If you have found only weak case authority, place the case law discussion here.
8. Finally, if there are any policy considerations not already covered by your discussion of case law or legislative intent, discuss those here.

This chapter has covered how to organize a discussion of multiple authorities for a single issue. Chapter 10 will cover the final kind of analytical situation—writing the analysis of multiple issues.

10

Writing the Analysis of Multiple Issues

Chapters 7 through 9 explained how to write an analysis governed by a single rule with no subparts (no subissues). Chapters 7 and 8 gave you a basic understanding of the paradigm for legal analysis and how to use a case in a legal discussion. Chapter 9 covered how to organize multiple authorities in a single-issue discussion.

This chapter moves to the next level of complexity—how to write an analysis when you must deal with multiple issues. When dealing with multiple issues, the basic principle is the same as when dealing with a single issue; the task is still to explain the law and then apply it. But because each issue and subissue will be governed by a separate rule, both rule explanation and rule application are more complicated.

Chapter 6 discussed the rule structures that commonly require you to deal with multiple issues. Take a moment to review them. You must deal with multiple issues when the rule that will govern your client's issue is an umbrella rule with subparts (pp. 69-73); or when the issue will be governed by several separate rules with no umbrella rule (pp. 73-74); or when the answer depends on which rule the court applies (pp. 76-77). We will look first at how to write the analysis of a single rule with subparts, such as the Shaffer burglary example from Chapter 3, pages 28-29.

 ## I WRITING THE ANALYSIS OF A SINGLE RULE WITH SUBPARTS

Recall our basic premise—that the structure of the rule will form the large-scale outline of the analysis. For the Shaffer issue, here is the structure of the rule:

> I. To obtain a burglary conviction, the state must prove *all* of the following elements:
>
> A. breaking
> B. entering
> C. dwelling house
> D. of another
> E. in the nighttime
> F. intent to commit a felony therein.

An analysis of the burglary rule requires analyzing the subissues one by one, stating, explaining, and applying the rule governing that *sub*issue before proceeding to the next one. The paradigm you learned in Chapters 7 through 9 will serve nicely for each of these separate discussions. However, before addressing the first subissue, you will need to write an "umbrella" section to introduce these separate discussions and place them in a context. After you have completed the discussions of each element, you will need to write a conclusion that pulls them all together and predicts a result. We'll look first at writing the umbrella section.

A. THE UMBRELLA SECTION

Assume that you have stated the question, using it as your roman numeral heading, just as we discussed in Chapters 7 through 9. The *umbrella section* is the material you place between this heading and the first of the subsections identified by the rule.

The umbrella section has two functions: (1) it states the umbrella rule[1] (with citation to the main authority establishing the rule), and (2) it begins rule explanation by explaining any information that applies to the rule generally rather than just to one subpart of the rule. Information that would apply to the rule generally includes information about the relationships among the rule's subparts, such as whether all elements are necessary or whether one is enough; whether the elements are evaluated separately or whether a heavy dose of one can make up for a skimpy dose of another; and whether some factors are more important than others.

Also, the authorities may set out standards that apply to all subparts. One party will carry the *burden* of proof.[2] A heightened *level* of proof may be required.[3] Some rules come with a presumption of some kind.[4] Some come

---

1. Recall from Chapter 6 that the *umbrella rule* is the larger rule that establishes the relationships among the subrules. *See* pp. 69-73.
2. *See* note 4 on p. 158.
3. *See* note 5 on p. 159.
4. A presumption is an assumption that something is true unless evidence shows otherwise.

with policy "leanings."[5] The procedural posture of a case may impose a particular standard more favorable to one party.[6] A canon of statutory construction may call for a strict reading of a statute.[7] Be sure to notice any such legislative or judicial "thumb on the scale" and explain it in the umbrella section as well.

Sometimes the umbrella section is fairly simple. For instance, in the Shaffer example, the umbrella section would state the rule defining burglary (and cite to the statute establishing it). The statement of the rule already includes the relationship of the elements: all are necessary. One item of rule explanation applies to all elements: the burden of proof. Since the rest of the rule explanation consists of explaining each element, one by one, the umbrella section of your working analysis need contain nothing else. It might look like this:

I.   Do the Shaffer facts establish the elements of burglary?

[Umbrella Section:]

To obtain a burglary conviction, the state must prove that Shaffer's conduct constituted a breaking and entering of the dwelling house of another in the nighttime with the intent to commit a felony therein. The state must prove each of these elements beyond a reasonable doubt. [Cite to the applicable authority.]

[Proceed with the discussion of each element, using for each the paradigm from Chapters 7 and 8.]

A. breaking
B. entering
C. dwelling house
D. of another
E. in the nighttime
F. intent to commit a felony therein.

Sometimes the authorities *expressly* state more general rule information than we see in the burglary rule. Sometimes the authorities only give *clues* from which you can surmise that general information; in that case, your rule explanation in the umbrella section must explain the clues you found and the inferences you draw from them. In either case, the depth of rule explanation in

---

5.   An example of such a policy leaning would be case law holding that, as between the criminal defendant and the prosecution, doubts are to be resolved in favor of the criminal defendant. *See* p. 125.

6.   For instance, for a motion for summary judgment, all factual inferences must be drawn in favor of the nonmoving party. *See* pp. 74-76.

7.   *See* p. 124.

the umbrella section would be greater than we see in the burglary example. The *Fox* example at the end of this chapter (p. 141) is an example of a more extensive umbrella section.

B.   THE DISCUSSION OF EACH SUBISSUE

When you have written the umbrella section, you are ready to write each subsection. For each subsection, use the basic paradigm structure discussed in Chapters 7 through 9. Begin by stating the particular subissue you will first analyze. You need not refer to any other subissue because the umbrella section has already explained how the subissues relate to each other. For your working draft, you can state the subissue by using it as the heading that sets off this part of your analysis from the rest. Let the identification of the *one* subissue you are about to discuss serve as a discipline to help you avoid confusing your analysis of *this* subissue with your analysis of others.

Then state the rule governing that element or factor, citing to the main authority establishing it. Remember that the "rule" governing an element or factor may not always look like a neat rule of law. You are looking for what the authorities identify as the way to decide that element. The authorities may state the rule expressly ("nighttime" means between thirty minutes after sunset and thirty minutes before sunrise); or you may have to deduce the rule (what the authorities identify as the way to decide this element) by noticing how the authorities decide that element. The *Fox* example at the end of this chapter is an example of having to deduce the rule.

Remember that you will be completing and refining your understanding of this rule as you write out the rest of the discussion. Don't be surprised if you need to return several times to your statement of the rule, revising it and refining it to comply with the analysis you are working out as you write.

Next *explain* the rule governing that element, using all the tools discussed in Chapters 7 and 8. Explain where you found the rule, how you decided that it was the rule, and what it means. After you have finished explaining the rule, *apply* it to your client's facts, just as Chapters 7 through 9 described.

When you have worked through your explanation of that element's rule and how it applies to your client's facts, you will have reached your conclusion on that element. State it with a brief summary of the key reasons supporting it. Finally, unless the transition to the next subissue is obvious, state briefly how your conclusion on this element connects back to the large-scale organization.

This intermediate conclusion—the conclusion you have reached about a subissue—is an important component of a multi-issue analysis. Professors Ray and Cox call this the "landing."[8] It is the spot at which your analysis returns to the firm ground of the rule structure before it jumps off again into the analysis of the next subissue.

8.   Mary Barnard Ray & Barbara J. Cox, *Beyond the Basics: A Text for Advanced Legal Writing* 205 (1991).

C. THE CONCLUSION

When you have written the analysis of each subsection, write a conclusion pulling together the results of each separate analysis and setting out the ultimate conclusion on the question presented. Include a summary of the primary reasons for the overall conclusion. This completes the written analysis of a rule with subparts.

BASIC MULTI-ISSUE PARADIGM

I. **Question Presented**

Umbrella section setting out all rule explanation common to the elements

  A. **First element**
- Rule statement and explanation unique to this element
- Rule application
- Landing
  B. **Second element**
- Rule statement and explanation unique to this element
- Rule application
- Landing

[Add the discussion of any other elements, organized in the same fashion as *A* and *B*.]

Conclusion

II WRITING THE ANALYSIS WHEN YOU HAVE NO UMBRELLA RULE

Chapter 6 described several kinds of assignments that require organizing without the aid of an umbrella rule. One assignment may require analyzing several separate rules, such as the example on pages 73-74. Another assignment may require analyzing which rule a court will choose to apply, such as the examples on pages 76-77. As Chapter 6 explained, whenever you must deal with multiple rules, you need an umbrella structure, whether you get it from an umbrella rule or you create it yourself. Whenever you have an umbrella structure, you need to write an umbrella section to explain that structure.

When you have an umbrella rule, the umbrella section explains the structure by setting out the umbrella rule and any parts of rule explanation that apply to the rule generally. (See section *A* above.) When you do not have an umbrella rule, simply introduce the subsections that will follow by identifying them, explaining briefly what part they play in the analysis, and explaining how they relate to each other. Here is one writer's umbrella section for a hypothetical answer to the Chapter 6 example on pages 73-74.

I.   Does the law impose a warranty on the Foster car sale?

In [name of jurisdiction], warranties governing transactions covered by U.C.C. warranty provisions are set out in [citation]. Warranties governing other transactions are set out in [citation]. Because these warranty provisions differ in critical ways, the first question this memo will discuss is whether U.C.C. warranty provisions would apply to this transaction.

The first section concludes that U.C.C. warranty provisions probably will govern this transaction, so the second section discusses the application of those provisions to this transaction. However, because the application of U.C.C. warranties is a close question, the final section of the memo discusses the possible application of non-U.C.C. warranties to this transaction.

   A.   Do U.C.C. warranty provisions govern this transaction?
        [rule, rule explanation, rule application, landing]

   B.   If U.C.C. warranty provisions govern this transaction, is it one of the kinds of transactions upon which those provisions impose a warranty?
        [rule, rule explanation, rule application, landing]

   C.   If non-U.C.C. law governs this transaction, does non-U.C.C. law impose a warranty on this transaction?
        [rule, rule explanation, rule application, landing]

   Conclusion

III   VARIATIONS OF THE MULTI-ISSUE PARADIGM

Like the paradigm for a single-issue analysis described in Chapters 7 through 9, the multi-issue paradigm gives you the basic format for a multi-issue analysis; however, it does not eliminate the need for your own skilled decision-making. You will need to make decisions about variations in *order* and variations in *depth*. The principles described in Chapters 7 through 9 apply equally here.

However, when you are using the multi-issue paradigm, you will need to make some additional decisions, such as the order in which you will discuss the elements; whether to truncate the analysis if one element seems to answer the question presented, thus eliminating the need to discuss other elements; and whether to complete rule explanation for all elements before beginning rule application for any one element.

A.   ORDER OF ELEMENTS

When you convert your working analysis to a document designed for a reader, the order of your discussion of the elements will be significant. We'll explore those reader-centered decisions in Chapter 12. At the working draft stage, however, the order of your discussion is much less significant. You can discuss the elements in the order in which they appear in the rule; you can begin with the elements about which you have the most information; or you can begin with the element(s) you think will resolve the question presented. (See the next section.) Use any order that makes logical sense and does not lead you into any inaccuracy of rule explanation or application.

B.   WHETHER TO TRUNCATE THE ANALYSIS

Sometimes your analysis must cover all parts of the rule no matter what your conclusion on any one part. Sometimes, however, one element of the rule will seem to resolve the question presented and eliminate the need to analyze the rest of the elements. For instance, if Mr. Shaffer's conduct occurred at 2:30 in the afternoon, you would not need to analyze whether it was a "breaking" or an "entering." Since all elements are necessary to establish burglary, the clear absence of the "nighttime" element would answer the question.

   Deciding whether to truncate the analysis after discussing one decisive element can be difficult. You must ask yourself how sure you are of the conclusion on the seemingly decisive element. If you have no doubt, such as in the Shaffer example in the last paragraph, you can discuss the decisive element first and stop the analysis right there. However, answers to legal issues often are not so clear. Lawyers truncate an analysis at their own risk. If another conclusion on the seemingly decisive element is possible, or if you are unsure of your own judgment, completing the analysis is the wiser course.

C.   WHETHER TO COMBINE RULE EXPLANATION AND
RULE APPLICATION FOR ALL ELEMENTS

Recall that the umbrella section of a multi-issue analysis begins rule explanation by setting out any information about the rule that applies to more than just an individual element. Under that paradigm, rule explanation for a particular element is postponed until the discussion of that particular element. Then for each element, rule application follows the rule explanation for that particular element. The outline of this basic paradigm looks like this:

I. Question Presented

[Umbrella section setting out all rule explanation common to the elements.]

A. First element
- Rule statement and explanation unique to this element
- Rule application and landing
B. Second element
- Rule statement and explanation unique to this element
- Rule application and landing

Conclusion

Notice that all rule explanation common to both elements has already been placed in the umbrella section, so the only rule explanation in each subsection is whatever explanation applies only to one element or the other, but not both. If all of your rule explanation applies to both elements, then your rule explanation will already have been set out completely in the umbrella section. The subsection for each element will begin directly with rule application. An outline of this variation on the basic paradigm looks like this:

I. Question Presented

[Umbrella section setting out all rule explanation common to all elements.]

A. Rule application and landing for first element
B. Rule application and landing for second element

Conclusion

Another variation on the basic paradigm is possible when each element has its own rule and rule explanation. In such a case, you may wonder whether you can state and explain the rules for *both* elements and then do the rule application section for both elements. An outline for such a discussion would look like this:

I. Question Presented

[Umbrella section setting out all rule explanation common to the elements.]

A. Rule statement and explanation
1. First element
2. Second element

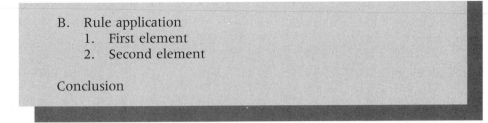

B. Rule application
    1. First element
    2. Second element

Conclusion

In *some* situations, you can explain all elements before you apply any of them. The rules and rule explanations for each element may be particularly interrelated in the authorities. The distinctions between them may be minor while the similarities are major. Separating the rule explanation sections may require you to repeat material. If the courts seem to take a more unified view of the elements, separating the rule explanation sections may even sacrifice some of the accuracy of the analysis. If your careful evaluation of the rule convinces you that these descriptions apply to your assignment, then you can opt for this variation of the multi-issue paradigm. Remember, though, that the virtue of the basic paradigm is that its structure forces you to think precisely about each element. Don't discard the advantages of that structure lightly.

 AN EXAMPLE

We'll use the Watson covenant-not-to-compete hypothetical and the *Fox* rule from Chapter 4 as an example of the multi-issue paradigm.[9] Take a moment to look back to pages 47-49, and Appendix D (p. 387) to refresh your recollection of the example and the *Fox* opinion. Assume that you have formulated a rule structured like this:

I. Is the Watson covenant-not-to-compete enforceable?

    A. Is the kind of activity restrained reasonable?

    B. Is the geographic scope of the restraint reasonable?

    C. Is the duration of the restraint reasonable?

9. For simplicity, we will only use *Fox* in this example, rather than working with both *Fox* and *Clein* from Chapter 5.

You know that you will be using the tools described in Chapters 7 through 9 for working with case authority: what the opinion *says* about the rule, how the opinion *applied* the rule, how the opinion did *not* apply the rule, the *facts* the opinion emphasized, what commentators said about the rule, and the *policies* implicated by the rule.

The first step is to write the umbrella section. First you state the umbrella rule and set out any part of rule explanation that applies to the rule generally. *Fox* seems to set out the rule expressly and relatively clearly, so you state the rule and its three elements. You also find, from *Fox*'s rule explanation, that all three elements are necessary before a court will enforce the covenant, so you include this information in the umbrella section as well.

Now you look for additional *general* information about how the decision-maker is to decide the reasonableness of the three elements. Does *Fox* seem to set out a standard that can be applied to all three elements? Look at the part of the *Fox* opinion where the court explains (using a quote from another opinion) that the best test of reasonableness is whether the restraint is only as large as is necessary for the protected party's needs and not so large as to impede the public interest. The opinion's author seems to be referring there to a standard that can be applied to all three elements. Since this rule seems to establish the test for analyzing all three elements, not just one, you include it in the umbrella section as well.

Finally, you look for any "thumbs on the scale." Does *Fox* set out any judicial or statutory leaning? Maybe and maybe not. The opinion does explain that contracts in general restraint of trade are against public policy. The opinion's author may be implying that this same policy that renders *general* restraints void suggests a skeptical attitude toward noncompetition covenants as well. On the other hand, the rest of the opinion's express language does not seem to reflect that leaning. You make a note to think about this question again after you have digested *Fox* further.

Since the *Fox* opinion does not elaborate further on the test for reasonableness in general, but rather goes directly to the analysis of each element, it appears that the remainder of rule explanation will apply individually to each element. Now you have a rough draft of the umbrella section:

I.   Is the Watson covenant-not-to-compete enforceable?

A covenant-not-to-compete is enforceable if all three of the following terms of the covenant are reasonable: (1) the kind of activity restrained; (2) the geographic scope of the restraint; and (3) the duration of the restraint. *Coffee System of Atlanta v. Fox*, 176 S.E.2d 71 (Ga. 1970). The test of reasonableness is whether the restraint is only as extensive as is necessary for the protected party's needs and not so extensive as to impede the public interest. *Fox*, citing *Shirk v. Loftis Bros. & Co.*, 97 S.E. 66 (Ga. 1918). [Note: Are covenants-not-to-compete disfavored because of the public policy against restraints of trade?]

Now, on to the first subsection. As you return to the opinion to find the discussion of your first subsection (the nature of the activities restrained), you notice that the opinion discusses the elements in an order different from yours and from its own statement of the rule. You decide to reorder your analysis so that you can follow the opinion's discussion more easily. So *A* becomes geography, *B* becomes time, and *C* becomes the nature of the activities restrained.

Now you turn your attention to the geography element. You know that the discussion under each subsection should begin with whatever rule explanation has not already been set out in the umbrella section. The opinion's general language seemed to lay out a test for determining reasonableness that would apply to each element, so you are looking now for any additional information about how that test applies to the geography element.

You identify the opinion's discussion of the geographic restraint. The court does not give any additional express explanation of the rule as it applies to that element. As a matter of fact, you notice that the opinion does not seem to apply its own articulated "test" at all, at least not directly. The opinion makes no effort to analyze the needs of the former employer or the public's interest. You wonder why not.

Relying on the court's initial statement about the rule, you had identified the two-pronged test as the standard for deciding reasonableness. Now, as you have returned to the opinion looking for rule explanation, you find that you must rethink whether the court really meant what it said. How can you reconcile the opinion's earlier statement with its own analysis? Since the opinion itself did not seem to use this two-pronged inquiry to decide the reasonableness of the activity term, you ask yourself what test it *did* use.

For both the geography term and the duration term, the opinion simply compares the terms of this covenant with the terms of other covenants in earlier precedent. The opinion even seems to say that these earlier opinions function as a "yardstick." This approach certainly does not seem consistent with the two-pronged test. Since each former employer's needs would be different, what would be the relevance of deciding Coffee System's need by reference to the needs of other former employers? And doesn't that same question apply to comparing the public's interest in restraining coffee sales and the public's interest in restraining other commercial activity?

So your next step is to read this earlier precedent to see if those opinions announce a "yardstick." Assume that you read those earlier opinions and discover that no such approach is announced. In those opinions, the court simply states that the terms must be reasonable, recites what the terms are for that particular covenant, and announces that those are reasonable. The earlier opinions neither announce a test for deciding reasonableness nor announce that the holdings in those cases can be used as yardsticks.

So you are back to *Fox* again. What does the court really seem to be doing there? You decide to read the opinion's discussion of the activity term to see if you find any hints, but that section is even more puzzling. The court does not apply the two-pronged inquiry there either. Rather, the opinion describes an even larger restraint on activity in an earlier case, and then states that, where the time and territory terms are limited, a restraint on soliciting customers of the employer is reasonable.

What exactly does this statement mean? You already know that *each* term must be reasonable—that if any one term is unreasonable, the covenant cannot be enforced. Therefore, the unreasonableness of the other two terms would already render the covenant unenforceable without regard for the activity term. So, if a prohibition on soliciting customers is reasonable *if the other terms are reasonable,* and if the other terms will always be reasonable (or else their unreasonableness would have already rendered the covenant unenforceable), perhaps you can conclude that a prohibition on soliciting customers generally will be reasonable.

But you are troubled by the illogic of the court's statement. If the opinion writer meant that prohibitions on soliciting customers generally would be reasonable, why not simply say that? Why did the author condition the activity element holding specifically on the reasonableness of the other two elements? You wonder if you are taking the author's language too literally, so you try to step back and read the court's statement with a more impressionistic eye.

Another possibility occurs to you. The author may be trying to tell you something about the way the elements of the rule relate to each other. While the court speaks in absolutes (a term either is or isn't reasonable), the fact that the court considered the other two terms in deciding the reasonableness of the activity term may imply that the *degree* of reasonableness of one term will impact the court's willingness to find another term reasonable. Does this make sense? Does this comport with your own experience of the way people reason?

It probably does. It makes sense that a judge would be more willing to approve one term that pushes the limits of reasonableness if the other two terms are eminently reasonable. While you cannot be entirely sure of this conclusion, the opinion's language and your common sense have given you some fairly good evidence. You are still most interested in figuring out the test for deciding reasonableness, but you make a note to yourself to go back to the umbrella section to add this additional information about how the elements relate to each other.

Having made that note, you turn your attention back to the primary question: What standard does a court use to decide reasonableness? You clarify for yourself that the conflict here is between what the opinion *said* and what the opinion *did.* As you reread what the opinion *did,* you are struck by the fact that the opinion analyzed all three elements in more or less the same way, that is, by comparison to earlier covenants. You also notice that the opinion's author did not expressly adopt the statement from the earlier opinion, but rather introduced it with a passive observation, "[i]t has been said that . . ."

Once again you rely on your common sense and your observations about the way people communicate. You find the opinion's own path through the analysis more convincing than its introductory quote from an earlier opinion. Perhaps the author of the opinion was simply quoting carelessly, and didn't mean to include those two inquiries as part of a "test" for reasonableness.

You begin to suspect that the concern for employers' needs and for the public interest functions more like a basic policy approach than as an actual test. Perhaps the opinion's author means that usually those two policies will not be offended by terms like the ones in the earlier opinions. In other words, perhaps a custom has arisen, originally defined by reference to these two standards, but now existing as a sort of presumption that terms within that scope are reasonable.

If this is the answer you decide on, you will need to return to the umbrella section and restate and explain the rule. Your new draft might look something like this:

I.   Is the Watson covenant-not-to-compete enforceable?

A covenant-not-to-compete is enforceable if all three of the following terms of the covenant are reasonable: (1) the kind of activity restrained; (2) the geographic scope of the restraint; and (3) the duration of the restraint. *Coffee System of Atlanta v. Fox,* 176 S.E.2d 71 (Ga. 1970). Restraints should be only as large as are necessary to protect the former employer and not so large that they unduly infringe the public interest. *Fox,* quoting *Shirk v. Loftis Bros. & Co.,* 97 S.E. 66 (Ga. 1918).

Courts usually decide reasonableness with reference to the kinds of restraints approved in earlier cases. Terms that fall within the customary range created by these earlier cases will probably be deemed reasonable without much in the way of individualized inquiry into the particular facts surrounding those terms. For instance, in . . . [here discuss *Fox* and several of the earlier cases, showing that your description accurately reflects how these courts decided those cases].

   A.   Is the geographic scope of the restraint reasonable?
        [Discuss the geographic scope of earlier cases and compare to this one.]

   B.   Is the duration of the restraint reasonable?
        [Discuss the duration of earlier restraints and compare to this one.]

   C.   Is the kind of activity restrained reasonable?
        [Discuss the nature of the activities restrained in earlier cases and compare to this one.]

We will leave this example now, though the writing process is not done. If you were to continue the project and complete the parts we've merely described, you would find that your analysis would continue to sharpen. But the example has served our purpose. It demonstrates the use of the multi-issue paradigm and how it can help you deepen and double-check your analysis.

EXERCISE 1.   Identifying the Parts of a Multi-Issue Discussion

Read the Discussion section of the office memo in Appendix A (p. 366) (a multi-issue discussion). Make a photocopy of the memo. On the photocopy, identify and label each part of the multi-issue discussion. Include the parts of the basic paradigm within each subsection of the discussion.

EXERCISE 2. Ethical Issues

a. Does the memo in Appendix A (see p. 365) assume that employees of Willis Chevrolet will lie? If so, is that appropriate? Does it trouble you? Why or why not?

b. While the doctrine allowing minors to disaffirm contracts is lawful and rests on sound policy, the doctrine would place the loss of Buckley's car on an arguably innocent third party. Assuming that Buckley has a reasonable chance of prevailing in such an action, should she pursue it? Do you see any moral issues for Buckley in this question? If so, would you raise them with her? How? If not, why not?

EXERCISE 3. Writing a Multi-Issue Discussion

Write a working draft of an answer to the Question Presented on page 143, using as your only authority the case summaries in Chapter 5 (pp. 66-68).

Facts

Mr. and Mrs. Carillo, each 64 years old, live in a neighborhood that includes older people, middle-aged people who have teenaged or young-adult children, and people with young children. The elementary school is about two blocks away, though most school children walk to school down the next street over. The closest neighbors who have children living at home are the Lupinos, three houses away from the Carillos.

About a year ago, the Carillos bought a trampoline for the use of their four grandchildren who visit from time to time. The trampoline is located in the Carillos' backyard. The yard is not fenced, but it is surrounded by a hedge and other shrubbery that effectively shield the backyard from view. Nonetheless, the neighborhood children know that the trampoline is there because they sometimes play with the Carillos' grandchildren. All of the children know that they are not permitted to jump on the trampoline unless an adult is present.

One day last spring, nine-year-old Jimmy Lupino was playing outside with a group of friends. One of the friends remembered the trampoline and suggested to the group that they ask the Carillos if they could play on the trampoline. They knocked, but the Carillos were not home. They huddled about what to do, and decided that they would each take just one turn on the trampoline. They went around the back and began to take their turns. When Jimmy Lupino's turn came, he climbed on. On his fourth jump he got too close to the edge, hit the metal side of the trampoline, and broke his spine. He is now partially paralyzed.

The Lupinos have asked if your firm will represent them on a contingency basis in a lawsuit against the Carillos. In order to decide whether to accept the case on this basis, you need an idea of what claims the Lupinos might be able to bring. One of the possible claims you need to evaluate is an attractive nuisance claim.

Question Presented

Do the Lupinos have a reasonable chance of recovery on an attractive nuisance claim?

EXERCISE 4. More Work with Facts

For each element of the rule you articulated in your answer to Exercise 3, list any other facts you would like to know about the *Carillo* case and, for each, explain why.

CONVERTING THE WORKING DRAFT TO AN OFFICE MEMO

11 The Office Memo and the Law-Trained Reader

Now that you have done a solid legal analysis of the question you were given, it is time to turn your attention to the document you are going to write and the reader for whom you will write it.

I OBSERVATIONS ABOUT READERS

A. FOCUS ON THE READER

We'll think first about the characteristics of law-trained readers. After all, the goal of writing is to communicate with a reader. A document is actually a conversation (see p. 151), and, as in any conversation, the better we know our partners, the more effectively we can communicate. Knowing the characteristics of the reader governs many of the writer's choices.

This need to know the person to whom we speak is more than a helpful tool; it is a fundamental part of the project of communication. We know this intuitively, just as we know that placing our weight on alternate legs is fundamental to walking. In conversation, we know without conscious thought that we need information about our conversational partner. In spoken conversation where we do not know each other already, we spend the early part of the conversation rapidly gathering information about each other. We pick up both verbal and nonverbal signals about who this other person is and what he or she is thinking. We may do this without realizing it; we often process the information and act on it without awareness that we have done so. But the fact that we do this automatically and unconsciously simply demonstrates how fundamental to the project is the information.

What about *written* communication, then? If we have to be reminded to focus on an audience, is the need less important? Less fundamental to the project? In reality, we do not have to be reminded to focus on an audience; we all do that just as intuitively in writing as in speaking. Whether we realize it or not, we always write to *someone*. But we are vulnerable in two ways: we may write to the wrong person, or we may write to the right person but with inaccurate or incomplete information about that person.

It is easy to write to the wrong person. Because we cannot rely on our eyes and ears to keep the image of our audience before us, we must rely on imagination instead. The picture is not clear and constant, and often we find that we are writing to ourselves rather than to the real reader. We are having a conversation with ourselves.

Also, it is easy to write with a fuzzy and incomplete picture of the reader in mind. Sometimes this lack of focus is caused by inaccurate information, but more often we simply fail to recognize and evaluate our assumptions. We forget to stop before we write and ask, "Who is this person, and what is she likely to be concerned about?"

When you undertake a legal writing task, you may not know your reader well—perhaps not at all. But you can still write with a fairly accurate focus on this unfamiliar reader because readers, particularly law-trained readers, tend to share certain characteristics. Even in large cities, lawyers and judges live in a "legal community" which shares certain values, customs, and forms of expression. Legal writing and analysis require you to present your message in a way that makes sense in the context of this legal community.

On the other hand, you may know your reader well. For instance, you may be writing a memo to another lawyer in your firm or to the judge for whom you work. In that case, your specialized knowledge of this particular reader is your best and most reliable source of information, but the observations in this chapter will still help you sharpen your picture of even this well-known reader.

The general characteristics of law-trained readers in this and later chapters can only invite you to begin your study of readers. Don't just accept the principles that follow. Notice your own reactions when you read. Try to be a "participant-observer" of the reading process. Your observations of your own reactions as a reader will be your best writing teacher. Observe too the other law-trained readers you know. This way, as the years of your legal practice go by, your writing will get better and better.

B.   ATTENTION LEVELS

Before a speaker can communicate, the audience must be listening. Here is some information about the attention levels of law-trained readers:

1.   A reader's attention is finite. Even the most diligent reader will run low or run out.

2. A reader's investment in the nuances of the topic may not be as great as the writer's. While the law-trained reader will have a particular need to understand the material, these readers are extraordinarily busy. The judge has many other cases and does not have a personal investment in this one. The senior partner has many other obligations and depends on the memo-writer to analyze thoroughly but communicate succinctly.
3. A reader's attention is not evenly distributed. It is greatest in the first several pages, and it decreases rapidly from then on.
4. Readers generally save some attention for the Conclusion. They are willing to invest attention there, but only if they can locate the Conclusion easily and if the Conclusion is clear and compelling enough to warrant the investment.
5. While readers spend more attention on the document's first few pages and on a compelling Conclusion, attention levels revive a bit at internal beginnings and endings, like the start of a new issue or the last few paragraphs of a statement of facts. This revival is more likely if the new issue is marked by a heading or subheading.
6. Stories, especially real life stories, are engrossing. Many readers pay more attention to facts than to abstract legal concepts. This means, for instance, that attention levels are higher in the middle of an effective Statement of Facts than in the middle of the Argument or Discussion section. It also means that, even in the middle of a Discussion or Argument section, a reader's attention level will rise a bit when the material begins to apply law to fact.
7. A reader's attention level is lowest about three-fourths of the way through the Discussion section of an office memo or the Argument section of a brief.

When you combine your thinking about these observations, you realize that *placement of material* is one of the important decisions a writer must make. While a reader will want the analysis to be complete, she also will want the most important parts of the analysis placed where she can find them quickly and give them first priority for her attention.

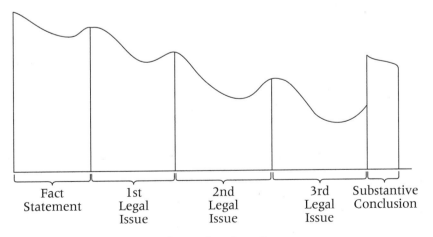

| Fact Statement | 1st Legal Issue | 2nd Legal Issue | 3rd Legal Issue | Substantive Conclusion |

Attention Levels

C. ROAD MAPS

Most nonfiction readers want a road map—some sense of where they are and where they are headed. But law-trained readers have an even greater need for an organizational structure. Here's why:

1. A reader's first priority is to understand the law. As you learned in Stage One, a law-trained reader's first step in the process of understanding the law is an "outline." This process of learning and applying law set out in outline form is how most lawyers and judges studied law. It is basic to the way law-trained readers think. In the first few semesters of law school this learning style and thinking process probably came more naturally to some than to others, but by the end of law school virtually all lawyers approach legal analysis by some variation of this method.[1] This process may even be the primary component of that nebulous concept "thinking like a lawyer."

2. Lawyers and judges do not read the law out of intellectual curiosity, but because they have a problem to solve. They are looking to your memo or brief to help them solve it. This means that your discussion of the law must be clearly and closely tied to the facts and issues of the case. Your organizational structure serves as the continuing reminder of how your legal discussion relates to the problem to be solved.

3. A law-trained reader reads skeptically, constantly assessing the strength and accuracy of the analysis. The most visible part of the analysis, the part the skeptical reader first evaluates, is its organization. Here the law-trained reader expects to find the "outline" of the law. If the reader doubts the organization of the analysis, the reader wonders whether the analysis is reliable.

4. Along with this skeptical assessment of the analysis itself, the law-trained reader is assessing the ability and credibility of the writer. Doubt about the writer's "outline" translates into doubt about the writer's ability, credibility, or both. This kind of doubt doubles the reader's natural skepticism.

5. At some point in their legal education or practice, law-trained readers have studied many of the more common rules of law. These readers will be used to thinking of those rules in a familiar order or structure. An example is the burglary rule from Chapter 3. Even if a reader is not already familiar with a particular rule of law, a statute or a leading case may set out the rule in a particular structure. A law-trained reader will be expecting to analyze the issue in this familiar order or structure. Law-trained readers are not comfortable with organizational surprises; and an uncomfortable reader is an unreceptive reader.

---

1. Some describe this thought process as the "categorical imperative": If *A, B, C,* and *D,* then *X.*

D. READERS AS COMMENTATORS

We have already seen how the reader's invisibility can cause the writer to forget the reader and unconsciously begin to write to himself. But the abstractness of the image of the reader can mislead the writer in another way as well.

It is easy to assume that writing is a one-way street, with the discourse all flowing in one direction. We tend to think that we, as writers, are the only speakers; we think this because we can't hear anyone else talking. The frightening reality is that the most important party to the conversation, the reader, *is* talking, but we can't hear her.

Think of it this way. Each of us has a little voice in his or her mind—an opinionated, skeptical, and talkative little "Commentator." We've already observed this character at work, because when a writer mistakenly begins writing to himself, it is to the writer's own internal Commentator that the writer is writing.

Well, the reader has such a Commentator too, and that little voice will chatter at every opportunity. The Commentator will be saying things like "No, that's not right, because . . .", or "What in the world do you mean by that?" or "But wait, where is the discussion about . . . ?" Think of yourself as a reader. Haven't you been reading this chapter listening to both the written word and to your own Commentator?[2]

The reader's Commentator will not remain completely silent, and there is nothing the writer can do to change that. The Commentator's participation can even be helpful. Yet each time the Commentator speaks, the reader is trying to listen to two voices at once; the writer must compete with the Commentator for the reader's attention. The writer, then, has two objectives: (1) The writer wants to keep the reader's Commentator relatively quiet, resolving its concerns at the point where they arise, and (2) when the Commentator does speak, the writer wants it to be saying "OK," "right," "yes," point by point by point.

A writer wants to calm the Commentator even from excited agreement. When the Commentator's imagination becomes engaged, even the chatter of agreement is distracting to the reader. More worrisome yet, the writer has lost control of the discourse because the writer has no way to predict where the Commentator's imagination will carry her.

Quieting the Commentator is not an easy task. As a writer you must anticipate the Commentator's chatter before the conversation occurs and try to preempt that chatter. Your goal is to craft your side of the conversation so that the Commentator is as quiet and agreeable as possible.

E. LAW PROFESSORS AS READERS

The two primary kinds of writing you'll do in law school course work will be the documents you write for your legal writing assignments and your answers

---

2. If so, be grateful to your Commentator. The sort of critical reading the Commentator inspires is essential to legal analysis. When you are studying the law and writing about it, your own Commentator is your best friend.

to law school exams. Your primary readers for these documents will be the law professors who drafted the assignments and examination questions. Undoubtedly these professors already understand a great deal about the relevant area of law and about the particular authorities on which your analysis will be based.

Ordinarily a writer should tailor the document to the reader's pre-existing knowledge. If the writer is certain that the reader knows some of the relevant information, the writer would only refer generally to the information when necessary to put new information in context. However, law school writing is a different matter. Unlike most readers, your professor is not reading to learn particular information. Instead, your professor is reading to evaluate what information *you* have learned and how well you can communicate it. If the information is not set out in your document, your professor will not know whether and how well you understand it.

Therefore, in law school writing, assume that you are writing to an intelligent, law-trained reader who has no particular expertise in the area you are discussing. This assumption will help you strike the right balance between including the information your professor wants to evaluate without explaining more than the assignment requires.

II   AN OVERVIEW OF THE OFFICE MEMO

In addition to knowing as much as possible about your reader, you need to know four more things: (1) your document's function, (2) its format, (3) its degree of formality, and (4) the rules of professional ethics that apply to the lawyerly task of memo-writing. How does the requesting attorney plan to use the document? What format and level of formality does she prefer for it? What are your ethical responsibilities in writing it? Since an understanding of function is necessary to an understanding of form, formality, and ethical requirements, we'll review function first.

A.   FUNCTION

Recall from Chapter 1 the primary function of an office memo. An office memo is an internal working document of the firm; it is not designed for outside readers. The function of an office memo is to answer a legal question. The question usually will seek an answer for a particular client in a particular situation. Often it will be the primary basis for making a decision with both legal and nonlegal consequences.

Also, the firm may have a "form file" in which it keeps, for future use, office memos dealing with particular legal questions. The idea is to eliminate the need to repeat research and analysis on topics that may recur. Keep in mind, then, that your document may have a long life, may impact many clients, and may create impressions about you in the minds of many future readers.

Remember also that your role is predictive rather than persuasive. You must take an objective view of the question rather than advocate for a certain result. Recall from Chapter 1 how easy it can be to forget this role. When your client's situation would be better served by a particular answer, it is easy to slip into advocating for that result rather than taking a balanced view of the question. Yet, if the answer to the question will be bad news for your client and for the requesting attorney, better that they learn that news now and from you; learning it later could be costly for the client, for the firm, and for you. Making an accurate prediction, then, is the function of an office memo.

B. FORMAT

The format of a memo is designed to fit its function and its reader's needs. Since a memo is an internal document, law firms are likely to have a preferred memo format. The firm's preferred format may use various words for the section titles, it may place the sections in an order different from that described here, or it may include other sections.

If your reader (your teacher or law firm) has a particular format preference, use it. If not, you can use the standard memo format this text describes. Variations in format are much less important than the accuracy and thoroughness of the analysis. This chapter will provide an overview of the suggested format, and Chapters 12 and 13 will take you through the process of creating each part of the document.

The components of a standard office memo format are:

1. Heading
2. Question Presented
3. Brief Answer
4. Fact Statement
5. Discussion
6. Conclusion (when appropriate)

Look at the sample memo in Appendix A to locate and review each component.

1. Heading.[3] The function of the heading is to identify the requesting attorney, the writer, the date, and the particular legal matter.

2. Question Presented.[4] The Question Presented identifies the question you have been asked to answer. It allows your reader to confirm that you have understood the question; it also may remind a busy reader of the question he or she asked you to analyze.

3. A more detailed discussion of this component appears at pp. 175-176.
4. A more detailed discussion of this component appears at pp. 176-180.

3.   Brief Answer.[5]   The Brief Answer comes next, and if you remember what we've already learned about law-trained readers, you'll understand why. Law-trained readers are nearly always in a hurry. They want answers quickly and right up front; then they can decide how much attention to invest in the explanation that follows. As the writer, you had to go through the analysis reflected in the discussion section before you could decide the answer. However, in the document designed for this busy reader, provide the answer first.

4.   Fact Statement.[6]   Next comes the section that sets out the facts on which your answer is based. If your reader is the requesting attorney, you probably obtained the facts from your reader in the first place. Why, then, would your reader want you to repeat them? There are at least five reasons.

First, your reader will want to be sure that you have not misunderstood any facts that could have affected the legal analysis. Second, your reader will want to have the facts freshly in mind while evaluating your explanation of the law and its application to this situation. Third, the requesting attorney may not be the only reader. Other attorneys or professionals working on this case may need access to the analysis in the memo.

Fourth, reading your fact statement in conjunction with your legal analysis may help the reader realize that she has neglected to give you a critical fact. This omission may have occurred because the reader did not know what facts would be important without knowing the law on the issue; or because the client neglected to provide the fact to the reader; or because of simple oversight.

Finally, if your memo is placed in the firm's memo file, attorneys working on future cases may read it as well. Such a reader may not be familiar with the facts of your case. Yet that reader will need to learn about the facts of your case to decide whether your legal analysis would apply to the reader's case. Including the facts in the memo addresses all of these reader concerns.

As the writer, you have an interest in reciting the facts as well. Your legal analysis will, of course, be based on the facts as you understand them. If the facts were to change, the result might change. If you memorialize the facts you have been given—the facts on which your answer is based—you insure that your work will be evaluated with reference to those facts. No future reader will think you had access to other, different facts and therefore expect you to have reached a different answer.

5.   Discussion.   The Discussion section explains to your reader the analysis that led to your answer. Your working draft, with some alterations, will become the Discussion section. Chapter 12 will explain how to convert your working draft into the Discussion section of the memo.

6.   Conclusion.[7]   Finally, you may choose to end with a Conclusion, a summary of the main points of your analysis. Why include a Conclusion when your Brief Answer has already stated the answer and the Discussion has already explained the analysis in detail? A Conclusion section can be helpful

---

5.   A more detailed discussion of this component appears at pp. 180-183.
6.   A more detailed discussion of this component appears at pp. 183-186.
7.   A more detailed discussion of this component appears at pp. 187-188.

in two ways. First, if the analysis has been complex or multifaceted, a Conclusion can tie together and summarize the Discussion. Sometimes this summary can add a clarity that the Discussion alone may not be able to achieve.

Second, a Conclusion can increase your reader's options for deciding how much attention to invest in understanding the details of your analysis. A Conclusion would go into more detail than the Brief Answer but not as much as the Discussion. Therefore a law-trained reader would have the option to read your Brief Answer first, then proceed to your Conclusion for somewhat more depth, and finally read your Discussion for even more depth. After reading each section, your reader can decide how far and how deeply to read on.[8]

C.   DEGREE OF FORMALITY

In practice you will find that the degree of formality a reader expects in an office memo will vary. Some firms expect formality in every memo. Some firms expect the memo-writer to follow the preference of the particular requesting attorney. Sometimes the preference of a particular attorney will vary depending on the kind of question, the particular client, time constraints, or other circumstances.

Choose the level of formality your reader desires. If you have no specific instructions, you can ask or you can look at examples of memos done by others in the firm. Resolve doubts in favor of formality. In law school, unless your teacher tells you otherwise, use traditional professional formality such as that demonstrated in the sample memo in Appendix A.

D.   ETHICAL REQUIREMENTS

Finally, remember the professional responsibilities that you, as a lawyer, must fulfill:

1. A lawyer must provide competent representation, including legal knowledge, skill, thoroughness, and preparation.[9]
2. A lawyer must act with diligence and promptness.[10]
3. Except with a client's permission, a lawyer must not reveal a client's confidences.[11]
4. A lawyer's advice must be candid and unbiased. The advice must not

---

8. Rest assured, however, that in law school your teacher will read and evaluate your entire document.

9. Model Rules of Professional Conduct Rule 1.1 (1994); Model Code of Professional Responsibility DR 6-101(A) (1980).

10. Model Rules of Professional Conduct Rule 1.3 (1994); Model Code of Professional Responsibility DR 6-101(A) (1980).

11. Model Rules of Professional Conduct Rule 1.6 (1994); Model Code of Professional Responsibility DR 4-101 (1980).

be adversely influenced by conflicting loyalties to another client, to a third party, or to the lawyer's own interests.[12]

5. While a lawyer's advice must provide an accurate assessment of the law, it also may refer to moral, economic, social, and political factors relevant to the client's situation.[13] However, the lawyer's representation of a client does not constitute a personal endorsement of the client's activities or views.[14]

6. A lawyer must not advise or assist a client to commit a crime or a fraud.[15] When the client expects unethical assistance, the lawyer must explain to the client the ethical limitations on the lawyer's conduct.[16]

7. Every lawyer is bound by the rules of professional conduct, no matter whether that lawyer is in charge of the case or working under the direction of another lawyer.[17]

While promulgated rules of professional responsibility cover only licensed lawyers, practically speaking, they govern law clerks and other support personnel as well. First, your work will affect a real client. Second, the lawyers for whom you clerk are responsible for the work you do as their clerk. Further, you may be held accountable for your work when you apply for membership in the bar yourself, not because the rules covered you at the time you did the work but because your prior work may be evidence of the kind of lawyer you would be, if admitted.

But the best reason to adhere to the rules is more personal. Your first legal work will be the raw material for developing your *own* professional standards. Begin now to expect yourself to meet or exceed the professional responsibilities of a lawyer. Do it for the sake of yourself and your craft.

———————————

Now that you have an introduction to your reader, to the office memo's function and format, to your choices about the appropriate degree of formality, and to your ethical responsibilities, it is time to begin creating your document. Chapter 12 explains how to convert your working draft into the Discussion section. Chapter 13 explains how to draft the remaining sections of the memo.

---

12. Model Rule of Professional Conduct Rule 1.7 (1994); Model Code of Professional Responsibility DR 5-101 and DR 5-105 (1980).

13. Model Rules of Professional Conduct Rule 2.1 (1994); Model Code of Professional Responsibility DR 5-107(B) and EC 7-8 (1980).

14. Model Rules of Professional Conduct Rule 1.2(b) (1994).

15. Model Rules of Professional Conduct Rule 1.2 (1994); Model Code of Professional Responsibility DR 7-102(A)(7) (1980).

16. Model Rules of Professional Conduct Rule 1.2(e) (1994); Model Code of Professional Responsibility DR 2-110(C)(1)(c) (1980).

17. Model Rules of Professional Conduct Rule 5.2 (1994).

Organizing for Your Reader: The Discussion Section

The rule's structure gave you the organization for the working draft of your office memo. This organization of the working draft has been your basic analytical tool. It has clarified for you how all parts of the rule fit together; it has allowed you to identify which elements are in question and which are not; it was your friendly disciplinarian as you wrote. Now you are ready to revise your working draft organization with your reader's needs in mind. This revised version of your working draft will become the Discussion section of your office memo.

 ## I CONVERTING YOUR WORKING DRAFT INTO THE DISCUSSION SECTION

When you convert your working draft into a document addressed to a reader, your *structure* should remain the same—that is, the question will still define your roman numeral and the applicable rule(s) of law will still structure your analysis. However, you may need to reorder the subparts of that structure by moving some of the sections around. The reason relates to the different functions of the drafts. Since the function of the working draft structure is primarily to help *you*, the writer, analyze the law and its application to the facts at hand, the working draft's outline must track the rule's structure so that your analysis doesn't miss any steps. Chapters 1 through 6 explained how this works.

However, the function of a subsequent draft is to serve the *reader's* needs,[1]

1. *See* Chapter 11.

so those needs should guide the selection of an organization for later drafts. The reader's needs and the working draft organization will not always conflict. Sometimes your structuring of the rule will constitute an organization that serves the reader best as well. Usually, though, this will be true only if the rule contains few subparts and if the parts of the analysis that turn out to be most important to the result happen to be those that the rule structure places right up front, where the busy reader will be looking for them. When this happy coincidence does not occur, you will need to make some organizational adjustments to better serve your reader.

For ordering subparts, you have at least four basic organizational plans to choose from: (1) dispositive issues, (2) important issues, (3) threshold issues, or (4) familiar order.[2] No matter which plan you choose, introduce your choice of organizational plans with an umbrella section. We'll look first at the umbrella and then at the organizational choices.

A.   THE UMBRELLA SECTION

Your working draft already contains an umbrella section,[3] so your task now is to revise it with your reader's needs in mind. The revised umbrella section should do the following four things:

1. Summarize the rule, setting out all subparts and clarifying how they relate to each other.
2. Identify any genuinely undisputed issues and provide a cursory explanation of why they are not in dispute.
3. State the order in which the remaining issues will be discussed, explaining the reason for this organizational choice.
4. If necessary to prevent confusion, identify any related legal issues *not* covered by the memo.

First, summarize the rule and cite the controlling authority. Your summary should be complete enough to give the reader a quick, clear overview of the rule, including all subparts. Be sure to explain how the rule functions. Clarify the relationships among the subparts, such as whether all subparts must be established or whether some subparts are prerequisites for proceeding to others.

In this rule summary, include any other information important to how the rule functions. For instance, one party will carry the burden of proof.[4] The rule may require a higher-than-normal level of proof (for example, clear and

---

2. These structures are not the only possibilities; you may well find or create others. Nor will you always adhere strictly to this book's descriptions of these structures; sometimes you will alter a structure to suit your reader's particular needs.

3. *See* Chapter 10.

4. The burden of proof places on one of the parties the responsibility of proving the facts necessary to resolve the legal issue in that party's favor.

convincing).[5] Some rules come with a presumption of one variety or another.[6] Some come with policy "leanings" (for instance, case law stating that doubts are to be resolved in favor of the criminal defendant). The procedural posture of a case, such as a motion for summary judgment, a motion to dismiss, or an appeal from a jury verdict,[7] may impose a particular standard more favorable to one party. A canon of statutory construction may call for a strict reading of a statute. Include any such special "instructions" as part of your explanation of the rule and how it functions.

Second, identify any genuinely undisputed issues. As you wrote the analysis in your working draft, you were able to identify each element not genuinely in dispute. For each such element, ask yourself whether your conclusion will be readily apparent to your reader or whether the reader will require some (although perhaps simple) analysis in order to be satisfied on the point. Make this decision based upon your assessment of (1) your reader's existing knowledge of the law, (2) the degree of your reader's faith in you as a legal thinker and writer, and (3) your reader's need for certainty. Make these assessments conservatively. If you are in doubt, err on the side of treating an issue as in dispute.

If you conclude that an issue is not genuinely in dispute, say so. Give the reader a cursory explanation of the basis for your conclusion—just enough to reassure the reader that your reasons for this conclusion are consistent with the reader's understanding. An example of an umbrella section that does this is the burglary example on pages 167-168 of this chapter.

If one of the undisputed elements also happens to be dispositive (that is, your answer to it, if correct, would dispose of the need for the rest of the analysis), do not treat it in a cursory fashion in the introductory paragraphs. All dispositive issues merit full analysis in the main body of the discussion, whether they appear clear to you or not. For instance, in a burglary case, if the facts conclusively establish the absence of the "nighttime" element, the charge of burglary cannot be sustained. Thus, the "nighttime" element is dispository and should be fully discussed in its own section rather than disposed of cursorily in the umbrella section.

Third, identify the remaining issues and explain the order in which you will address them. Explaining your choice of structures is particularly important if your structure is different from the one the reader may be expecting.

---

5.   The most common standard for a burden of proof in a civil case is proof by the preponderance of the evidence. That means that the party bearing the burden must present stronger evidence than that of the opposing party in order to win. However, in a criminal trial, the prosecution must meet a higher standard of proof—proof beyond a reasonable doubt. In some circumstances, a party may be required to prove certain facts by a higher standard than a mere preponderance, but not beyond a reasonable doubt. Courts often refer to this intermediate standard as "clear and convincing evidence."

6.   In the determination of most legal and factual issues, the decision-maker starts from a neutral posture. However sometimes, as a matter of policy, the law will impose a "presumption" supporting a certain result. For instance, the law imposes a presumption that service of process in a judicial proceeding has been accomplished lawfully. In such a case, the decision-maker presumes the truth of the presumption until sufficient evidence to the contrary has been offered.

7.   *See* the discussion of procedural rules on pp. 74-76, Chapter 6.

An effective umbrella section provides the reader with the context for the analysis, and it clears away the underbrush—the issues that the reader need not ponder. It presents the road map for the remaining issues and enlists the support of the reader's Commentator[8] for the organizational choice to follow. In other words, the introduction meets the reader where he is, deals with his immediate needs, and leads him to the starting point of the analysis.

Finally, clarify any potential confusion about the scope of your analysis. If a reader could assume that your analysis includes all relevant legal issues pertaining to the question, but it does not, be sure to say so. For example, if the requesting attorney has asked you to analyze claims under only one statute, but claims might exist under other statutes. In such a case, clarify that your memo covers only possible claims under the identified statute. Your reader will appreciate this clarity, and you will be protected from later misunderstandings.

B. ORGANIZATIONAL CHOICES

After an effective umbrella section, the Discussion begins immediately with the issues at the heart of the analysis. Set out those issues in an organization that fits both the analysis and the reader's needs. Here are the most common organizational plans and some examples of how to decide among them.

1. Dispositive Issues

If you are working with a rule that has several elements or other subheadings, seldom will all of the subheadings be equally likely to be dispositive of the Question Presented. As you wrote your working draft, you should have been able to identify those subheadings that are most likely to be dispositive. If the discussion deals with several subheadings, and if some are more likely to be dispositive than others, your reader's needs may be best served by a dispositive issues structure.

For instance, assume that to enforce a covenant-not-to-compete, the plaintiff must prove that the duration, geographic scope, and nature of the activity restrained are reasonable. Since all three terms must be reasonable, the most dispositive term (that is, the term most likely to decide the issue) will be the term most likely to be found *un*reasonable. The dispositive issues organization would place it first.

Organizing according to dispositive issues is an effective tool to help your reader manage a number of issues or elements. This organization places the issues most likely to be dispositive at the spot where the reader's attention and patience are at their greatest. It minimizes the time a busy reader must devote to the analysis. It maximizes the busy reader's flexibility by enabling the reader to choose how far into the latter parts of the analysis to read and with what degree of care. It preempts the Commentator's impatient complaints. It

---

8. *See* p. 151.

assures the reader that the writer's analysis is complete enough to separate the issues that are dispositive from those that are not.

To use the dispositive issues organization, order the issues according to their likelihood of disposing of the Question Presented. First come any issues that you believe to be dispositive. These are ordered from those you are most sure of to those you are least sure of. Then come issues you believe are *not* dispositive, but beginning with those where your assessment may be wrong and ending with those where your assessment is most likely right.

One more reminder of the importance of the umbrella section: Be sure to explain your decision to order the subsections this way. Your reader will welcome this structure, but only if the reader understands the reasons for and accepts the wisdom of the choice.

2.   *Important Issues*

The important issues organization orders subheadings by their importance to the reader and to the analysis.[9] This organization is often a good choice when a rule of law contains a list of factors the decision-maker must consider. Usually, no one factor is dispositive; yet some will be more important to the analysis than others.

We'll use an issue of child custody as an example. Assume that the law of your jurisdiction requires the judge to decide custody according to the "best interests of the child." The statute sets out a number of factors that the judge should consider in determining "best interests." No doubt, some of the factors will be more important in some cases than in others. For one family, religion might be an important factor because the children have been raised to adhere strictly to the tenets of a certain faith, and the disruption of that faith would be traumatic to them. In another case, however, religion may not be important because the children have not been involved in any particular faith. Perhaps in that family, the lifestyle of one of the parents will be a more important factor.

In a discussion of the application of the child custody statute to a particular child, organizing according to important issues makes sense. This organization offers the same sorts of advantages and works much the same way as the dispositive issues organization. The "important issues" organization simply orders the subheadings with reference to their importance to the analysis, beginning with the most important and ending with the least important.[10]

---

9.   The importance to the reader and the importance to the analysis should be the same, unless the writer and the reader have differing views of the analysis. If the writer suspects a difference, the writer should either (1) use the introductory paragraphs to convert the reader to the writer's view of the analysis, or (2) order the subpoints by their importance to the *reader's* analysis.

10.   This structure is a workhorse of objective legal analysis (analysis such as that in an office memo). However, it may be a bad choice for persuasive writing, such as a brief to the court. If, for instance, the most important subpoint yields an unfavorable result, you will want to look for an organizational structure that allows you to reduce rather than maximize the impact of this particular factor. *See* Chapter 18.

3.   *Threshold Issues*

As we have already seen, the analysis of a Question Presented may require two or more steps, and the first may be a threshold issue. A *threshold issue* is one that determines the direction of the analysis from that point on. For instance, assume that a rule of law tells you that if a business is a "lending institution," it may not do certain things. The issue of whether your client is a "lending institution" within the meaning of that rule of law determines the direction of the analysis from that point on. If your client is *not* a "lending institution," the rule of law prohibiting certain conduct does not apply to your client, and the analysis can move on to any other rules of law that may apply to your client. But if your client *is* a "lending institution," the rule of law does apply, and the analysis must continue to determine whether your client's proposed conduct falls within the category of conduct prohibited by the rule. Thus the issue of whether your client is a "lending institution" is a threshold issue.

When you are working with a rule that has a threshold issue, the best organizational choice usually is to place the threshold issue first. The reader probably will expect the analysis to begin with the threshold issue. Also, remember that a reader's attention and patience are limited. If you conclude that the threshold step in the analysis is not met, then the reader's need to ponder the second step is not so great. The reader's only objective in reading further is to understand the probable result should the memo's prediction about the threshold issue prove to be inaccurate.[11]

Occasionally, however, you may be working with a rule where the analysis of the threshold issue is complex and your answer to a remaining issue makes the complex analysis of the threshold issue unnecessary. For instance, perhaps the issue of whether your client is a "lending institution" (and therefore whether the statute would apply to your client at all) is a close and complex question. However, even if the statute applies to your client, the statute rather clearly would not prohibit your client's proposed conduct.

If this second conclusion is relatively clear and easily explained, your reader may be best served by the dispositive issue organization. Simply explain your organizational choice in the introductory paragraphs. Your reader will appreciate the dispositive issue organization if she understands your reasons for the choice.

4.   *Familiar Order*

Many rules of law are familiar to law-trained readers, and the elements of those rules are often listed in a certain familiar order. Often the familiar order is the order the rule uses. Common law burglary is a good example. The definition of burglary is traditionally stated as "the breaking and entering of

---

11.   Even the best and most thorough prediction of what a judge might decide on a given issue is, after all, only a prediction of human conduct. The prediction may be better reasoned than the judge's ultimate decision, but even then a prediction that mispredicts is inaccurate.

the dwelling house of another in the nighttime with the intent to commit a felony therein." On a burglary issue, a law-trained reader will be accustomed to thinking of the elements in the order recited in that sentence, and your first draft probably would have analyzed them in that order.

Even if no rule establishes a familiar order of elements, the common habit of ordering issues chronologically may establish a familiar order. If the subissues pertain to events occurring in a chronology, a law-trained reader probably will expect to analyze the issues in that order. For instance, contracts issues are often ordered by the chronology of events constituting the formation and performance of the contract: offer, acceptance, modification, and performance.

Unless the reader's other needs require a different choice, order your discussion in the way the reader is expecting.[12] You don't want to add unnecessarily to the reader's natural skepticism by imposing an unfamiliar organization. Familiar order organization can serve as a default position—your choice unless there is a reason to prefer a different plan for this particular writing task.

You can see that the underlying *structure* of the analysis addressed to a reader remains the same. The sections of your document are still defined by (structured by) the applicable rule(s) of law. However, your assessment of the reader's needs has governed the *order* of your discussion of these sections. Some sections of the working draft have been moved into the umbrella section, some have been moved up to the beginning of the main Discussion section, and some have been moved to the end. After you have selected and implemented your organizational plan, all that remains to be done to the draft of the Discussion is to check your subsection lengths, revise your section headings, and smooth out the transitions between the sections.

C. Check Subsection Lengths and Revise Headings

Now that you have your organization in place, check the length and complexity of each of the subsections. If several subsections are short and this troubles you, you may choose to combine them. Remove the original subheadings, leaving the material under one heading that covers it all. Within that new and larger section, use clear transitional phrases or sentences to mark the beginning and end of your discussion of each of these smaller issues. Don't be too hasty to obscure the rule's structure like this, however. Law-trained readers generally are less troubled by short sections than by confusion about rule structure.

If a subsection strikes you as particularly long and complex, consider further subdivisions with headings. These subdivisions can reflect different lines of authority, different tests set out in case law, rule explanation versus rule application, or any other points of division that would be helpful to the reader. For length, use three pages as a rough outside limit. Headings and subheadings

---

12. Of course, the umbrella section may have dealt already with some of the subparts of the rule. For instance, in the burglary example, seldom would all of those elements genuinely be disputed; thus those undisputed points would be removed already from their place in the familiar order and placed in the umbrella section.

will constitute your reader's road map. Most busy readers want to orient themselves in the text at least every three pages or so. Also remember that reader attention wanes between subheadings and can be renewed with a subheading.

Finally, check your headings and subheadings to be sure that they communicate your points to your reader. Headings are important to readers because they make the large-scale organization visible at a glance. They mark the reader's progress through the analysis, so that the reader always knows where she has been, what is coming next, and where she is headed. They allow busy readers to find the conclusion on a particular issue by locating the heading for the next issue and then reading the paragraph immediately before it. They mark the spots where the reader might choose to invest a bit more attention. They assist the reader in evaluating the analysis itself, and through it the writer's ability and credibility. They quiet the Commentator's impatient chatter,[13] allowing the reader to consider preliminary issues with the assurance that awaited sections are coming. They allow busy readers to jump immediately to the particular section they need to review.

Your working draft headings (those marked by roman numerals) were questions, but for subheadings you may have used phrases instead of complete sentences. Phrases were fine for your working draft because you were using the working draft to work out your own analysis. Now that you are communicating with a reader, revise at least your major subheadings into complete thesis sentences.

As for whether those complete sentences should be questions[14] or declarative sentences asserting your conclusions,[15] you will encounter differing preferences. Now that you have worked out your answer for each issue and subissue, your busy reader probably will prefer to see your *answer* asserted in the heading rather than a question. If you have received no instructions on this point, the better course is to phrase the headings and subheadings as conclusions.

D. EDIT THE PARADIGM

Whether or not you have asserted your conclusion in the subheading, consider inserting a statement of your conclusion in the first paragraph under the heading. If you did not state the conclusion in the heading, your busy reader is waiting eagerly to see it. Even if you did state the conclusion in the heading, a distracted and impatient reader may have missed it, looking for it instead in the text right under the heading. If stating the conclusion both in the heading and in the first paragraph seems repetitive, simply use slightly different words or sentence structure for the second statement.

---

13. *See* p. 151.

14. An example of a subheading that states the question rather than the conclusion is: "Did the defendant's conduct constitute a 'breaking' pursuant to the burglary statute?"

15. An example of a subheading that states the conclusion is: "The defendant's conduct constituted a 'breaking' pursuant to the burglary statute."

I. The court will probably grant custody of Bonnie to Ms. Hutchinson.

Because Ms. Hutchinson maintains a stable home, only works part time, and is not required to travel, the court will probably grant her custody of Bonnie.

 **EXAMPLES**

A. BURGLARY

Now let's look at some examples of when you might choose which organizational plan. Consider once again the burglary statute and the case of Gerald Shaffer. Mr. Shaffer was arrested and charged with committing an assault and battery upon his estranged wife. The prosecutor is considering charging Shaffer with burglary as well. She has asked you to tell her whether the facts as she understands them arguably establish probable cause to believe that Shaffer committed burglary.[16] Here are the facts the police have given her:

On February 1, Mr. and Mrs. Shaffer paid the February rent on the house where they both lived, using funds from their joint checking account. The account contained the proceeds of Mrs. Shaffer's salary as a grocery clerk and Mr. Shaffer's salary as a construction worker. On February 10, the couple separated. Mr. Shaffer moved into an apartment across town. His departing words were "I'm gone. You'll never see me again." Mrs. Shaffer continued to live in the house.

At about 3:30 P.M. on February 20, Mr. Shaffer was served with a copy of his wife's divorce complaint. He spent the next couple of hours in his favorite bar contemplating his fate and getting angrier and angrier. After several drinks, he was not entirely sober, but the bartender says that Shaffer was completely coherent and in control of his motor abilities. Shaffer told the bartender that he was going to go "have a little chat" with his estranged wife. Though he cannot be entirely sure, the bartender is pretty certain that Mr. Shaffer left the bar at about 5:45 P.M. Sunset that day was at 6:00.

Mr. Shaffer says that he drove directly to the house where his estranged wife still lived. The distance between the bar and the house would take approximately 15 minutes to drive, assuming normal traffic. When Mr. Shaffer arrived, he knocked on the door, but no one answered. He tried his old key but discovered that the locks had been changed. He then began kicking the door until the lock gave 'way. He entered the living room where he encoun-

---

16. A prosecutor has an ethical duty to refrain from prosecuting criminal charges that the prosecutor knows are not supported by probable cause to believe that the acts constitute the charged offense. Model Rules of Professional Conduct Rule 3.8 (1994).

tered his estranged wife. He yelled that this was still his house and asked her why she had changed the locks. The situation quickly became violent, and Mr. Shaffer struck Mrs. Shaffer, knocking her down, causing her to lose consciousness, and causing other significant injuries. Mrs. Shaffer cannot recall what time it was when Mr. Shaffer arrived.

Mr. Shaffer says that he had been hoping that a reconciliation would be possible, but when he was served with the divorce complaint he realized that the marriage was over. He says that he went to the house to talk to his estranged wife about a property settlement. He says that this was still his only intent when he entered the living room. He says that he doesn't know what came over him during the argument about the locks. Suddenly he found himself hitting Mrs. Shaffer.

The attack constitutes a felony under the state criminal code. The question presented is whether these facts reasonably might constitute burglary as well. You have already written your working draft, using the organization set out on page 130. Now you must select an organization for your presentation to your reader.

First, identify any elements that you have concluded are not genuinely disputed and move them, along with their cursory explanation, to the introduction. In your first draft you probably concluded that the elements of "breaking," "entering," and "a dwelling" are not genuinely disputed here. The Shaffer facts establish these elements without much doubt.

Now you must decide the order for the remaining three elements: "of another," "nighttime," and "intent to commit a felony therein." Ask yourself whether there is a familiar order for these elements of burglary. You will probably conclude that there is and that it is the order stated here. This is probably the order you used in your first draft. This familiar order is your default choice—the order you will use unless you can identify a reason that one of the other choices will serve your reader better.

Next ask yourself whether there are any threshold issues among your subheadings. You will conclude that there are not. All of the subheadings are elements of the crime, and none is dependent on the outcome of any other. Thus, the threshold issues organization does not apply here.

Finally, ask yourself whether some of your remaining subheadings are likely to be dispositive. Since the burglary rule is made up of elements each of which must be established and since several are in dispute, the answer is "yes." Any one of the remaining elements could be dispositive. The facts do seem to raise some doubt about whether the house was the dwelling place "of another," about whether the breaking and entering occurred in the "nighttime," and about whether Mr. Shaffer entered with the "intent to commit a felony." Since several elements are in dispute and may be dispositive, you can be pretty sure that the dispositive issues organization will serve your reader best.

So you move the remaining elements into order by the odds that each will be dispositive. Let's assume that the law in your jurisdiction establishes that "nighttime" is any time between thirty minutes after sunset and thirty minutes before sunrise. On these facts, this issue will be close. Without more information, you cannot confirm whether Mr. Shaffer entered the house later than 6:30. The bartender's estimate could be mistaken by thirty minutes or more, although he says he is "pretty certain."

Although the facts do not look strong on the nighttime issue, the question is only whether the prosecutor could have a reasonable belief that the facts constitute the crime. This element is weak, but given the low standard, the lack of certainty of the bartender, the important role of the jury's assessment of witness credibility, and the chance to do further factual investigation before trial, you conclude that the facts on this element are probably sufficient at least to support the charge.

The "intent" element is even more unpredictable, but at least here there is evidence favorable to each side. Intent will be a subjective factual determination, and on these facts a jury could decide the question either way. However, the wide latitude of reasonable interpretations on the intent issue actually lends support to the reasonableness of a prosecutor's belief of probable cause. You decide that the prosecutor reasonably could conclude that Mr. Shaffer did intend to commit a felony when he entered the house, despite his story to the contrary. Therefore, this element would not prevent the prosecutor from charging Mr. Shaffer with burglary.

Finally, consider the "of another" element. Assume that you have found mandatory case law in your jurisdiction holding that a dwelling is "of another" if the defendant has voluntarily waived all rights to the dwelling, even if his funds had constituted part of the rent payment. You conclude that Mr. Shaffer's departing statement on February 10 probably would constitute a waiver of his claim that the house was still his dwelling. Thus, the facts on this element are strong enough to support a charge.

Since *all* elements must be established in order to constitute the crime, any element that is missing is dispositive. The more likely the element is to be missing, the more dispositive it is likely to be. Your analysis has convinced you that the "nighttime" element is probably the weakest element, and therefore it is most likely to be dispositive. You place it first. You conclude that the remaining two are roughly equal, but that the "of another" element might be more easily resolved by further investigation, so you place it second. This leaves the "intent" element, which prosecutors nearly always have to guess about anyway, so you place it last.

Now you have cleared away the elements not in dispute and ordered the remaining elements by the odds that they will dispose of the question. Assuming that the discussions under the Shaffer subsections are not too long to need further division, here is the final organization of the Discussion section of the memo:

I. The facts establish sufficient probable cause to support a charge of burglary against Shaffer.

The facts establish sufficient cause to believe that Shaffer committed burglary when he entered the building on West Third. The elements of burglary are: (1) a breaking, (2) entering, (3) the dwelling house, (4) of another, (5) in the nighttime, (6) with the intent to commit a felony therein. [citation]

The Shaffer facts establish the first three elements without dispute. Shaffer kicked down the door (a "breaking"); he admits entering the building; and the building is a home where the Shaffers resided for a number of years. The remaining three elements are not conclusively established, but the facts are strong enough to support the charge. Because the closest question arises on the "nighttime" element, the memo will discuss it first.

A.   The facts are sufficient to support a belief that the breaking and entering occurred in the nighttime.

B.   The facts are sufficient to support a belief that the house was the dwelling "of another."

C.   The facts are sufficient to support a belief that Shaffer intended to commit a felony when he entered the house.

Think back over the two-stage process we used to get to this final draft of the outline. The stages recognize the two functions of an organizational plan. The structure of the working draft functioned primarily as *your* tool, organizing your process of legal analysis and serving as your check for accuracy and completeness. The second draft's organization functions primarily to serve your *reader,* organizing the analysis in the order that best meets the reader's needs.

B.   EMPLOYMENT DISCRIMINATION

Dr. Aaron Lowenstein applied for a newly created position as a psychologist at Holy Word College, a college sponsored by a small evangelical denomination of the Christian religion. The position entails offering counseling to Holy Word students who are experiencing personal problems. Lowenstein is a highly qualified and experienced psychologist; he also happens to be a Conservative Jew. Holy Word College hired someone else for the job, and Lowenstein believes that Holy Word declined to hire him because of his religion. He has come to your law firm to ask if Holy Word's actions violated the law. He tells you about his application and job interview and all he knows about the other applicants, including the applicant who was hired.

When you research the law, you find Title VII of the Civil Rights Act of 1964.[17] The relevant part of the provision making discrimination illegal reads as follows:

> § 703. It shall be an unlawful employment practice for an employer . . . to . . . refuse to hire . . . any individual . . . because of such individual's . . . religion. . . .

17.   Holy Word's actions may raise issues under other statutes, but we will here focus only on Title VII of the Civil Rights Act of 1964, 42 U.S.C. § 2000e-17.

You determine that if the facts establish that Holy Word refused to hire Lowenstein because of his religion, then Holy Word appears to have violated this act.[18] At this point in your research, it appears that the answer to Lowenstein's question will depend on one issue: Did Holy Word refuse to hire him because of his religion?

However, as you continue reading the act you also find this provision:

> § 702. This title shall not apply to . . . a religious . . . educational institution . . . with respect to the employment of individuals of a particular religion to perform work connected with the carrying on by such . . . educational institution . . . of its activities.

Now the question becomes more complex, and you have several more issues. Can you identify them? *If* Holy Word is a "religious educational institution," *and if* the work Lowenstein would have been performing would have been "connected with the carrying on" of the institution's "activities," *then* Holy Word's refusal to hire Lowenstein is not prohibited by the act after all because the act does not apply.

So, here is the structure of your working draft:

I.   Did Holy Word's actions violate Title VII of the Civil Rights Act of 1964?

    A.   Does Title VII's prohibition of religious discrimination apply to Holy Word College?

        1.   Is Holy Word a "religious educational institution" pursuant to § 702 of the act?—AND—

        2.   Is the work Dr. Lowenstein would have been performing "connected with the carrying on" of the "activities" of the institution pursuant to § 702 of the act?

    B.   Do the facts seem to establish that Holy Word refused to hire Dr. Lowenstein because of his religion?

Now, assume that your research and analysis lead you to believe that Holy Word is undisputably a "religious educational institution" pursuant to § 702. You further conclude that both of the remaining issues (*A-2* and *B*) are going to be close questions—and therefore they are about equally dispositive. What organization will you select? Stop before you read on, and write out an outline of your organizational choice.

_____

18.   The act defines relevant terms such as "employer" and "religion." For simplicity's sake, we'll assume that you have read all definition sections and determined that these terms do apply to the parties to this dispute. We'll also assume that you have not found any other provisions relevant to your inquiry.

You should have come up with a threshold issues organization that looks something like this:

I. Did Holy Word's actions violate Title VII of the Civil Rights Act of 1964?

   UMBRELLA SECTION
   - Identifying and briefly setting out the coverage issue from § 702 and the discrimination issue from § 703.
   - Explaining that the issue of whether Holy Word is a "religious educational institution" is not genuinely in dispute.
   - Explaining that the memo first will discuss the issue of whether the work is "connected with" carrying on the institution's "activities" because if so, then § 703 does not apply.

   A. Is the work Dr. Lowenstein would have been performing "connected with the carrying on" of the "activities" of the institution pursuant to § 702 of the act?

   B. Do the facts seem to establish that Holy Word refused to hire Dr. Lowenstein because of his religion?

Threshold issues organization works well here because you have concluded that both of the issues in dispute are roughly equally dispositive. If one of them had been much more likely than the other to be dispositive, your reader might have preferred a dispositive issues organization.

C. "INTENT" AND ADMISSIBILITY OF EVIDENCE

Reread the Shaffer facts described in Example 1, pp. 165-166. Assume that you work for the firm defending Mr. Shaffer rather than the prosecutor's office. The prosecutor has offered a plea bargain and Mr. Shaffer's lawyer needs to advise him about whether to agree to the plea. As part of that process, she needs your best estimate of the odds that a jury would find that Mr. Shaffer intended to assault his wife when he entered the living room on February 20. Let's add one new fact: One of the other bar patrons present that fateful afternoon has told the police that Mr. Shaffer said as he left the bar, "I'm going to go show my wife what I think of her, and when I'm done, she's going to need a doctor."

Predicting what a jury might do is always a dicey task, but it is nonetheless fundamental to deciding whether to make a plea bargain. You quickly realize that the most important fact relating to whether a jury might find "intent" is Mr. Shaffer's alleged statement to the other bar patron. If the jurors hear and believe the bar patron's testimony, they probably will find that the intent element is met. If the jurors do not hear this statement, they might be persuaded that at the time of his entry, Mr. Shaffer had not yet formed the intent to commit a felony. Thus the question requires not only an analysis of the facts pertaining to the intent issue, but also an analysis of whether the bar patron's testimony will be admissible as evidence at trial.

Assume that you researched the applicable rules of evidence and found that the statement almost certainly would be admissible.

For your first draft organization, you probably used two subheadings, one for the evidentiary issue and one for the intent issue. You would have used the structure of the rule of evidence to organize the evidence subheading and the structure of the rule on intent to organize the intent subheading.[19] Because the first draft structure is primarily a tool to aid your own analysis and writing process, you probably used subheadings under the intent issue, so that you could separate your analysis of the intent issue according to whether the statement is admitted. Your working draft structure might have looked like this:[20]

I. Is a jury likely to conclude that the Shaffer facts establish the intent element of burglary?

    [Umbrella section setting out the rule on intent and explaining the need to address the evidentiary rule governing the statement's admissibility.]

    A. Is the alleged statement to the bar patron admissible?

    B. Are the facts likely to establish intent?
        1. Are the facts, including the statement to the bar patron, likely to establish intent?

        2. Are the facts, excluding the statement to the bar patron, likely to establish intent?

Now how will you order the subheadings (*A* and *B*) in your final draft structure? There is no familiar order here, because these are two unrelated rules of law. The rule of evidence is not a threshold issue since the decision does not change the direction of the next step of the analysis. The same rule of law will apply whether the statement is admissible or not.

What about dispositive issues? While the admissibility of the statement is important for an accurate prediction of the jury's findings on the intent ele-

---

19. *See* pp. 133-134. In the example on p. 134, the writer would have three rules of law because there were two different rules of law governing the transaction, depending on the rule of law governing the applicability of the U.C.C. Here there would be only two rules of law because the *rule* on intent will be the same whether or not the statement is admissible. What will change is the batch of facts to which the rule will be applied.

20. In a real case, the evidentiary issue would be a bit more complex than this structure reflects, but for the purposes of this example, we'll assume that this first draft structure adequately covers the issue.

ment, the answer on admissibility does not dispose of the question. The discussion must still include an analysis of both issues, so neither issue disposes of the other.

The remaining structure is the important issues structure. If your analysis had concluded that excluding the statement from evidence was a realistic possibility, the discussion of that possibility would be critical to the intent issue. In such a case, the evidentiary issue might well be more important, more central, to the analysis of the intent issue than any particular definition of "intent" that the rule of law might set out.

But your analysis has concluded that the statement will be admissible. Thus, you know that the most important part of the analysis will be the impact of the statement on the jury—in, other words, the discussion of the intent issue. If your reader understands the relative importance of the two issues, your reader will appreciate placement of the most important issue (the intent issue) first.

Thus, the important issues structure requires you to assess your reader's starting point. Your reader (Mr. Shaffer's lawyer) probably knows that the statement will be important and may be hoping that the statement will be inadmissible. This reader will have a fairly intense investment in the evidentiary issue. By placing the intent issue first you would be asking this reader to trust your naked assertion that the reader's fond hopes are in vain, with the explanation that the analysis that leads to this bad news is so clear that it is not important enough to place first. You would be asking this reader to give up those hopes without the opportunity to think through the analysis; to plunge immediately into the analysis of the impact of the very "fact" the reader had hoped to avoid. This asks the reader to travel a long way in a very short time, and on very little basis. If this is your assessment of your reader, then your reader is invested in a starting point that views the evidentiary issue as the most important. You had better order your discussion that way too.

On the other hand, your reader may not be focusing on the evidentiary issue at all. Perhaps your reader has not had the opportunity to give the particular facts much thought yet, or perhaps your reader is an experienced trial lawyer who knows the rules of evidence well enough to expect the evidentiary answer. This reader probably will be prepared to accept your explanation of the relative importance of the two issues and will be willing, even grateful, to postpone the evidentiary analysis in favor of the more central issue. In such a case, you probably should choose the important issues organization—placing the intent issue first.

Assume that you have decided that your reader already expects the evidentiary conclusion and will accept your judgment that the most important part of the analysis is the intent issue. You will still need to explain, in the umbrella section, the reasons for your conclusion that the intent issue is the most important issue, but you know that your reader will not resist you there.

In keeping with your organizational choice, reverse the order of A and B, so that the intent discussion comes first. If your discussion of the subparts of the evidentiary issue is not too long and complex, you can remove the subheadings from the final draft. If you are confident that the statement almost certainly will be admitted, you also can condense the discussion of how the intent issue plays out if the statement is excluded. In that case, you can remove the subheadings from the intent issue as well. Your final draft organization probably will look like this:

I. A jury is likely to conclude that the Shaffer facts establish the intent element of burglary.

   [Umbrella section setting out the rule on intent and explaining the choice to postpone the discussion of the evidentiary rule governing the statement's admissibility.]

   A. The facts are likely to establish intent.

   B. The alleged statement to the bartender will be admissible.

So now you have converted your working draft of the analysis to a discussion designed for a reader. When you become experienced at both legal analysis and the process of legal writing, the first stage—the working draft—may be so easy for you that it seems like second nature. If so you may collapse the processes of creating the working draft and of creating a reader-centered document into one stage. Even if you are new to legal thinking and writing, you may be able to collapse the two stages if your issues are few and simple. But most of us, in our first legal writing tasks, need to keep these two stages separate in order to be sure that each is serving its special function. Remember the adage: Two hands while learning, please.[21]

---

21. *See* pp. 189-190 for checklist for Discussion section.

Completing the Draft of the Office Memo

Now that a draft of the Discussion section is in place, it is time to add the remaining sections.[1]

I DRAFTING THE HEADING

Draft a Heading in the format of standard business interoffice communications:

    TO: [Name of requesting attorney]
    FROM: [Your name]
    DATE: [Date]
    RE: [Include client's name and the file number, if your firm uses a
              numbering system; the particular legal matter; and a phrase
              identifying the particular issue.]

1. Since a memo is an internal document, law firms are likely to have a preferred memo format. The firm's preferred format may use different words for the section titles, it may place the sections in an order different from that described here, or it may include other sections. If your reader (your teacher or law firm) has a particular format preference, use it. If not, you can use the standard memo format this text describes. Variations in format are much less important than the accuracy and thoroughness of the analysis.

175

The date is important to both you and your readers. Your readers need the date because the law is subject to change and because your readers may refer back to your memo months or even years later. The memo's date will tell them whether and for what period of time the analysis in your memo must be updated. You need the date because you want your work to be evaluated on the basis of the law to which you had access, not later developments you could not have known without a crystal ball.

The "RE" section should identify the client and the file number, both for your current reader and so that the memo can be returned in case it is later separated from the file. This section also should identify both the legal matter you are working on and the particular issue you have been asked to analyze. Identify the *legal matter* because your firm may be handling a number of matters for this particular client, and your reader will want to know at a glance which of those matters your memo concerns. Identify the *issue* because this legal matter may raise a number of issues that will be the subject of an office memo. Your reader will want to know at a glance which issue your memo concerns, and to be able to distinguish this memo from the others in the file.

Here is an example of a heading:

```
TO:      Ramon Caldez
FROM:    Marcia Willingham
DATE:    August 17, 1996
RE:      Sharon Watson (file #96-24795); covenant-not-to-compete
         against Carrolton; enforceability of the covenant.
```

 II   DRAFTING THE QUESTION PRESENTED[2]

The Question Presented states the question you have been asked to answer. It serves several functions: It helps your reader confirm that you have understood the question, it reminds a busy reader of the question he or she asked you to analyze, and it allows lawyers working on other cases in the future to decide whether the analysis in your memo will be relevant to those other cases.

A.   Content and Format

If you have been asked only to find out the state of the governing law on a particular question, the Question Presented simply states the legal question:

2. Some law firm formats title this section the "Issue."

Under what circumstances does Iowa law allow recovery on a claim for the wrongful death of a fetus?

However, if you have been asked to apply a rule to a set of facts and predict a result, drafting a readable Question Presented can be more of a challenge. Here are three format options.

1. One format option organizes the content of the Question Presented in two sections: a statement of the *legal* question and a concise statement of the major relevant fact(s).

Can . . . [state the legal question] . . . when . . . [state the major facts]?

This format does not state the rule of law as part of the Question. Here is an example:

Can Carrolton enforce the Watson covenant-not-to-compete when the covenant prohibits Watson from making sales contacts for three years and applies to the three counties closest to Carrolton's headquarters?	Legal issue Major facts

Common verbs for beginning a Question Presented in this format are: "Can . . . ?" "Did . . . ?" "Was . . . ?" "May . . . ?" and "Is . . . ?" Common transitions into the factual description are: "when . . ." and "where . . ." as the examples demonstrate.

2. An even simpler version of a Question Presented is the format beginning with "whether" and constituting a clause rather than a complete sentence. This format still begins with the legal question and ends with the significant facts:

Whether Carrolton can enforce the Watson covenant-not-to-compete when the covenant prohibits Watson from making sales contacts for three years and applies to the three counties closest to Carrolton's headquarters.	Legal issue Major facts

When the Question Presented uses the "whether" format, the clause can be followed by a period and treated as a complete sentence although it is not.

3. A third format option is the "under/does/when" format. This format

usually results in the longest and most complex Question Presented, though it allows for a shorter Brief Answer. The Question Presented is longer and the Brief Answer shorter because this format puts the statement of the law in the Question rather than in the Answer. Here is an example:

Under the Georgia common law rule that allows covenants-not-to-compete only when the area restrained, the activities restrained, and the duration of the restraint are reasonable, can a covenant-not-to-compete be enforced when the covenant prohibits the covenantor from (1) making sales contacts, (2) for three years, and (3) applies to the three counties closest to the headquarters of the covenant's beneficiary?	**The rule** **Legal issue** **Major facts**

Notice that the middle verb can vary, using the same common verbs identified above: "can," "did," "was," "may," or "is."

Use the format your teacher or the requesting attorney prefers. If you can identify no preference, consider using the first format, since it results in a simpler, more understandable sentence and since locating the applicable rule of law is usually part of the question you are asked to answer.

B.   GENERIC VERSUS SPECIFIC REFERENCES

No matter which format you choose, you will need to decide whether to use a general or a specific Question Presented. For example, the first two examples (p. 177) refer specifically to Watson and Carrolton, while the third example does not. The third example is phrased as a generic legal question without reference to the parties involved in the situation that has raised the issue. Here is an example of a generic Question Presented drafted in the first format described above:

Can a covenant-not-to-compete be enforced where the covenant prohibits the covenantor from making sales contacts for three years and applies to the three counties closest to the headquarters of the covenant's beneficiary?	**Legal issue** **Major facts**

You will find proponents of both the generic and the specific Question Presented. The specific Question Presented directly states the question the requesting attorney wants to know. Ramon Caldez is not asking an academic legal question; rather, he wants to know the fate of a particular client—Sharon Watson. While this memo may someday be placed in the firm's memo file and be examined by a future reader for purposes of another case, the primary function of this memo is to answer a question about the *present* client.

The abstract version of the Question Presented refers to the parties involved by characterizing them rather than by naming them. When Ramon Caldez reads this characterization, he will probably have to stop as he reads it to substitute in his mind the names of the parties in place of the characterizations. He also will have to ask himself whether the characterizations accurately refer to the parties in this particular case because if they do not, then the answer set out in the memo may not apply to these parties. But the question of whether the law set out in the memo applies to these parties is part of what Caldez wants *you* to analyze *for* him.

Finally, as a practical matter, a Question Presented that uses the parties' names rather than characterizations of the parties generally uses fewer words and is more easily readable. Notice how this is true for the examples above. Since some Questions Presented must include a great deal of information, finding ways to reduce the number of words and to simplify the sentence structure can be helpful.

On the other hand, a busy attorney with a heavy caseload may not remember the names of the parties as easily as the characterizations (the landlord, the contractor, the lender). If you suspect that your reader is not familiar enough with the case to remember the names, either use generic references or use names with characterizations in parenthesis, like this:

> Can Carrolton (the beneficiary) enforce the Watson covenant-not-to-compete when the covenant prohibits Watson from making sales contacts for three years and applies to the three counties closest to Carrolton's headquarters?

Again, use the phrasing you think your teacher or requesting attorney will prefer. As with most other third-stage writing decisions, your assessment of your reader's starting point should be the most important factor.

C. DEGREE OF DETAIL

Try to limit the Question Presented to one readable sentence. Packing both the legal issue and the major facts into one readable sentence can be quite a challenge. If your draft of the Question Presented is unwieldy, first use the editing techniques described in Chapter 15. If those techniques do not allow you to achieve a readable sentence, consider shortening the facts you include. If all else fails, use two sentences; two sentences that are easy to read are better than one sentence that requires rereading.

D.   ROLE

Finally, remind yourself of your role. As you worked through the analysis of the question, you convinced yourself of a particular conclusion. Having done so, you'll have a tendency to state the Question Presented (especially the facts) as an advocate for the conclusion you reached rather than as an objective legal analyst. Resist that tendency and stick to your objective role.

EXERCISE 1

For each of the following Questions Presented, use a different format. Use specific references for one and generic references for the other.

   a.   Draft a Question Presented for an office memo addressing Ms. Ryan's question on pages 101-102.

   b.   Draft a Question Presented for an office memo addressing Ms. Pyle's question in the hypothetical on page 89 of Chapter 7 and continuing with the working draft of the analysis on pages 97-99 and 108-110.

III ▷ DRAFTING THE BRIEF ANSWER

A.   CONTENT AND FORMAT

The Brief Answer gives your busy reader the answer (the conclusion) quickly and right up front. Since Questions Presented come in several formats, their Brief Answers do as well. A Brief Answer responding to a Question that does not articulate the rule of law (those described in formats 1 and 2 on p. 177) should state the answer forthrightly ("yes," "probably yes," "no," or "probably not"). The remainder of the Answer should set out, either directly or indirectly, the rule of law governing the issue and a summary of the reasoning leading to the answer. We'll assume that you have concluded that Carrolton will be able to enforce the Watson covenant. Your Brief Answer might be:

> Probably yes   **[forthright statement of the answer].**   A covenant-not-to-compete is enforceable under Georgia law if the activity restrained, the geographic area of the restraint, and the duration of the restraint are all reasonable   **[statement of the governing rule of law].**   Several Georgia courts

> have held that covenants restraining sales contacts are nearly always reasonable as to the activity restrained. Georgia courts have also held covenants reasonable when the duration of the restraint was up to three years and when the area restrained included up to ten counties **[summary of reasoning]**.

Brief Answers that respond to Questions in the third format on pages 177-178 (Questions that have already stated the law) can be shorter. When you are using this format, state the answer in the first few words ("yes," "probably yes," "no," or "probably not"). Then state, in several complete sentences, the reasons for your answer, like so:

> Probably yes   **[forthright statement of the answer]**.   Several Georgia courts have held that covenants restraining sales contacts are nearly always reasonable as to the activity restrained. Georgia courts have also held covenants reasonable when the duration of the restraint was up to three years and when the area restrained included up to ten counties **[summary of reasoning]**.

B.   GENERIC VERSUS SPECIFIC REFERENCES

Use references that match those in the Question Presented. If you used the parties' names in the Question, use them in the Brief Answer. If you used characterizations in the Question Presented, use those characterizations in the Brief Answer as well.

C.   DEGREE OF DETAIL

An average length for a Brief Answer is one moderate paragraph (about one-third to one-half of a double-spaced page). Remember that the function of the Brief Answer begins to be compromised when the Answer gets much longer than that. Occasionally you will be dealing with a rule that is so complex that even a Brief Answer will take more space, but usually not. Try to limit this section to five sentences or less, like the example above.

D.   DEGREE OF CERTAINTY

For many memo assignments, the hardest decision you must make is the degree of certainty of your answer. Perhaps the answer seems clear and certain.

Yet how can you be sure that you are not missing other possible ways of construing law or facts or whether you have simply received a straightforward, easy assignment? Perhaps you think the answer could go either way, and you cannot decide which is more likely; yet you know that the requesting attorney wants an answer, not a coin toss.

There is no easy solution to this discomfort. You are just beginning the lifelong project of developing the legal judgment to gauge the certainty of a predicted result. As the years of your legal practice pass, you will get better and better at making these judgments.[3] For the time being, you must research and analyze thoroughly and then make the best judgment you can.

When you are struggling with the question of the degree of certainty of your answer, keep in mind the possible spectrum:

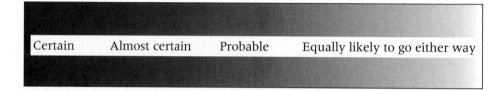

Certain   Almost certain   Probable   Equally likely to go either way

Regard with suspicion an answer on either end of the spectrum. Some issues actually have certain answers, but before you conclude that yours is one of them, be sure you have done a complete and accurate legal and factual analysis. Some issues actually will be a coin toss, but before you conclude that yours is one of them, ask yourself whether you are simply resisting the discomfort of having to make a prediction in an uncertain area.

Finally, once you decide where your answer fits on the spectrum, communicate that decision clearly in the Brief Answer. Search your draft of the Brief Answer for the words that will tell your reader your degree of certainty, and be sure that you have not sent mixed signals within the Brief Answer itself or between the Brief Answer and the Discussion section.

So, here is how the office memo looks so far:

TO: Ramon Caldez
FROM: Marcia Willingham
DATE: August 17, 1996
RE: Sharon Watson (file #96-24795); covenant-not-to-compete
         against Carrolton; enforceability of the covenant.

QUESTION PRESENTED

Can Carrolton enforce the Watson covenant-not-to-compete where the covenant prohibits Watson from making sales contacts for three

---

3. In practice (and in a law school class, if your teacher permits it), you often can discuss the law and the facts with other more experienced lawyers.

years and applies to the three counties closest to Carrolton's headquarters?

BRIEF ANSWER

Probably yes. Carrolton should be able to enforce the Watson covenant. A covenant-not-to-compete is enforceable under Georgia law if the activity restrained, the geographic area of the restraint, and the duration of the restraint are all reasonable. Several Georgia courts have held that covenants restraining sales contacts are nearly always reasonable as to the activity restrained. Georgia courts have also held covenants reasonable when the duration of the restraint was up to three years and when the area restrained included up to ten counties.

EXERCISE 2

For each of the Questions Presented you drafted for Exercise 1 (p. 180), draft a corresponding Brief Answer.

IV ⬦ DRAFTING THE FACT STATEMENT[4]

In drafting the fact section your primary tasks are (1) selecting which facts to include, (2) organizing those facts in an effective way, and (3) remembering your predictive role.

A. FACT SELECTION

Often you will know many facts about a particular client's situation. However, your busy law-trained reader will want to know only two kinds of facts: (1) facts relevant to the question presented and (2) background facts necessary to provide context for these legally significant facts. Contextual facts will come

---

4.   You may have written a draft of the fact statement early in the process of writing your working draft, as suggested on p. 83. Writing a working draft of the fact statement along with the working draft of the analysis can help you understand both the law and the facts better and earlier. If you have already written a working draft of the fact statement, simply revise it with the following principles in mind.

to you naturally as you write, so we'll focus on identifying the legally significant facts.

Relevant facts are those that help you decide how the rule of law will apply to your client's situation. For instance, for the rule we devised from the *Fox* case in Chapter 10, the relevant facts are those that tell you about the kind of activity restrained, the geographic scope, and the duration of the restraint.

Writing your working draft already has given you a good sense of the facts that will be relevant to the issues. Especially as you wrote the "rule application" part of your analysis, you considered how the legal rule would apply to your client's situation. Review your Discussion section to make a list of the facts that will be relevant. Consider each subissue separately so that your thinking will be more precise and focused. While your list certainly should include all facts you discussed in your analysis, do not limit your list to those facts. Let the process of reexamining each part of your legal discussion be an occasion for double-checking your fact application. You may be surprised at how often you will see a fact in a significant new way when you are working on the fact statement.

Also, include any facts that may have a powerful emotional impact on the decision-maker, even if those facts are not technically relevant to the legal issues. Remember that judges and other decision-makers are human.[5] Few of us can separate completely our objective legal analysis from our reaction to compelling parts of a story. While legally irrelevant facts theoretically should not affect a result, judges may be more swayed by these inevitable responses than theory contemplates.

For instance, in a divorce case, the judge deciding property issues might be influenced by knowing that one spouse has seriously battered the other spouse, even if the applicable law does not make fault relevant to property division. If your case includes an emotionally powerful fact, do not ignore it, especially if the legal rule you are working with gives the decision-maker some discretion.

Finally, include facts only. Save the coverage of legal authorities and arguments until the Discussion section. For cases already in litigation, include the current procedural posture of the case and, if relevant, a summary of the procedural history.

As you compile your list of *known* relevant facts, ask yourself what *other* facts you would like to know—what unknown facts might affect your prediction. Once again this will serve both your reader's purposes and your own. First, even if the requesting attorney has not asked you to identify important unknown facts, she almost certainly will appreciate ideas about factual investigation. Second, you will find that legal analysis and fact investigation are inextricably intertwined. Often the process of identifying important unknown facts will yield new insights about rule application, rule explanation, or both. Fact identification is yet another opportunity to deepen your analysis of the question presented.

Judge whether and how to pass on the list of unknown facts by your assessment of the requesting attorney's preference. One fairly easy way would be to attach the list at the end of the memo as a helpful and practical bonus for your reader, but one that does not interrupt the flow of the material your

---

5.   In Chapter 16 we'll consider judges in more detail.

reader is expecting. If an unknown fact is particularly important, you might even mention it in the Fact Statement. Your goal is to provide your reader with all appropriate information, placed at the most helpful spot.

B. ORGANIZATION

Once you have identified the facts, think about how you want to organize them. Normally your first paragraph should identify your client and briefly describe the client's problem or goal. This paragraph will give your reader a context for the facts that follow. The first or the last paragraph should describe the current status of the situation, including the procedural posture of any litigation. For the material between, the most common format choices are organizing chronologically, topically, or using a combination of the two.

1. Chronological. If the legal analysis has not identified complex and distinct factual topics, if the *order* of events is particularly important, or if there are a number of factual developments in the story, a simple chronology may be best. For instance, turn back to the description of the Ryan/Kaplan facts on pages 101-102. Notice how those facts are organized. Recall that the legal issue there is whether a reasonable person would have thought that Kaplan was serious. Now review the factual description of the Shaffer facts on pages 165-166. Each story has a number of factual developments, and the chronology is particularly important. In each of those situations, a chronological organiza- tion works well.

2. Topical. When the facts are complex and cover a number of topics, or when they include more description than a series of discrete events, a topical organization may work best. For example, review the recitation of the Tobin/Carletta facts on page 35. There, chronology is not important. The facts simply describe topics: Carletta's statement, the circumstances surrounding it, the possible consequences of it, and Tobin's reaction to it. If we had more detailed facts about each of those topics, perhaps each topic might become one or more paragraphs. This would be an example of a topical organization.

3. Combination of chronological and topical. If, as is common, the facts have characteristics of both patterns, using a combination may be the best approach. Turn back to the Carillo facts on pages 142-143. There, some of the facts have chronological importance, but many are descriptive. Notice how they fall roughly into four topics: (1) an introduction of the Carillos and a description of their neighborhood; (2) facts surrounding the purchase of the trampoline, its placement in their yard, and the rules for its use; (3) the events on the day of the accident; (4) the present status of the matter. The overall organization of that fact statement is topical, devoting a paragraph to each factual topic. However, the topics appear chronologically, and the facts within topic 3 are presented in a chronology.

Identifying format choices will be helpful as you organize your first few fact statements. You may even create other options when the situation calls for other results. Many writers find it best to write a preliminary draft, letting the story unfold according to the writer's intuition. Then they can identify the format that emerged, evaluate where it works and where it doesn't, and edit it in a second draft. Your goal is to use the format that will best meet your reader's needs for clarity and logical presentation.

C.   REMEMBERING YOUR ROLE

As you begin to write the Fact Statement, be particularly attentive to your role. Remember that both your legal analysis and your factual description must be as objective as possible. Watch for the tendency to slip into trying to "prove" something by the way you tell the story. Here are three techniques that will help you resist this role confusion:

1. Check to be sure that you use neutral language and objective characterizations wherever possible. Rather than writing, "the defendant was speeding through the school zone," write instead "the defendant was traveling 50 MPH through the school zone." Rather than writing, "Wade brutally beat the victim," write instead, "Wade struck Baker on the head, resulting in a cut over the left eye."
2. Check to be certain that you have included the unfavorable facts as well as the favorable facts and the facts that run counter to your prediction as well as those that support it. You may have to remind yourself to identify and include these unfavorable or conflicting facts, but the discipline will help you stay in role.
3. Where appropriate, identify one or two important unknown facts. Pointing out a potentially important fact that is currently unknown will help counteract the unconscious tendency to slip into describing the facts with more certainty and more advocacy than a balanced, objective perspective would support.

 **EXERCISE 3**

Critique the following Fact Statement, using the criteria described above and any others you choose. Write an improved version.

Fact Statement (first version)

On March 1, 1996, our client Karen Berry, a lawyer, loaned $50,000 to her client, Morgan Cox. Cox was to use the money to purchase a lot in order to construct a warehouse for his wholesale distribution company, ABC Distributing. The loan was to be repaid over ten years. As security for the loan, Berry took a mortgage on the lot and assumed a 51% partnership status in ABC.

The partnership documents give Berry both control over ABC and joint ownership with Cox of all company assets.

ABC had been operating out of leased space, but the lease would soon expire, and the owner had served notice that the lease would not be renewed. ABC had only four months to vacate the leased premises. Berry had learned of this fact during the course of her representation of Cox and ABC in the negotiations to renew the lease. Upon learning that the owner had decided not to renew the lease, Berry suggested to Cox that he buy a particular lot in the heart of the industrial district and build a warehouse on the lot. Cox responded that he did not think he could come up with a downpayment. Berry offered to loan him the $50,000 at 8% per anum. She said that as security she would take a mortgage on the lot, and she would assume 51% partnership status in ABC.

The law requires that Berry refrain from misrepresenting or concealing any material fact. Berry knew that the lot was close to one of the routes proposed for a planned interstate connector. She knew that the value of the lot would increase if that route was chosen for the highway. Berry says that she told Cox about this possibility. Whether Cox will confirm Berry on this point is presently unknown.

On the matter of the $50,000 loan, Berry says that she explained all aspects of the transaction to Cox. However, she says that Cox already understood the proposed transaction clearly since he has over twenty years of business experience. Cox has a Masters degree in Business Administration, and he was at one time a licensed real estate broker. Clearly, with this kind of background, Cox should have been aware of the nature and effect of the proposed transaction. Being sure that the client is aware of the nature and effect of the proposed transaction is one of the key elements required by *Goldman v. Kane*.

Shortly after completing the transaction Berry discovered that Cox had a gambling problem and was draining ABC of its cash. The business was in serious trouble. Fortunately for Berry, she was able to dissolve the partnership agreement before she incurred significant liabilities. Since Cox was in default on the loan payments, Berry foreclosed on the lot. However, true to her promise, she did not claim interest in any other company asset.

Within a month after Berry took title to the lot, the proposed connector route nearest the lot was selected for the new highway. Two months later Berry sold the lot for $80,000. Cox has filed a disciplinary grievance against Berry, alleging that Berry violated the ethical rule governing a lawyer's business transactions with a client.

DRAFTING THE CONCLUSION

Now you have completed the sections of the memo that precede the Discussion section. Your document first identifies the question you have been asked to analyze (Question Presented), then states the answer (Brief Answer), then sets out the facts (Fact Statement), and then provides a complete explanation of the analysis leading to the answer (Discussion).

If your Discussion is relatively short and clear *and* if your teacher or requesting attorney does not have a preference, you need not add a separate Conclusion section. However, if your analysis has been complex or multifaceted, a Conclusion section can tie together and summarize the Discussion. It also can increase your reader's options for deciding how much attention to invest in understanding the details of your analysis. A Conclusion should go into more detail than the Brief Answer but not as much as the Discussion. This allows a law-trained reader to read your Brief Answer first, then proceed to your Conclusion for somewhat more depth, and finally read your Discussion for even more depth. After reading each section, your reader can decide how far and how deeply to read on.

Therefore, don't choose to add a Conclusion if you will only be repeating the Brief Answer. Add a Conclusion only if your reader expects it or if a middle level of detail summarizing the law and the facts would be helpful to your reader.

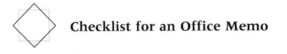 **Checklist for an Office Memo**

HEADING

1. Have you included the name of the requesting attorney, your name, the date, the client's name; the file number; and a phrase identifying the particular legal matter and issue?

QUESTION PRESENTED

2. Have you made an appropriate choice of format?
3. If you chose the "legal issue/major facts" format, did you state the legal question in the first half of the sentence and the significant facts in the second half?
4. If you chose the "whether" format, did you state the legal question first and the significant facts second, all in a clause and ending with a period?
5. If you chose the "under/does/when" format, did you state the rule, then the legal question, and then the significant facts?
6. Have you made an appropriate choice of generic or specific references?
7. Have you edited to achieve one readable sentence?
8. Have you maintained an objective perspective?

BRIEF ANSWER

9. Have you stated the answer in the first several words?
10. Have you included a statement of the rule if the Question Presented did not already state it?

11. Have you stated a summary of the reasoning leading to the answer?
12. Have you chosen either generic or specific references to match the Question Presented?
13. Have you kept the Brief Answer to a maximum of one-third to one-half a double-spaced page?
14. Have you taken a position, even if you are not sure?
15. Have you avoided sending your reader mixed signals about how sure you are of your answer?

FACT STATEMENT

FACT SELECTION

16. Have you included all legally significant facts?
17. Have you included sufficient facts to put the legally significant facts in context?
18. Have you included any major emotional facts?
19. Have you avoided including discussion of legal authority?
20. Have you avoided "arguing" the facts or drawing legal conclusions?
21. Have you pointed out any important unknown information?

ORGANIZATION

22. Have you identified the client and the client's situation at the beginning of the Fact Statement?
23. Have you selected an appropriate organization (chronological, topical, combination) for the facts?
24. Does your last paragraph give the facts closure and lead into the Discussion section by explaining the procedural posture of the legal issue or by some other device?

ROLE

25. Have you maintained neutral language and objective characterizations?
26. Have you included both favorable and unfavorable facts?

DISCUSSION

UMBRELLA SECTION

27. Have you summarized the rule, setting out all subparts and clarifying how they relate to each other?
28. Have you included any important information about how the rule functions generally, such as a burden of proof or a relevant presumption?
29. Have you identified any genuinely undisputed issues and provided a cursory explanation for why they are not in dispute?

30. Have you stated the order in which the remaining issues will be discussed, explaining the reason for this organizational choice?
31. If necessary to prevent confusion, have you identified any related legal issues not covered by the memo?

DISCUSSION OF ISSUES

32. Have you selected an appropriate organization for the issues?
33. Have you checked section lengths, combining or dividing subsections where appropriate?
34. Have you revised your headings into complete thesis sentences?
35. Have you stated your conclusion on each issue at the beginning of the discussion of that issue?

CONCLUSION

36. Have you added a Conclusion section only if the Discussion has been long and complex?
37. Is your Conclusion more detailed than the Brief Answer but significantly less detailed than the Discussion?

stage
four

REVISING TO ACHIEVE A FINAL DRAFT

Citations and Quotations

Now that you have a completed draft of the document, the next step is editing quotations and citation form.

I CITATION IN LEGAL WRITING

In legal writing, as in other writing, you must cite to your sources for both words and ideas. Citation to authority has twin purposes: (1) to provide your reader with the authority that supports your assertions about the law, and (2) to attribute the words and ideas of another author to that author.

Providing your reader with authority to support your assertions about the law is essential to legal analysis and persuasive argument. Your citations should "prove" that the law is what you say it is and that it means what you say it means.

A citation is also your attribution to another author, recognizing that the ideas (and the words, if you are quoting) came from that author. Recall from the discussion of plagiarism on pages 8-9 the importance of careful attribution. Since a reader will attribute uncited material to you, a citation is your way of disclaiming credit for the words and ideas you did not create for yourself. Therefore, you should cite when you quote and when you paraphrase (that is, when you rephrase the authority's words but make the same point the authority made).

USE CITATIONS

1. When you state the facts from an opinion.
2. When you state the opinion's holding.
3. When you state the opinion's reasoning.

EXERCISE 1.   Recognizing Ideas That Need Citations

Read the following passage[1] and identify the statements for which a citation is either necessary or desirable. Be prepared to say why.

The lawyer has a fiduciary relationship with his or her client. The fiduciary aspect of the relationship is said to arise after the formation of the attorney-client relationship, and it applies to a fee agreement reached after the attorney-client relationship has been entered.

There are at least three reasons for imposing fiduciary obligations on a lawyer. Once the relationship is established, the client will likely have begun to depend on the attorney's integrity, fairness, and judgment. Second, the attorney may have acquired information about the client that gives the attorney an unfair advantage in negotiations between them. Finally, the client will generally not be in a position where he or she is free to change attorneys, but will rather be economically or personally dependent on the attorney's continued representation.

Several cases illustrate the contours of the attorney's fiduciary duty. In *Benson v. State Bar*, the attorney borrowed money from a current client. He "was heavily in debt, and insolvent, at the time he approached [the client] for these loans." In return for the loans, he gave the client unsecured promissory notes. In disbarring the lawyer, the court described the client's trust in the lawyer's judgment and wrote:

> The gravamen of the charge is abuse of that trust, and regardless of petitioner's contention that he never specifically recommended the unsecured loans to [the client], it is undisputed that in soliciting them he failed to reveal the extent of his preexisting indebtedness and financial distress.

In *People v. Smith*, James Smith, an attorney, was under investigation for drug use. He offered to cooperate with Colorado police as an undercover informant. He secretly recorded a telephone conversation with a former client in which he asked the former client to sell him cocaine. He then met with the former client wearing a body microphone. The recorded conversations

---

1.   Modified from Stephen Gillers, Regulation of Lawyers: Problems of Law and Ethics 61-62 (4th ed. 1995).

were ultimately used to convict the former client of three felony charges. The Colorado Supreme Court held that although Smith

> no longer represented the [former client], the conduct in all probability would not have occurred had [Smith] not relied upon the trust and confidence placed in him by the [former client] as a result of the recently completed attorney-client relationship between the two. The undisclosed use of a recording device necessarily involves elements of deception and trickery which do not comport with the high standards of candor and fairness to which all attorneys are bound.

For these and other offenses, Smith was suspended from the practice of law.

Now that you have decided *when* to cite to authority, turn your attention to *how* and *where* to cite.

 # II CITATION FORM

A citation is your representation to your reader that the cited material stands for the proposition for which you cited it. It also allows a reader to find the source, and provides the reader with some basic information for gauging the precedential weight the authority carries. Several commercially published citation authorities exist, and some courts have adopted their own citation rules. However, by far the most widely used authority for citation form is *The Bluebook: A Uniform System of Citation* (15th ed. 1991), better known as "the Bluebook."[2]

Learning to use the Bluebook (or whatever other citation authority your jurisdiction or teacher requires) is unavoidable. As much as you might like to, you cannot simply copy the citations you find in the authorities your research reveals. Many citations in opinions, annotations, and secondary sources do not conform to current citation requirements. So gather your courage and start using the Bluebook. Ultimately, no supplemental source, including this chapter, can replace your own mastery of it.

A. USING THE BLUEBOOK

The Bluebook will intimidate you if you let it. The best way to approach the Bluebook is to cut it down to size mentally by identifying the primary parts

---

2. The future may bring significant changes in citation form. Increased use of electronic techniques for finding law has led to pressure to change citation practice. The next few years will reveal much about the future of citation form.

you'll use. Notice the larger sections of the Bluebook as they are set out on the outside back cover:

1.   Sections of Bluebook

1. Introduction. The Bluebook begins with a seven-page Introduction expressly designed for novices. The Introduction describes the parts of the Bluebook, gives an overview of basic citation principles, and provides a number of examples. After you finish your preliminary tour of the Bluebook, read these seven pages.
2. Practitioners' Notes. This section is necessary because the rest of the Bluebook focuses on citation form appropriate for law review publishing. The Practitioners' Notes explain how to adapt the rules in the rest of the Bluebook to practitioner-writing—the kind you will be doing in your legal writing class and in practice. These notes also cover some citation situations that arise primarily in law practice. Most of what you will need to know from this section is found in notes P.1 through P.4.
3. Rules. The rules themselves come next, divided into chapters. The first chapter covers general rules and the remaining chapters are devoted to the particular kinds of sources to be cited (e.g., cases, statutes, periodicals). You will use the first four chapters most often.
4. Tables. After the rules comes a section of tables. These are simply reference sources for the standard abbreviations for courts, case names, publications, and other commonly used terms. You certainly need not learn these tables; simply use them for reference when you need to look up an abbreviation.

The parts of the Bluebook you will use most often are the first four Practitioners' Notes, the first four chapters of rules, and a couple of the reference tables. This is already starting to seem more manageable, isn't it?

2.   How to Locate the Rules You Need

Now for ways to find the rules you need in the Bluebook. Here are the best strategies for locating particular rules:

WAYS TO LOCATE THE BLUEBOOK RULES YOU NEED

1. Use the Bluebook's index, which is quite good.
2. Use the Table of Contents.
3. When reading a particular rule, look at the listed cross-references.
4. Use the Quick Reference for Court Documents and Legal Memoranda set out on the *back* inside cover. (The one on the front inside cover is for law review citations.)

3. Understanding Bluebook Terms

Three Bluebook concepts are especially puzzling to many new legal writers: typeface requirements, the distinctions between "citing in text" and "citing in a footnote," and the differences between a "citation sentence" and a "citation clause." Knowing what the Bluebook means by these concepts should make deciphering the mysteries of the Bluebook a little easier.

1. Typeface requirements. The Bluebook's rules (the white pages following the blue Practitioners' Notes) are designed primarily for law review writing rather than for practitioner-writing. Law review writing uses, on different occasions, large and small capitals, regular typeface, and italics. The examples and explanations in the rules section employ those distinctions among typefaces.

Practitioner-writing is simpler, using only regular type (such as courier) and *either* italics or underscoring. Practitioners' Note 1 sets out what to underscore or italicize. Simply type everything else in regular typeface, and don't worry about the more complicated distinctions in the rules section of the Bluebook.

2. Citing in text versus citing in a footnote. Law review articles are notorious for footnotes, so it is no wonder that the rules section of the Bluebook provides special requirements for citations in law review footnotes. However, footnotes should be the exception rather than the rule for practitioner-writing. When practitioners *do* use a footnote, they often simply use the same citation principles they have been using in the text. If your teacher or law firm allows this approach, don't concern yourself with the distinctions between text and footnotes in the Bluebook's rules section.

3. Citation sentences versus citation clauses. The Bluebook sometimes refers to "citation sentences" and "citation clauses." These strange-sounding phrases simply refer to the two places to put a citation—inside or outside a sentence of text. You can put a citation inside a sentence of text, like so:

> The Supreme Court has observed that employers and unions must have significant freedom in the creation of seniority systems, *California Brewers Ass'n v. Bryant,* 444 U.S. 598, 608 (1980), but this freedom is not unlimited, *see, e.g., Nashville Gas Co. v. Satty,* 434 U.S. 135 (1977).

Each of these citations is called a "citation *clause*" because the citation is *part* of a sentence of text and not a free-standing unit unto itself.

The cite to *California Brewers Ass'n* is placed immediately after the part of the sentence that it supports. The writer has not placed it at the end of the sentence because the writer is citing it as support only for the proposition stated in the first part of the sentence. The cite to *Nashville Gas Co.* is placed immediately after the part of the sentence it supports, but the writer has not

placed it outside the period because it is not cited as support for the entire sentence, but only for the proposition stated in the last half of the sentence.[3]
    A citation also can be placed outside the sentence of text, like so:

> The Supreme Court has observed that employers and unions must have significant freedom in the creation of seniority systems. *California Brewers Ass'n v. Bryant*, 444 U.S. 598, 608 (1980).

This citation is called a "citation *sentence*" because the citation is *not* a part of a sentence of text. The citation is placed outside the period because the writer is citing the case as support for all of the material in the sentence of text.[4] Strange as it may sound, the Bluebook treats a citation outside a sentence as a "sentence" unto itself.

B. INTRODUCTION TO CITATION FORM

While the applicable rules are more detailed, an overview of the basic components of a legal citation will help you put the more detailed rules into a context. Here are the basic components of a citation to a case, a statute, a book, and a law review article:

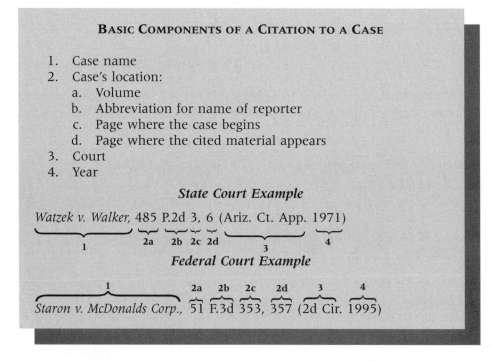

BASIC COMPONENTS OF A CITATION TO A CASE

1. Case name
2. Case's location:
    a. Volume
    b. Abbreviation for name of reporter
    c. Page where the case begins
    d. Page where the cited material appears
3. Court
4. Year

State Court Example

Watzek v. Walker, 485 P.2d 3, 6 (Ariz. Ct. App. 1971)

Federal Court Example

Staron v. McDonalds Corp., 51 F.3d 353, 357 (2d Cir. 1995)

---

3. See pp. 200-201.
4. See pp. 200-201.

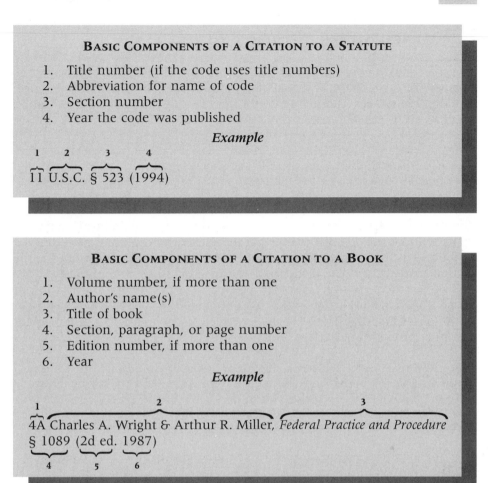

BASIC COMPONENTS OF A CITATION TO A STATUTE

1. Title number (if the code uses title numbers)
2. Abbreviation for name of code
3. Section number
4. Year the code was published

Example

1   2   3   4
11 U.S.C. § 523 (1994)

BASIC COMPONENTS OF A CITATION TO A BOOK

1. Volume number, if more than one
2. Author's name(s)
3. Title of book
4. Section, paragraph, or page number
5. Edition number, if more than one
6. Year

Example

1   2   3
4A Charles A. Wright & Arthur R. Miller, *Federal Practice and Procedure*
§ 1089 (2d ed. 1987)
 4   5   6

BASIC COMPONENTS OF A CITATION TO A LAW REVIEW ARTICLE

1. Author's name
2. Title of article
3. Location of article:
   a. Volume number
   b. Abbreviation for name of law review
   c. Page where article begins
   d. Page where cited material appears
4. Year

Example

1   2
Murray M. Schwartz, *The Exercise of Supervisory Power By the Third
Circuit Court of Appeals,* 27 Vill. L. Rev. 506, 508 (1982)
        2   3a   3b   3c   3d   4

C. Matching the Citation to the Text

A writer tells the reader which proposition the citation establishes by the *placement* of the citation. If the citation appears outside the textual sentence, standing alone as a citation sentence, the reader knows that the citation supports all of the material in the preceding sentence, like so:

> To prove a claim for sexual harassment without showing an adverse employment action, a plaintiff must show that the harassment created a "hostile or abusive work environment" and that the plaintiff indicated that the harassment was unwelcome. *Meritor Sav. Bank v. Vinson,* 477 U.S. 57, 66 (1986).

This sentence says two things: that the plaintiff must show a hostile environment and that the plaintiff must show that he or she communicated that the conduct was unwelcome. The placement of the citation to *Meritor* outside the textual sentence tells the reader that *Meritor* establishes both of these points.

However, if *Meritor* only established one of these points, the citation to *Meritor* should go inside the textual sentence and immediately after the proposition that it supports. The writer would need to cite to another authority for the other proposition, like so:

> To prove a claim for sexual harassment without showing an adverse employment action, a plaintiff must show that the harassment created a "hostile or abusive work environment," *Meritor Sav. Bank v. Vinson,* 477 U.S. 57, 66 (1986), and that the plaintiff indicated that the harassment was unwelcome [cite to the other case].

A similar situation exists when the writer has authority for one part of the sentence but no authority for the other part of the sentence. In that case, the writer should still take care to place the citation immediately after the proposition it supports, simply leaving the other proposition unsupported, like so:

> Though a plaintiff can prove a claim by showing that the harassment created a "hostile or abusive work environment," *Meritor Sav. Bank v. Vinson,* 477 U.S. 57, 66 (1986), Willingham has made no such showing in this case.

Sometimes a writer points out an aspect of an authority and then uses that aspect of the authority to reason her way to another point about that authority. The first point came from the authority but the second point did not; the second point came from the writer's own reasoning process. Once again, the writer should place the citation to the authority immediately after the point that came from the authority rather than after the writer's reasoning process, like so:

> In *Newcomb v. Roberts,* the court allowed recovery on an attractive nuisance claim to a child who came into the defendants' yard to hide from her friends and fell into a swimming pool while there. [the citation to *Newcomb* goes here.] Though *Newcomb* made no mention of the issue, the court's allowance of recovery on these facts shows that the older authority requiring that the child be drawn by

the artificial condition is no longer valid. [The citation to *Newcomb* does *not* go here because *Newcomb* does not say that the requirement is no longer valid.]

EXERCISE 2. Identifying the Text the Citation Supports

Identify the proposition(s)[5] each of the following citations supports.

A malpractice action can be based on conduct other than a failure to exercise the proper standard of care. It also can be based on violation of a duty the lawyer owes the client as a fiduciary. For example, a fiduciary's duty of loyalty requires her to avoid conflicts of interest. *See Simpson v. James,* 903 F.2d 372 (5th Cir. 1990). Ethics rules require the same, Model Rules of Professional Conduct Rules 1.7-1.9, and a violation of a rule of ethics is considered evidence of malpractice, *Beattie v. Firnschild,* 394 N.W.2d 107 (1986). If a client suffers a loss as a result of a lawyer's conflict of interest, the client will be able to recover in malpractice. *Simpson,* 903 F.2d at 377; *Miami Int'l Realty Co. v. Paynter,* 841 F.2d 348 (10th Cir. 1988).

Similarly, except in limited circumstances, a fiduciary may not reveal a client's confidential information to the client's disadvantage. Not only is this an ethical rule, Model Rules of Professional Conduct Rule 1.6, but if a lawyer improperly reveals confidential information, a malpractice action will lie. *Tri-Growth Centre City, Ltd. v. Silldorf, Burdman, Duignan & Eisenberg,* 216 Cal. App. 3d 1139, 265 Cal. Rptr. 330 (1990).

Breach of fiduciary duty also can occur if a lawyer helps another agent of a client violate the agent's fiduciary duties to the client. *Avianca, Inc. v. Corriea,* 705 F. Supp. 666 (D.D.C. 1989).

D. Citing with Style and Grace

Citations in the text of a document can make the text hard to read. A reader has to jump over all the names, numbers, and parentheticals; find the spot where the text begins again; and pick back up on the message of the text. Granted, law-trained readers become fairly good at these mental and visual gymnastics, but even law-trained readers can use all the help a writer can give them. Here are four suggestions for minimizing the disruption caused by citations:

1. Case names and citations placed in the middle of the sentence make it hard to find the key parts of the sentence and combine them into a coherent thought. For instance, notice how a reader must hop through this sentence:

A majority of the Court in *General Electric Co. v. Gilbert,* 429 U.S. 125 (1976), followed *Geduldig v. Aiello,* 417 U.S. 484 (1974), and held that pregnancy classifications were not gender classifications.

5. Modified from Stephen Gillers, Regulation of Lawyers: Problems of Law and Ethics 686-687 (4th ed. 1995).

When possible, use the following techniques to clear the reader's path from subject to verb to object:

a.   Move the citation to the end of the sentence. Let it stand alone as a citation sentence. If the textual sentence identifies the case name (and your teacher permits), you do not need to repeat it.

b.   When the sentence contains two propositions, each requiring its own authority, consider dividing the sentence into two sentences. Thus you can move the citations outside the sentences.

c.   When possible, move even the case *names* to the beginning or end of the sentence.

d.   Consider moving less important material into a parenthetical in the citation.

Notice how techniques *a, c,* and *d* have improved the readability of the sentence:

> In *General Electric Co. v. Gilbert,* a majority of the Court held that pregnancy classifications were not gender classifications. 429 U.S. 125, 136 (1976) (following *Geduldig v. Aiello,* 417 U.S. 484 (1974)).

2. Avoid beginning a sentence with a citation. Here is an example of a sentence with this flaw and an improved version:

> *Change*   Public Law 95-555, 92 Stat. 2076, October 31, 1978, included a new § 701(k).
>
> *To*   Congress added a new version of § 701(k) when it enacted Public Law 95-555, 92 Stat. 2076, October 31, 1978.

3. If you state the full case name in the sentence, you do not need to repeat it at the beginning of the citation sentence unless your reader prefers the repetition.

> In *Marafino v. St. Louis County Circuit Court,* the court held that an employer could refuse to hire a pregnant applicant if the employer would have refused to hire *any* applicant who would need a leave of absence shortly after beginning work. 707 F.2d 1005, 1007 (8th Cir. 1983).

4. As a general rule, avoid long string citations. *String citation* is the term lawyers use for "stringing" a number of citations together to support the same proposition. Lawyers often cite several authorities for an important proposition, but the longer the "string," the more the citations impair readability. Further, as citations devoid of discussion, the long list seldom adds much to the legal analysis.

Generally, you are better off to cite and discuss the several most important authorities and omit the others. However, string cites are appropriate when your reader needs every relevant authority or when you wish to demonstrate, graphically on the page, the strength of the proposition the citations support.

EXERCISE 3. Editing the Placement of Citations

Use the techniques described in section D to make the following passage more readable and to be sure that the placement of the citation accurately identifies the textual material it supports.

42 U.S.C. § 2000e-2(a) prohibits employers from discriminating against applicants or employees based on the individual's race or sex. The act, titled the "Civil Rights Act of 1964," protects individuals of all races and both genders, not just minorities and women. *McDonald v. Santa Fe Trail Transp. Co.*, 427 U.S. 273, 280 (1976); *Hall v. City of Brawley*, 887 F. Supp. 1333 (S.D. Cal. 1995); *Hannon v. Chater*, 887 F. Supp. 1303 (N.D. Cal. 1995); *Curler v. City of Fort Wayne*, 591 F. Supp. 327 (N.D. Ind. 1984).

However, the Court has never been comfortable with the issues raised by the application of Title VII to the racial majority or to men. In *United Steelworkers of Am. v. Weber*, 443 U.S. 193 (1979), the Supreme Court upheld a voluntary race-conscious affirmative action plan, but several years later the Court held that, to be permissible, a voluntary affirmative action plan had to benefit only "actual victims of the discriminatory practice." *Firefighters Local 1784 v. Stotts*, 467 U.S. 561, 579 (1984).

Just three years later, the Court, in *Johnson v. Transportation Agency of Santa Clara County*, 107 S. Ct. 1442 (1987), seemed to reaffirm its holding in *Weber* when it expressly followed the *Weber* holding. The Court wrote that the *Johnson* issues "must be guided by our decision in *Weber.*" *Johnson* dealt with a voluntary affirmative action plan designed to improve the representation of racial minorities and of women in traditionally male jobs. *Johnson v. Transportation Agency of Santa Clara County*, 107 S. Ct. 1442, 1449 (1987).

E. EDITING CITATION FORM

This section assumes that you have looked up the relevant citation rules in the Bluebook. What follows is an editing checklist to help you flag the most common citation errors for beginning legal writers.

Checklist for Editing Citations

GENERAL PRINCIPLES

1. Have you placed each citation immediately after the proposition it supports?
2. Have you cited to the available legal authority for each point you have made about the law or the authority?

3. Have you placed your citations at the end of your sentences whenever possible?
4. Have you avoided unnecessary string citations?
5. Have you minimized the number of sentences beginning with a citation?
6. Have you underscored, using an unbroken line, or italicized:
    a. Case names, titles of books, and articles?
    b. Signals (such as *e.g.* or *see*)?
    c. Phrases giving prior or subsequent history (such as *aff'd* or *cert. denied*)?
    d. Terms introducing related authority (such as *citing*)?
    e. Terms used in short citation forms in place of repeating the name of the source (such as *id*)?
7. For citing all authorities other than names of periodicals, have you closed up all adjacent single capitals, individual numerals, and ordinals (for example, "3d"), and initials in personal names? R.6.1(a).
8. Have you left a space between single capitals and multiple letter abbreviations (for example "F. Supp.")? R.6.1(a).
9. When you put the citation outside the sentence, have you placed a period at the end of the citation?
10. When you put the citation in the middle of a sentence, have you placed a comma at the end of the citation?
11. When you have cited to several authorities together, have you separated them with a semicolon?
12. When you have cited to several authorities together, have you put them in the order set out in R.1.4?
13. Have you used *supra* only for secondary sources and *not* for cases, statutes, and constitutions? R.4.2.

QUOTATIONS

14. For all cites to the quotation, including parallel citations, have you included the pinpoint cite to the page where the quoted material appears? R.3.3(a).
15. When you have used a block quote, have you placed the citation at the normal left margin on the line immediately following the block quote? R.5.1(a).
16. When the source to which you are citing has quoted the material from another source, have you used an explanatory parenthetical? R.5.2.
17. When you have added or deleted citations or indications of emphasis, have you used an explanatory parenthetical? R.5.2.

CASES

LONG FORM

18. Have you used only the last names of the parties? R.10.2.1(g).
19. Have you omitted all parties other than the first party listed on each side? R.10.2.1(a).

20. Have you avoided using "et al." to signal that you have omitted the names of additional parties? R.10.2.1(a).

21. Have you used "v." (rather than "vs" or "v" or "V") and have you included it in the underscoring of the case name? P.1(a).

22. Have you abbreviated case names in citations according to R.10.2.2, T.6 & T.10?

23. Have you refrained from abbreviating the first word in the name of a party? R.10.2.2.

24. Have you refrained from abbreviating "United States" in a case name?

25. Have you placed a comma after the case name and refrained from underlining the comma?

26. For federal district court and circuit court cases, have you closed up the spaces in "F.3d" but left a space in "F. Supp."? R.6.1(a).

27. Have you included a pinpoint cite to the page(s) of the opinion where the referenced material is located? R.3.3(a).

28. Have you refrained from placing any punctuation between the page number of the case and the parenthetical?

29. Have you included the opinion's date in parentheses? R.10.5.

30. For state cases where the state is not unambiguously conveyed by the reporter title, have you included the name of the state in the parentheses? R.10.4(b).

31. For state cases where the court deciding the case is not the highest court of the state, have you included the court's name, properly abbreviated, in the parenthetical? R.10.4(b) & T.10.

32. For cases from federal circuit courts, have you identified the circuit in the parenthetical and used the correct abbreviation for it (D.C. Cir., 1st Cir., 2d Cir., 3d Cir., 4th Cir., 5th Cir., 6th Cir., 7th Cir., 8th Cir., 9th Cir., 10th Cir., 11th Cir., Fed. Cir.)? R.10.4(a) & T.7.

33. For federal district courts, have you identified the district in the parenthetical (for example, "S.D. Cal.")? R.10.4(a).

34. Have you refrained from putting a comma between the date and any other information within the parenthetical?

35. Have you included the subsequent history, if any, in the full citation to a case? R.10.7.1, T.9 & P.1(d).

36. Have you separated the subsequent history from the citation to the case with a comma? P.1(a) & P.1(d).

37. Have you included an explanatory phrase in a second parenthetical (and before any subsequent history) when additional information would be helpful for evaluating the weight properly given to the authority? R.10.6.

38. Where a phrase of information would help the reader understand the significance of the cited authority, have you included that information in an explanatory parenthetical? R.1.5.

39. Have you used an appropriate signal to introduce cited authorities that:
    a. support the proposition but do not clearly state it,
    b. offer a profitable comparison,
    c. contradict the proposition, or
    d. provide background material? R.1.2.

40. Have you underscored all signals? P.1(c).

41. When you are citing to a concurring or dissenting opinion, have you disclosed in a parenthetical this potential limitation on the weight of the cited material? R.10.6.

42. Have you indicated by parenthetical any other limitations on the weight of the cited material (for example that the cited language is dictum or that your proposition is contained in the cited material only by implication)? R.10.6.

PARALLEL CITATIONS

43. When citing state cases from state *A* to the courts of state *A*, have you included all parallel citations? P.3.

44. When citing cases from states other than state *A* to the courts of state *A*, have you cited to the regional reporter? R.10.3.1(b).

45. When citing United States Supreme Court cases, have you cited to the official reporter (U.S.) where possible? T.1.

46. When you have cited parallel citations, have you placed the citation to the official reporter, if any, first?

SHORT FORMS

47. Have you used a full citation the first time you cite to a particular authority?

48. Have you used a short citation form (1) only within the same general discussion where you gave the full cite, and (2) only where the reader will be able to find the full cite easily? P.4.

49. When you have used a short citation form, is it clear to the reader which prior authority you are referencing? P.4.

50. When you have used *id.*, have you been referring to the case cited immediately prior to the *id.* cite? R.4.1.

51. Have you underscored the cross-referencing term (for example, "*id.*")? P.1(f).

52. Have you refrained from using *supra* to refer to a case? R.4.2.

53. Have you underlined the period after *id.*? P.1(f).

54. When using a short citation form for cases that require parallel cites, have you conformed the short form to the examples given in P.4(a)?

STATUTES

55. Have you used the citation form listed in T.1?

56. If the information would be helpful, have you given the statute's name (official or popular) or the original section number? R.12.3.1.

57. If possible, have you cited to the official code rather than to an unofficial code? R.12.2.1 & T.1.

58. Have you included in parentheses the year of the code you are citing to (*not* the year the statute was enacted)? R.12.3.2.

59. Have you identified the title, chapter, or volume number, if any, in the manner required by T.1? R.12.3.1(b).

60. Have you refrained from using *"et seq.,"* but rather designated the exact sections you are citing? R.3.4(b).

61. Have you left a space after the section symbol? R.6.2(b).

62. If your computer cannot make a section symbol, have you used the abbreviation "sec." or written out the word "section," whichever your teacher or law firm prefers? R.6.2(b).

63. If you have cited to a privately published version of the code, have you identified the publisher in the parenthetical that contains the year? R.12.3.1(d) & T.1.

64. If you are citing to material contained in a supplement, either alone or in addition to material contained in the main volume, have you followed the format shown in R.3.2(c)?

65. If you are citing to a statute that has been amended or repealed, have you followed the format shown in R.12.6?

66. If you are citing to rules of evidence or procedure, uniform acts, model codes, or restatements of the law, have you followed the format provided in R.12.8.3, R.12.8.4 & R.12.8.5?

67. Have you used a full citation the first time you cite to the statute?

68. If you used a short form for later cites to the statute, is the short form in the same general discussion in the text? R.12.9(a).

69. If you used a short form of citation, have you followed the format set out in R.12.9(b) & P.4(b)?

BOOKS

70. For the first citation to the book, have you used the author's full name and followed it with a comma? R.15.1.

71. If the book has more than two authors, have you used only the first author's name followed by "et al."? R.15.1.1.

72. If the book has an editor or translator, have you followed the provisions of R.15.1.2 & R.15.1.3?

73. Have you underlined the name of the book? P.1(b).

74. Have you capitalized the name of the book as set out in R.8 & R.15.2?

75. Have you cited to the latest edition and identified the edition in the parenthetical? R.15.4.

76. Have you identified the year of publication in the parenthetical? R.15.4.

77. If the cited material appears in a supplement, have you followed the format set out in R.3.2(c)?

78. If you have cited to *Ballentine's Law Dictionary, Black's Law Dictionary,* C.J.S., or Am. Jur., have you followed the format set out in R.15.7?

79. If you have used a short form for later citations to the same book, have you complied with P.4(d), R.4, R.15.8, R.16.6 & R.17.7?

80. Have you used a pinpoint cite to identify the page(s) on which the cited material appears? R.3.3(a).

PERIODICALS

81. Have you provided the author's full name followed by a comma? R.16.1 & R.15.1.1.
82. Have you underscored the title of the article and followed the title with a comma (*not* underscored)? P.1(b).
83. Have you abbreviated the periodical as set out in T.13? If your periodical is not included in the list, have you used T.13 & T.10 as your guides for constructing the periodical's abbreviation?
84. Have you followed R.6.1(a) for spacing between the letters abbreviating the periodical name?
85. Have you included the volume number of the periodical (before the abbreviated title of the periodical)? R.16.2.
86. Have you identified the page on which the article begins, placing it after the abbreviated title of the periodical and refraining from using a "p." or "pp."? R.16.2.
87. Have you included a pinpoint cite to the page(s) where the cited material is found? R.3.3(a).
88. Have you refrained from putting a comma between the page number and the parenthetical? R.16.2.
89. Unless the periodical uses the date for the volume number, have you included the date of the volume in the parenthetical? R.16.2.

 EXERCISE 4.   Editing for Citation Form

Edit the following citations for correct citation form. Use the checklists in section E. If you spot an error that you cannot correct without additional information, simply note the error and identify the information you would need to correct it.

1. <u>Leibel vs. Raynor Manufacturing Co.,</u> 571 S.W. 2nd 640 (1978).
2. Brown v. New Haven Civil Service Comm., 474 F.Supp. 1256, 1263, (1979).
3. <u>Equal Pay Act of 1963</u>, 29 USC §206(d), <u>et seq.</u>
4. <u>Connecticut V. Winnie Teal, et al.,</u> supra at 444.
5. Harold S. Lewis, Jr., Litigating Civil rights and Employment Discrimination cases, 1996.
6. <u>Humphrey v. McLaren</u>, 402 N.W.2d 535 (Minn, 1987). [cited in a brief filed before a trial court in Minnesota]
7. <u>Prandini v. National Tea Co.,</u> <u>Id.</u> at 49.
8. Jack Lee Sammons, <u>The Professionalism Movement: the Problems Defined,</u> 7 Notre Dame Journ. of Law, Ethics & Public Pol. 269, 1993.
9. e.g., <u>U.S. Dept. of Labor v. Triplett</u>, 494 US 715, 716 (1990).
10. <u>Laffey v. Northwest Airlines, Inc.,</u> 567 F.2d 429, 431 (1978).

◆III◆ QUOTATIONS

The most common quotation problems are (1) failing to use quotation marks for borrowed language, (2) using too many quotations, (3) insufficiently editing quotations, and (4) making errors in the mechanics of quoting. The remainder of this chapter deals with these common quotation problems.

A. WHEN QUOTATION MARKS ARE REQUIRED

Quotation marks are required to designate places where a writer has used the words of another. Requiring quotation marks furthers several important policies.[6] First, the quotation marks insure that the creator will have the credit (or blame) for the creation. Second, the quotation marks allow the writer to avoid claiming undeserved credit; for even if the creator does not desire recognition, you should not take credit for someone else's work. Finally, the quotation marks inform readers of the source of the creation. Irrespective of the interests of the two authors, readers deserve accurate information about who created what.

For these policy reasons, quotation marks are necessary when you quote the words of another but unnecessary when you paraphrase. However, sometimes it is hard to know whether a particular passage is a quotation or a paraphrase. When are the words yours and when are they "the words of another"?

Start with the proposition that you should attempt to rephrase the thoughts of others into your own words and sentence structures. However, even if you are not looking at the source while you write, you may find that your text turns out to be similar to your source's text. This result can occur because the source uses words that are commonly used to express the idea; because the sentence structure the source used is commonplace; because without realizing it, you have been thinking of the topic in the source's words; or some combination of all three.

Now, if the original text used the word "table" and you use it too, no one would argue that you must put quotation marks around "table" in your document. However, if your draft shares a whole paragraph in common with the original text, everyone understands that the paragraph must be designated by quotation marks or by blocking the material.[7] Somewhere between these two extremes lies the point at which the words are those of another (and quotation marks become necessary), but no bright-line test will tell you precisely where.[8]

---

6. Copyright law can create legal requirements in addition to the policies described here.

7. *See* section D; Rule 5.1, The Bluebook.

8. *Ideas* that come from another author must always be attributed to the other author. This section assumes that you are attributing the *ideas* to their source, according

The absence of a clear test is particularly unfortunate for legal writers. Legal writers rely heavily on sources, and most legal writing texts advise writers to paraphrase rather than quote the majority of those sources;[9] if you follow this good advice, you will be doing a lot of paraphrasing. How can you know whether your paraphrase is sufficiently different from the original author's text to free you from the requirement of using quotation marks?

To gauge how similar your text is to another writer's text, consider the *combined effect* of these factors: (1) the length of the common unit of text; (2) the number of units in common; (3) whether the sentence structure is the same or similar; and (4) whether the common units include language that the original author used in particularly effective ways.

Some writers use a seven-word benchmark for measuring the length of a common unit requiring quotation marks; if seven or more words used together in your text match the text of the source, use quotation marks for those words. The benchmark recognizes the unlikelihood of a common seven-word unit appearing in text by different authors inadvertently. It also acknowledges that a passage of at least seven words is sufficiently long to merit recognition of the original author for assembling the words into a unit of text, even if it is the only common unit and even if the unit has no distinctive characteristics or particular merits. So be sure to use quotation marks *at least* for any unit of seven or more words that your text shares in common with another.

However, don't think you can avoid using quotation marks simply by changing every seventh word. The seven-word benchmark is only an approximate measure of when the writing is similar enough to require quotation marks, and it only applies when no other similarities are present. You also must consider whether there are other common units of text and whether the sentence structure is similar. Would an objective reader think that this passage is fundamentally someone else's, with just a few surface changes?

Finally, consider the nature of the common text, for you must use quotation marks for language an author has used in a particularly vivid, creative, or unusual way. Attributing the word or phrase to the original author recognizes that author's use of those words to convey the idea so effectively.

For instance, the first sentence of the prior paragraph uses the words "you must use quotation marks." The words number only five, so if there are no other similarities, they probably do not constitute a phrase long enough to merit recognition of the author simply for putting them together as a unit. Nor was the author particularly original or effective in selecting those words, in combining them, or in applying them to the idea being discussed. Using these words probably would not require quotation marks attributing the words to the first author.

However, sometimes an author's use of particular words for a particular idea makes the words uncommon. For instance, in *Griggs v. Duke Power Co.*, Chief Justice Burger condemned employer practices that function as "built-in headwinds" impeding employment for minority groups.[10] In *Watson v. Fort*

---

to proper citation form. Here we deal only with deciding when to attribute the *words* as well.

9.   *See* p. 92
10.   401 U.S. 424, 432 (1971).

Worth Bank and Trust, Justice O'Connor described the positions argued by the parties as "stark and uninviting alternatives."[11] In his dissent in *Wards Cove Packing Co. v. Antonio,* Justice Stevens described the living and working conditions at the defendant's canneries as "a plantation economy."[12]

These are examples of words and phrases used in distinctive ways. In each case, the author was especially effective in selecting the words to express the idea. In each case, the author's effective use of language merits recognition, and other writers who use these phrases should give the credit to the original author by using quotation marks.

Like the "reasonable person" standard or the "best interests of the child" standard, the "using the words of another" standard is open to interpretation. It is far better either to use quotation marks or to paraphrase the passage more thoroughly than to risk questions about whose writing the passage really reflects.

B. CHOOSING TO USE QUOTATION MARKS

Even if quotation marks are not required, a legal writer may choose to use them anyway—to communicate information important to the reader. The most common occasions for this kind of quoting are when the analysis must apply a particular legal test or when the analysis must construe particular words of a statute. Here are examples of each:

PARTICULAR LEGAL TEST

A lawyer must use the degree of skill commonly exercised by a "reasonable, careful and prudent lawyer." *Cook, Flanagan & Berst v. Clausing,* 438 P.2d 865, 867 (1968).

PARTICULAR WORDS OF STATUTE

Title VII makes it unlawful for a labor organization "to exclude or expel" an individual because of religion. 42 U.S.C. § 2000e-2(c)(1).

Even though quotation marks would not be required for these words, the writer should use them anyway, to let the reader know that these are the words at issue in the analysis.

---

11.   487 U.S. 977, 989 (1988).
12.   490 U.S. 642, 662 n.4 (1989).

C. OVERQUOTING

Chapter 7 warned against using too many quotations.[13] There, in the working draft stage, the reason for the warning was the danger of confusing copying the authorities with analyzing them. The editing stage brings two more reasons to minimize quotes. First, many readers are tempted to skip quoted material entirely. Perhaps they assume that the quoted material simply supports the points already asserted by the current writer. Perhaps they are discouraged by the single-spacing of a block quote. Whatever the reason, busy readers do tend to skim or skip quoted material.

Second, a quotation seldom communicates your point as clearly, directly, and succinctly as you could. After all, the original writer was not writing about *your* case. Your paraphrase can do what quotations cannot, that is, tie the substance of the precedential source directly to the issues of *your* case.

As a general rule, limit yourself to quoting only in the following circumstances:

1. Quote when the issue will turn on the interpretation of particular words of a statute, rule, or key case, as described above. Limit the quotation to *those particular words* so your reader will understand the issue and your analysis of it.

> A lawyer must use great care in deciding whether to undertake representation of a new client when that representation might be directly adverse to an existing client. The existing client must consent to the lawyer's representation of the new client. Model Rules of Professional Conduct Rule 1.7(a)(2). However, even if the client consents, the lawyer must not undertake the new representation unless the lawyer "reasonably believes" that the new representation will not "adversely affect the relationship" with the existing client. *Id.* at § 1.7(a)(1).

2. Quote *key* language from an authority with a great deal of precedential value. This could be mandatory authority or highly respected persuasive authority such as an opinion of the United States Supreme Court,[14] a provision of a Restatement of Law, or an opinion written by a respected judge.
3. Quote *key* language when the author has found a particularly effective way to express the idea you want to convey.

> Under Rule 60(b) the court possesses "a grand reservoir of equitable power" to accomplish justice. *Thompson v. Kerr-McGee Ref. Corp.,* 660 F.2d 1380, 1385 (10th Cir. 1981).

---

13. *See* p. 92.
14. Remember that opinions of the United States Supreme Court are not automatically mandatory authority. *See* p. 58.

D.   THE MECHANICS OF QUOTING

Use this section as an editing checklist; it identifies the most common quotation errors. For other quotation questions, see Rule 5 of the Bluebook.

1. Quotations of fifty or more words should be indented from both side margins. The indentation signals that the material is quoted, thus eliminating the need for quotation marks around the quoted material. Indented quotations should be single-spaced.[15]

2. Quotations shorter than fifty words should not be indented or single-spaced and should be enclosed within quotation marks.[16]

3. Place end punctuation within the quotation marks if it is part of the material you are quoting. For punctuation you add, place commas and periods inside the quotation marks, but place other added punctuation outside the quotation marks.[17]

> "Discriminatory employment practices are prohibited." [The period is part of the quoted material.]

> The statute prohibits "discriminatory employment practices." [The period is not part of the quoted material.]

> Does the statute prohibit "discriminatory employment practices"? [the question mark is not part of the quoted material.]

4. Signal changes in the quotation by using brackets and ellipses. Use brackets when you replace letters or words or when you add material to the quotation:[18]

> "[R]egulations [of employee appearance] making distinctions on the basis of sex will not support allegations of discrimination unless [the regulations] are unreasonable or unevenly enforced."

In the first bracket, the upper-case *R* replaces a lower-case *r* because in the original the quoted language did not constitute the beginning of a sentence. The second and third brackets identify material added or substituted to clarify, simplify, or shorten the quoted material.

5. To signal the omission of letters, use empty brackets.[19] For instance, write "draft[]" when omitting the "ing" from "drafting."

6. To signal the omission of one or more words within the quotation, use ellipses. An ellipsis is a series of three dots with a space before, between, and after.[20]

> "The evidence included a communication . . . suggesting that the employee should wear clothing of a more feminine style."

---

15.   *See* Rule 5.1(a).
16.   *See* Rule 5.1 (b).
17.   *See* Rule 5.1 (b).
18.   *See* Rule 5.2.
19.   *See* Rule 5.2.
20.   *See* Rule 5.3.

7. Do not use an ellipsis at the beginning of a quotation.[21] A reader will assume that the original source may include material ahead of the quoted material.

8. Similarly, do not use an ellipsis at the end of a quotation *to signal the omission of material beyond the end of the quoted sentence.*[22] A reader will assume that the original source may contain material after the quoted sentence.

9. When you are using material that was a *part* of a sentence in the original but you are using it as a complete sentence in your text, indicate the omitted material at the end of the quotation by placing an ellipsis between the last quoted material and the punctuation at the end of the sentence.[23]

> "The mere existence of a grievance procedure does not insulate an employer from liability . . . ."

The ellipsis will tell your reader that in the original the sentence contained additional material.

10. Use a parenthetical clause after the citation to signal citations or footnotes you have omitted from inside the quotation or to signal emphasis you have added or deleted:[24]

> The court observed that a partner's interest in partnership property "is a derivative interest subject to significant limitations. [A partner] has *no right to use this property for other than partnership purposes* without the consent of the other partners." *Bellis v. United States,* 417 U.S. 85, 98 (1974) (citations omitted) (emphasis added).

The original material contained citations after "limitations" and before the next sentence. The italicized phrase was not italicized in the original.

11. If you find an error in the quoted material, signal the error by following it with "sic" enclosed in brackets,[25] like so:

> "The party least anxious to settle was her [sic]."

E.   EDITING QUOTATIONS

Edit quotations down to the key words so your reader doesn't have to sift through the quoted material for your point. Editing must not change the meaning, but within that constraint you have great latitude to clear away the underbrush. Often the most effective quotation has been edited down to a short phrase or even a single word, perhaps with the key language italicized

21. *See* Rule 5.3.
22. *See* Rule 5.3(b).
23. *See* Rule 5.3(b)(iii).
24. *See* Rule 5.2.
25. *See* Rule 5.2.

or underlined. Moderate use of italics and underlining in quoted material can help overcome the tendency of busy readers to skim quotations. They may still skim the rest of the quotation, but an italicized or underlined word may draw their attention at least to the most important part.

For instance, assume that you represent the defendant in a case in which the plaintiff alleges that she was sexually harassed when her supervisor pressured her into going to dinner with him and kissing him. You are writing a brief to the trial court on the issue of what the plaintiff must prove. Compare the following quotations:

> The Supreme Court has held that "the District Court in this case erroneously focused on the 'voluntariness' of respondent's participation in the claimed sexual episodes. The correct inquiry is whether respondent by her conduct indicated that the alleged sexual advances were unwelcome, not whether her actual participation in sexual intercourse was involuntary." *Meritor Sav. Bank v. Vinson,* 477 U.S. 57, 68 (1986).

> The Supreme Court has held that a plaintiff cannot prove a sexual harassment claim merely by showing that she participated in the sexual conduct involuntarily. She must prove that "by her conduct [she] *indicated* that the alleged sexual advances were unwelcome . . . ." *Meritor Sav. Bank v. Vinson,* 477 U.S. 57, 68 (1986) (emphasis added).

Which manner of quoting distills the key distinction and highlights it for your reader? Which states the legal principle as it would apply to the procedural posture of your case? Which states the legal principle in language that would be applicable to the facts of your case? Which is more readable?

Now that your citations and quotations are in proper form, turn your attention to editing the rest of the document.

15 Revising for Usage and Style

The final step in the writing process is editing. Good editing requires reading the document as if you've never seen it before; that is hard to do if you have been working on it intensely. Try to arrive at the editing stage with enough time to put the document down for at least a day. Even if you do not have that luxury, let at least a couple of hours pass; then try to read as if you were a complete stranger to the document.

Use the sections of this chapter as a checklist to help spot problems. These sections identify many of the most common trouble areas. You also may want to check your draft against the material on paragraphing and transitions in Chapters 7 and 8. Confirm that your paragraphs are not too long and that they do not wander. Be sure that the transitions between topics and theses are clear and accurate.

Watch for other errors not highlighted here and for typographical errors. Have a good composition handbook or style manual handy to check grammar or punctuation questions.[1] You can use computer programs for checking grammar, punctuation, style, and cite form. Remember, however, that no computer program can replace your own skilled decision-making. A computer program can only flag something in the document, allowing *you* to decide whether and how it should be revised.

At first you may need to go through your document once for each of the sections that follow. As you learn the material in this chapter, your early drafts will get better and better. These better early drafts will help you decrease the number of times you revise the document.

---

1. Examples include Terri LeClercq, *Guide to Legal Writing Style* (1995); H. Ramsey Fowler & Jane E. Aaron, *The Little, Brown Handbook* (6th ed. 1995); Texas Law Review, *Manual on Style* (7th ed. 1992).

PROFESSIONAL TONE AND LEVEL OF FORMALITY

1. Legal writing calls for the degree of formality appropriate for traditional business and professional writing. Therefore, do not use contractions, colloquialisms, slash constructions (such as "either/or"), and abbreviations appropriate only for note-taking or citations:

The plaintiff *will not* [rather than "won't"] be able to argue that . . . .

Clayton's *children* [rather than "kids"] were visiting their grandmother.

The corporate president, vice president, *and* [rather than "&"] secretary all testified.

The stockholders can sue the corporate president or vice president *or both* [rather than "president and/or vice president"].

The defendant's employment policy prohibits sexual harassment such as unwanted touching, verbal intimidation, displaying pornography, *and other sexually offensive conduct* [rather than "etc."].

2. Do not omit articles (a, an, the) as you may be accustomed to doing when taking notes or as the writers of case headnotes do.

3. Avoid unnecessary references to yourself, your firm, or opposing counsel. In legal matters, the focus is on the parties and the law rather than on the lawyers.

"The covenant is not enforceable" rather than "*I believe that* the covenant is not enforceable."[2]

For briefs, references to counsel are necessary only when the legal issue makes the conduct of the lawyers legally relevant. For example, if the brief concerns a dispute about scheduling a deposition, some references to correspondence and telephone calls exchanged by the lawyers may be necessary. However, even then, do not use the first-person pronoun "I." Rather, use a characterization such as "counsel for plaintiff."

For office memos, the practice in your firm may be as formal as that for a brief, but more likely it will be slightly less formal, allowing for occasional references to the firm as "we" or the writer as "I." For instance:

Formal memo	Before filing the complaint, it will be necessary to confirm the defendant's correct corporate name.
Informal memo	Before filing the complaint, we need to confirm the defendant's correct corporate name.

2. *See also* "throat-clearing" p. 228.

Follow the practice of your firm or the guidance of your teacher in deciding whether occasional personal references are permissible for your office memo. For briefs, avoid personal references entirely unless they are legally relevant, and do not use "I."

4. Adopt a tone of respect for your reader. Assume that your reader is intelligent and competent, no matter what you actually believe.

5. Sarcasm and detectable anger have no place in legal writing. In the rough and tumble of litigation, other parties (or even judges) will make you angry. Allowing your own emotional response to color your writing is both unprofessional and counterproductive.

6. Unfortunately, humor is rarely appropriate or effective in legal writing either. It nearly always backfires. Legal matters and the parties involved in them deserve to be taken seriously.

7. Do not use rhetorical questions (questions asked merely for effect, with no response expected). An example of a rhetorical question: "How can the plaintiff argue that her claims are just?"

 # LEGAL USAGE AND CUSTOMS

Legal *usage* refers to the accepted way lawyers use legal language. The Bluebook covers primarily citation form rather than legal usage. However, the Bluebook does address some questions of capitalization, quotations, and titles of judges, officials, and court terms.[3] For other legal usage questions, consult a legal usage dictionary.[4] The items that follow represent some of the most common legal usage questions for people new to the study of law.

1. Courts "find" facts and "hold" rules of law. Use "find" and "finding" when referring to decisions the court made about facts and "hold" and "holding" when referring to decisions the court made about the law:

Compare	The court's *finding* that the car was traveling fifty miles per hour was supported by the evidence.
With	The court *held* that driving fifty miles per hour constituted negligence.
Compare	The court *found* that the officer had not advised the defendant of his right to remain silent.
With	The court *held* that the failure to advise the defendant of his right to remain silent violated the defendant's Constitutional rights.

3. Capitalization is covered in Rule 8 and Practitioners' Note 6; questions relating to quotations are covered in Rule 5; titles of judges, officials, and court terms are covered in Rule 9.

4. Two good references are Bryan A. Garner, *A Dictionary of Modern Legal Usage* (1987) and David Mellinkoff, *Mellinkoff's Dictionary of American Legal Usage* (1992).

2. Reserve the verb "held" for the court's holding. For example, you would write: "the court held that a valid offer must include a price." But when you describe dicta, you would use verbs like "observed" or "stated."

3. The court need not persuade anyone of anything; therefore, the court does not "argue." Courts decide the issue after the lawyers have "argued" it.[5]

4. Similarly, the court need not bargain with anyone; therefore, it does not "stipulate." Parties "stipulate" (agree), and a court may take some action based on that agreement.

5. Capitalize "Court" when naming a particular court in full ("the United States District Court for the District of Idaho"), when referring to the United States Supreme Court ("In *Brown v. Board of Education* the Court held . . ."), or when referring to the court to which the document is addressed ("The Court has not yet considered the Defendant's Motion for a New Trial.").[6] Otherwise do not capitalize "court."

6. Capitalize a party's procedural designation (plaintiff, defendant, appellant) when referring to the particular parties of your case ("The Appellant did not file its motion within the statutorily required time."), but not when referring to a party in another case ("In *Bell v. Burson* the plaintiff . . . .").[7]

7. Capitalize the actual titles of court documents filed with the court in the matter that is the subject of your document ("Plaintiff's Motion for Summary Judgment was filed within the required time limit."), but not the generic name for a kind of document ("The parties must file all motions for summary judgment by April 27.")[8]

8. If a court issued an opinion ten years ago, or even ten minutes ago, the court's action is a *past* legal event; therefore, reference to that event calls for a verb in the past tense. However, a rule of law is a current reality and calls for a verb in the present tense.

Court opinion *(past tense)*	The court *held* (or "observed," "stated," "applied," "rejected," "adopted") [rather than "holds," "observes," "states," "applies," "rejects," "adopts"] . . .
Rule of law *(present tense)*	The court adopt*ed* the rule that a covenant not to compete *is* [rather than "was"] enforceable if . . . .

9. Cases do not decide issues; courts do. Therefore, a case cannot "hold" an opinion.[9]

Change	*Bell v. Burson* held that . . .
	The *Bell* opinion held that . . .
To	The court in *Bell v. Burson* held that . . .
	The *Bell* court held that . . . .[10]

5.   Some lawyers use the verb "argue" when referring to the content of a *dissenting* opinion.

6.   The Bluebook, Rule 8 and Practitioners' Note 6(a).

7.   The Bluebook, Practitioners' Note 6(b).

8.   The Bluebook, Practitioners' Note 6(c).

9.   Many practicing lawyers use the incorrect usage, however, and some would say that this rule is fading away. Write for your particular reader; if you do not know your reader well, opt for the technically correct usage.

10.   Some lawyers object to identifying the court by the case name ("the *Bell* court"). If you are writing for such a lawyer or judge, write "the court in *Bell*" instead.

10. Although the human beings who actually decide cases are called "judges," it is customary to refer to them as "the court." This is especially true of appellate courts, where several judges will usually participate in most decisions. For a one-judge court such as a trial court, you may use either "court" or "judge," but lawyers tend to prefer "court" there as well.

In *Bell v. Burson* the *court* [rather than "judge" or "judges"] held . . .

11. A "court" (even a court with more than one judge) is an entity rather than a group of several judges. Therefore, "court" takes a singular pronoun:

The appellate court overruled *Janace v. Harbison. It* [rather than "they"] held that . . . .

12. Material found in a legal source is not a geographical location. Therefore, use "in which" rather than "where" to refer to it:

Our client can rely on the holding of *Bell v. Burson in which* [not "where"] the court . . . .

13. A criminal defendant may "be found guilty" or may "be convicted" of a crime. In civil litigation, the comparable term is "liable":

Shaffer was *convicted of* burglary.

After the criminal prosecution, Shaffer's former wife sued him for damages resulting from the assault. He was *held liable* for $50,000.

14. When you refer to more than once to a party or an entity with a long name, you may select a shorter form of reference for the second and subsequent references. Use the full name for the first reference, but take that occasion to introduce the shorter reference in parentheses.

The Department of Human Services (DHS) denied the claim.

15. Footnotes should be scarce or absent altogether in most legal documents. While scholarly writing is usually filled with them, they are used sparingly in practitioner-writing. Footnotes are often places to put material that detours away from the main point of the document. Most detours are counterproductive in practitioner-writing.

 GENDER-NEUTRAL WRITING

While the use of masculine nouns and pronouns for general reference is technically correct, most of today's good writers avoid or minimize it. Professor Dworsky explains one reason.

[I]t perpetuates the habit of thinking of the male as the model of a human being from which females deviate. And for a reader who thinks visually, the masculine pronoun will momentarily create the image of a man in the reader's mind. Test yourself on the following sentence:

> A lawyer should zealously represent his client. Quickly now: What did the lawyer look like in your mind?[11]

Two other reasons are relevant to your writing even if you have no political or cultural agenda. First, your professional reputation will be made, in part, by your writing. If your writing reflects knowledge and careful use of modern standards of style, your readers will notice. They will suspect that you are skilled and careful in performing other lawyering tasks as well.

Second, reader-centered writing requires gender-inclusive writing. Roughly half of each year's law graduates are women.[12] Women-owned businesses make up one of the fastest growing segments of the United States economy.[13] More and more, the attorneys, judges, and clients for whom you write will be women. Further, even if your initial reader does not notice gender-specific language, you can never be sure who will be reading your document in the future. Smooth and easy use of gender-neutral language is by far the wiser strategy.

Before exploring technique, we need to clarify what *gender-neutral writing* is and is not. Gender-neutral writing does not mean that you should avoid referring to gender when you are writing about a particular person. That person has a gender, and there is nothing wrong with recognizing this fact. Therefore, use language appropriate for the person's gender, like this:

> Mr. Cole retrieved *his* raincoat.
> Ms. Dantzler has requested that *her* deposition be rescheduled.

Gender-neutral language simply means that you try to avoid using masculine nouns and pronouns for *general* reference. For example:

Change	A person cannot recover damages for injuries sustained primarily as a result of *his* own negligence.
To	A person cannot recover damages for injuries sustained primarily as a result of *that person's* own negligence.

Using gender-neutral language smoothly is not always easy. Our language is still struggling to find ways to avoid referring to the general population as male. Here are some strategies for achieving gender-neutral writing in the smoothest way possible.

---

11.   Alan L. Dworsky, *The Little Book on Legal Writing* 16 (1990).

12.   *See* Laura N. Gasaway & Judith W. Wegner, *Women at UNC and in the Practice of Law,* 73 N.C. L. Rev. 705, 709 (1995); Patricia McKeown, *Diversity in the Workplace: What Does It Mean for Your Bottom Line?,* 67 Wis. Law. 10, 11 (Apr. 1994).

13.   *See* Deborah Graham, *Law's New Entrepreneurs,* 81 A.B.A. J. 54 (Feb. 1995); Anne S. Gallagher, *Widening the Net,* 81 A.B.A. J. 60 (Feb. 1995).

A. TECHNIQUES FOR NOUNS: ELIMINATION OR SUBSTITUTION

1. Where possible without loss of clarity, eliminate the noun entirely. For instance, you could probably eliminate the term "bat boys" from the following sentence without altering the meaning.

> . . . to all players, coaches, [bat boys,] ticket takers, concession workers, or other employees whose jobs are related to the sport of baseball.

2. Substitute gender-neutral synonyms where the noun is needed.

Use	*Rather than*
worker	workman
mail carrier	mailman
chairperson	chairman
supervisor	foreman
server	waitress
reporter	newsman
housekeeper	maid
spouse	husband/wife
sibling	brother/sister
firefighter	fireman
police officer	policeman
flight attendant	stewardess
supplier	materialman
humans, persons, individuals	man, men, mankind
humanity, humankind	mankind
staffing	manning

B. TECHNIQUES FOR PRONOUNS (HE, SHE, HIS, HERS)

1. Where showing possession is not necessary to the meaning, substitute "the" or "an" for the pronoun.

> . . . a plaintiff may petition the court for relief, attaching to *the* [rather than "his"] complaint a copy of . . .

2. Repeat the antecedent. The antecedent is the noun to which the pronoun refers. In the following sentence, "doctor" is the antecedent:

> . . . a doctor and the nurses, secretaries, and receptionists in *the doctor's* [rather than "his"] office . . .

3. Make the antecedent plural so you can use the plural (nongendered) pronoun "their."

The license fee applies to *taxi drivers* [rather than "a taxi driver"] driving *their* [rather than "his"] own taxi*s*.

Do not use the plural pronoun without pluralizing the antecedent. The following is an example of this error:

Anyone who rides a roller coaster must assume the risk, and cannot recover for *their* injuries.

4. Rephrase to use a clause beginning with "who."

Change   A person must assume the risk of injury if he rides a roller coaster.
To   A person who rides a roller coaster must assume the risk of injury.

5. Eliminate the pronoun by using a passive-voiced verb.

If the examining physician knows that the person *being examined* [rather than "he is examining"] has been under treatment . . .

Warning: Use this technique sparingly. As section IV explains, overusing the passive voice is not good style.

6. Substitute "one." This technique is a little stilted, but it may suffice from time to time.

Change   A person should always tell the truth in order to preserve his reputation.
To   One should always tell the truth in order to preserve one's reputation.

The less formal "you" or "your" may work in less formal documents, but *not* in court documents.

You should always tell the truth in order to preserve *your* reputation.

7. Rephrase the clause entirely.

Change   For each speaker, enclosed is an outline of his presentation, a copy of
           the exercise he has prepared, and a memorandum explaining his
           exercise.
To   Each speaker has prepared a presentation outline, an exercise, and an
           explanatory memorandum. Copies are enclosed.

8. Where elimination, substitution, and rephrasing fail, use both pronouns separated by a conjunction, such as "and" or "or."

A parent may enroll his or her child . . .

9. Several techniques you will see in other contexts are *not* recommended for formal professional writing. Examples include:

his/her; he/she
s/he
"her" in place of "his"
alternating between "his" and "her"

You have no doubt noticed that this text intentionally does not use formal professional style. One of the several ways in which it does not is its use of both "him" and "her" for general reference. This choice is designed to reflect the reality that the world in general and lawyers in particular are made up of people of both genders. Simply avoiding gender reference does nothing to change the unconscious assumptions we have all inherited; yet those assumptions impoverish us all. A few mental pictures of women as lawyers, judges, and clients can help to counteract the thousands of years that the mental images of those groups were entirely men.

However, the purposes of a legal document are different from the purposes of this text. A legal document is designed to represent a client. Legal documents should avoid writing that calls attention to the writer's own personal causes, no matter how certain the writer is of them. Therefore, in legal documents, avoid using either gender for general references. If you cannot avoid gendered references, use both as described in item 8 above.

C.　Techniques for Proper Names and Titles

Refer to a client in the way the client prefers. However, if the client does not have a preference, gender-neutral writing requires consistency of treatment. Unless you have a strategic reason for different treatment, decide whether to use courtesy titles, like Mr. or Ms., and treat all names in the same fashion, regardless of gender.

1.　Be consistent in the use of courtesy titles. If you do not use "Mr." for men, do not use "Miss," "Mrs.," or "Ms." for women.

2.　Unless you have a good reason, use "Ms." rather than "Mrs." or "Miss." The object is to treat men and women the same. Since the courtesy title for men ("Mr.") does not indicate a marital status, the title for women should not do so either. You can decide to use "Mrs." or "Miss" when a reader prefers it, when the legal issue makes marital status relevant, when using the title will eliminate confusion, or when you have a particular strategic reason.[14]

3.　Be consistent in the use of first names and last names. You can use last names only, first and last names together, or (rarely) first names only. However, unless you have a good strategic reason,[15] apply your decision equally to both genders.

14.　*See* Chapter 21.
15.　*See* Chapter 21.

FOCUS ON STRONG SUBJECTS AND VERBS

Perhaps the most important goal for improving your writing style is developing techniques to keep your writing focused on strong subjects and verbs. Here are some of the best techniques for accomplishing this goal.

1. Passive voice. Much legal writing is filled with unnecessary passive verbs. Learn to spot them, evaluate whether they serve a purpose, and get rid of them if they do not. You can learn to recognize passive verbs by checking the subject of the sentence. Identify the subject and ask yourself whether the subject performed the action described by the verb. If it did, then you have used a verb in the active voice. If it did not, but instead was acted *upon,* you have found a passive-voiced verb. You'll be surprised at how soon you develop the ability to spot passives easily.

> *Active*   Ms. Watson signed a covenant-not-to-compete.
> *Passive*   A covenant-not-to-compete was signed by Ms. Watson.

The subject of the first sentence is Ms. Watson. Did she do what the verb describes? Did she "sign"? Yes she did, and therefore you know that the first sentence uses the active voice. However, the subject of the second sentence is the covenant. Did the covenant sign? Of course not. The covenant was acted upon; the signing happened *to* the covenant. Therefore you know that the second sentence uses the passive voice.

Why are sentences overloaded with passive verbs undesirable? First, writing in the passive voice uses more words. You can see this on a small scale in the example above, and the effect can compound in a sentence with more than one passive verb.

> *Passive*   It was insisted by Carrolton that the covenant had been breached by
>   Ms. Watson.
> *Active*   Carrolton insisted that Ms. Watson had breached the covenant.

Locate the passive verbs in the first sentence, which contains fourteen words. Notice that the second sentence contains only nine words, a reduction of 36 percent. Avoiding verbs in the passive voice will help to reduce wordiness.

Second, sentences in the passive voice often omit altogether the identity of the actor; yet the actor's identity is usually (though not always) important. These versions of our earlier examples reflect this problem of ambiguity (or complete mystery):

> A covenant-not-to-compete was signed. [Who signed?]

> It was insisted that the covenant had been breached. [Who insisted? Who breached?]

Perhaps the context surrounding the sentences will supply the answer, but perhaps not. Writing in the active voice will help you write clearly.

Finally, writing in the active voice is more forceful. A sentence in the active voice drives forward in a straight line; the subject "does" the action to the object. But a sentence in the passive voice moves in reverse, backing in stops and starts toward the subject. Like a car, a sentence driving ahead moves more smoothly and forcefully than a sentence in reverse.

While writing in the active voice is generally preferable, an occasional passive-voiced verb can serve a particular function. For instance, section III explained that a passive verb can sometimes eliminate the need for using a masculine noun or pronoun. In persuasive writing, as Chapter 21 will explain, a number of strategic considerations may call for a passive verb. Also, sometimes the identity of the "actor" really is unimportant, and a passive verb can appropriately focus the attention on the object of the action. A passive verb may allow you to avoid references in court documents to yourself or your firm. And sometimes using a passive verb can allow you to begin the sentence with a smooth transition from earlier material.

However, most legal writing, including the case opinions you spend so much time reading, relies far too much on verbs in the passive voice. Because so much of what you are reading everyday is infected with passivitis, you will have to struggle against developing the habit yourself.

2. Nominalizations. The second technique for focusing on strong subjects and verbs is to avoid nominalizations. Nominalizations are nouns that began life as a verb and should have been content with their lot in life. When such a verb aspires to upward social mobility, it finds that it needs a crowd around it. Suddenly, your sentence has several more words than it used to.

No nominalization	The sellers decided to accept the buyer's offer.
One nominalization	The sellers *made a decision* to accept the buyer's offer.

If your sentence contains several nominalizations, the party can get really out of hand.

No nominalizations	The sellers decided to accept the buyer's offer, so they authorized their broker to announce their decision.
Three nominalizations	The sellers *made a decision* to accept the buyer's offer, so they *issued an authorization to* their broker to *make an announcement of* their decision.

Wordiness isn't the only problem nominalizations cause. Sentences using nominalizations are both weaker and less clear than sentences in which the verbs stay where they belong. Since nominalizations are still verbs at heart, they don't do a very good job of being nouns; they are by nature more vague than "real" nouns. Worse yet, when the hole left by the departed verb is filled, the substitute verb is usually weaker than the departed verb.[16] These

---

16. Verbs like "make," "issue," "is," or "had" are much weaker than action verbs like "agree," "announce," "object," "collide," or "revise."

consequences combine to weaken the sentence and obscure the meaning.

Here are examples of common nominalizations and the verb forms to which they should return.

Change	*To*
enter into an agreement	agree
contains a provision	provides
have a collision	collide
file a motion	move
give consideration to	consider
had knowledge that	knew
effect a termination	terminate
make an assumption	assume
make a decision	decide
places emphasis on	emphasizes
it is a requirement of the contract that	the contract requires that
commencement of discovery will occur	discovery will commence

3.   Throat-clearing.   Another major obstacle to focusing on strong subjects and verbs is the habit of "throat-clearing"—using introductory phrases that communicate little more than "I'm getting ready to say something here." In the judicial opinions and practitioner-writing you see, you'll notice an abundance of it. Often throat-clearing phrases begin with "it is" and end with "that." Here are some examples:

It is interesting to note that . . .
It is important to remember that . . .
It seems that . . .
It is clear (or obvious) that . . .
It is widely understood that . . .
As noted above . . .
As to . . .
With respect (or regard) to . . .

Other examples introduce an assertion by claiming responsibility for it, such as "The defendant submits (or believes, argues, or contends) that . . ."

One can speculate about why these phrases slip into our writing. They may reflect a natural human insecurity about the material that is to follow; they may reflect an inaccurate perception that these phrases elevate the tone or convey an objective perspective; they may simply be habits born of reading the legal writing of others. Whatever the reason, throat-clearing phrases impede rather than advance good writing. If some of these phrases slip into your writing in the working draft stage, edit them out in revision. Let your sentences proceed directly to your point without working into that point with a throat-clearing phrase.

4.   Placement of modifying phrases: Keep the subject and verb close together.   The basic components of a sentence are the subject, the verb, and the object, and a reader tackles a sentence by searching for those components. First, a reader looks for the subject. Once the subject is found, the reader's urge to find the verb is strong. The primary meaning of a sentence is communicated by the *combination* of the subject and the verb. A reader who can't find and mentally combine them quickly will be frustrated and confused.

The primary impediment to finding and mentally combining the subject and verb is the placement of long modifying phrases between them. Legal writers are especially prone to this weakness. Usually the problem is caused by trying to say too much in one sentence. For example, consider this sentence:

> In the first month of his marriage, the defendant, who was only nineteen at the time and who had not completed high school or developed a trade and who had just lost his part-time job, was charged with robbing a convenience store at the corner of Bayside and Tenth Avenue.

This writer has a lot to say about the defendant—probably more than one sentence should carry. The result is the placement of several modifying phrases or clauses between the subject and the verb.

The solution is to remove those interrupting modifying phrases and clauses. Since the sentence really has no other place for them, they indicate that another sentence is necessary. Notice that the information about the defendant falls into two categories: general information about the defendant and specific information about a particular event. The solution is to use separate sentences, one or more for each category of information.

> In the first month of his marriage, the defendant was charged with robbing a convenience store at the corner of Bayside and Tenth Avenue. He was only nineteen at the time. He had not completed high school or developed a trade, and he had just lost his part-time job.

Not only is the second version easier to read, but it helps the reader organize the information as well.

Use these guidelines to manage long modifying phrases:

- Where clarity is not a problem, move the long phrase to one end of the sentence. This placement allows the reader to read quickly; it places the primary emphasis on the main clause, where it usually belongs; and it maximizes clarity.
- If clarity is a problem, place the modifying phrase close to the word it modifies. Placing a modifying phrase some distance from the word it modifies jeopardizes clarity. If the resulting sentence separates the subject and verb by too great a distance, separate the material into two or more sentences.
- Place a long phrase in the middle of the sentence only when you have a good rhetorical reason for doing so,[17] and only when the placement will not cost the sentence its readability.

---

17. *See* Chapter 21.

5.   Break up long sentences.   Remember that the more complex the message, the simpler the medium must be. Break up sentences that are longer than roughly twenty-five words. Long sentences bury the subject and verb.

6.   Avoid beginning sentences with forms of "It is" or "There is." Sentence constructions beginning with forms of "it is" or "there is" always lack force and often lack clarity. Like the constructions described above, they obscure the subject and verb. Try to reword these constructions to put the "real" subject and action up front in their usual spots.

Change   It is unethical to contact a party represented by another lawyer.
To   Contacting a party represented by another lawyer is unethical.

Change   There are four defendants seeking dismissal on jurisdictional grounds.
To   Four defendants are seeking dismissal on jurisdictional grounds.

Change   It was that kindness that may have cost David his life.
To   That kindness may have cost David his life.

 AVOID WORDINESS

1.   Watch for phrases that can be replaced by a single word.   Unnecessary phrases abound in poor legal writing. Phrases beginning with "the fact that" are nearly always culprits, but many other phrases constitute clutter as well. Here are examples of common unnecessary phrases and their single-word synonyms.

Change	*To*
at the time when	when
at the point in time when	when
as a result of	because
by reason of the fact that	because
due to the fact that	because
for a period of one week	for one week
for the purpose of	to
for these reasons	therefore
inasmuch as	since
in many cases	often
in order to	to
it was formerly the case that	formerly; previously
previous to	before
that was a case where	there

Also watch for substantive points that take up more than their fair share of space.

Change	the contract between Wigby and Matthews
To	the Wigby/Matthews contract
Change	The buyer discovered six violations of code requirements. All of the violations dealt with plumbing.
To	The buyer discovered six plumbing code violations.
Change	. . . for the purpose for which it was intended . . .
To	. . . for the intended purpose . . .

2. Avoid matched pairs. At the time of the Norman conquest in 1066, English legal language was already a blend of Anglo-Saxon and Latin terms. Then came the Normans, with their own terms for legal matters. Because the conquering Normans had to establish a legal system that would govern the people of the land—whether Norman or Anglo-Saxon—the language of the legal system had to be understandable by each group. A common solution was to use Norman and Anglo-Saxon terms, side by side. Thus, English legal language developed *matched pairs,* two words commonly used together but having the same or nearly the same meaning. We see examples of this practice today in the following terms:

adjudged and decreed	full and complete
alter and change	good and sufficient
attorney and counselor	null and void
bind and obligate	stipulate and agree
by and through	true and correct
cease and desist	use and benefit
covenant and agree	will and testament
each and every	

The need that created matched pairs nearly ten centuries ago is gone. Today, matched pairs not only unnecessarily clutter good writing, but they can cloud meaning as well. Intelligent readers unfamiliar with the strange custom assume that the words must mean something different, or why would the writer have used them both? Since some of your most important writing will be addressed to nonlawyers (clients, for instance), it is best to avoid using matched pairs. When the two terms mean the same thing, choose the shorter or more familiar of the two and discard the other.

3. Avoid legalese. For the same reasons, purge your writing of unnecessary legalese. When writing to a law-trained reader, you may choose to use some legal terms unfamiliar to laypersons because those terms communicate legal concepts more clearly and concisely than nonlegal terms would. But do not resort to the jargon of law unless it is necessary to convey your point clearly and concisely. Here are examples of unnecessary legalese:

assuming *arguendo*
the *instant* case
the *above-captioned* case
the *said* defendant
the *aforementioned* contract

the items *hereinafter* described
to remove *therefrom*
to wit
whereas
the party of the first part
supra (except when properly used in a legal citation)
all Latin words except those few that have become true terms of art (such as "pro
se," "res ipsa," "pro bono," "prima facie")

4.   Avoid redundancies.   Redundancies can slip into language easily. Here are examples:

advance planning	past experience
final outcome	point in time
first and foremost	reason is because
honest truth	whether or not
old adage	

5.   Unnecessary variations.   Clear legal writing requires consistency in terms. Once you pick a term, use the same term for each reference. Otherwise your reader will have to decide, with each new term, whether you mean something different from the prior term. Professor Wydick uses this example:

> The first case was settled for $20,000, and the second piece of litigation was disposed of out of court for $30,000, while the price of the amicable accord reached in the third suit was $50,000.

> The readers are left to ponder the difference between a *case*, a *piece of litigation*, and a *suit*. By the time they conclude that there is no difference, they have no patience left for *settled, disposed of out of court*, and *amicable accord*, much less for what the writer was trying to tell them in the first place.[18]

In legal writing, consistency is important. Don't worry about seeming repetitious; it is far more important to be understood.

6.   Avoid intensifiers.   Because generations of writers have overused words like "clearly" or "very," these and other common intensifiers have become virtually meaningless. As a matter of fact, they have begun to develop a connotation exactly opposite their original meaning. So many writers (lawyers and judges alike) have used those labels in place of well-reasoned analysis that some readers see these intensifiers as signaling a weak analysis. Rid your writing of these words:

clearly	quite
extremely	very
obviously	

---

18.   Richard C. Wydick, *Plain English for Lawyers* 66 (3d ed. 1994).

7. Avoid unnecessary qualifiers. While editing, watch for these and other unnecessary qualifiers that may have slipped into your document.

"hopefully"[19]	probably
in my opinion	rather
maybe	somewhat
perhaps	

 VI **MISCELLANEOUS**

1. Tabulate. When your document deals with several items (elements of a rule, factors, guidelines, categories of facts), tabulating the items will help your reader navigate through the substance of your text.

> The plaintiff must prove (1) that the defendant owed a duty to the plaintiff; (2) that the defendant breached that duty; (3) that the plaintiff suffered compensable damages; and (4) that the defendant's breach proximately caused those damages.

Not only will a tabulated list be easier for your reader to understand, but the process of listing and tabulating gives you another chance to double-check your analysis, and demonstrates to the reader that you are controlling the content rather than the other way around.

2. Names of Parties. You have three basic choices for referring to people: (1) use some form of the person's name, such as last name only, first and last name, or last name with a courtesy title; (2) use a procedural designation, such as plaintiff or appellee; or (3) use a characterization based on the person's role in the factual story, such as "landlord" or "tenant." Unless you have a strategic goal that counsels otherwise,[20] choose the reference that will be easiest for your reader to follow.

If your document refers only to a few people, the reader probably will have no difficulty in following references either by name or by procedural title. If your document refers to more people or to a group of individuals, or if the litigation has several parties with the same procedural title, consider creating a reference based on the person's role. For instance, the document might refer to Fitzpatrick, Cramer, Burns, and Wells, who are joint venturers in a business enterprise. You could refer to them all as "the joint venturers." Or the document may refer to Baldwin and Sammons, the buyer and seller, respectively, of real property. You could refer to Baldwin as "the buyer," to Sammons as

---

19. "Hopefully" appears in quotation marks because it is not a qualifier at all, but is often misused as one.

20. *See* Chapter 21.

"the seller," and to both of them together as "the contracting parties." Whichever you choose, be consistent. Readers are easily confused by encountering several different references for the same person.

3.   Names of Things.   If the document refers to only one of a certain thing, the generic name will be the best form of reference. For instance, if the document refers to only one contract, "the contract" is the clearest and easiest reference. If the document refers to several contracts, find an easy identifying characteristic and use the same characteristic to distinguish between the contracts. For instance, common distinguishing characteristics for several contracts are the dates or the parties of each: "the September 5 contract" and "the December 23 contract," or "the Owens contract" and "the Guzman contract." Just as with references to people, be consistent.

4.   Numbers.   Write out numbers from zero to ninety-nine using letters. For numbers over ninety-nine, use numerals unless the number begins a sentence. Irrespective of the general rule, use numerals if the number contains decimal points, when numbers appear in a series, or when material repeatedly refers to percentages or dollar amounts.[21]

5.   Avoid multiple negatives.   As a general rule, affirmative statements are easier to understand than are negative statements. This difference in readability is magnified when the sentence uses two negatives, and more than two makes a sentence nearly impossible. For instance, consider this sentence:

> A plea setting up a contract of settlement of the plaintiff's claim is insufficient where it does not allege that the infant had not dissipated the consideration and was able to restore it and had not restored it.

This sentence has four negatives. Most readers will be unable to make sense of this sentence without four or five slow readings. Now consider this revision:

> A plea setting up a contract of settlement of the plaintiff's claim must allege that the infant has retained the consideration, is able to restore it, and has not done so.

This revision cuts the four negatives down to one. The first two negatives were eliminated by making an affirmative statement of the required pleading rather than a negative statement about the lack of the required pleading. The third negative was simply omitted because the allegation that the infant has retained the consideration necessarily means that the infant has not dissipated it. The one remaining negative, stated clearly, does not cause the reader any difficulty.

The remedies for multiple negatives will be as varied as the sentences that contain them. The key is to develop the habit of noticing them so you can edit them out.

---

21.   *See* The Bluebook Rule 6.2.

6. Notice unintended humor. Finally, notice and correct any unintended humor.

The owner was attached to the renovations.

Lewis relieved himself of the notebook.

The failure to connect the light switch to the outlet is a defect in my mind.

When asked for a little more detail, the skeleton of the problem began to form.

He discussed the fact that the chemical was being stored in a concrete surface impoundment basin with both Ms. Blair and Mr. Shore.

 Checklist for Language and Usage Errors

1. Have you avoided using contractions, slang, and note-taking abbreviations? p. 218.
2. Have you avoided unnecessary personal references? pp. 218-219.
3. When referring to material in a legal authority, have you used "in which" rather than "where?" p. 221.
4. Have you used "found guilty" or "convicted" for a criminal matter and "held liable" for a civil matter? p. 221.
5. Where possible, have you used short form references to parties with long names? Have you introduced the references with a parenthetical (DHS)? pp. 233-234.
6. Have you used footnotes sparingly or not at all? p. 221.
7. Have you used a past tense verb when referring to something the court did ("the court held")? p. 220.
8. Have you used "find" for a court's decision about facts and "hold" for a court's decision about law? pp. 219-220.
9. Have you used a present tense verb for the rule set out in an authority ("the court held that a covenant *is* enforceable")? p. 220.
10. Have you avoided saying that the court "argued" or "stipulated"? p. 220.
11. Have you said that the *court* held or decided rather than that the *opinion* held or decided? p. 220.
12. Have you capitalized particular documents actually filed, but avoided capitalizing names of categories of documents? p. 220.
13. Have you capitalized "Court" only when appropriate? p. 220.
14. Have you capitalized the procedural titles of the parties in your case but not the procedural titles of parties in legal authorities? p. 220.
15. Have you purged your document of sarcasm, anger, humor, and rhetorical questions? p. 219.
16. Have you avoided gendered writing? pp. 221-225.
17. Have you avoided overusing passive verbs? pp. 226-227.
18. Have you avoided nominalizations? pp. 227-228.
19. Have you edited out throat-clearing phrases? p. 228.

20. Have you kept your subjects and verbs close together? pp. 228-230.
21. Have you broken up long sentences? p. 230.
22. Have you avoided unnecessarily beginning sentences with "it is" or "there is"? p. 230.
23. Have you edited wordy phrases, replacing them with shorter synonyms? pp. 230-231.
24. Have you avoided matched pairs? p. 231.
25. Have you avoided legalese? pp. 231-232.
26. Have you checked for redundancies and unnecessary variations? p. 232.
27. Have you deleted unnecessary intensifiers and qualifiers? pp. 232-233.
28. Have you tabulated lists? p. 233.
29. When appropriate have you used generic references for people and things? pp. 233-234.
30. Have you confirmed whether to write out numbers or use arabic numerals? p. 234.
31. Have you avoided multiple negatives? p. 234.

At last you are done. You have been through a long and difficult process. The process required you to (1) formulate a rule of law, (2) articulate it in a rule structure, (3) use that structure to create the large-scale organization of your analysis, (4) write out a working draft of the analysis for each subpart of the rule, (5) convert the working draft to the Discussion section of a memo designed for a particular reader, (6) add the other components of an office memo, (7) edit for proper and effective citation form and quotations, and (8) edit the draft for tone, formality, usage, gender-neutral writing, grammar, punctuation, and style.

Working through this process is among the hardest and most complex of all tasks a lawyer must perform, but certainly among the most important as well. Congratulations for making it through each step. Your conscious use of each stage of the process to achieve the particular goals of that stage has helped you deepen your analysis and confirm its accuracy. It has also helped you produce a complete and useful document, free from technical errors. If you continue to use this process, consciously and carefully, it will dramatically improve your skills of both analysis and expression for many years to come.

THE PROCESS OF WRITING PERSUASIVELY: THE BRIEF

II

STRUCTURING FOR PERSUASION: OUTLINING THE WORKING DRAFT

stage one

Ethics, Judges, and Briefs

In Part I, we saw that the process of writing an office memo divides into four stages. Brief-writing does too, but in some ways the stages are more complex. In the two working draft stages (Chapters 16-19), you must do more than structure a rule from the authorities; you must structure the most favorable rule you reasonably can. In the third stage, converting your working draft into a brief (Chapters 20 and 21), you must do more than organize logically; you also must organize to persuade. Finally, in the fourth stage, editing the brief (Chapter 22), you must edit not only for style and compliance with technical rules, but also for persuasion.

The briefs you write will be vital to your clients. The outcome of most cases depends on the judge's rulings on numerous legal questions arising during the litigation. Most of those issues will be decided after you have filed a brief. The judge is usually more influenced by the brief than by any other form of argument the lawyer makes. Therefore, for your client's sake, your brief must be thorough, well-written, accurate, honest, free of technical errors, and in compliance with the court's rules.

Your brief-writing will be important to you as well. Your reputation as a lawyer will be built, in significant part, by the care you take in brief-writing. And reputation is more than just a personal matter; it is an integral part of your professional effectiveness. Over the course of her career, a lawyer with a reputation for honest and careful work will be able to accomplish much more for her clients than a lawyer with a reputation for dishonesty or slipshod work. Thus, every brief you write is a document with persuasive impact, for good or for ill, not only on the pending case, but on all cases you will handle in the future.

Finally, your brief-writing will be important to your firm. A firm's reputation is built by the quality of the work its lawyers produce, and especially by the quality of the writing the firm allows to pass through its doors. Your firm's reputation will affect its ability to attract clients and its ability to represent them effectively. So write as if your practice depends on it, because it does.

We begin our study of brief-writing with these three cardinal rules: Be honest. Be accurate. Be clear. The honesty, accuracy, and clarity of the lawyers' arguments will affect a judge's decision far more than any strategy or rhetoric the lawyers could employ. The starting points for thinking about these cardinal rules are the characteristics of judges as readers, the ethical duties that govern lawyers as advocates, and an overview of the document that must comply with these rules—the brief.

 # THE ETHICAL RESPONSIBILITIES OF A BRIEF-WRITER

In addition to the ethical duties set out in Chapter 1 (competence, diligence, loyalty, promptness, confidentiality), formulating persuasive rules and arguments raises several other professional duties. You will need to be aware of these duties as you explore possible rule formulations and legal or factual arguments.

1. A brief-writer must not knowingly make a false statement of law.[1] This means, for example, that the writer must not assert that a particular case stands for a proposition of law when no reasonable interpretation of the case would yield that proposition. It also means that the writer cannot rely on a holding without disclosing that the case has been reversed or overruled. Many law-trained readers maintain that citing an authority is an implicit representation that the writer has read the authority itself (not just the headnotes). Whether it is or not, citing an authority you have not read and updated is unprofessional and extraordinarily risky. Never do it.

2. A brief-writer must not knowingly fail to disclose to the court directly adverse legal authority in the controlling jurisdiction.[2] The writer is not required to disclose the adverse authority if it has been disclosed already by other counsel. However, omitting the authority from an opening brief probably cannot be justified by the argument that the lawyer was simply waiting to see if opposing counsel would raise it in reply.[3]

Disclosure is not only ethically required, but it is strategically wise as well. If you wait for the opposing lawyer to raise the adverse authority, you forgo

---

1. Model Rules of Professional Conduct Rule 3.3(a)(1) (1994). *See also* Model Code of Professional Responsibility DR 7-102(A)(5) (1980).

2. Model Rules of Professional Conduct Rule 3.3(a)(3) (1994). *See also* Model Code of Professional Responsibility DR 7-106(B)(1) (1980).

3. *Jorgenson v. County of Volusia,* 846 F.2d 1350 (11th Cir. 1988) (applying Fed. R. Civ. P. 11).

the chance to be the first to interpret the authority and explain its impact. Allowing opposing counsel the first shot at interpreting the authority means that you start out behind and must make up that lost analytical ground.

The scope of the duty to disclose can be articulated in several ways, most often focusing either on the question of whether the case is one that the judge should consider or on the more subjective reactions of a "reasonable judge." In a pre-Model Rules Formal Opinion, the ABA Ethics Committee adopted both articulations.

> The test in every case should be: Is the decision which opposing counsel has overlooked one which the court should clearly consider in deciding the case? Would a reasonable judge properly feel that a lawyer who advanced, as the law, a proposition adverse to the undisclosed decision, was lacking in candor and fairness to him? Might the judge consider himself misled by an implied representation that the lawyer knew of no adverse authority?[4]

The ABA Model Rule expressly requires disclosure only if the authority is in the controlling jurisdiction, but some jurisdictions broaden the requirement. For instance, the New Jersey Supreme Court requires, on federal questions, disclosure of adverse decisions of any federal court.[5]

3. A brief-writer must not knowingly make a false statement of fact or fail to disclose a material fact when disclosure is necessary to avoid assisting a criminal or fraudulent act by the client.[6] The duty to refrain from false statements of fact applies throughout the brief, not merely to the section of the brief labeled "Statement of Facts" or "Statement of the Case."[7]

4. A brief-writer must not assert a legal argument unless there is a nonfrivolous basis for doing so. A position that argues for an extension, modification, or reversal of existing law is not frivolous. When defending the accused in a criminal matter, it is not frivolous to require that every element of the case be established.[8]

A claim is not frivolous merely because the lawyer believes that ultimately it will fail.[9] But when a lawyer cannot "make a good faith argument on the merits of the action" the claim is frivolous.[10] The attorney's subjective belief is not sufficient to meet the standard. The test is whether a reasonable, competent attorney would believe that the argument could have merit.[11]

---

4. ABA Committee on Ethics and Professional Responsibility, Formal Op. 280 (1949).

5. *In re Greenberg,* 15 N.J. 132, 104 A.2d 46 (1954).

6. Model Rules of Professional Conduct Rule 3.3(a)(1) and (2) (1994). *See also* Model Code of Professional Responsibility DR 7-102 (A)(3) and (5) (1980).

7. *See* Chapter 21.

8. Model Rules of Professional Conduct Rule 3.1 (1994). *See also* Model Code of Professional Responsibility DR 7-102(A)(1) (1980); Fed. R. Civ. P. 11 (establishing an affirmative duty to investigate the law and the facts).

9. Model Rules of Professional Conduct Rule 3.1 cmt. 2 (1994).

10. *Id.*

11. *See, e.g., Beeman v. Fiester,* 852 F.2d 206, 211 (7th Cir. 1988).

The meaning of "frivolous" in this context often is subject to debate, even among experienced lawyers. In the early years of law study, while you are still observing the kinds of arguments that do and do not have persuasive value for judges, you may feel particularly at sea with this standard. When you suspect that you may be approaching the line, consider doing two things: (1) Ask a more experienced lawyer whether the argument might be frivolous.[12] (2) Ask yourself (and the more experienced lawyer) whether making such a marginal argument is good strategy, even if the argument is permissible. If you are wondering whether the argument is so weak that it might be considered frivolous, your position may be stronger without it.[13]

5.   A brief-writer must not communicate ex parte[14] with a judge about the merits of a pending case, unless the particular ex parte communication is specifically permitted by law.[15]   In the context of brief-writing, this means that you must provide each party (through counsel, if any) with a copy of your brief. Court rules require certification that you have done so.[16]

6.   A brief-writer must not intentionally disregard filing requirements or other obligations imposed by court rules.[17]   Virtually all courts operate under rules of procedure that set out the applicable time deadlines and format requirements for your brief. Many courts impose page limits, and some prescribe the margins and number of permissible characters per inch. You can guess the purpose behind these rules. It may be tempting to change the font or ignore the margin requirements so that you can file a longer brief, but it is neither ethical nor wise to do so. Resist the temptation, both in practice *and* in your legal writing course.

II ◇ JUDGES AS READERS

Judges share the characteristics of other law-trained readers.[18] Their attention is finite. They are busy and impatient with delay in getting to the bottom line. They generally focus more attention on the beginning and end of a document or a section than on the middle. They find facts engrossing. They want a road

---

12.   Take care not to violate any honor code regulations pertaining to your law school assignment or your duty of confidentiality to a client.

13.   *See* Chapter 17.

14.   *Ex parte,* in this context, means without notice to other parties in the litigation.

15.   Model Rules of Professional Conduct Rule 3.5 (1994); *See also* Model Code of Professional Responsibility DR 7-110 (B) (1980).

16.   *See* pp. 250-251.

17.   Model Rules of Professional Conduct Rules 3.4 and 3.2 (1994). *See also* Model Code of Professional Conduct DR 7-106(A) (1980).

18.   *See* section I of Chapter 11.

map. They value clear organization that sets out the rule of law. But judges tend to have some additional characteristics as well. Here are some other observations about how judges read.

1. While any law-trained reader is a skeptical reader, testing the analysis at each step, a judge is particularly so. This skepticism and testing is the heart of a judge's job. Girvan Peck explained it by describing judges as "professional buyers of ideas."[19] However, even a skeptical judge will be less skeptical of the analysis of a lawyer known for careful and honest work than of the analysis of a lawyer with a poor reputation for either competency or candor.

2. Because judges are human, a judge who is already convinced of the equities of your position will be more receptive to your legal arguments. This judge will *want* you to be right on the law. This human desire can help to overcome a little of the judge's natural skepticism.

3. Most of us are more willing to accept the analysis of one whom we like and of one who has been considerate of our needs. This is true of judges as well. This does not mean that judges decide cases on the basis of social and political connections. But a lawyer who treats the judge professionally, with respect and consideration, will be a more effective advocate than the lawyer who does not.

4. As public servants with public responsibilities, judges are concerned about the social policy implications of their decisions. However, trial judges and judges serving on intermediate appellate courts know that their role requires them to apply the law the way the jurisdiction's highest court would. Not only do judges prefer having their orders affirmed rather than reversed, but reversals often mean having to deal with the case again. A judge's goal is to resolve cases, not protract them.

Therefore, trial judges and judges serving on an intermediate appellate court are most persuaded by authorities that help them predict how the higher court would decide the question. Before these judges, policy arguments are secondary to mandatory authority. Judges serving on the highest appellate court in the jurisdiction are much more amenable to policy arguments than are their colleagues on lower courts.

5. Because most judges plan to spend many years on the bench, they take a long-term view of each legal issue. Judges are concerned about how an individual ruling may constrain or empower them in future cases.

6. Lawyers as a group tend to be personally conservative (though not necessarily politically so). This is particularly true of judges. Because of the public nature of their job and the fact that they are seen as safeguarders of public morality, lawyers who become judges tend to be conservative in their personal lifestyle.

7. People tend to cling more tenaciously to conclusions they think they have reached themselves than to those asserted by others. Judges are no different. Thus, when a judge notices that the writer is using a particular technique for persuasion, the technique loses its effectiveness. Heavy-handed use of a persuasive technique will usually hurt more than it helps. By far, the most effective persuasive techniques are invisible to the reader.

---

19.   Girvan Peck, *Writing Persuasive Briefs* 77 (1984).

8. A reader who feels pushed will resist. An effective legal argument will not push an unwilling reader down a path. Rather, an effective legal argument will place the reader at a vantage point that allows the *reader* to see and take the best path. Thus, as a brief writer, you must decide how far you can take the judge without losing the judge's cooperation in the process. The consequences of pushing a judge to accept an unreasonable argument go beyond the judge's rejection of the *un*reasonable parts of the argument. The judge will tend to reject the *reasonable* parts of the argument as well.

9. Judges read briefs in order to decide between legal positions. When such readers are presented with categories, particularly categories identified with point headings, they tend to keep score. They may not even realize that they are doing it, and they often will not observe that the rhetorical effect of keeping score is to weight each category equally. As Chapter 17 will demonstrate, knowing this tendency should help a writer select an organizational plan and decide how to subdivide the argument.

10. As decision-makers encounter arguments, one by one, they tend to label each argument as "weak" or "strong" before going on to the next argument. Decision-makers are more likely to be convinced by one strong argument than by a series of weak ones. Also, a strong argument will lose some of its force if it follows or is followed by weak arguments on the same point.

11. The reader's perception of the strength of the first argument affects the reader's perception of the strength of the arguments that follow. As law-trained readers, judges expect to find the strongest argument first. Unless the judge knows of a reason that the weak argument had to be discussed first, the judge will presume that the strongest argument is first, and thus that subsequent arguments are even weaker.

12. Judges often relate to the lawyers who practice in their courts much like parents relate to children. Those of you who are parents know that there is nothing quite as tiresome and irritating as constant fighting and bickering among children. Most judges have little tolerance for bickering and blustering lawyers. Judges much prefer to focus on legal issues rather than on the personalities or practices of the lawyers in the case.

13. One final observation about judges as readers—the judge may not read your brief at all; the judge may ask a law clerk to read and summarize the briefs for both sides. So you need to think, too, about the characteristics of law clerks as readers.

Law clerks tend to be young and recent law graduates, with little or no practice experience. They probably have not had much experience in dealing with most of the issues raised in the briefs they see. They may not be as personally conservative as their judges, though remember that the judges did the hiring. Usually clerks' positions last only one to two years, so their perspective on the consequences of individual results may not be as far-sighted as the judge's. They may be more politicized on certain issues, bringing to those questions the vigor of an advocate.

The impact of a law clerk on the brief-reading process is a bit of a wild card. If the judge has law clerks, you probably will not know whether the judge has assigned your brief to one of them. Even if you knew, the high turnover rate and the relative invisibility of those positions probably means that you will have little access to information about this person. Attempting to apply general characteristics to an unknown law clerk is problematic since law clerks as a group tend to be more diverse than their employers. However, despite the personal predilections of a law clerk, the strongest motivation of most law clerks is to please the judge.

There are two general observations that you *should* keep in mind, however. First, is the relative inexperience of most law clerks as compared to most judges. This means that you will want to take care not to leave out steps in the analysis on the assumption that your reader is the judge and that the judge is an expert.

Second, while these readers are often inexperienced, they also tend to be bright. Many judicial clerks served on their school's law review and received much of their formative training in that context. Thus, they expect the details of a brief to be right. They tend to draw conclusions about the reliability of the analysis based on the lawyer's attention to these details. They may well scrutinize every aspect of your brief more thoroughly than a busy judge could.

 ## III   AN OVERVIEW OF THE BRIEF

While it might seem that a brief, being a court document, would have a more standardized format than would an internal document like an office memo, a comparison of sample briefs will quickly dispel this notion. Trial-level briefs differ from appellate-level briefs; state court briefs of each level differ from federal court briefs of each level; briefs filed in one jurisdiction differ from briefs filed in another; briefs originating from one firm differ from briefs originating from another; response and reply briefs differ from opening briefs. It may seem that the most one can say about the components of all briefs is that they all have an Argument!

This variety is no cause for concern, however. The following sections describe each component you may see or be asked to include in your brief. Simply include those required by the applicable court rule, by local or firm custom, or by the particular circumstances and legal issues of the case. The trial- and appellate-level briefs in Appendices B and C can serve as examples of customary formats. When in doubt about whether to include a particular section, ask your teacher or the attorney for whom you are writing the brief. If no instructions are available, here are guidelines for which components to include and the order in which to place them.

Component	Trial-Level Brief	Appellate Brief
Caption	Yes	Yes
Table of Contents	Yes, if the brief is long and complex	Yes
Table of Authorities	Only if the brief cites many sources	Yes

Component	Trial-Level Brief	Appellate Brief
Statutes Involved	Yes, if providing the text would help the reader	Yes, if feasible; otherwise provide statute's text as an Appendix
Opinion Below	No	Optional
Jurisdiction	No	Optional
Standard of Review	Only if the trial court is reviewing a matter decided in another forum	Yes[20]
Preliminary Statement[21]	Optional	Optional
Questions Presented[22]	Yes, if the brief covers several issues	Yes
Statement of Facts[23]	Yes	Yes
Summary of Argument	Only if the brief is long and complex	Yes
Argument	Yes	Yes
Conclusion	Yes	Yes
Certificate of Service	Yes	Yes

   1.   Caption.   The function of the Caption is simply to identify the case and the document. For examples of customary formatting on the page, refer to the captions and titles for the briefs in Appendices B and C. In cases with multiple parties, the brief's caption need list only the first plaintiff and the first defendant followed by "et al."[24] The caption must include the case number assigned by the court.[25] Court rules may require additional information such as the name and address of the attorney or the name of the assigned judge. The caption also must include the title of the document, for example, "Brief in Support of Defendant's Motion to Dismiss." For an appellate brief, the caption will appear on a cover sheet of the color prescribed by the court rules. For a trial-level brief, the caption can appear on a cover sheet (as shown in the sample trial-level brief in Appendix B) or simply at the top of the first page of the brief.

   2.   Table of Contents.   The Table of Contents should include each component that follows the Table of Contents and should designate the number of the page on which that component begins. For the Argument section,

---

   20.   Some court rules require the Standard of Review to constitute its own section. If the court rules are silent as to placement, the writer can cover the Standard of Review early in the Argument section rather than in a separate section.
   21.   Sometimes called "Introduction."
   22.   Sometimes called "Statement of Issues." Some court rules require the Questions Presented to appear as the first item after the Caption.
   23.   Sometimes called "Statement of the Case."
   24.   *Et al.* is an abbreviation for *et alli,* meaning literally "and others." See Fed. R. Civ. P. 10(a) and 7(b)(2).
   25.   *See* Fed. R. Civ. P. 10(a).

include each point heading and subheading, using the same style of print (all caps or initial caps only) as used for that heading in the body of the argument.

3. Table of Authorities. List the authorities cited in the brief and the page(s) on which each is cited. If the authority is cited so frequently throughout the brief that listing individual page numbers would be unwieldy, use the term *passim* (meaning "throughout") instead. List the authorities in separate categories, such as, cases, statutes, treatises, articles, and miscellaneous. If the brief cites many cases, consider organizing the cases by issuing court, starting with the highest level and going to the lowest level. Within each list of cases, order the entries alphabetically.

4. Statutes Involved. This section sets out the text of the relevant part(s) of any statutes at issue. It allows the reader to refer conveniently to the statutory language. If the relevant language is short enough, place it in a section entitled "Statutes Involved." If its length would make placement within the brief unwieldy, consider placing it in an Appendix and referring the reader to the Appendix on your first mention of the statute.

5. Opinion Below. This section of an appellate brief tells the reader where to find the opinion from the court below. Provide the page numbers within the court record and, for a reported opinion, the citation.

6. Jurisdiction. This section provides the citation to the statute conferring on the court the jurisdiction to hear this type of case.

7. Standard of Review. Set out the appropriate standard for the court's review of the legal issue(s) raised by the brief. Include citations to relevant authority establishing the standard.[26] If the brief addresses more than one issue, remember that the standard of review might be different for each.

8. Preliminary Statement (or Introduction). The Preliminary Statement summarizes the procedural history that has led to the occasion for the brief, that is, the pending motion or appeal.

9. Question(s) Presented (or Statement of Issues). The Question(s) Presented section states the legal issues addressed by the brief and the factual context in which they have arisen. Articulating Questions Presented offers an important opportunity for advocacy, requiring skill and care. Chapter 20 explains the drafting of Questions Presented in more detail.

10. Statement of Facts (or Statement of the Case). This section sets out the facts relevant to the legal issues addressed by the brief, as well as the context necessary for understanding those facts. Like the Questions Presented, the Statement of the Case is an important opportunity for advocacy, requiring skillful and careful drafting. Chapter 21 explains drafting a Statement of Facts in more detail.

26. *See* section III of Chapter 18 for a discussion of standards of review.

11.   Summary of Argument.   The Summary of the Argument is exactly that—a concise statement of the nub of your argument on each issue. It is often the first place a reader looks to answer the question, "OK, so what is this case about?" Consequently, it should be drafted to make the strongest, most effective presentation of the core of your argument(s). The Summary must not simply repeat the argument headings.[27] For each issue, it should set out, more fully than a point heading can, the application of the relevant rule to the most compelling facts. Usually one paragraph covers each issue.

12.   Argument.   The Argument contains the fully articulated argument on the legal issues. Just as your working draft became the Discussion section of the office memo, your working draft will become the Argument section of the brief. Chapters 17-20 will cover the process of creating the Argument section of the brief.

13.   Conclusion.   Two schools of thought exist on Conclusions. The more traditional approach is a pro forma statement of the precise relief sought.[28]

> For the foregoing reasons, the Court should grant the Defendant's Motion to Dismiss.

For appellate briefs, use this more traditional form of conclusion.

However, for trial-level briefs, if court rules and local customs permit, consider a Conclusion that gives you one last opportunity for advocacy. This sort of Conclusion should still be short—no more than half a double-spaced page. But it could gather together the most compelling arguments on each issue in support of its assertion of the correctness of the result you seek.

> Therefore, as this brief has demonstrated, the circumstances of this case render the covenant's terms unreasonable. The covenant would protect Carrolton to a degree far greater than necessary, while devastating both Ms. Watson's fledgling business and her personal finances. Further, it would significantly infringe the public's interest in reasonably priced health care equipment, merchandise vital to the community's well-being. For these reasons, Carrolton's Motion for Summary Judgment should be denied.

14.   Certificate of Service.   Ethical rules prohibit ex parte contact with the judge about the merits of a legal matter.[29] Court rules require copies of all filings to be served upon all parties, via their attorneys.[30] Also, ethical rules prohibit all contact with a party represented by an attorney except through the party's attorney.[31] Therefore, the copy of the brief must be served on the party's attorney rather than directly upon the party. The Certificate of Service

27.   Fed. R. App. P. 28 (a)(5).
28.   Fed. R. App. P. 28 (a)(7).
29.   Model Rules of Professional Conduct Rule 3.5(b) (1994); Model Code of Professional Responsibility DR 7-110(B) (1980).
30.   *See, e.g.,* Fed. R. Civ. P. 5(a).
31.   Model Rules of Professional Conduct Rule 4.2 (1994); Model Code of Professional Responsibility DR 7-104(A)(1) (1980).

demonstrates compliance with these rules. The Certificate is placed on a separate page at the end of the brief. It certifies that copies of the brief have been mailed or delivered to all parties via their attorneys.

This chapter has described the ethical responsibilities of a brief-writer[32] and the general characteristics of judges as readers. It has provided an overview of the components of trial-level and appellate briefs. Now you are ready to begin work on the brief you have been assigned.

---

32.   For exercises and discussion questions about the material in this chapter, see the exercises at the end of Chapter 17.

Formulating and Structuring a Favorable Rule

17

Creating the working draft of a brief is much like creating the working draft of an office memo.[1] But a brief also must persuade. It must meet its reader—the judge—wherever she is and move her to the spot where the client needs her to be. In addition to presenting an honest, accurate, and clear legal discussion, the brief-writer also must (1) formulate the most favorable rule possible, a rule that will present the client's story most compellingly; (2) order the points and subpoints to maximize persuasive impact and write out compelling arguments under each section; and (3) use the facts to tell a compelling story.

These tasks are among the most challenging and interesting parts of a lawyer's job, but they do complicate the writing process. The rule you first formulate may be well reasoned and faithful to the sources, but may not be particularly favorable. You want the rule to give maximum legal significance to your client's strongest facts and to limit the legal significance of your client's weakest facts. How well does your rule measure up? Will your formulation of the rule help or hurt your client?

If you are troubled by the prognosis for your client under your first rule formulation, you'll need to think again about the rule. You may be able to formulate a better one.

---

1. Chapters 2 through 6 have described analyzing the sources of law on your client's legal issue, formulating a rule from those sources, and outlining the rule organized a working draft. Chapters 7 through 10 have described writing a draft, explaining the law from the sources you found, and applying that law to the facts of your client's case.

I **FORMULATING A FAVORABLE RULE**

One of the hardest lessons of the first year of law school is learning that the law is pliable. Most of us come to law school expecting that legislatures will have created rules for all occasions. The lawyer's task is simply to learn them, tell the client about them, and point them out to the judge. The judge will, without further ado, apply these rules of law and decide the case.

Instead we find that the rules are created mostly piecemeal, some in the form of statutes and some in the form of case law. They are created by many different legislatures and judges. They evolve over a period of time. They are not always thoroughly thought out or well articulated by their creators. Rules made by case law are often articulated in varying forms by different judges, even in the same jurisdiction. Rules made by statutes have one official written version, but even they are the subject of explanation and commentary by a number of different writers. Ambiguity, in both the legislative and judicial processes, facilitates compromise and resolution of differing viewpoints. Most rules of law are achieved through such compromises.

As a result of how our laws are made and of the human frailties of those who make them, ambiguities abound. The rule could be this or it could be that. The lawyer writing a brief seeks to resolve those ambiguities in the way most favorable to the client. The lawyer must provide the judge with the relevant statutes and case law and must be scrupulously honest about what these sources say. The lawyer must not deceive the judge about the statutes or the cases. Rather, the lawyer recognizes the ambiguities that exist in these sources, selects the rule formulation most favorable for the client, and seeks to persuade the judge to adopt that one.

As we saw in Chapters 4 and 5, ambiguities in rule *formulation* exist, especially in legal rules created by case law.[2] First, such legal rules usually are not written in the literary form of a "rule," but rather in the more loosely written prose of a case opinion. Second, the opinion may not articulate the complete rule, but rather may expect readers to surmise the complete rule by noticing how the court discusses the facts of that particular case.

Third, rules created by case law may be authoritatively articulated in different forms by different opinions. Some of those opinions may articulate the rule fairly clearly and some may not. Some may use the language from earlier cases to articulate the rule, and some may create an original articulation of the rule.

When you are confronted with case law that seems to establish a troublesome rule, that is, a rule that hurts your client's case, you will need to look for the ambiguities in the opinion's articulation. If you find ambiguity on a point relevant to your client's situation, you can try to persuade the judge to

---

2.   Statutes may be ambiguous as well, but most often ambiguity in a statute derives from uncertainty about what the enacting legislature meant by the words of the statute rather than in rule formulation.

resolve those ambiguities in your client's favor. In other words, you try to formulate a more favorable rule.

A. Tools for Formulating a Favorable Rule

You have two primary methods for dealing with a case seeming to set out a troublesome rule: (1) You can try to discount the troublesome case, or (2) you can try to reconcile its language with your client's position. An advocate can use a number of ways to discount or reconcile a case. Here, roughly in the order of their force, is a list of some of the primary ways:

1. Appeal to stronger authority. You may be able to discount the opinion by trumping it with stronger authority. For instance, remember that mandatory authority controls over persuasive authority.[3] The opinion of a higher court overrides the opinion of a lower court of the same jurisdiction. The opinion of the highest state court overrides the opinion of a federal court applying state law. A more recent opinion usually carries more weight than an older opinion.[4]

Sometimes you will find no mandatory authority, but only persuasive authority from other jurisdictions. Authorities from other jurisdictions are likely to disagree. While legal analysis is never a matter of mere "nose counting," it helps your case if you can claim majority support for your proposed rule, especially if the majority is substantial. Then you can appeal to "the great weight of authority."

One of the rules you find articulated by the persuasive authority may have been the settled law on this issue for many years. The antiquity of such a well-settled rule may give it greater persuasive authority than a more recent holding, particularly if that more recent holding is not carefully reasoned and thoroughly discussed in the opinion. On the other hand, several recent holdings may constitute a "modern trend" in the law, and thus may have greater persuasive authority than an older rule. When persuasive authorities are in conflict, there is no rigid formula for deciding which rule is more persuasive. You are free to argue for the greater merit of the rule you prefer.

2. Distinguish the facts. You can sometimes argue that the law articulated by the troublesome case does not apply to your client's situation. You do this by showing that your client's facts are different from the facts of the troublesome case, *and* by showing that the differences are legally significant. It is best to show that your factual distinctions are significant in light of the express reasoning of the precedential case. You will be looking for language that either states or implies that the law in that opinion was meant to apply to a factual situation different from your client's situation. But if you cannot find express support for this argument in the opinion, appeals to reason,

---

3. *See* Chapter 5.
4. Always check to be sure that the opinion has not been reversed or overruled, either expressly or by implication.

common sense, and justice may also support a claim that a factual distinction is material.

3. Distinguish the policy. Your case may be factually different from both the favorable and unfavorable precedents. Your task then is to show that the policy considerations of the favorable authorities—and not those of the unfavorable authorities—apply to your client's case. The policies behind a rule are the goals to be served or the problems to be avoided by that rule. For instance, the policies behind a rule imposing liability on a home owner for maintaining an attractive nuisance would include the goal of protecting children from dangers they are not yet old enough to realize.

4. Reinterpret the opinion. Carefully reread the opinion and all other authority from the jurisdiction asking yourself whether you have misread the opinion's troublesome language. Look particularly at the terms the opinion uses to be sure that your initial understanding of their meaning is the meaning the court intended. Ask yourself whether the court has simply used language carelessly. Did the court really mean to be saying something different from the law articulated by the other cases? Read any cases the court said it was following.

One of the best ways to check the court's articulation of the law is to measure what the court *said* against what the court *did*. The court may have articulated a statement of law carelessly or unclearly, but rendered a result consistent with your client's needs. The court's discussion of the application of that law to the facts of the case before the court may yield good clues about what the court really meant. You may be able to formulate the rule of the case more favorably than you initially thought.

5. Attack the bad authority; defend the good. You can sometimes demonstrate that the law articulated in the troublesome opinion is not well reasoned, that it does not lead to a just result, or that it is not in keeping with current developments of the law. You probably won't persuade a lower court to reject the controlling decision of a higher court expressly, though this occasionally happens. A court may, however, reject persuasive authority. Even where you are attacking controlling authority, you may be laying the groundwork for an appeal in which you will ask the higher court to reverse existing law.

B.   EXAMPLE: FORMULATING A FAVORABLE RULE FROM *FOX* AND *CLEIN*

Let's look at an example of how some of these strategies might work. We'll use a variation of the Watson covenant-not-to-compete example. You recall that Sharon Watson was a sales employee of Carrolton Company. She was interested in leaving Carrolton to form her own company that would compete with Carrolton. Thus, she needed to know the likelihood that Carrolton could enforce the covenant.

Now, suppose that Watson decided to leave Carrolton and begin her own competing business. The history of her decision goes like this: Originally Carrolton had been owned by Watson. Since its founding it has been the only retailer of in-home health care equipment in the area. Consequently, it does a large volume of business each year and is profitable.

One year ago Watson sold Carrolton to its present owners. She stayed on, accepting employment in a sales position for the company. She agreed to the covenant-not-to-compete as one of the terms of the sale. The covenant applies only to making sales contacts, not to any other aspect of the business. The covenant restricts her only in the three counties closest to the company head-quarters. The covenant restricts her for three years after leaving Carrolton's employ.

When Watson owned Carrolton, she used a reasonable markup so that customers paid fair prices. She tried to be responsive to customer needs in other ways as well. She viewed the business as a responsible commercial citizen of the community. However, the new owners of Carrolton have taken a different approach to the business. They are aware of the lack of competition in the area, and therefore have substantially raised prices. They are not concerned about customer requests and complaints, knowing that customers have nowhere else to go for the health care equipment they need. Watson became increasingly frustrated as she watched the slow destruction of the business reputation she had built over many years. She also saw in this situation an entrepreneurial opportunity.

For these reasons, Watson has left Carrolton and formed Acme. Acme has begun to compete with Carrolton, and Watson has begun to make sales contacts for Acme. Start-up costs for a health care equipment retailer are high. Ms. Watson is dealing with those costs in two ways: She has incurred substantial personal debt to pay some of the costs, and she has postponed some of the costs by planning to start small, selling equipment in only several of the categories of products currently sold by Carrolton. In the first two years of business, Acme will do well to break even. It cannot expect to garner more than 20 percent of Carrolton's business in the particular products it will sell and none of Carrolton's business in the other categories. The loss of that much business would still leave Carrolton with healthy profits.

Carrolton has filed suit against Watson, seeking to enforce the covenant-not-to-compete. You represent Watson. You must write a brief setting out the law the court should apply in deciding whether to enforce the covenant. As Watson's lawyer, you want to prevent Carrolton from enforcing the covenant. Therefore, you'd like to set out a rule of law that Carrolton would find harder to meet.

Recall that your research had led you to *Coffee System of Atlanta v. Fox* and *Clein v. Kapiloff.*[5] Reread these two cases.

In Chapter 4 we first formulated this rule from *Fox*:

---

5. *See* App. D, pp. 387 *(Fox)* and 393 *(Clein)*.

A covenant is enforceable if all of the following elements are reasonable:

1. the kind of activity that is restrained;
2. the geographic area where it is restrained; and
3. the time period of the restraint.

Then in Chapter 5 we formulated this rule from *Clein*:

To be enforceable, a covenant-not-to-compete:

1. must be supported by sufficient consideration, and
2. must be reasonable. The test for determining reasonableness is:
   a. whether the covenant is reasonably necessary to protect the interests of the party who benefits by it;
   b. whether it unduly prejudices the interests of the public; and
   c. whether it imposes greater restrictions than are necessary.

We worked with synthesizing these two cases, and finally formulated the following rule:

I. IS THE WATSON COVENANT-NOT-TO-COMPETE ENFORCEABLE?

The covenant is enforceable if the contract is valid in all other essentials and if the activity restrained, the geographic area of the restraint, and the time period of the restraint are all reasonable.

A. Is the contract valid in all other essentials, including sufficiency of consideration?

[Discuss any relevant cases pertaining to contract essentials including *Fox* and *Clein.*]

B. Is the kind of activity restrained reasonable?

[Discuss any relevant cases pertaining to the nature of the restrained activity, including *Fox* and *Clein.*]

C. Is the geographic scope reasonable?

[Discuss any relevant cases pertaining to the geographical limits of a restrained activity, including *Fox* and *Clein.*]

D. Is the duration of the restraint reasonable?

[Discuss any relevant cases pertaining to the duration of a restraint, including *Fox* and *Clein.*]

Having formulated this rule, you begin your analysis. You do not need to worry about the other contract essentials since they are not at issue in Watson's case, so you set about to find all of the Georgia cases that give clues about the relevant prongs of the *Fox/Clein* test: the reasonableness of what is restricted, where it is restricted, and how long it is restricted.

As you begin organizing and writing your working draft, you notice that Watson's case is not looking good. You have found many Georgia cases upholding restrictions of the same kind, geographic scope, and duration as the Watson-Carrolton covenant. Should you simply advise your client to give up, close down her new business, and go job hunting so that she can try to repay the debts she incurred for start-up expenses?

Watson's case might look much different, though, under some of the language from the rule you originally formulated from *Clein*. If the judge could assess Carrolton's need for the covenant, the judge might find that Watson's competition during the period of the restraint would do little harm to Carrolton. If the judge could consider the interests of the public, the judge would probably conclude that the public has a significant interest in the benefits that would result from competition with Carrolton. If the judge could consider whether the restrictions are larger than necessary to protect Carrolton, the judge might be more willing to refuse enforcement of the covenant.

Moreover, as an advocate, you know that it is important to present the judge with a sympathetic and compelling personal story, a set of *facts* that will make the judge want to agree with your client's argument on the *law*.[6] Generally, though, you may present to the judge only the facts that have *legal* significance—that is, only the facts the judge needs to know in order to apply the relevant rule of law. If the Georgia rule only compares the terms of the Watson-Carrolton restraint to the terms of restraints enforced by past Georgia cases, without regard to the needs of the public and the parties, then your ability to tell the judge Watson's full story is impaired. You cannot present her compelling personal goals and the strong public policy that represent the heart of Watson's position.

So, you need to find a way to articulate the Georgia rule in a form that includes the *Clein* considerations for the needs of the public and of both parties. Yet you cannot ignore the way the *Fox* opinion seemed to set out the Georgia test. *Fox* is mandatory authority, it is a more recent opinion than *Clein*, and its holding has not been overturned. What can you do?

Recall from Chapter 5 that you have already searched for a way to argue that the *Fox* rule does not apply to your client's factual situation. The only possible distinction you noticed was the distinction that the *Fox* covenant was part of an employment contract while the *Clein* covenant, like the Watson covenant, was part of the sale of a business. However, you found that the test for determining enforceability would be the same. Further, you found that covenants made as part of the sale of a business are *more* easily enforced than those made as a part of an employment contract. Because this is not the result you want, you do not pursue this distinction.

Your next option is to ask yourself what the court must have meant by the troublesome language, that is, the language seeming to restrict the test to the

6. *See* Chapter 21.

elements of the covenant. Does the language of the *Fox* opinion really exclude the parts of *Clein* you want to use? In other words, did the court in *Fox* really *mean* to be saying that a judge is not supposed to consider the interests of the public or the situation of the parties when deciding whether to enforce a covenant? You also look for clues beyond the seemingly conflicting language. Has a later opinion already discussed and explained the seeming inconsistency?

Fox does not discuss the particular interests of the restrained party. The opinion does not reject that consideration expressly, but neither does it seem to consider those interests in deciding the case before it. By quoting from an earlier case, however, *Fox* does describe the *public's* interests as part of judging reasonableness.

This is your clue. Perhaps what seemed to be a *complete* statement of a test for deciding the enforceability of a covenant was really just a part of the test. Perhaps it was merely the identification of the aspects of the restraint that the court should examine. You read the *Fox* language again and this time you notice that the opinion introduces the list as "elements" the court has considered in determining whether a covenant is "reasonable."

Now you're onto something. If the *Fox* opinion's list of three only identifies the *elements* (the terms) of the covenant that the court should examine, and if the *standard* that each aspect must meet is reasonableness, then perhaps the *Fox* opinion does not mean to be setting out the complete, exclusive statement of how to decide enforceability of a covenant. After all, we would still need to know *how* a court is to judge whether the elements of the covenant (what, where, and how long) are reasonable. *Fox* itself implicitly supports this understanding: After *Fox* sets out the list of three elements, the opinion goes on to consider each element of the covenant before it. In the process of examining the reasonableness of the nature, scope, and duration of the restraint, *Fox* seems to discuss "reasonableness" in part by reference to the interests of the public and the needs of the restraining party.

In other words, perhaps in *Fox* the Georgia Supreme Court intended to list the *terms* of the covenant a court should test for reasonableness, but not *what factors* to use to judge the reasonableness of those terms. If so, then the *Fox* opinion did not purport to list the factors for judging reasonableness. It merely gave us some good clues by letting us "listen in on" the factors it chose to use in deciding the case before it.

More fortunate yet, two of the three factors you want to salvage from *Clein* (the interest of the public and the needs of the restraining party) were mentioned in the *Fox* opinion. And since *Fox* does not announce that its "reasonableness" analysis of the *Fox* covenant is exclusive, you can argue that a judge can consider the remaining factor you'd like to include, the needs of the restrained party. You even notice some language from another portion of *Clein* that supports consideration of the needs of the restrained party: "The agreement must be considered with reference to the situation, business and objects of the parties in light of all of the surrounding circumstances." As a matter of fact, this language seems to give you a chance to identify other relevant and helpful factors as well.

So, it looks as if you can formulate a rule that harmonizes the *Fox* and *Clein* opinions more favorably for Watson's case. First, try to state your rule using *simple* sentences. When you have several items, include "and" or "or" to indicate whether all must be considered. After each part of your statement of the rule, indicate the source of that part of the rule. You might come up with something like this:

> A covenant-not-to-compete is enforceable only if it is reasonable. [*Fox* and *Clein*]
>
> The terms of the covenant that must be reasonable are (1) the kind of activity restrained, (2) the geographic scope of the restraint, and (3) the duration of the restraint. [*Fox*]
>
> The way a court judges "reasonableness" is by considering (1) the needs of the restraining party [*Fox* and *Clein*], (2) interests of the public [*Fox* and *Clein*], (3) the needs of the restrained party [*Clein*], and (4) all other circumstances [*Clein*].

Notice how much stronger Watson's legal arguments are since she can argue that the covenant is unreasonable in *her* case (based on the needs of the parties and interests of the public) rather than simply by comparing the terms of her covenant with the terms of the covenants enforced in other cases. Because you looked for the ambiguities in the language of the controlling opinions, you have been able to formulate a rule more favorable than the one you initially thought *Fox* and *Clein* set out.

Notice also how this formulation of the rule allows you to put Watson's whole story before the judge. Because you were paying attention to your client's story, you formulated a rule that gives legal significance to Watson's best facts. The combination of narrative and rule-based reasoning has made this result possible.

Finally, notice how the struggle to find a way to articulate a more favorable rule has actually led you to a more complete and more accurate understanding of the law.

One word of caution. *Credibility is essential to advocacy.* The more a judge feels pushed by an argument and the closer to the limits of credibility the lawyer's formulation of a rule comes, the more a judge will resist the brief-writer's purpose. Even more important, once a brief-writer's formulation of the rule has crossed the credibility line, once the judge believes that the brief-writer is proposing a rule that the sources can't reasonably be said to support, the judge will tend to reject everything else the lawyer offers. Thus, a brief-writer is better off proposing a slightly less favorable rule than running the risk that the judge will decide that the writer's proposed rule is outside the bounds of any reasonable construction of the statutes and case law.

II ◆ **STRUCTURING A FAVORABLE RULE**

A.   SUBPARTS

After you have *formulated* a favorable rule, your work with the rule still may not be done. You must take your statement of the rule and *structure* it in the way most helpful to your client. By "structuring the rule," we mean organizing the rule into a structure (an outline format) like those described in Chapter 2. The primary task of rule-structuring is identifying the rule's subparts and their relation to each other. Often the rule's structure will be inherent in the way the authorities state the rule, and you will not have choices to make. The burglary rule is an example of such a rule.

But sometimes the authorities will leave you more latitude in identifying the rule's subparts, and you can exercise that latitude to your client's advantage. Keep in mind that the subparts you identify will probably become the organizational groupings for your discussion, either formally, as subheadings, or informally, as the organizational scheme within rule explanation and rule application. So you want to look for subparts that (1) emphasize and de-emphasize the material in a helpful way, and (2) appeal to the reader's interest and thus claim more of the reader's attention.

The parts of the rule that become subheadings in the final draft are especially important. Recall two major characteristics of how subheadings function: (1) Subheadings emphasize their own content and obscure other content, and (2) subheadings often serve as the reader's mechanism for keeping score.

1.   *Choosing Subheadings for Emphasis*

Subheadings emphasize their own content and de-emphasize other content. Therefore, issues that are favorable to the writer ideally should be stressed in the subheadings, while less favorable issues are addressed less conspicuously in the body of the brief. Using a subheading insures emphasis of that part of the analysis by providing visibility, repetition, and substantive focus. Further, emphasizing a particular part of the rule necessarily draws attention *from*, and therefore de-emphasizes, parts not used as subheadings.

As long as the subheadings fairly and completely cover the rule, a reader will seldom ponder what the writer's other choices for subheadings might have been—that is, why some elements were broken out separately and others lumped together; why some exceptions were given subheadings and others mentioned in sections on the basic rule. Even if other choices for subheadings occur to a reader, the reader will not mentally reorganize the argument according to that other possible set of subheadings. So, the selection of subheadings is another decision the advocate must make, another choice invisible to the reader but effective upon the reader nonetheless.

Strategic selection of subheadings, then, requires the writer to identify the facts and law the writer wishes to emphasize and de-emphasize, the facts and law that help most and that hurt most. Much of this process of identifying strong and weak facts and law will be unique to each client's case and to each legal issue. However, some general principles apply. Recall the characteristics of judges as readers. Remember, for instance, the power of the equities and of social policy. Remember the natural attraction of readers to facts. Remember that judges care about how today's ruling may limit or enhance their ability to "do justice" in tomorrow's case. Such characteristics of judges apply to each case and give you some good standards for evaluating choices of subheadings, no matter what the characteristics of the particular facts and law.

2. Subheadings as a Tallying Mechanism

Subheadings are the reader's tallying mechanism. Recall that readers, whether they realize it or not, keep score. This process is particularly true when the reader encounters separately identified categories—that is, subheadings. A reader tends to stop at the end of the discussion of a subheading and do a little preliminary evaluation of the strength of that subheading. The reader will mentally label each subheading as either "weak" or "strong."

In order to make this tallying mechanism work to your advantage, try to maximize the *number* of strong subsections and minimize the *number* of weak subsections. Look for ways to break the stronger part of your case into several strong arguments with separate subheadings. Look for ways to lump the weaker parts of your case into as few subheadings as possible. Not only does this minimize the number of weaker points, but sometimes several weaker points, combined, can become one stronger point. A reader will be far more convinced by one strong argument than by a series of weak ones.

B. EXAMPLE: STRUCTURING A FAVORABLE RULE FROM *FOX* AND *CLEIN*

Once again, let's consider an example to see how this process works. We'll use the rule we most recently formulated from *Fox* and *Clein*.

A covenant-not-to-compete is enforceable only if it is reasonable. [*Fox* and *Clein*]

The terms of the covenant that must be reasonable are (1) the kind of activity restrained, (2) the geographic scope of the restraint, and (3) the duration of the restraint. [*Fox*]

The way a court judges "reasonableness" is by considering (1) the needs of the restraining party [*Fox* and *Clein*], (2) interests of the public [*Fox* and *Clein*], (3) the needs of the restrained party [*Clein*], and (4) all other circumstances [*Clein*].

Notice that this formulation of the rule gives you two options for structuring the rule: You can organize the rule by the terms of the covenant to be judged or by the interests used to judge them.

Terms of Covenant	*Interests*
I. REASONABLENESS OF COVENANT	I. REASONABLENESS OF COVENANT
A. Activity restrained **[Discuss interests of parties and public.]**	A. Needs of restraining party **[Discuss activity, territory, and time.]**
B. Territory restrained **[Discuss interests of parties and public.]**	B. Needs of public **[Discuss activity, territory, and time.]**
C. Time restrained **[Discuss interests of parties and public.]**	C. Needs of restrained party **[Discuss activity, territory, and time.]**
	D. Any other circumstances **[Discuss activity, territory, and time.]**

Both structures are accurate representations of the rule. But notice the difference in emphasis. How well does each set of subheadings accomplish your goal of emphasizing and de-emphasizing in a strategically helpful way? Ask yourself which structure will focus more attention on the arguments most helpful to Watson. The structure on the left, organized by the *terms* of the covenant, will focus the judge's attention on what is restrained, where it is restrained, and how long it is restrained. Watson's facts on those comparisons are not compelling. Her covenant restrains only limited activities in a limited geographical area for a limited time.

The structure on the right, organized by the *standards* for judging reasonableness, will focus the judge's attention on how little Carrolton needs the restraint, on how the public's interests are hurt by it, and on how much Watson would be hurt by it. Watson's facts on these standards are stronger.

How well does each set of subheadings accomplish your goal of appealing to your reader's interest and therefore keeping the reader's attention? Notice that the set on the left emphasizes uninteresting facts (categories of jobs and numbers of counties and years) while the set on the right emphasizes compelling facts about people. Notice that the set on the right emphasizes equities and social policy—topics of interest to many judges. Notice, too that the set on the right emphasizes the breadth of factors the judge may consider in deciding this case, thus appealing to the judge's concern about the effect of this ruling on deciding future cases.

Your decision here is easy; the rule structure on the right is the better choice. This rule structure will form the structure of your legal discussion.

In Chapter 4 we formulated a rule directly from *Fox*. In Chapter 5 we formulated a somewhat different rule from *Fox* by harmonizing it with *Clein*. Now we have formulated a third rule from *Fox* and *Clein*. Further, we have structured this third rule in two ways, ways so different that they seem like two distinct rules rather than merely two ways of structuring the same rule. Each of these rule statements and structures is supportable from the two cases we have worked with. Let this example of the diversity of rule formulations be another reminder of the pliability of many rules of law.

 # RULE FORMULATION AND STRUCTURING IN A RESPONSIVE OR REPLY BRIEF

Usually the party seeking relief files an opening brief; then the opposing party files a responsive brief. Generally the party who filed the opening brief can respond to the responsive brief by filing a reply brief. Rule formulation and structuring require some additional decisions when you are writing a responsive brief or when you are filing a reply brief.

A. RESPONSIVE BRIEF

Every litigator has this common experience: You are sitting at your desk working on the matters of the day. The mail arrives, and you open an envelope from a law firm representing an opposing party. There you find a motion asking for some ruling—a ruling either harmful or downright fatal to your client's position. Your anxiety level starts to rise. A brief accompanies the motion, and you quickly read it. "Uh oh. We may be in trouble!" you think. "Does the law really say that? Do the facts really establish that? Oh no! Am I going to lose this case? How will I explain this to my client?"

The first thing you do is find the cases cited in the opening brief and start to read them. "Oh good," you think. "This may not be quite as bad as I thought. I can argue that this case doesn't apply because . . . and this statute doesn't apply because . . ." You switch on your computer or grab your Dictaphone, put your opponent's brief on top of all those case reporters stacked, open, on your desk, and start to tackle your opponent's brief, point by point and case by case. Your anxiety level starts to decrease as you take apart your opponent's arguments. Before long you've got a draft. You read it over, do some editing, feel much better, and file it.

This common scenario may make the lawyer feel better, but unfortunately it seldom results in a strong responsive brief. The scenario leads the lawyer into three traps: (1) being unable to see other, more favorable rule formulations or structures, (2) allowing the opponent's argument to remain the center of the judge's attention, and (3) conceding that the opponent's brief should be the one the judge uses as the overall exposition of the law governing the issues.

First, when the lawyer organizes the responsive brief by responding to the opponent's points, the lawyer has accepted the opponent's rule structure. This mistake can be particularly serious because the party who controls the structure of the argument stands a much better chance of controlling the outcome. The Watson/Carrolton example above demonstrates this basic principle of advocacy.

This is not to say that the responding attorney should always formulate or structure the rule differently from the opening brief. The rule structure from the opponent's brief may be the only available option, it may be as favorable as the other options, or it may even be the best structure for the responding lawyer's arguments. In such cases, use the same structure because your brief won't have to ask the judge reading the briefs to shift from one structure to another. The important principle here is to remember to *ask* whether the opponent's rule formulation and structure constitute the most favorable options. If so, use them, but make the decision consciously, after considering the options, rather than unconsciously by assuming the opponent's structure.

Second, even if the authorities will not support any other, more favorable rule formulation or structure, a responsive brief written like the one in our scenario never has a chance to present its own message in a coherent and powerful way. It spends its pages trying to poke holes in the opponent's arguments rather than affirmatively establishing the strength of its own arguments. Thus the judge's attention remains centered on the opponent's arguments.

Finally, if the content of the responsive brief primarily refers back to the arguments set out in the opening brief, the judge cannot use the responding attorney's brief as the primary exposition of the law, but rather must use the opening brief as the basic point of reference for the legal analysis. The responding attorney would be in a far better position if the judge at least had the option to choose the responsive brief as the starting point for deciding what the law is. And if the responsive brief is better written and researched, the judge will probably do just that.

So what would be a better scenario than the one described above? Try this instead: Your day is interrupted by the arrival of a brief accompanying the motion from an opposing party. You panic. This time, however, instead of frantically trying to respond to the brief, you take a deep breath and put the opening brief aside for a few days. You work on other matters, using your focus on them to distance yourself from the arguments you read in the opening brief. Then you return to the task of responding to the brief, beginning by researching the issue as if you were going to file an opening brief seeking the opposite ruling—as if the opposing brief has not been filed. You use your standard methods for finding authority. Some of the authorities you find will have appeared in the opening brief, but probably some will be new. When you have found the relevant authority, you formulate and structure the most favorable rule you can.

At this point, you check to be sure that you have read all the cases your opponent has cited, updated them, and read the main authorities on which those cases relied. You can now use your critical reasoning to devise ways to minimize the damage those cases can do to your position.

Next you write a draft of an argument *as if you were writing an opening brief seeking the ruling you want.* When you have your own analysis written out, you convert that draft of an argument to the argument section of a responsive brief. Now you insert your specific responses to the opponent's points into *your affirmative argument.* Place these responses after your own affirmative arguments in the draft rather than ahead of them. With a little editing here and there, you'll have a stronger responsive brief than did the first lawyer described above.

B.   REPLY BRIEF

A reply brief allows the writer of the opening brief to accomplish three important but potentially inconsistent goals: (1) to counter arguments made in the opponent's responsive brief, (2) to return the judge's attention to the writer's own arguments, and (3) to avoid losing the judge's attention by *unduly* rehashing material from the opening brief. (A little repetition is necessary so the important arguments, obscured by pages devoted to less important points, will not fade from memory.) The particular challenge of the reply brief is to accomplish these three goals in the same document.

Use the structure from your opening brief, and write a summary of the heart of *your* argument. Then, just as described above for a responsive brief, insert your responses to the opponent's points into the summary of your affirmative argument. Generally these responses should go after your own arguments in the draft rather than ahead of them. If you do need to intersperse your responses within your own points, be sure that the emphasis remains on your points.

Reasserting your own structure is particularly important if the responsive brief has used a different (presumably less favorable) structure. The reply brief that can pull the argument back to your large-scale structure, incorporating the opponent's points into that structure and rebutting them there, stands a far better chance of retaining control of the argument.

If the judge reads the briefs in the order of filing, the reply brief-writer controls the material the judge reads last and therefore material the judge may remember longest. The chance to control the "last word" is a powerful strategic opportunity. Draft a compelling summary of your main points, getting right down to the nub of the matter and showing why your position is the best resolution of the issue. Try to keep your summary short so you won't lose the judge's attention and so the rhetorical impact of your summary won't be diffused over too many pages.

Both office memo-writers and brief-writers must find the descriptions of the rule written in case law and statutes, analyze the language and context of those versions of the rule, and then formulate and structure a written version of that rule. The brief-writer's job may seem harder, though, because the brief-writer must do more than take the rule as she finds it. She must use the authorities as raw material for formulating and structuring, not the most *likely* rule, but the most *favorable* rule, and she must "sell" the rule to the judge.[7]

But, actually, the job of predicting requires the memo-writer to do these same analytical tasks. Since an office memo should predict the written version of the rule a judge would adopt, the writer must recognize the possible rules brief-writers might formulate and the possible arguments they might make in support of those rule formulations. Tougher yet, the memo-writer must evaluate the strength of those arguments and predict which the judge will "buy."

Persuasion also requires the skill of objective analysis because the writer must evaluate the marketability of the rule formulation the writer would like to sell. So, each writing task—prediction and persuasion—requires skill in the other. Each time you practice one, you are improving your skills at the other as well.

 # EXERCISES IN FORMULATING AND STRUCTURING A FAVORABLE RULE—ETHICS AND STRATEGY

The exercises that follow are based in Fort Lauderdale, Florida and deal with Florida law on constructive eviction. The Florida state court system has a supreme court, a set of intermediate-level appellate courts (called District Courts of Appeal), and trial-level courts. Fort Lauderdale is within the jurisdiction of the fourth District Court of Appeal. A decision of a District Court of Appeal is mandatory on all lower Florida courts within that district, and it may be regarded as persuasive by Florida courts outside that district.[8]

For the purposes of these exercises, assume that the only Florida Supreme Court case dealing with constructive eviction is *Hankins v. Smith*. Assume that the only Fourth District appellate cases dealing with constructive eviction are *Barton v. Mitchell Co.* and *Boulevard Shoppes v. Pro-1 Realty, Inc.* Assume that appellate courts from other Florida districts and the Eleventh Circuit have issued four other constructive eviction cases. The significant portions of these cases are printed on pages 403-413.

Assume that Florida has no statutes that deal with constructive eviction.

---

7. Recall Girvan Peck's description of a judge as a "professional buyer of ideas." Girvan Peck, *Writing Persuasive Briefs* 77 (1984).
8. Niki L. Martin, *Florida Legal Research and Source Book* Chapter 3, pp. 1, 4-5(1989).

EXERCISE 1

Facts

You are a staff attorney in the local legal aid office. The office represents people who do not have sufficient income to pay an attorney. One of your clients is Sophia Guzman. Guzman has five children. Her husband died three years ago, and she has had to resort to public assistance to support herself and her children.

Guzman and her children rent a two-bedroom apartment in a dilapidated building owned by A-1 Realty Co. Neither Guzman nor the other tenants have a lease; the tenants can move anytime they choose, and the landlord can evict them anytime it chooses. However, Guzman and her neighbors live there because they cannot afford to pay higher rent or the costs of moving, including the security deposit. They don't think they could find an apartment where the rent is this low. But the building is in terrible shape and they have become concerned that it may be a health risk as well. The water and sewer system work sporadically, the power surges and wanes, and the rat population is increasing.

Guzman and a group of her neighbors have been complaining to their landlord for over a year. A-1 Realty's president admitted that the building needed work and promised to fix these problems, but nothing has been done. The tenant group then tried complaining to the appropriate municipal agencies, but to no avail. Their next strategy was to sue the landlord, alleging constructive eviction.

Believing that the facts about the property's condition are compelling, you have decided to move for summary judgment. This seems a good strategy because, even if the judge does not agree, the judge will become educated about the egregious facts of the case and may pressure the defendant to consider settling. Also, you know that you will learn much about the defendant's defense by forcing a response to your motion. This knowledge will improve your trial preparation if a trial proves necessary. So, you must file a brief in support of your motion for summary judgment, arguing that Guzman's facts constitute constructive eviction.

Assignments and Discussion Questions

1. Formulate the constructive eviction rule and structure it in the outline form you will use for your brief.
2. Write out a draft of the argument.
3. List additional facts you want your paralegal to gather.
4. Intent could be a problem for your case, since the facts don't seem to establish that the landlord is trying to get the tenants to move. (The landlord could evict the tenants at any time; therefore the landlord does not need to resort to these strategies to retake possession.) If

you ignore *Hankins* (the old Florida Supreme Court opinion) and the opinions from the other districts and simply cite the two recent fourth District cases, you can avoid mentioning intent entirely. Is there anything wrong with that? What are your ethical and professional responsibilities regarding troublesome mandatory authority? What about troublesome persuasive authority inside the controlling jurisdiction?

5. Even if the applicable rules of professional ethics permit ignoring the troublesome authority, are there other reasons that such a decision would be problematic?

 **EXERCISE 2**

Facts

Your firm represents Gloria and Sam McSwain. The McSwains own and lease several pieces of business property, including a building across the street from the area hospital. This building is divided into two offices. Since the building was first built, both offices have been leased as doctors' offices. Most of the other buildings nearby are used as doctors' offices as well.

About three years ago, the doctors renting the suite on the building's east side relocated. The McSwains advertised the space but found the commercial leasing market depressed. Ultimately they were able to lease the suite for a period of ten years to Dr. Anne Chambless and Dr. Harold Mendez, family practitioners. However, Chambless and Mendez demanded that the McSwains complete substantial renovations as a condition for leasing the suite. The McSwains spent $65,000 on the renovations, which they financed by giving a second mortgage on the property. They will be able to pay off the second mortgage from the lease payments by the eighth year of the ten-year lease.

About two years ago, the doctor leasing the suite on the west side of the building retired and closed his practice. The McSwains considered themselves fortunate when they were able to re-lease the west suite quickly. Their new tenant is Dr. Richard Lewis, an obstetrician and gynecologist. The McSwains knew Lewis because the McSwains are members of the local pro-choice organization, and Lewis was an occasional guest speaker for the group. He spoke about the medical aspects of abortion and about his own experiences as a doctor who sometimes performs the procedure. The McSwains happened to see Lewis at K-Mart shortly after learning that the west suite would be vacant. They asked him if he knew of any doctors interested in new office space, and discovered that he was interested in moving closer to the hospital. The lease was negotiated promptly, and Lewis moved in.

Three months after Lewis moved in, the local pro-life organization targeted several doctors who perform abortions and conducted massive demonstrations outside their offices. Lewis was one of the targeted doctors. His office was picketed for eight days. Groups of 20 to 60 people spent each day chanting, playing music, using loudspeakers, and accosting people who approached the building. The demonstrations significantly disrupted the normal operations in both the east and the west suites of the McSwains' building. When the demonstrations concluded, the pro-life group promised to return periodically for more demonstrations.

On the first day of the demonstrations, Chambless and Mendez contacted the McSwains and demanded that they do something to make the demonstrations stop, including evicting Lewis if necessary. They explained that their family practice patients were upset by having to confront the demonstrators in order to enter and leave the building. They also explained that a number of their patients were members of the pro-life group. These pro-life patients were threatening to organize a movement to convince other Chambless/Mendez patients to boycott the practice while it was located next to Lewis.

The McSwains responded that they did not know how to stop the demonstrations and that they did not think they could evict Lewis until his lease expired, since Lewis had not breached any provision of his lease. They also explained that evicting Lewis would be unacceptable to them personally because they believe strongly in Lewis's right to offer abortion services, and that they were happy to be able to provide office space to Lewis since other medical landlords might have been reluctant to lease to a doctor who offered abortion services.

Chambless and Mendez found the situation intolerable and immediately began looking for other office space. About three months later, they found acceptable space and moved. The McSwains knew that the combination of the depressed commercial lease market and the threat of renewed demonstrations would make re-leasing the east suite difficult. Yet they must have lease income to repay the second mortgage.

The McSwains have sued Chambless and Mendez for the balance of their lease payments. Your firm represents the McSwains. Defendants Chambless and Mendez have counterclaimed, alleging that they were constructively evicted by the McSwain's decision to lease the west suite to a doctor performing abortions. Chambless and Mendez have moved for summary judgment on their constructive eviction counterclaim.

Defendants' Authorities and Rule Formulation

Defendants have formulated the constructive eviction rule from *Barton* (4th Dist.), *Hankins* (Fla. Sup. Ct.), *Boulevard Shoppes* (4th Dist.), and *Richards* (2d Dist.). Here is a summary of the Defendants' attorney's argument:

I.   CHAMBLESS AND MENDEZ WERE CONSTRUCTIVELY EVICTED BY THE PRESENCE OF THE ABORTION SERVICE NEXT DOOR.

Constructive eviction occurs when (A) a tenant is deprived of the beneficial enjoyment of the leased premises because the premises are rendered unsuitable for the purposes for which they were leased, and (B) the tenant vacates the premises within a reasonable time.

A. The premises were rendered unsuitable.

- [Discussion of facts and holding of *Barton.*]
- *Boulevard Shoppes* is an example of conditions not severe enough, while *Barton* is an example of conditions sufficiently severe. [Explain facts and rulings of each case.]
- Counter-analysis: An old case, *Hankins,* mentions an intent element, but later Fourth District cases have ignored that element (*Barton* and *Boulevard Shoppes*) or have construed it as met by implication from the condition itself (*Richards*).
- Here, the abortion demonstrations are far more disruptive than the noise from the exercise studio in *Barton.* The landlords' act of knowingly and intentionally leasing, for a fixed term, the neighboring suite to a tenant performing abortions satisfies whatever is left of the intent requirement.

B. Defendants vacated within a reasonable time.

- [Explanation of "reasonable time" from other cases.]
- Here, Defendants began looking for acceptable space immediately after the demonstrations began and moved promptly after finding space.

Assignments and Discussion Questions

1. Formulate the constructive eviction rule and structure it in the outline form you will use for your brief.
2. Write out a draft of the argument on behalf of the McSwains.
3. List additional facts you want your paralegal to gather.
4. What if you believe strongly in the pro-life cause? What are your professional and ethical obligations?

stage two

DRAFTING FOR PERSUASION: WRITING THE WORKING DRAFT

Drafting Working Headings

Now that you have formulated the most favorable rule you reasonably can and selected the most persuasive structure for the rule, you are ready to organize the arguments into working headings. These working headings will guide your thinking as you use the writing process to work out the best arguments. In the next stage, converting the working draft into a brief, you'll convert these working headings into the point headings and subheadings of the brief.

ORGANIZING ARGUMENTS UNDER WORKING POINT HEADINGS

A. IDENTIFYING WORKING POINT HEADINGS

Review the rule, component by component, identifying those for which you have a reasonable argument. The next step is to identify which of these components will become point headings.

A *point heading* is the statement of your argument on a *dispositive* legal issue—that is, an independent and freestanding ground that entitles your client to the relief you seek.[1] To tell if your argument on an element or set of elements is an independent ground for the relief you seek, ask yourself this question: If the judge agrees with me on *only* this component of the rule,

---

1. Richard K. Neumann, Jr., *Legal Reasoning and Legal Writing: Structure, Strategy, and Style* 209 (2d ed. 1994); Helene S. Shapo et al., *Writing and Analysis in the Law* 283 (3d ed. 1995).

is that enough to get the ruling I seek? If your answer is "yes"—if the judge would not need to consider other legal issues before granting the ruling you seek—then your argument on that part of the rule is an independent ground for the relief you seek. A heading that states your argument on that element is a point heading.

This definition will be clearer if we look again at the burglary case. The state must prove *all* of the elements to win a burglary conviction. Thus, the defense attorney's brief need only show that any one of these elements is missing in order to show that the state cannot prove the burglary charge. In the defense attorney's brief, then, each challenged element will constitute an independent ground for the desired result. If the attorney challenges the state's proof on three elements ("nighttime," "intent," and "of another"), the defense attorney will have three independent, freestanding ways to win the desired ruling. The defense attorney can prevail by persuading the judge on any *one* of these elements. Therefore, the argument on each element will constitute a *point,* and the defense attorney's brief will contain three point headings.

However, the prosecution's brief in response must argue that the state can prove all of the elements of burglary. The state cannot obtain the ruling it seeks (submission of the case to the jury) simply by showing that the facts will prove any *one* element; the prosecutor's brief must show that the facts can prove *all* of the challenged elements. In the prosecutor's brief, then, each challenged element will be a subpoint. The prosecutor's brief will have only one *point* heading—a point arguing that all elements are provable. As in an office memo, having only one roman numeral is fine. In a brief, let the roman numerals identify for your reader the freestanding arguments that entitle your client to the result you seek.

B.   DRAFTING WORKING POINT HEADINGS

Next, draft a *working point heading* for each point. A working point heading should be a single, complete sentence that identifies and asserts the correctness of the ruling your client seeks and states how the legal rule applies to your client's facts, entitling your client to that ruling. A good way to draft working point headings is to think of the point heading in halves, using this basic formula:

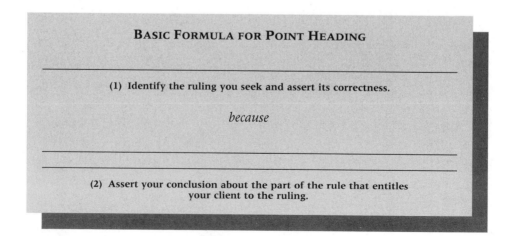

BASIC FORMULA FOR POINT HEADING

(1) Identify the ruling you seek and assert its correctness.

because

(2) Assert your conclusion about the part of the rule that entitles your client to the ruling.

For example, assume that the defendant is challenging the state's proof on the "nighttime" element in the burglary charge. Assume further that the rule on what constitutes "nighttime" is any time between thirty minutes after sunset and thirty minutes before sunrise. The defendant's working point heading might look like this:

The burglary charge should be dismissed

[(1) Identifying the ruling you seek and asserting its correctness.]

because

the alleged breaking and entering occurred earlier than thirty minutes after sunset.

[(2) Asserting your conclusion about the part of the rule that entitles your client to the ruling.]

Don't try to identify the rule simply by a legal citation ("The motion to dismiss should be granted because the contract complies with the rule in *Smith v. Jones*."). Articulating the key part of the rule in the working point heading will help keep your thinking focused. Also, when you later convert the working draft to a document designed for a reader, you'll need to articulate the rule. Your reader probably will not have the content of a particular statute or the holding of a particular case memorized.

 EXERCISE 1. Identifying Working Point Headings

Facts: Several years ago Clifford Foodman defended Raymond Carson on hit-and-run charges (*State v. Carson*). Now Foodman represents Alice Janoff, the defendant in a contract dispute. Carson is the plaintiff in the case. Before Foodman accepted representation of Janoff, Foodman wrote to Carson informing him that Janoff had asked Foodman to represent her in *Carson v. Janoff*. The letter told Carson that Foodman would assume that Carson consented to the proposed representation if Carson did not contact Foodman. Carson did not respond. Now, eight months later, Carson has filed a motion in *Carson v. Janoff* seeking Foodman's disqualification from representing Janoff. The judge has asked both parties to submit simultaneous briefs on the issue. Assume that this is the applicable rule:

A lawyer who has formerly represented a client in a matter shall not thereafter represent another person in the same or a substantially related matter in which that person's interests are materially adverse to the interests of the former client unless the former client consents after consultation.

Assuming that reasonable support exists for each, which of the following arguments would qualify as a subject for *point* headings for Carson, arguing that Foodman should be disqualified? Which would qualify as a subject for *point* headings for Janoff, arguing that Foodman should not be disqualified?

a.   *Carson v. Janoff* [is] [is not] substantially related to *State v. Carson.*
b.   Carson [did] [did not] consent to Foodman's representation of Janoff.
c.   Janoff's interests in *Carson v. Janoff* [are] [are not] materially adverse to Carson's interests.

EXERCISE 2.   Evaluating Working Point Headings

Using the facts and rule from Exercise 1, identify the best working point heading. Why is it the best? Identify the components of each.

a.   Carson consented to Foodman's representation of Janoff.
b.   The motion to disqualify should be denied because Janoff's failure to respond to Foodman's letter constituted consent to the representation.
c.   The motion to disqualify should be denied because Janoff consented to the representation.
d.   The motion to disqualify should be denied.

II   IDENTIFYING AND DRAFTING WORKING SUBHEADINGS

After you have identified and drafted working point headings, turn your attention to working subheadings. The first level of subheadings should define any separate "single issues" your analysis of the point heading will cover.

A.   HOW TO IDENTIFY A SINGLE-ISSUE DISCUSSION

First, remember how to identify a "single issue." Look at your rule structure and distinguish between the parts of the rule that must be considered together and the parts of the rule that can be decided separately. The parts of the rule that can be decided separately constitute separate issues. The parts of the rule that must be considered together are all part of the same issue. Before going on, review pages 84-85 to be sure that this concept is clear.

Use as many levels of subheadings as you need to reflect the single issues represented in the rule's structure. Even if the rule has several subparts, the facts and procedural posture of your particular assignment may place only one of those subparts at issue. If you have only one component necessary to establish the point heading, do not use a subheading. That component should be the subject of the point heading itself.

B.   DRAFTING WORKING SUBHEADINGS

The content of a working subheading can be simpler than the content of a working point heading. A subheading need not assert the entitlement to a particular ruling since the point heading already did that. The subheading can be limited to the second half of the formula for a working point heading:

> **Assert your conclusion about the part of the rule that entitles your client to the ruling.**

Back to the burglary example. The lack of any single element would entitle the defendant to a dismissal of the burglary charge. Therefore, every element the defendant challenges would constitute a point heading. If the defendant challenges the state's ability to prove three of the elements, the defendant's brief would contain three point headings, one for each disputed element.

The prosecutor, however, must establish all disputed elements to prevail on the motion. Therefore, the state's responsive brief (arguing that the charges should *not* be dismissed) would contain only one point heading. Since working subheadings represent each single issue necessary to establish the point heading, the state's brief would have three subheadings, one for each challenged element. The state's working point heading and subheadings would look like this.

> I.   THE BURGLARY CHARGE AGAINST THE DEFENDANT SHOULD NOT BE DISMISSED BECAUSE THE EVIDENCE AT TRIAL WILL ESTABLISH ALL OF THE ELEMENTS OF BURGLARY.
>
> A.   The evidence will show that the crime occurred in the nighttime.
>
> B.   The evidence will show that the Defendant intended to commit a felony when he entered the house.
>
> C.   The evidence will show that the dwelling was not the Defendant's own.

A working point heading that attempts to state the writer's position on a number of elements would be unwieldy. In such a case, the working point heading can simply make an umbrella statement covering all disputed elements, as this one does.

◆ EXERCISE 3.   Drafting Working Point Headings and Subheadings

In a disciplinary proceeding, a partner in a law firm has been charged with responsibility for disciplinary violations committed by an associate in the firm. The rule governing the responsibility of the partner is:

> A lawyer shall be responsible for another lawyer's violation of the rules of professional conduct if:
>
> (1) the lawyer orders or, with knowledge of the specific conduct, ratifies the conduct involved; or
>
> (2) the lawyer is a partner in the law firm in which the other lawyer practices, or has direct supervisory authority over the other lawyer, and knows of the conduct at a time when its consequences can be avoided or mitigated but fails to take reasonable remedial action.

Facts: The associate, Barbara Wendell, was working on the case of *Jaynes v. Darien* under the direct supervision of the partner, Willis Treyburn. The firm represented the defendant. Wendell was preparing a response to the plaintiff's request for production of documents. One of the requests asked for all of the defendant's interoffice memos concerning the plaintiff. Wendell had examined all of the defendant's interoffice memos and knew that one of them was devastating to the defendant's position. Wendell had found the memo buried in the defendant's files, and she believed that no one recalled the existence of the memo.

Wendell destroyed what she believed to be the only copy of the memo. She prepared a response to the plaintiff's request for production and did not disclose any information about the memo. She presented the response to Treyburn for his signature. Treyburn signed the response and Wendell filed it with the court.

Upon receiving a copy of the response, the plaintiff's attorney, Allison Bell, called Treyburn and demanded a copy of the missing memo. It seems that someone employed by the defendant had remembered the memo. This employee, sympathetic to the plaintiff's cause, had made a copy of the memo and given it to Bell. Treyburn honestly told Bell that he knew nothing about such a memo, but he assured Bell that the defendant would stipulate to the authenticity of the document, assuming it was genuine.

When Treyburn asked Wendell about the memo, Wendell admitted her conduct to Treyburn. Although he was distraught, Treyburn reasoned that no damage had been done to the plaintiff. Bell had the memo and the defendant would stipulate to its authenticity. Treyburn took disciplinary action against Wendell within the firm, but decided to say nothing about Wendell's conduct to anyone outside the firm.

Unfortunately, the same sympathetic employee who provided Bell with the copy of the memo had seen Wendell destroy the original. Now all of the facts are known to the bar disciplinary authority.

The issue is whether Treyburn can be held responsible for the actions of Wendell under the rule set out above. (Treyburn may well have violated other disciplinary rules as well, but this example deals only with the rule above.) Treyburn is filing a brief arguing that he is not responsible for Wendell's actions. The bar disciplinary authority is filing a brief arguing that Treyburn is responsible under the rule.

Outline the rule and then draft a set of working point headings and subheadings for the disciplinary authority and another set for Treyburn.

Compare the point headings and subheadings for each party. Are the topics they cover different? Why or why not?

IDENTIFYING THE APPROPRIATE STANDARD OF REVIEW

If you are writing an appellate brief rather than a trial-level brief, you must determine the appropriate standard of review for the issues addressed in the brief. Your brief will be required to identify the standard of review. Court rules may require that the standard be identified in its own labeled section,[2] or the standard may simply be set out early in the Argument section. More relevant for our purposes in this chapter, the point headings and subheadings should ordinarily reflect the standard of review.[3]

What is a standard of review? The *standard of review* defines the level of deference the appellate court must give to the trial court's decision on the question appealed.[4] Can the appellate court freely decide the question on its own, without any regard for the decision of the trial court? This standard would be good news for the *appellant*, who objects to the trial court's decision. It would be like starting over, as if the trial court had never decided the question.

Or must the appellate court give some level of deference to the trial court's decision? This more limited standard would be good news for the *appellee*, who agrees with the trial court's decision. This standard increases the odds that the trial court's decision will prevail. The question of which party will have the good news, and just how good the news will be, depends on the kind of trial court decision being appealed.

---

2.   *See* p. 249.

3.   If the standard of review is unfavorable, you may not wish to reiterate it in each point heading. A simple acknowledgment of the standard early in the brief may be sufficient.

4.   *See generally* Ruggero J. Aldisert, *Opinion Writing* 53-69 (1993); Daniel J. Meador et al., *Appellate Courts: Structures, Functions, Processes, and Personnel* 154-226 (1994); Alan D. Hornstein, *Appellate Advocacy In A Nutshell* 31-36 (1984).

A.   CATEGORIES OF TRIAL COURT DECISIONS

In a proceeding before a trial court, the judge must decide both the law and the facts. A trial court also must decide many discretionary questions, often procedural in nature. Errors in making any of these decisions—decisions of law, decisions of fact, or decisions left to the court's discretion—can lead to an appeal. The following sections describe these categories of decisions and the standard of review and policy rationale applicable to each.

1.   Questions of Law

A pure question of law can be decided without reference to the facts of the case at all. Does this jurisdiction recognize a claim for the wrongful death of a fetus? Within what time period must a notice of appeal be filed? Must a contingent fee agreement be put in writing? Must a will be signed? These are all purely questions of law. They can be researched and answered without reference to any particular set of facts.

A trial court's decision on a pure question of law is subject to de novo review by an appellate court. De novo review allows the appellate court to grant no deference to the trial court's opinion. The appellate court is free to substitute its own opinion on the question of what the jurisdiction's law provides.[5] The principle of stare decisis encourages the appellate court to pay some deference to the existing law, but this deference is unrelated to whether the lower court adopted and applied that law.

Therefore, an appellate court need not give any deference even to a trial court ruling that is *correct*—correct in the sense that it accurately states the rule of law at the time of the lower court's decision. Depending on the level of the appellate court and on the nature of the issue being appealed, the appellate court may decide that the trial judge was right in concluding what the law *was*, but that the law *ought* to be something else. The appellate court might take the opportunity presented by this case to announce a change in the law.[6] As a matter of fact, the primary rationale for the de novo standard is the function of appellate courts to make new law.

2.   Questions of Fact

A pure question of fact is a question that can be decided only on the basis of evidence. What the law is or is not has absolutely nothing to do with the question. What speed limit was posted? Did the defendant enter the building? Is the signature on the contract that of the plaintiff? These are all purely questions of fact. They can be decided without reference to any rule of law. You could have decided such questions long before you came to law school.

A trial *judge's* decision of a pure question of fact is nearly always subject to

---

5.   *See, e.g., Watzek v. Walker,* 485 P.2d 3 (Ariz. Ct. App. 1971).
6.   Whether that change in the law will apply to the case then before the court is a separate legal issue that is the subject of a separate body of law.

review using a "clearly erroneous" standard.[7] To overturn a trial judge's decision using the "clearly erroneous" standard, an appellate court would have to decide that, while *some* evidence supporting the decision may exist in the trial court record, the appellate court "is left with the definite and firm conviction that a mistake has been committed."[8] It is not enough that the appellate court would have made a different decision. As long as the lower court's decision is plausible, given the record as a whole, the opinion must be upheld.[9]

The most common policy rationales for the "clearly erroneous" standard are (1) the better opportunity of trial courts to judge the credibility of witnesses and the weight to be accorded to testimony; (2) the function assigned to trial courts as the primary fact finders; (3) the inadvisability of expending judicial resources on duplicating functions and responsibilities; (4) the unfairness of requiring the parties to convince two different courts of their facts; (5) the concern for crowded appellate dockets; and (6) the advantage of a trial judge's expertise in fact-finding.

A *jury's* decision of a pure question of fact usually is subject to an even more limited standard of review—a "competent evidence" standard. If the jury was properly instructed and if the record contains some modicum of competent evidence supporting the jury's decision, the appellate court must allow the jury's decision to stand.[10] In other words, the appellate court's only function in reviewing a jury verdict is to be sure that the jury's verdict is not irrational.[11] In addition to some of the same policies supporting the limited review of a judge's fact-finding, the primary rationale for this "competent evidence" standard, the most limited of reviews, is the parties' constitutional right to a trial by jury.

3. Mixed Questions of Law and Fact

Identifying purely factual or purely legal questions and the corresponding standards of review is fairly straightforward. The matter becomes confusing when the question involves a mixture of law and fact. For example, consider the following example drawn from a case in which the plaintiff is suing the defendant for damages arising from a car accident. Here are some questions of fact and the trial court's decisions on them:

Questions of Fact	*Trial Court's Answers*
What speed limit was posted?	55 MPH
What speed was the defendant traveling?	65 MPH
Was it raining?	yes
Did the driver signal an intention to turn?	no

---

7.   *See* Fed. R. Civ. P. 52(a).
8.   *Anderson v. City of Bessemer,* 470 U.S. 564, 573 (1985).
9.   *Id.* at 573-574.
10. *See, e.g., I.M.A. v. Rocky Mountain Airways, Inc.,* 713 P.2d 882 (Colo. 1986).
11. Robert J. Martineau, *Fundamentals of Modern Appellate Advocacy* 133-134 (1985).

Here is a question of law and the trial court's answer to it:

Question of Law	*Trial Court's Answer*
What is the duty of care owed by an automobile driver to other drivers?	A driver must exercise the degree of care that would be exercised by a reasonable person under those same circumstances.

Having decided the *facts* and decided the relevant *law,* the trial court now decides *how the law applies to the facts of this case.*

Question of Mixed Law and Fact	*Trial Court's Answer*
Is driving 65 MPH in the rain when the speed limit is 55 and not signaling the intention to turn **[Facts]**	No

consistent with

the degree of care that would be exercised by a reasonable person under those same circumstances? **[Law]**

Now, assume that the defendant appeals. She does not disagree with the trial court's answers deciding the speed limit, her speed at the time of the accident, whether it was raining, and whether she signaled. Assume also that she does not disagree with the trial court's answer defining the duty of care owed to other drivers. Rather, she disagrees with the trial court's decision that driving at that speed under those conditions and turning without signaling *was inconsistent with* the way a reasonable person would drive. In other words, she disagrees with the way the trial court applied the law to the facts. This is a disagreement about a mixed question of law and fact (an "ultimate fact").

The reviewing court must decide whether to use a de novo standard or a "clearly erroneous" standard for a mixed question of law and fact. Usually the court chooses the standard on a case-by-case determination of whether factual questions or legal questions will predominate. The majority of mixed questions are subject to de novo review, and mixed questions of constitutional law are nearly always subject to de novo review.[12] Questions of negligence generally are subject to "clearly erroneous" review.[13]

4.   *Questions Within the Trial Court's Discretion*

A trial judge has no discretion about whether to apply the relevant rule of law. A trial judge has no discretion about whether to decide the facts of the dispute and be bound by those facts in resolving the case. However, during the course of a legal proceeding, a trial judge must decide other questions, questions that the applicable rule of law leaves within the judge's discretion.

---

12.   *See, e.g., United States v. McConney,* 728 F.2d 1195 (9th Cir. 1984) (en banc).
13.   *Id.*

As we saw in Chapters 2 through 4, the applicable rule of law may provide the judge with factors or guidelines to help the judge know *how* to make the decision, but the applicable rule doesn't tell the judge *what* to decide. Instead, the rule recognizes that the best answer to that particular question will differ from situation to situation and will depend on circumstances that no single rule of law could anticipate, describe, and evaluate.

Questions left in the trial court's discretion are usually either matters of equity or matters of procedure and case management. For instance, after the initial stages of litigation, a party who has filed an answer must obtain the judge's permission to amend that answer.[14] Case law construing the applicable rule may give the judge some guidelines about when to give permission, but under most court rules, the decision is left to the judge's discretion. The trial judge's duty in making such decisions is to refrain from acting unreasonably or arbitrarily.

This scope of authority gives a trial judge broad latitude and, correspondingly, it gives appellate courts a narrow role in reviewing such lower-court decisions. An appellate court is not free to overturn a trial judge's decision just because the appellate court would have made a different decision. To overturn a decision left to the trial court's discretion, the appellate court must hold that the decision was "an abuse of discretion."[15] As long as the trial court's decision was not unreasonable or arbitrary, the appellate court must affirm it.

Some lawyers evaluate the "abuse of discretion" standard as allowing roughly the same degree of deference as the "clearly erroneous" standard for reviewing facts.[16] Others view "abuse of discretion" as allowing slightly more latitude on appeal than does "clearly erroneous."[17] Still other lawyers believe that "abuse of discretion" actually covers several subtle sublevels of deference.[18]

The most common policy rationales for the "abuse of discretion" standard are: (1) the need for flexibility in case management; (2) judicial economy and the crowded appellate docket; (3) judicial *comity* (respect for the decisions of other judges); (4) the ability of the trial judge to assess the circumstances firsthand; (5) the need for flexible rules of law to address satisfactorily all possible circumstances; and (6) the need to support the trial judge's authority and control of her own courtroom.

B. Advocating a More Favorable Standard of Review

Section A sets out the general rules that usually determine the appropriate standard. Courts, however, do not always follow the general rule; the first

---

14. *See, e.g.,* Fed. R. Civ. P. 15(a).
15. *See, e.g., Napolitano v. Compania Sud Americana De Vapores*, 421 F.2d 382 (2d Cir. 1970); *Kern v. TXO Production Corp.*, 738 F.2d 968 (8th Cir. 1984).
16. *See, e.g.,* Robert J. Martineau, *Fundamentals of Modern Advocacy* 138 (1985).
17. *See, e.g.,* Ruggero J. Aldisert, *Opinion Writing* 65 (1993).
18. Maurice Rosenberg, *Standards of Review, in* Arthur D. Hellman, ed., *Restructuring Justice* 48-49 (1990).

and best way to identify the appropriate standard of review for your case is to look for opinions issued by the court that will be deciding your case. Search for cases deciding issues similar to yours, and see what standard of review the court used in those cases.

If you are relying on appellate cases from your own jurisdiction for some of your argument on the merits of your case, those cases probably also mention the appropriate standard of review for the issues your brief addresses. If not, look for cases on your issue from other appellate courts, and look for opinions from your own jurisdiction on similar issues. Find out what the standard is, what it means, and how it might apply to a case like yours.

It should go without saying that an advocate should look for authority, including policy arguments, supporting the most favorable standard of review possible. Where doubt exists as to the proper standard, an appellant should argue for the *least* restrictive standard—a standard that maximizes the appellate court's authority to overturn the challenged decision. An appellee should argue for the *most* restrictive standard—a standard that limits the appellate court's authority to overturn the trial court's ruling.

On pure questions of law, the de novo standard of review is well settled, and few, if any, distinctions will affect it. On pure questions of fact, the "clearly erroneous" or "competent evidence" standards are fairly well settled as well. However, an advocate may still be able to influence, subtly, an appellate court's application of the standard for reviewing fact-finding. For instance, in an appropriate case the lawyer might point out that the evidence was entirely documentary (requiring no assessment of witness credibility) or that the evidence was uncontested. In either situation, the policy rationales listed on page 285 would be less applicable.

However, the standards applicable both to questions of mixed law and fact and to questions left to the trial court's discretion may leave some room for advocacy. For questions that might be categorized as mixed law and fact, the advocate can sometimes influence the appellate court's decision on whether the particular question *is* a mixed question, and if so, what standard should apply to it. Should the appellate court decide by examining the nature of the particular question on appeal? If so, how does this particular question fare under such an examination? Does the *factual* aspect or the *legal* aspect predominate? Were the facts contested? Was the law well settled and construed by many cases? Were the facts established by a judge or by a jury? Does the case involve an important issue of constitutional rights?

For questions that may be left to the trial court's discretion, the advocate can sometimes influence the appellate court's decision on (a) whether the applicable rule *does* leave the question to the trial court's discretion; and if so, (b) just how much discretion the appellate court should allow the trial court to exercise in deciding this particular kind of question. Though the cases do not expressly identify sublevels within the "abuse of discretion" standard, such sublevels probably exist.[19]

---

19.   A number of commentators have identified levels within the abuse of discretion standard. *See, e.g.,* Henry J. Friendly, *Indiscretion About Discretion,* 31 Emory L.J. 747, 760-762, 771-772, 783-784 (1982); Federal Civil Appellate Jurisdiction: An Interlocutory Restatement, 47 Law & Contemp. Probs. 62-63 (1984); Maurice Rosenberg, *Standards of Review,* in Arthur D. Hellman, ed., Restructuring Justice 48-49 (1990).

So compare the policy rationales for the "abuse of discretion" standard to the circumstances of your case. Consider the rule that grants the trial court discretion. Use your common sense. What small points can you make to subtly convince the appellate court to narrow or widen the deference it will give to the trial court? For instance, do the authorities announce standards or factors that are to guide the trial court's discretion? Did the trial court have to make factual findings as part of the decision of the question left to its discretion? How important are the rights at stake? How possible and how desirable is it to increase the uniformity of approach among trial courts on this issue? Has the trial court deviated from a common custom or practice? Is this a relatively new question that could benefit from a period of experimentation at the trial court level before an appellate court takes a position on it? The answers to these sorts of questions can provide the raw material for influencing the way the appellate court applies the standard.

C. EDITING HEADINGS TO CONFORM TO THE STANDARD OF REVIEW

Once you have identified the applicable standard of review, edit your point headings and subheadings to conform to the relevant standard. Here are examples of headings phrased according to the appropriate standard:

No competent evidence	The burglary conviction should be overturned because the record contains no competent evidence that the breaking and entering occurred later than thirty minutes after sunset.
Clearly erroneous	The judgment should be overturned because the trial court's finding of intent to discriminate was clearly erroneous.
De novo	The trial court should have denied the defendant's motion to dismiss because this jurisdiction allows parents to bring a claim for the wrongful death of a fetus.
Abuse of discretion	The trial court did not abuse its discretion when it issued a preliminary injunction prohibiting the defendant from concealing or disposing of his assets.

Notice that the de novo standard does not change the phrasing of the argument because that standard puts no gloss whatsoever on the question. That standard imposes no limitations on the appellate court's decision.

A brief is far more effective when it establishes the most favorable standard of review supportable by the authorities and makes a few points about how that standard should be applied to the pending case. Consider the policy rationales that underlie each standard of review, comparing them to the circumstances of your case. Now, as you write the argument, make whatever points you can in favor of applying the standard most favorable to your position.

As Senior United States Circuit Judge Ruggero J. Aldisert explains, "[s]tandards of review are critically important in appellate decision making."[20] Yet, many lawyers forget to research the proper standard and to couch their arguments according to its terms. As a matter of fact, Judge Aldisert describes his experience of observing the "psychological block" that seems to prevent some lawyers from recognizing and dealing with the standard of review.[21] If, from the beginning of your practice, you pay careful attention to the standard of review, you will never be one of the lawyers Judge Aldisert describes.

EXERCISE 4.   Identifying Categories of Trial Court Decisions

For each of the following issues on appeal, decide whether the issue is a question of law, a question of fact, a mixed question, or a question of the trial court's exercise of discretion. Review the facts of the case on page 269.

a.   Assume that the trial court ruled against Guzman and in favor of A-1 Realty. The trial court held that, to prevail on a claim for constructive eviction, the plaintiff must prove that the property was unsuitable for occupancy for the purposes for which the occupancy was intended. The court decided that the apartment had been leased as a residence and that the condition of the apartment was suitable for occupancy as a residence. Guzman has appealed the court's decision that the apartment was suitable for occupancy as a residence.

b.   Assume that the trial court ruled against Guzman and in favor of A-1 Realty. The trial court held that, to prevail on a claim for constructive eviction, the plaintiff must prove that the property was unsuitable for occupancy for the purposes for which the occupancy was intended. The court decided that the building does not contain rats. Guzman has appealed the court's decision that the building does not contain rats.

c.   Assume that the trial court ruled against Guzman and in favor of A-1 Realty. The trial court decided that, to prevail on a claim for constructive eviction, the landlord must have intended to force the tenant to move. Guzman

---

20.   Ruggero J. Aldisert, *Opinion Writing* 53 (1993).
21.   *Id.*

appeals the trial court's decision that intent is an element of a claim for constructive eviction.

d.   In pretrial discovery, A-1 Realty refused to answer ten of Guzman's interrogatories. Guzman moved for an order requiring A-1 to answer the ten interrogatories. The trial court decided that five of the interrogatories were proper and five were objectionable. The court ordered A-1 to answer the five proper interrogatories and refused to order A-1 to answer the other five.

The applicable rule of procedure provides that when a motion to compel discovery is granted in part and denied in part, the court "may" apportion the expenses of bringing and resisting the motion among the parties "in a just manner."[22] The trial court ordered that each party bear its own expenses on the motion. Both parties appeal the court's order apportioning expenses, each arguing that the court should have required the other party to reimburse that party's expenses.

Your research on this question will yield case opinions that tell you the applicable standard of review on this issue, but what is your best guess about what standard these opinions will identify?

---

22.   *See, e.g.,* Fed. R. Civ. P. 37(a)(4)(C).

Writing the Working Draft

The headings and subheadings have provided the structure of your working draft; the next step in creating the working draft of the Argument section is writing out the arguments for each section. Just as in the working draft stage of the office memo, you may find it helpful to write out a working draft of the Statement of Facts[1] before you proceed with the working draft of the Argument section. If you are experiencing "writer's block," this strategy may help you get started. Also, you may find that immersing yourself in your client's story is excellent preparation for the more linear reasoning required in the Argument section.

I UMBRELLA SECTION[2]

For a single-issue brief where the reader needs no context, you may not need an umbrella section; but for a brief with several issues or for a single-issue brief where context would help the reader, an umbrella section can serve important functions. An umbrella section sets out the writer's organizational choices so

---

1. *See* Chapter 21.
2. Your teacher or law firm may ask you to use a format that includes a separate section labeled "Introduction to Argument." The content and function of this separate section are different from the content and function of the umbrella paragraphs at the beginning of the Argument section. *See* Chapter 16 for a description of the Introduction to Argument.

the judge will be receptive to the writer's legal analysis.[3] In addition, by providing context, the umbrella section functions as another tool of persuasion. Ideally, a brief should *teach* the judge your argument;[4] most learners learn best when they have a context in which to place new material. An umbrella section provides the judge with the context for the heart of the argument to follow.

As you recall, an umbrella section should be concise—generally limited to one or two short paragraphs. The function of an umbrella section is to introduce the components that follow; therefore, you can use an umbrella section at the beginning of the Argument section (before the first roman numeral) to introduce the roman numeral(s), or you can use an umbrella section to introduce subparts within a roman numeral. Customary content of an umbrella section includes:

1.   Summarizing the umbrella rule of law.
2.   Explaining the status of any relevant elements you will *not* discuss.
3.   Asserting the correctness of the ruling you seek on the elements your brief *will* discuss.
4.   Identifying the relevant standard(s) of review, if any.
5.   Explaining the order in which the points will be presented.

1.   Summarize the rule and cite the controlling authority defining the rule.   Your summary should be complete enough to give the reader a quick, clear overview of the relevant parts of the rule. Include any other principles that favorably affect the functioning of the rule, such as presumptions, burdens of proof, or policy leanings.[5]

2.   Explain the status of any elements *not* discussed in the brief. Your argument may omit some of the elements either because the element is undisputed or because it is not at issue at this stage in the litigation. If the status of these undiscussed elements might be initially unclear to your reader, identify these elements and clarify their status. If the unargued element favors your client's position and the opposing party does not contest it, say so here.

What if the element favors the opposing party, and *you* do not contest it? What if the rule contains elements on which you have no reasonable argument? Consider conceding those elements here, at the outset of the argument. Such a concession may allow you to harvest valuable credibility with your reader. A concession presents your reader with rhetorical evidence that your argument on the *contested* elements is legitimate, because you have been straightforward enough to concede the *uncontested* elements.

3.   Assert the correctness of the ruling you seek on the elements your brief *will* discuss.   You can add a persuasive summary, in one or two sentences, of your argument on each element.

---

3.   *See* Chapter 16.
4.   "Teaching" the judge does not mean that the brief should employ a condescending or pedantic tone, however.
5.   *See* Chapter 12, pp. 158-159.

4. Identify the relevant standard of review. In an appellate brief where the standard of review will not have its own labeled section, the umbrella section also may cover the standard of review. Cite to authority that supports your position on which standard applies.

If the standard will not be disputed, you can rely on minimal authority and omit lengthy explanation. If you expect the standard of review to be disputed, however, you will need to set out your authority, policy rationale, and arguments in more depth. If the discussion will be lengthy, consider making the standard of review a subheading unto itself.

As you write the argument that follows, be sure it is phrased in terms that comply with the relevant standard of review. Since the de novo standard does not apply any particular gloss to the question, you probably won't need to refer to it throughout the section, unless it is helpful to your argument. For the other standards of review, be sure that your argument is focused on "whether the trial court abused its discretion," or "whether the factual findings were clearly erroneous," or "whether the record contains competent evidence to support the jury's verdict."

5. Identify the elements your argument will cover and, where helpful, explain the order. The umbrella section can summarize your argument on these elements in one or two sentences. If you anticipate that your reader will resist your chosen order, explain the choice.

⬥ **EXERCISE 1.   Labeling the Components of the Umbrella Section**

Here is an example of an umbrella section immediately before the roman numeral and an umbrella section between the roman numeral and the subsections. Identify each component of the two umbrella paragraphs.

ARGUMENT

To find the defendant guilty of burglary, the jury must find that the defendant (1) broke and (2) entered (3) the dwelling (4) of another (5) in the nighttime (6) with the intent to commit a felony therein. [citation] The defendant does not contest the sufficiency of the evidence to establish the first four of these elements. The defendant challenges only whether the breaking and entering occurred in the nighttime and whether the defendant had formed the requisite intent when he entered the dwelling. This brief will show that the evidence establishes these final two elements as well.

I. THE BURGLARY INDICTMENT AGAINST THE DEFENDANT SHOULD NOT BE QUASHED BECAUSE THE EVIDENCE WILL ESTABLISH BOTH CHALLENGED ELEMENTS OF BURGLARY.

> To defeat a motion to quash the indictment, the state need only show that a reasonable jury *could* consider the expected trial evidence and find each challenged element present. [citation] The state's expected trial evidence more than meets this standard.
>
> A. <u>The evidence will show that the crime occurred in the nighttime.</u>
>   **[one paradigm]**
>
> B. <u>The evidence will show that the defendant intended to commit a felony when he entered the house.</u>
>   **[one paradigm]**

II THE PARADIGM FOR AN ARGUMENT

Now write out a draft of the argument under each heading, using the paradigm on page 296 to organize the argument on that point. If you have a point heading and no subheadings, write out one paradigm. If you have subheadings, write an umbrella paragraph for that point heading and write a separate paradigm under each subheading. The order of the subheadings is not important at this stage of the writing process (except that all subheadings must stay beneath the appropriate point heading). Later, after you have written a draft of each point and can evaluate the strength of each, you can decide the order of the point headings and subheadings.

Chapters 7 and 8 explained the paradigm for organizing a predictive legal analysis. The same paradigm, with only slight variation, applies to brief-writing. The first half of the paradigm states and explains the rule; the second half applies the rule to the client's facts. Just as we saw in predictive writing, rule explanation should remain distinct from rule application, with rule explanation coming first.

All of the reasons we saw earlier for keeping rule explanation separate from rule application still apply, but in persuasive writing another important reason applies as well. Presenting the reader with rule explanation first and separate from rule application capitalizes on one of the principles of persuasion: readers are more persuaded by ideas they have first thought of themselves than by an idea first asserted by another.[6] This is especially true when the reader knows that the person doing the asserting is an advocate with an admitted persuasive agenda.

The strategy goes like this: The reader first reads the brief's fact statement, and has those facts in mind when reading the rule explanation. During the

---

6. *See* Chapter 16, p. 245.

rule statement and explanation, the reader will be thinking of those facts and anticipating rule application. The reader's Commentator[7] will be applying each point the writer is explaining about the rule to those facts. Presenting rule explanation first, without explicit application to the facts, allows the rule explanation to lead the reader to the desired conclusions about rule application, *before the writer asserts those conclusions.* Then, when the writer reaches the rule application phase, the writer is only asserting the conclusions the reader has already reached on his own.

The paradigm for persuasive writing differs from predictive writing slightly. Because the task for a *predictive* legal analysis is to decide the most likely conclusion, the working draft paradigm for a predictive analysis guides the writer to that conclusion. The writer begins with the *issue* and writes her way through the legal reasoning process, ultimately reaching a conclusion—an answer to the question posed. She may not know for certain what her conclusion will be until she writes her way to it.

The brief-writer, however, already knows both the legal and factual conclusions she wants to reach. Her goal in writing the working draft is to find the best *route* to that destination rather than to choose the destination itself. Therefore, rather than beginning with a statement of the issue, the brief-writer can begin directly with a statement of the *conclusion* about the issue. The conclusion is the result the writer wants her reader to reach. A brief's final draft takes this form anyway, and beginning by stating the conclusion is a good way to keep focused on what the writer wants to "prove."

In the working draft of a brief, the conclusion replaces the statement of the issue in the point heading or subheading, and it also generally appears in the first paragraph of text beneath the heading.[8] A version of the conclusion also appears at the beginning of the rule application section, right before the writer shows how the client's facts establish the conclusion. Here, it reminds the writer of exactly what she must use the facts to "prove." Finally, the conclusion appears at the end of the paradigm, just as in the paradigm for predictive writing. This repetition not only contributes to an orderly route through rule-based reasoning, but its subtle repetition is an effective technique for emphasis.[9]

Occasionally, later drafts can vary the normal multi-issue paradigm by combining the rule explanation section for each element into one comprehensive explanation of the rule and then combining the rule application section for each element into a comprehensive application of the rule. If you think that your situation may call for this approach, review the description of this variation on pages 135-137. However, don't use this variation for the first draft. Let the discipline of separately writing out the rule explanation and rule application for each individual element help you deepen your understanding of that element. Only after you are sure that you have mined the depths of analysis and argument possible for each individual element can you decide whether a combined discussion is appropriate.

---

7. *See* Chapter 11, p. 151.
8. *See* the examples on pp. 297-298.
9. Mary Barnard Ray & Barbara J. Cox, *Beyond The Basics: A Text for Advanced Legal Writing* 179 (1991).

	PARADIGM FOR AN ARGUMENT
Conclusion	State the conclusion you want your reader to reach (in the heading and in the first paragraph).
Rule statement	State the applicable legal rule (in the form and structure most favorable to your client's position).
Rule explanation	Explain where the rule comes from (to satisfy your reader that the rule you've stated really is the rule).
	Explain what the rule means (in the terms most favorable to your client's position).
	Rebut any counter-analysis you can weaken by a preemptive discussion.
Factual conclusion	State the conclusion you want your reader to reach about the facts.
Rule application	Apply the rule to your client's facts (emphasizing the favorable facts and de-emphasizing the problematic facts).
	Rebut any counter-application you can weaken by a preemptive discussion.
Conclusion	Restate your conclusion with a one-paragraph summary of the key points supporting it.

A hint about writing the rule application section of each separate issue: A brief must refer only to facts that are a part of the court record.[10] When the brief recites a fact, it must cite to the location of the fact in the record. Since your finished brief will have to contain these cites, start inserting them now, as you write the working draft of the rule application sections. Use the citation form described in section IV of this chapter.[11]

EXERCISE 2. Labeling the Components of the Paradigm

Here is a skeletal example of a prosecutor's trial-level argument on two of the elements of burglary. It shows the paradigm for advocacy. Locate and label the parts of the paradigm.

10. *See* pp. 329-330.
11. Pp. 303-304.

ARGUMENT

To find the defendant guilty of burglary, the jury must find that the defendant (1) broke and (2) entered (3) the dwelling (4) of another (5) in the nighttime (6) with the intent to commit a felony therein. [citation] The defendant does not contest the sufficiency of the evidence to establish the first four of these elements. The defendant challenges only whether the breaking and entering occurred in the nighttime and whether the defendant had formed the requisite intent when he entered the dwelling. This brief will show that the evidence establishes these final two elements as well.

I. THE BURGLARY INDICTMENT AGAINST THE DEFENDANT SHOULD NOT BE QUASHED BECAUSE THE EVIDENCE WILL ESTABLISH BOTH CHALLENGED ELEMENTS OF BURGLARY.

To defeat a motion to quash the indictment, the state need only show that a reasonable jury *could* consider the expected trial evidence and find each challenged element present. [citation] The state's expected trial evidence more than meets this standard.

A. The evidence will show that the crime occurred in the nighttime.

The state's trial evidence will show that the time of the defendant's entry into the dwelling was within the period of time defined as "the nighttime." For the purposes of the burglary statute, [citation], an event occurs in the nighttime if it occurs more than thirty minutes after sunset and less than thirty minutes before sunrise. [cite to primary authority]

[Rule explanation continues, beginning with a discussion of the primary authority and proceeding to other authorities. Discuss the most favorable and persuasive authorities first.]

The state's trial witnesses will establish that the defendant entered the victim's dwelling at 6:30 P.M. or later.

[Rule application continues, discussing each piece of evidence leading to conclusion that the time was 6:30 or later.]

Thus, the state's evidence will establish the time of the defendant's departure from the bar; the normal time required to drive to the dwelling; the time of the victim's arrival at her neighbor's house; and the time of the neighbor's call to the paramedics. The evidence on these points will establish beyond a reasonable doubt that the crime occurred in the nighttime, as defined for the purposes of the crime of burglary.

B. The evidence will show that the defendant intended to commit a felony when he entered the house.

The trial evidence will show that the defendant formed his intent to assault and batter the victim before he left the bar and drove to the dwelling. [State your formulation of the rule on what the state must prove to establish intent; cite to primary authority.]

[Rule explanation continues, beginning with a discussion of the primary authority and proceeding to other authorities. Discuss the most favorable and persuasive authorities first.]

The state's trial witnesses will establish that by the time he left the bar the defendant had formed the intent to assault his victim.

[Rule application continues, discussing each piece of evidence of the defendant's intent at the time he entered the dwelling.]

Therefore the state's trial evidence will establish that the defendant had formulated the requisite intent at the time he entered the dwelling. The state need only show that . . . [one-sentence summary of what the state is required to show for the intent element]. Here, the testimony of *X, Y,* and *Z* will more than meet this standard.

For completed examples of each section of the paradigm, review the Argument sections of the briefs in Appendices B and C. For a review of the components of rule explanation and application, see Chapters 7 through 9. Use working labels to help you stay on track with the paradigm as you write and to help you evaluate your draft. Use thesis sentences wherever you can. Since thesis sentences assert positions, they are even more important for a strong *argument* (in a brief) than for an accurate *prediction* (in an office memo).

III   RULE APPLICATION FOR RULES WITH PERMISSIVE SUBPARTS: ADVANCED TECHNIQUES

The organizational pattern usually best for the rule *explanation* of a rule with permissive subparts (factors or guidelines) is organizing according to the factors.[12] However, a writer can organize the rule *application* section of the paradigm in several different ways. These organizational decisions can significantly affect the persuasiveness of a brief.

A.   First Organizational Option: By Factor

Since rule application generally mirrors rule explanation, the factor-by-factor pattern often organizes rule *application* as well. The working draft using this pattern would explain the factors, one by one, and then apply them one by one:

12.   *See* Chapter 9.

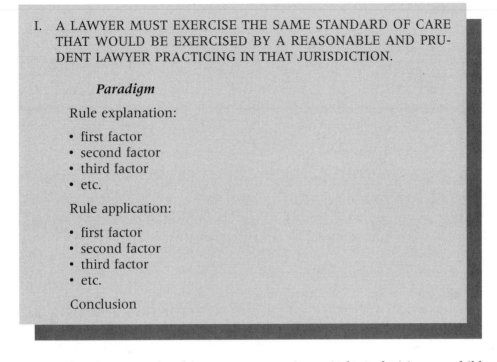

I.   A LAWYER MUST EXERCISE THE SAME STANDARD OF CARE
     THAT WOULD BE EXERCISED BY A REASONABLE AND PRU-
     DENT LAWYER PRACTICING IN THAT JURISDICTION.

> ***Paradigm***
>
> Rule explanation:
>
> - first factor
> - second factor
> - third factor
> - etc.
>
> Rule application:
>
> - first factor
> - second factor
> - third factor
> - etc.
>
> Conclusion

Consider, for example, this statute governing a judge's decision on child custody in a divorce:

> As between the parents, custody is to be decided according to the best interests of the child. The court may consider the following factors in deciding the best interests of the child:
>
> 1. the fitness of each parent
> 2. the appropriateness for parenting of the lifestyle of each parent
> 3. the relationship of the child to each parent
> 4. the placement of other children
> 5. the child's living accommodations
> 6. the district lines of the child's school
> 7. the proximity of extended family and friends
> 8. religious issues
> 9. any other factors relevant to the child's best interests

In rule application, the writer *could* simply apply each factor, one by one, just as the rule explanation explained each factor.

To evaluate this choice, look first at the effect of organizing rule application according to the statute's list of factors. Recall that readers keep score. Recall that keeping score, factor by factor, implicitly tends to equalize the importance of the factors; yet few readers will compensate consciously for the effect of this phenomenon. Thus, organizing according to the statute's list of factors tends to equalize the emphasis on favorable and unfavorable factors.

Second, organizing according to the list will expose any weaknesses of the client's facts on any particular factor. Such an organization limits flexibility. The writer cannot combine weaker factors with stronger factors that may offset the particular weakness. Nor can the writer identify a strategic theme (sometimes called a "theory of the case") and use the organization of the legal argument as one way of explaining this theme to the judge.

The *theory of the case* is your version of what really happened or what the case is really about. It usually has a theme that incorporates and makes sense of the facts proven at trial. For instance, in the child custody case, one theory of the case might be that the father is an unfit parent. A different theory of the case would be that the father is a fit parent, but that the mother would be a better custodial parent for this particular child at this particular time. These theories would use the same facts to tell different stories about the case. These different theories would require significantly different strategies, both in writing and in many other aspects of handling the case.

If you suspect that organizing rule application by the list of factors may not be your best choice, ask yourself (1) if the statute and its context offer any other possibilities for categories; and (2) what categories you would like to use if the statute hadn't created any. For our custody example, both inquiries will give you other possibilities.

B.   Second Organizational Option: By Party

The procedural context of this statute offers at least one other organizational choice because the statute operates when the judge is deciding which parent will be awarded custody. Thus, one option is to organize the rule application by party. Such a discussion, written on behalf of the mother, might look like this:

I.   BEST INTERESTS OF THE CHILD

As between the parents, custody is to be decided according to the best interests of the child. The court may consider the following factors in deciding the best interests of the child: [list]

Rule explanation [explaining the factors one by one]

Rule application:

- Interests served by awarding custody to mother:
  [Discuss, in the best light possible, the statute's identified factors that favor the mother. Since the statute allows consideration of other factors, discuss also any unidentified factors that favor the mother.]

- Interests served by awarding custody to father:
  [Discuss, in a less favorable light, the factors that favor the father. Compare these to the interests served by awarding custody to mother, showing that the latter outweighs the former.]

We cannot fully evaluate an organizational plan without reference to the facts and legal authorities controlling the particular case. Yet, we can observe at least four advantages of this organization, even without reference to facts and authorities. First, this organization would be flexible; it would allow the writer to combine factors, to emphasize and de-emphasize, and to advance a theme within each subsection. The writer could communicate a primary theme about the advantages of placement with the mother and could communicate a different primary theme about the disadvantages of placement with the father. Second, this organization has the appearance of objectivity. It is the classic "on the one hand this; on the other hand that" structure. Because its *structure* appears neutral, it may reduce the reader's skepticism.

Third, it immediately equalizes the score being kept by a reader. If the majority of the statute's identified factors would favor the opposing party, using this "balancing" format invites the reader to keep score using a much more favorable method. Finally, this organization may be the one most like the judge's natural thought process on this issue. Thus, if the brief-writer has used this organization and has already laid out the analysis in this format, the judge may choose to use that writer's analysis (rather than the opposing writer's analysis) as the starting point for the judge's own reasoning about the issues.

This organizational plan looks like an interesting option—one the brief writer will want to consider. First, though, the writer must finish identifying other possible plans.

C. THIRD ORGANIZATIONAL OPTION: BY THEME

Recall that the second question on page 300 invited you to be more creative. It asked you to imagine that the statute did not identify a set of categories and to decide what categories you would prefer.

Here is the brief-writer's best chance to think about themes. In the final analysis, why should this child be placed with the mother? Why not the father? If the lawyer steps back even further from the categories of the statute, the real heart of the client's position is likely to appear. For instance, perhaps the court-appointed social worker has identified this child's two greatest present needs as stability and a sense of control over his own fate in the midst of this frightening process of divorcing parents. You can see how the statute's identified factors and probably a number of other, unidentified factors would fit under these two categories. You could organize the statute's factors (and any others you want to add) beneath categories defined by these two identified needs. The application section might look like this:

I.   BEST INTERESTS OF THE CHILD

As between the parents, custody is to be decided according to the best interests of the child. The court may consider the following factors in deciding the best interests of the child: [list]

Rule explanation [explaining the factors one by one]

Rule application:

Child's need for stability [Discuss each factor that impacts stability:]

- Personal fitness of each parent to provide stability [Argue that placement with the mother would provide more stability because she has a more stable personality, keeps daily activities on a predictable schedule, etc.]
- Personal lifestyle of each parent as it affects stability [Argue that the father travels sometimes and would need either to take the child with him or leave him in the care of a baby-sitter, who would be a new person in the child's life.]
- Relationship of the child to each parent as it affects stability [Argue that, while the child cares deeply for each parent, the child has spent more time with his mother than with his father.]
- Living accommodations as they affect stability [Argue that, while the father's new home is nicer, the mother will be living in the former family home and the child would not have to move.]
- District lines of the child's school as they affect stability [Argue that, while the father's new house is closer to the child's school, stability counsels for having the child continue to ride the same school bus with the same group of children.]
- Any other factors relevant to stability

Child's need for sense of control over his own fate

- Personal fitness of each parent as it affects the child's sense of control [Argue that, while both are fit parents, the mother is more likely than the father to allow the child to make decisions in appropriate areas of the child's life.]
- Other factors affecting the child's sense of control [Argue that the child has decided that he wants to operate a paper route and placement with the father would interfere with his ability to carry out that decision, etc.]
- Any other factors relevant to sense of control.

Such a fact discussion organizes by *theme* or theory of the case rather than by factors. This organization is the most flexible of the three. First, it allows the most room for combining the discussions of some factors, so that they strengthen each other, while isolating other factors, to expose the weakness of the other party's position.

Second, and even more important, this organization allows the writer to mold the statute to suit the client's goals in the particular case. The writer can identify, apart from the statute, this particular child's greatest needs. After these particular needs are identified (and who could argue that the child does *not* need stability and some sense of control?), the fact discussion reorganizes the statute's identified factors, and any others as well, around these strategically identified needs.

Third, this organization allows the writer to emphasize larger and more compelling categories than the factors listed in the statute. Thus, the writer can pit these larger needs of the child against the individual factors that favor the other party. For instance, assume that the father has moved close to the child's grandparents, and placement with the father would have the advantage of proximity to the grandparents. Under this organization, the writer could weigh the child's need for stability against the advantage of proximity to the grandparents rather than weighing the child's need to avoid changing schools against the advantage of proximity to the grandparents. The judge is more likely to agree that, while proximity to grandparents is nice, the need for stability in a child's life is a vital.

Using themes or facts to organize the rule application part of a legal discussion is an advanced writing technique. While it will sometimes be the most effective choice, take care not to use it unless you are sure that you understand the rule itself and that the rule's meaning will remain identifiable in your organization.

IV   CITATIONS TO THE RECORD

Because the judge needs more than your assertion that the *rule* is what you say it is, your rule explanation section cites to the sources that establish the legal rule. Similarly, the judge needs more than your mere assertion that the *facts* are as you say they are. Citations to the sources for facts serve the same function for facts that citation to legal authority serves for the law. Use factual citations when you discuss your client's facts in the rule application section of the paradigm. You'll need the citations for your final draft anyway, and inserting them in your working draft will keep you from making factual arguments that you won't be able to substantiate when you convert your draft into a brief.

If your case has already proceeded through the trial stage and is now on appeal, you will have a formally prepared "Record." You or another lawyer representing your client will have selected the relevant parts of the trial court's case file for inclusion in the Record on appeal. An appellate brief must rely for its facts solely on this Record; therefore, the factual citations in an appellate brief must refer to and only to the Record. The most common form for these citations is "R. at [page number]."

If your case is still before the trial court, you will need to establish the facts by citation to whatever item in the trial court file establishes that fact best. If the item is not already part of the court record before you file your motion, court rules provide the procedure for filing it simultaneously with your motion. Therefore, you might file several affidavits (with or without documents attached) along with your motion. You can cite to a transcript of deposition or court testimony ("T. at *xx*" or "Anderson dep. at *xx*"); to pleadings ("Compl. Para. *xx*"); to an Affidavit (Watson Aff. Para. *xx*"); or to any other part of the record. See Practitioners' Note 7 in the Bluebook for form.

◆ V ◆ THE STRATEGY OF COUNTER-ARGUMENT

Lawyers often struggle with how to treat counter-analysis and counter-applica-tion in an opening brief.[13] On the one hand, the writer wants to respond to the arguments she anticipates. On the other hand, she does not want to raise arguments the opposing party might not have thought of or articulate them better than the opposing brief would have. (This concern applies to adverse *arguments,* but not to directly adverse *authorities.* As you know, the lawyer has a duty to disclose directly adverse authorities in the controlling jurisdiction.[14]) Nor does she want to sacrifice her affirmative stance—the primary advantage of the opening brief—by turning her own brief into a defensive document. Resolving these strategic questions is always a case-by-case task, but here are some helpful guidelines:

1. Include counter-argument in an opening brief when you are relatively sure that the opposing brief or the court itself will raise the argument and when you can weaken it by a preemptive discussion. More often than not, a well-crafted preemptive discussion will weaken an oppo-nent's argument.

2. As a general rule, the most effective forms of counter-argument do not identify the opposing arguments as such ("The defendant may argue that . . . . However, . . . "). Rather, the effective counter-argument "disproves" the opposing arguments primarily by affirmative "proof" of the writer's own position.

3. In a preemptive discussion that does identify the opposing party's argu-ment, describe that argument briefly and in general terms. Articulate your position on that argument in more detail than you use in articulat-ing the opposing party's argument. Detail is a technique for emphasis and lack of detail is a technique for de-emphasis.[15]

4. Never place an identified counter-argument ahead of your own affirma-tive argument; rather place it after you have made all of your *own* points. Otherwise your brief will take on a defensive tone and will lose much of its rhetorical power.

---

13.   An opening brief is the first brief filed on an issue. Usually one side files an opening brief and the opposing party files a responsive brief. Then, generally, the party who filed the opening brief has an opportunity to file a reply brief. *See* Chapter 17, section III.

14.   *See* Chapter 16.

15.   Mary Barnard Ray & Barbara J. Cox, *Beyond the Basics: A Text for Advanced Legal Writing* 176 (1991).

5.   After you have a draft of the argument, compare the space devoted to counter-argument with the space devoted to affirmative argument. The great majority of the draft should be devoted to your own affirmative argument.

 # VI ▷ VARIATIONS ON THE PARADIGM

Like memo-writing, brief-writing sometimes calls for a variation on the paradigm. For instance, if the rule has mandatory elements but the discussion for each will be simple, you can treat them all comprehensively in one discussion. In such a situation, you would write a rule explanation section covering all elements and then write a rule application section applying each element, one by one, to your client's facts. Chapter 10's discussion of several possible variations on the paradigm applies to brief-writing as well. However, even if you suspect that ultimately you will choose to vary the paradigm, use the classic version of the paradigm for the first draft. Writing your way through it for each issue will deepen your analysis and lead you to stronger arguments.

EXERCISE 3.   Writing Out a Working Draft

Write out the working drafts described below. Review the Carillo facts on pages 142-143. Use the case summaries from pages 66-68 as your only authorities. For the purposes of the exercise, do not assume any procedural posture requiring a gloss on the facts. Simply use the exercise to practice the principles set out in this chapter.

a.   Write out a working draft of an argument on behalf of the Lupinos, seeking a ruling that the facts, if proven, would constitute a legally sufficient attractive nuisance claim.

b.   Write out a working draft of an argument on behalf of the Carillos, seeking a ruling that the facts, if proven, do not constitute a legally sufficient attractive nuisance claim.

stage
three

CONVERTING THE WORKING DRAFT TO A BRIEF

20

The Argument and the Format of the Brief

Once you have a solid working draft of the argument, turn your attention toward converting it to the Argument section of the brief and to adding the other components of the document. To convert the working draft to the Argument section of the brief, your two primary tasks are reordering the arguments in the most effective manner and converting the working headings into point headings and subheadings for the brief.

 I **CHOOSING AN ORDER FOR THE ARGUMENTS**

A. ORDERING POINT HEADINGS

Your draft already has working point headings, but you have not yet decided the *order* in which they should appear. While no one right order exists, the most common choices for ordering point headings are (1) ordering by strength on the law, (2) ordering by strength on the equities, (3) ordering by the reader's priorities, and (4) ordering by familiarity.

1. Order by Strength on the Law

If one or two points are significantly stronger on the law than the others (and this will usually be the case), you will nearly always want to order them by strength, placing the strongest point first. You already have a good idea of the virtues of this order. A reader's attention to the argument is greatest at the beginning and drops off rapidly after the first few pages. Judges are busy and want to see the strongest arguments first. As a matter of fact, some busy judges will read only the first fifteen pages or so. Since the first fifteen pages includes the Introduction and Statement of Facts, such a judge is reading only the first eight to ten pages of the Argument.

A judge who does read beyond the first arguments will become frustrated with the writer and with the client's position if the judge finds that the first arguments are the weaker arguments. Judges usually presume that the strongest argument is first, and thus prejudge the subsequent arguments as even weaker.

2.   *Order by Strength on the Equities*

Some arguments rely primarily on rules of *law* and some rely primarily on the equities, that is, on *facts* that speak to the judge's sense of justice. If your points are of relatively equal legal strength, you may choose to order them according to their equitable (factual) strength. You will be able to identify which is which by asking yourself, "Which of these points really sounds like an appeal to justice? Which convinces me that one or more of these parties *should* win, as opposed to which party is *supposed* to win?"

If you have a point that relies heavily on the equities and those equities favor your client, you should capitalize on those favorable equities up front. A reader whose sense of justice is already convinced will be much more willing to accept your legal analysis. Such a reader will *want* you to be right on the law. You can capitalize on the equities in two ways: by placing the point strongest on the equities first or by placing it last. If your points are relatively equal in legal strength, you might decide to order your points by their equitable strength, placing the strongest first.

However, strange as this may sound, sometimes you can capitalize more effectively on a point with favorable equities by placing it last in the Argument section. This makes more sense when you remember that your reader will read the brief's Fact Statement before reading the Argument section. In Chapter 21 we will see that a brief-writer can make an argument implicitly (especially an equitable one) by doing a careful job on the brief's Statement of Facts. The Statement of Facts precedes the Argument section. It tells the story of the events that lead to the pending issues. It should make no express reference to the law, and yet it may well be the section of the brief with the most potential for persuasion. Of course your argument section must still make the argument expressly, but a well-drafted Fact Statement may allow you to present the reader with the equities even earlier than the first legal argument.

In such a case, placing the point with favorable equities last has additional advantages. First, it lets the favorable facts convince your reader without any express argument from you. This can work well because the Fact Statement does not seem like the argument of a litigant and thus the reader's level of skepticism is not as high as when reading an express legal argument.

Second, leaving space between the presentation of the facts and the argument you will make about them allows the reader to reach the desired conclusion before you articulate it. Thus, she may think of the conclusion as primarily her own. As you recall from Chapter 16, a reader clings more tenaciously to a position she thinks she reached herself than to a conclusion first argued by another. Then, when the reader encounters the argument articulated by the writer at the end of the Argument section, the writer's argument will seem to confirm the reader's own well-grounded conclusions.

Third, presenting the favorable equities first in the form of the fact statement and then last in the form of the legal argument allows you to place the favorable equities at the points of greatest reader attention.[1] Fourth, this organizational choice allows you to surround more technical, less compelling legal arguments with the favorable equities.

Finally, finishing the argument with strong equities allows you to use them to capture the reader who still has some doubts about the law, but who could be convinced to resolve those doubts in your favor. The equities can be the last nudge such a reader needs.

3. Order by Your Reader's Priorities

Occasionally your brief will have a point heading that will have priority in the mind of your reader, the judge. This priority will stem from the judge's preference for basing a judicial opinion on some kinds of legal rulings rather than on others. For instance, courts normally decide issues on jurisdictional grounds first, on procedural grounds second, and on substantive grounds last. Judges often prefer to decide issues on narrow grounds rather than on broad grounds. When both a constitutional ground and a nonconstitutional ground are dispositive, constitutional jurisprudence requires courts to decide as many of the issues as possible on the nonconstitutional ground.

Because your reader will have these preferences, you must take them seriously when choosing an order for your point headings. If the issues with priority for the judge also happen to be your strongest arguments, your decision is easy—order the points according to the judge's priorities. However, if your client's position on the judge's priority argument is weak, you must decide whether you can afford to place it first. Usually your best choice will be to place your strongest points first, but to use an umbrella section to assure the judge that your argument will address the other point as well.[2] Of course, you will not want to announce that you have placed that point last because your client's position on it is weak, but rather that your client's argument on the first point is so dispositive that consideration of the remaining point may be unnecessary.

4. Order by Familiarity

Recall from Chapter 11 that the order of the elements of some legal rules has become familiar to law-trained readers. Judges, however, seldom expect

1. *See* Chapter 11.
2. *See* pp. 291-293.

to see a preordained order in a brief because they are used to seeing points ordered by strength. For brief-writing, ordering by familiarity is useful if your points are of relatively equal legal and equitable strength and if your reader has no particular priorities for considering the issues.

For instance, in a negligence case where all aspects of the claim are at issue in the brief, the familiar order would be (1) duty, (2) breach, (3) causation, and (4) damages. In a similar contracts brief, the familiar order would be (1) offer, (2) acceptance, (3) consideration, (4) modification, and (5) performance. Like most decisions the writer must make, the important question is the reader's expectation. If the reader expects to see the arguments in a familiar order, the writer must either meet that expectation or convert the reader to a different expectation in the umbrella section.

B.   ORDERING SUBHEADINGS

Subheadings have three primary functions in a brief. First, they provide your reader with an easily identifiable road map of your argument. Second, they allow your reader to pause for a moment, and thus invite increased attention levels at the beginning and end of each subsection.[3] Third, they make visible the persuasive rule structure you formulated.

The working draft has already identified the primary subheadings.[4] Now, as you convert the working draft to the Argument section, order subheadings of equal rank according to the organizational principles described above for point headings.

Usually, further subdivisions are not necessary and can even be confusing. Occasionally, however, when the paradigmed discussion under a subheading is long or complex, further divisions within the discussion can help the reader follow the argument. If you need additional demarcation to help your reader follow the paradigmed argument, you can subdivide by any logical categories. The first level of subheadings, however, should be the issues addressed by the brief and should reflect rather than obscure the rule's structure.

 ## II   CONVERTING WORKING HEADINGS TO THE BRIEF'S POINT HEADINGS

In the working draft, the point headings and subheadings guided you in drafting the argument. In the brief designed to persuade the judge, they will serve as a tool of persuasion. Headings can persuade because (1) they assert your position in compelling language; (2) they make visible the persuasive structure you have selected for your rule and your argument; and (3) they allow the judge to find a quick, persuasive summary of your entire argument

3.   *See* Chapter 11, pp. 148-149.
4.   *See* Chapter 18, pp. 279-280.

by reading only the point headings and subheadings, either in a Table of Contents or by paging through the body of the Argument itself.

Converting your working headings to the final headings involves two steps: adding the key facts (where helpful) and editing for readability and persuasion.

A.   ADDING THE KEY FACTS

If the issue requires the application of a rule of law to your client's facts, the final version of the point headings ideally should refer to the key facts entitling your client to the desired result. For example, review the working point heading example on page 277. This working point heading simply asserts the correctness of the desired ruling and asserts your position on the part of the rule that entitles the client to the ruling. It says, "We win because the nighttime element is missing." It does not refer to the *facts* that establish that the nighttime element is missing. But to win on that issue, the defendant must apply the "nighttime" element to the facts of his case to show that the element is not met. Therefore, the final version of the "nighttime" point heading should refer to the defendant's key fact(s) on that issue.[5]

In the first stage of the brief-writing process, you thoroughly thought through the facts and the way they apply to the rule. The process was recursive, so at several stages along the way, you probably had new insights about the significance of particular facts. With the benefit of those insights, you are now better able to identify the key facts than you would have been before writing the working draft.

To convert the working headings into headings for the brief, again think of the point heading in halves, this time adding the key facts to the second half of the formula:

FINAL VERSION OF POINT HEADING

_____

(1) Identify the ruling you seek and assert its correctness.

because

_____
_____

_____

(2) Identify the key *facts* and state how they establish the correctness of the ruling.

---

5. If the issue is a pure question of law, not requiring fact application, then you have no facts to add. However, the heading should still state, to the extent feasible, the supporting rationale.

The second half of the point heading implicitly identifies the part of the rule that entitles your client to the result when it states how the facts establish the correctness of the ruling. Here is an example of the final version of the burglary point heading. Notice how the second half of the point heading implicitly identifies the part of the rule that determines the result.

BURGLARY POINT HEADING IN THE BRIEF

The burglary charge should be dismissed

[(1) Identifying the ruling you seek and asserting its correctness.]

because

the testimony of the bartender and other bar patrons establishes that Mr. Shaffer arrived at the house earlier than thirty minutes after sunset.

[(2) Identifying the key *facts* and stating how they establish the correctness of the ruling.]

When the point heading must cover more than one element, placing the key facts for all of those elements in one sentence along with the other required information results in an unwieldy heading. In that situation, move the facts for each element into the subheading dealing with that element. For example, here are the prosecutor's revised headings for a brief responding to the defendant's challenge of three elements. Since the prosecutor must win on all three challenged elements to prevail, the point heading must cover all three elements with separate *sub*headings for each.[6]

I.   THE BURGLARY CHARGE AGAINST THE DEFENDANT SHOULD NOT BE DISMISSED BECAUSE THE EVIDENCE AT TRIAL WILL ESTABLISH ALL OF THE ELEMENTS OF BURGLARY.

A.   The evidence will show that the crime occurred in the nighttime because it occurred at 6:45 P.M., more than thirty minutes after sunset.

B.   The evidence will show that the defendant intended to commit a felony when he entered the house because he alluded to his intent to batter Mrs. Shaffer before he left the bar for her home.

---

6. *See* pp. 279-280.

> C.   The evidence will show that the dwelling was not the defendant's own because he had waived his claim to the premises and did not retain any right of access.

One last point: This section began by stating that point headings "ideally" should include key facts, so before we leave this section we must explore what might make a situation less than "ideal."

A situation is less than ideal when the key facts, stated in isolation from other facts and from your explanation of them, are not persuasive. Sometimes the facts of a particular case are persuasive only in combination with each other. Or perhaps they require some explanation before their significance will be apparent to the judge. In either case, including the key facts in the point heading probably will hurt rather than help your effort to persuade the judge. In either case, then, leave the facts out of your point heading.

In summary, try to include in the final version of the point heading (or the combination of the point heading and its subheadings) the following information:

1.   the correctness of the ruling you seek,
2.   your position on the part of the rule that entitles your client to the ruling, and
3.   the key facts that establish your position on the determinative part of the rule (when helpful).

After you try to pack all of this information into one sentence, edit for readability and persuasion. The next two sections will tell you how to tame unmanageable point headings.

EXERCISE 1.   Evaluating the Content of Point Headings

Review the facts set out in Exercise 1, Chapter 18 (pp. 277-278) and read the following versions of the "consent" point heading for Foodman's brief. Identify the point heading that contains each component for a complete point heading. For the others, identify which part is missing.

a.   Carson consented to Foodman's representation of Janoff when he did not respond to Foodman's letter.
b.   The motion to disqualify should be denied because Janoff did not respond to Foodman's letter.
c.   The motion to disqualify should be denied because Janoff consented to the representation.
d.   The motion to disqualify should be denied because Janoff's failure to respond to Foodman's letter constituted consent to the representation of Janoff.

B. EDITING FOR PERSUASION

The most important quality of a persuasive point heading is readability, for the judge will not agree with a proposition she cannot understand. Editing for readability is the subject of the next section. Other strategies for persuasion impact the rhetorical structure of the point heading, and this section describes several of those rhetorical strategies.

1. Affirmative language versus negative language.   Most briefs focus on certain conduct: Is it or is it not lawful? proper? desirable? Sometimes the writer can articulate the client's position either by using affirmative language or negative language. In addition to being more readable,[7] affirmative language generally is more forceful and appealing than negative language.[8] Here are examples of two point headings, one using affirmative language and one using negative language.

Negative language   Carrolton's Motion for Summary Judgment should be granted because Watson is unable to show that the terms are unreasonable or that she has not breached those terms.

Affirmative language   Carrolton's Motion for Summary Judgment should be granted because the terms of the covenant-not-to-compete are reasonable and the uncontested facts establish Watson's breach.

2. Varying the structure of the point heading.   The point heading structure described in this chapter is the easiest structure for learning to draft a readable point heading. It begins with the relief you want and follows with the facts and law supporting that relief. After you have a little practice with drafting point headings, however, you can vary the formula and sometimes achieve a more persuasive version. For instance, consider these versions of the Shaffer heading. What differences in effectiveness do you notice?

VERSION 1

The burglary charge against Mr. Shaffer should be dismissed because the alleged breaking and entering occurred at 6:15 P.M., which was earlier than thirty minutes after sunset.

VERSION 2

Because the alleged breaking and entering occurred at 6:15 P.M., which was earlier than thirty minutes after sunset, the burglary charge against Mr. Shaffer should be dismissed.

VERSION 3

The alleged breaking and entering occurred at 6:15 P.M., which was less than thirty minutes after sunset, and therefore the burglary charge against Mr. Shaffer should be dismissed.

7. *See* p. 318.
8. *See, e.g.,* Helene S. Shapo et al., *Writing and Analysis in the Law* 287 (3d ed. 1995).

Tinker with the structure of the point heading until you are satisfied that it is as persuasive as it can be.

3.   Phrasing alternative arguments.   When you have more than a single point heading, one or more of the headings may be an alternative argument, presented in case the judge does not agree with the first argument. The trick here is to avoid seeming to reduce the credibility of the first argument by making alternative arguments. The following example demonstrates this flaw:

I.   THE LAW OF THIS JURISDICTION DOES NOT ALLOW RECOVERY FOR THE WRONGFUL DEATH OF A FETUS, EVEN IF THE FETUS IS VIABLE AT THE TIME OF THE INJURY.

II.   THE LAW OF THIS JURISDICTION ALLOWS RECOVERY FOR THE WRONGFUL DEATH OF ONLY A *VIABLE* FETUS, AND THE LAWRENCE FETUS WAS NOT VIABLE AT THE TIME OF THE INJURY.

Rather than following a strong argument with a second argument that seems to undercut the first, relate alternative arguments to preceding arguments in terms that *assume the correctness* of the first argument. One way to do this is to restate the first argument expressly, like this:[9]

I.   THE NEGLIGENCE CLAIM IS BARRED BY THE STATUTE OF LIMITATIONS BECAUSE THE PLAINTIFF DID NOT FILE THE COMPLAINT UNTIL FOUR YEARS AFTER THE ALLEGED NEGLIGENT ACT.

II.   NOT ONLY IS THE CLAIM BARRED BY THE STATUTE OF LIMITATIONS, BUT THE PLAINTIFF'S ASSURANCE THAT HE WOULD NOT PURSUE AN ACTION BARS THE CLAIM UNDER THE EQUITABLE DOCTRINES OF ESTOPPEL AND WAIVER.

Reiterating the first point in the course of making the second can make the second point heading unwieldy, however. Another way to avoid seeming to disavow the first point heading is to use, in the second point heading, a verb tense that communicates that any assumption of a flaw in the first point is contrary to fact:

I.   THE LAW OF THIS JURISDICTION DOES NOT ALLOW RECOVERY FOR THE WRONGFUL DEATH OF A FETUS, EVEN IF THE FETUS IS VIABLE AT THE TIME OF THE INJURY.

II.   EVEN IF THE LAW *DID* ALLOW RECOVERY FOR THE WRONGFUL DEATH OF A VIABLE FETUS, THE LAWRENCE FETUS WAS ONLY IN THE FIFTH MONTH OF GESTATION, AND THEREFORE WAS NOT VIABLE.

Examine any alternative point headings to be sure that they do not undermine other arguments.

---

9.   Modified from Girvan Peck, *Writing Persuasive Briefs* 135-136 (1984).

C.   EDITING FOR READABILITY

Often the addition of the key facts to a point heading results in a long, complex, and obtuse sentence. Yet a point heading cannot persuade a judge of something the judge cannot decipher. And readability is especially important for point headings because the format for point headings (all capital letters) already hinders readability.

The best editing techniques for simplifying and clarifying such a point heading have already been described in sections IV through VI of Chapter 15. This chapter reminds you of the techniques most important for taming point headings.

1.   *Keep the subject and the verb close together.*   In other words, avoid intrusive phrases and clauses.
2.   *Avoid nominalizations.*   Remember that nominalizations are verbs pretending to be nouns. "Investigate" is a verb, but "investigation" is a nominalization. Nominalizations require more words and make sentences harder to understand.
3.   *Avoid unnecessary passive-voiced verbs.*   Passive-voiced verbs make the sentence's subject something other than the actor. Passive verbs generally require more words and make sentences harder to understand.
4.   *Keep the facts and reasoning at the end of the sentence.*   Placing the desired result first and the facts and reasoning second generally results in a point heading that is easier to read.
5.   *Avoid vague words.*   Vague words cause the reader to puzzle over the writer's meaning. Purge your point headings of words like these:

this matter	with regard to
it involves	it deals with
it pertains to	it concerns

6.   *Avoid negatives.*   Negatives, especially multiple negatives, can make a sentence harder to understand.[10]
7.   *Review and use all other techniques from section VI of Chapter 15 for reducing the number of words.*

If you have tried all of these editing techniques and still cannot produce a readable point heading, the best solution is to remove one of the items of information, generally either the key facts or the relief requested. Decide which based on persuasiveness. If the key facts are particularly persuasive, remove the relief requested; generally your reader can easily refer to the record for a reminder of the relief you request. As a last resort, remove the facts. An easily readable point heading that asserts the party's legal argument but lacks supporting facts is more persuasive than a point heading that includes the facts but can't be understood.

---

10.   Veda R. Charrow et al., *Clear and Effective Legal Writing* 165 (2d ed. 1995).

EXERCISE 2. Editing Headings for Readability

Edit the following headings to make them more easily readable. Use the techniques identified in the prior section and in section VI of Chapter 15.

1. It is clear that Crawford's actions of sitting peacefully in the parking lot of an open store, entering the store and leaving therefrom without incident, and driving lawfully out of the parking lot do not give rise to a reasonable, articulable suspicion of criminal activity to make a valid stop of said defendant.

2. The Defendant's Motion to Dismiss should be granted in as much as the contract involved provided that the escrow account under consideration could be closed by the escrow agent at the point in time when at least three days have passed from the date the notice of default was issued by the lender.

3. The Motion to Attach Assets should be denied because the Court should take into consideration the defendant's reduced line of credit and the unavailability of other sources for cash for the purpose of operating the business during the litigation in this matter.

4. The Motion for Summary Judgment filed by the Defendants, Mr. and Mrs. Carillo, should not be denied due to the fact that the evidence will show that the injured child understood the danger involved in a trampoline.

5. There is no reasonable, articulable suspicion to justify a stop of Salavar where the testimony of the officer is contradicted on virtually every point, where the officer has no facts to support a claim of criminal activity, and where the officer only witnessed Salavar's car in an area of criminal activity and therefore the Defendant's Motion to Dismiss should be granted.

6. The leased premises, which are subject to the constant threat of very disruptive demonstrations, are not suitable with regard to the purpose for which they were leased, and therefore the lessees have been constructively evicted.

7. A minor who induces another to enter into a contract with him by making a false representation of his age is estopped from a disaffirmance of the contract if the other party demonstrated reasonable and justifiable reliance on the minor's representation.

III ◇ QUESTION PRESENTED

After you have a draft of the Argument section of the brief, you are ready to draft the Question Presented (or Statement of Issues). A Question Presented has two functions: (1) to apprise the judge of the legal issue to be decided and (2) to begin persuading the judge to decide that issue in your client's favor. To draft Questions Presented that accomplish both purposes the writer must walk a fine line between neutrality and overzealous advocacy. The goal is to draft a Question that accurately states the issue *and* suggests a favorable answer. For example, here are examples of Questions Presented from opposing briefs:

[BRIEF ON BEHALF OF CARROLTON]

Is a covenant-not-to-compete enforceable where the covenant was a bargained-for term of the sale of a business, where the term was negotiated as part of the agreement to allow the seller to continue working for the business, and where the sale specifically included the company's customer lists and good will?

[BRIEF ON BEHALF OF WATSON]

May a larger, established business enforce a covenant-not-to-compete where the covenant would eliminate all competition within the market area and where the prohibited activity would affect only four percent of the covenant-holder's profits?

Notice how each accurately recites the legal issue and several key facts while suggesting an answer favorable to the client for whom the brief is written.

A.   CONTENT AND FORMAT

1.   Format for a pure question of law.   A Question Presented that deals only with an issue of law is a straightforward statement of the legal issue. It should identify the particular legal issue, rather than simply asking whether one side's position is correct. For instance, the first of the following Questions simply asks whether one party's position is correct, without identifying the legal issue; the second actually poses a legal question.

Can Dole bring a claim for malicious prosecution?

Can a criminal defendant bring a civil action for malicious prosecution prior to the resolution of the criminal proceedings that give rise to the claim?

2.   Format for a question involving facts.   The easiest way to draft a Question Presented that involves the application of law to fact is to think of the Question in two parts, the first part stating the legal issue and the second part stating the key facts.

Can [state the legal question] . . . where . . . [state the major facts]?

Common verbs beginning the Question Presented are: "May . . . ?" "Does
. . . ?" "Is . . . ?" and "Did . . . ?" Common words used for the transition
to the second part of the Question, referring to facts, are "when" and "where."
   The Question Presented also can be phrased as a clause beginning with
"whether" and ending with a period:

> Whether a large, established business can enforce a covenant-not-to-compete
> where the covenant would eliminate all competition within the market area
> and where the prohibited activity would affect only four percent of the covenant-
> holder's profits.

3.   Standard of review.   The Question Presented for an appellate brief
should focus on the alleged error of the trial court. Lawyers disagree about
whether the Question Presented must always be phrased in the terms of the
relevant standard of review.[11] An example of phrasing the Question Presented
in terms of the standard of review is:

> Did the trial court abuse its discretion to allow the plaintiff to reopen his case
> when . . . ?

Follow the directions of your supervising attorney or teacher. If you receive
no directions, consider these guidelines: Omit the standard when you are
dealing with a pure question of law and you know that the judge will already
know that the relevant standard of review is de novo. Include the standard
when the court must decide whether the lower court abused its discretion.
When the standard is "clearly erroneous" and the standard is favorable for
your argument, be sure to include it. If the "clearly erroneous" standard is
unfavorable to your argument, leave it out if you can phrase the Question
Presented accurately without emphasizing the unfavorable standard.

4.   References to parties.   For references to the parties, a Question Presented can use (1) the parties' names, (2) generic descriptions (property owner,
retailer, buyer, lessor), or (3) procedural titles (plaintiff, defendant, appellant,
respondent). Procedural titles force the judge to stop to remember who the
parties are in this particular case; thus they make the Question less readily
understandable.[12] Avoid using procedural titles unless the legal issue concerns
the law applying to a party in that procedural posture, for example:

> Can a criminal defendant bring a civil action for malicious prosecution prior to
> the resolution of the criminal proceedings that give rise to the claim?

In such a case, the procedural title is actually the generic description of the
kind of person to whom the question would pertain.
   In other cases, however, the better choices are generic descriptions or the
parties' names. Choose the alternative that better serves your strategy. Some-

---

11.   *See* Chapter 18, section III.
12.   *See* Fed. R. App. P. 28(d).

times using the parties' names can serve the strategic function of humanizing the parties and the legal issues in dispute.[13] Using names can serve a practical function, allowing the drafter to use fewer words. For instance, in the Carrolton example third above, the generic description "a large, established business" is longer than the name "Carrolton" would have been.

On the other hand, using generic descriptions may allow the writer to give additional helpful information about the party. For instance, in the Carrolton example, the generic description allowed Watson's lawyer the chance to convey some helpful information about Carrolton—that it is a "large, established business." In such a situation, the additional information may be worth the added length. Experiment with both alternatives and select the one that works best for that particular case.

5.   Don't avoid the actual question the judge must decide.   Some writers are tempted to assume the answer to the question the judge must decide, like so:

> May Carrolton enforce the terms of the covenant-not-to-compete where the terms are unreasonable?

Neither party argues that Carrolton can enforce a covenant with unreasonable terms. The governing case law clearly states that Carrolton cannot. Neither party is asking the court to adopt a different rule. Rather, the question the judge must decide is *whether the terms are reasonable.* Perhaps the drafter of this Question Presented was hoping that the assumption would slip past the judge, but it will not. Don't avoid the real issue and thus miss the opportunity to state it in the most persuasive way you can.

6.   Don't overdo the advocacy.   Some court rules require that Questions Presented not be argumentative. Even in the absence of court rules, overzealous advocacy is counterproductive. It causes the skeptical reader to discount the material because the writer's agenda is too heavy-handed. The goal is to state the Question Presented allowing the *facts* to speak for themselves. Facts persuade more effectively than rhetoric ever can. Here is a Question Presented that has crossed the line into argumentativeness:

> Can a reckless defendant, whose callous conduct caused the death of a precious new life, escape liability for wrongful death just because the baby's guardians had not yet completed an adoption proceeding?

To avoid argumentative Questions Presented, limit adjectives and adverbs, using facts instead of such characterizations. Edit out heated rhetoric or language that smacks of name-calling. Stick to facts the opposing party cannot dispute.

> Can legal guardians recover for the wrongful death of a child when the guardians had raised the child as their own for four years, had instituted adoption proceed-

---

13.   *See* Chapter 21.

ings two years prior to the child's death, and had believed, reasonably and in good faith, that a final adoption decree had been issued?

7.   Do try to phrase the question in a way that suggests a favorable answer.   Generally, a question that suggests an affirmative answer is more persuasive than a question that suggests a negative answer.[14] Sometimes, however, the rhetorical impact of a negative structure can outweigh the advantage of calling for an affirmative response. For instance, a structure that asks, "Can *X* require *Y* to do *Z*?" implies that *X* is being oppressive to *Y*, simply by virtue of the structure of the question. The structure invites the reader to respond with a resounding "No." For example, consider this Question Presented:

> Can an employer, in order to collect urine samples, require employees to urinate in the plain view of a supervisor?

8.   Multiple questions presented.   A brief can raise several questions and thus have several Questions Presented. Simply draft a separately numbered Question Presented for each legal question. Order the Questions Presented in the order in which the issues appear in the Argument.

B.   DRAFTING HINTS

Creating a Question Presented is like creating a haiku. Each of these literary forms requires meticulous attention to word selection and placement, sentence structure, and theme. Unlike poetry, however, no one would argue that obscurity of message is desirable for a Question Presented. Rather, a Question Presented should be a powerful sentence that is *easily understandable on first reading.*

Keep reworking the Question Presented for readability and subtle persuasiveness. Use the techniques covered in Chapter 15 and in section II of this chapter. Try to achieve a concise, clear, and direct style, and a persuasive framing of the Question.

EXERCISE 3.   Critiquing Questions Presented

a.   Review the Carillo facts on pages 142-143. Assume that the matter is now in litigation. Critique these two versions of the Question Presented drafted by the lawyer for Jimmy Lupino. Write a better version.

---

14.   John C. Dernbach et al., *A Practical Guide to Legal Writing and Legal Method* 221 (2d ed. 1994).

Can the Carillos maintain an attractive nuisance in their backyard?

Does a trampoline constitute an attractive nuisance?

b.   Assume that a construction firm, M & L Construction, and one of its customers, Quincy Development, entered into a contract for the construction of a shopping center. The construction contract contained an arbitration clause prohibiting either party from suing the other over "disputes pertaining to M & L's performance of the construction contract" unless the parties first go through nonbinding arbitration of their dispute. Construction began. About two months later, Quincy decided that M & L was not keeping to the construction schedule and it withheld one of its scheduled interim payments to M & L. M & L has filed suit without going through arbitration, taking the position that the nonpayment is not a dispute that is controlled by the arbitration clause. The following Question Presented appears in Quincy's brief arguing for dismissal. Critique it.

Is the plaintiff's interpretation of the arbitration agreement fundamentally flawed?

c.   Review the Guzman facts on page 269. Critique these two versions of the Question Presented to appear in a brief filed by the lawyer for Guzman. Write an improved version. The issue is whether the premises have become unsuitable for the purposes for which they were leased.

Has an apartment become unsuitable for use as a dwelling when the utility services are unreliable?

Has a slum lord constructively evicted poor tenants who cannot afford to move elsewhere when he callously forces children to live with rats and without heat, water, and toilet facilities?

 **EXERCISE 4.   Writing a Question Presented**

Review the McSwain facts on pages 270-271. Assume that you are writing a brief on behalf of Chambless and Mendez. The issue is whether the doctors vacated the premises within a reasonable time after the abortion demonstrations began. Draft the Question Presented.

◈ IV ◈ FORMATTING THE BRIEF

Now it is time to decide what other sections the brief will include. Refer to the instructions you received with your assignment, to section III of Chapter 16 for a description of the various sections, and to the sample briefs in Appendices B and C. Draft all of the components your finished brief will contain except the Statement of Facts. For formatting information, follow first the applicable court rules and your law firm's or teacher's instructions. To whatever extent they do not contradict your other instructions, follow these guidelines:

1. Caption. The court's name, the parties' names, and the document title should appear in all capital letters (all caps). The parties' procedural titles (for example, Plaintiff, Appellant, Defendant, Appellee) should appear in initial caps.

2. Components of the brief. The titles of the components of the brief (for example, Question Presented, Statement of the Case, Argument, Conclusion) should be centered and underlined and should appear in all caps. Some court rules require the Question Presented to appear on a page by itself.

3. Point headings. The point headings (those marked by roman numerals) should appear in all caps, single-spaced but not underlined. Some writers center them, but this can make a long point heading even harder to read. A better choice may be to use the full width of the line so the reader isn't confronted with a block of capital letters resembling a ten-story building.

4. Subheadings. Subheadings should be indented one tab space, underlined, and single-spaced. They should use capitalization as if they were a normal sentence of text.

5. Table of Contents. The section titles for the components of the brief (such as Question Presented, Statement of the Case, Argument, Conclusion) should appear in initial caps in the Table of Contents, using Rule 8 of the Bluebook as a guide for determining which words to capitalize.

Point headings should appear in the Table of Contents in the same typeface as they appear in the text of the Argument, that is, all caps, single-spaced, not underlined. Some writers make the typeface for subheadings in the Table of Contents consistent with the typeface in the text as well. However, underlining the subheadings in the Table of Contents, where they appear together, makes them hard to read. Consider omitting the underlining for subheadings.

6. Text. Briefs should be double-spaced except where otherwise indicated. Insert two spaces between sentences. Do not justify the right margin. Page numbers should be centered at the bottom of the page.

———————————

Now all of the brief's components are in place except the Statement of Facts. The next chapter covers drafting a persuasive Statement of Facts.

21

The Statement of Facts

There is an adage among trial lawyers: If you have to choose between the law and the facts, take the facts. The adage reflects the experience of many lawyers that a judge or jury convinced of the justice of your cause will find a way around unfavorable law. Conversely, if the judge or jury perceives that justice is on the other side, favorable law may not be enough.

The Statement of Facts is the primary place where your reader's sense of justice about the case will be formed. As a general rule, narrative is more effective at creating attitudes than is intellectual analysis. *The Jungle* persuaded countless readers of the inhumanity of the meat-packing industry. *Cry the Beloved Country* persuaded people around the world of the injustice of apartheid.

Consider your own reactions. Imagine reading a well-reasoned analysis arguing that Hitler should not have imprisoned and killed German Jews. The analysis explains and applies certain abstract moral principles. Imagine your response. Now compare it to your response to *The Diary of Anne Frank* or *Schindler's List* or *Sophie's Choice*. Which would you find more powerful—the analysis or the stories of the people who lived the facts? Which would you remember longer? Which would persuade you more?

Stories grab us, persuade us, motivate us. Your client's story can persuade a judge, just as a movie or book can persuade you. But to be persuasive, your client's story must be told skillfully. Many lawyers believe that the brief that tells the most effective story is the most likely to prevail.

The writing techniques required for an effective Statement of Facts are more challenging than those required for writing a short story or novel. It is harder because the writer must use the facts to persuade without *appearing* to use the facts to persuade. Rather, the writer must recite the facts in a manner that is objective enough to be fair and simultaneously persuasive enough to be compelling. As Professors Ray and Cox put it:

If briefs to the court were gymnastics events, the statement of facts would occur on the balance beam. Writing a persuasive statement is accomplished not by following one set of rules, but by balancing your use of various techniques to maintain credibility while achieving the stance needed to highlight favorable facts. It does not require the brute force of emphatic language so much as a subtle blend of strength and control of structure and detail. It involves much thought, consideration of alternatives, and monitoring the interactions of various techniques. Yet an excellent statement of facts looks natural and effortless, just as a complex routine looks easy when completed by a skilled gymnast.[1]

It takes years to master the art of legal storytelling. This chapter will give you some techniques to practice as you begin your career.

I   FACT ETHICS, READERS, AND THE CONVENTIONS OF FACT STATEMENTS

Before beginning, a writer does well to remember the general principles that apply to Fact Statements and their readers.

A.   REMINDERS ABOUT FACT ETHICS

Remember from Chapter 16 that a lawyer must not misrepresent facts.[2] Misrepresentation includes both stating facts untruthfully and omitting material facts when the result of the omission is to create a false inference. The rule further requires lawyers to disclose material facts when disclosure is necessary to avoid assisting the client in a criminal or fraudulent act.

In virtually every case, you'll find some facts you wish weren't there, generally because they are unfavorable for your client's case. The more material the facts are, the more you wish they didn't exist. But they exist nonetheless, and leaving them out of your Fact Statement won't make them go away, for they will certainly appear in the opposing brief. Omitting them from your brief will only damage your credibility before the judge, causing the judge to wonder how much she can rely on the other facts you assert. Few things make a judge angrier than feeling misled by a lawyer.

The omissions also force the judge to use the opposing party's Fact Statement, rather than yours, as the court's primary factual reference. These conse-

---

1. Mary Barnard Ray & Barbara J. Cox, *Beyond the Basics: A Text for Advanced Legal Writing* 162 (1991).

2. A lawyer shall not knowingly make a false statement of fact or fail to disclose a material fact when disclosure is necessary to avoid assisting a criminal or fraudulent act by the client. Model Rule of Professional Conduct 3.3(a)(1) and (2); See also Model Code of Professional Responsibility DR 7-102(A)(3) and (5).

quences are serious for both lawyer and client. Therefore, both ethics and good strategy require inclusion of all material facts, whether favorable or not.[3]

B.   REMINDERS ABOUT READERS

Review the sections in Chapters 11 and 16 about law-trained readers in general and judges in particular.[4] Remember that (1) judges want to do justice and will be more receptive to your arguments on the law if the facts have convinced the judge that your client *should* win; (2) stories, especially stories about people, are compelling; (3) readers devote more attention to the beginning of the document (which is where the Fact Statement appears) than to any other part; and (4) readers devote more attention to the beginning and end of a section than to the middle.

C.   THE CONVENTIONS OF A STATEMENT OF FACTS

Certain formal requirements and generally accepted conventions apply to the Statement of Facts. Refer to the Statement of Facts of the briefs in Appendices B and C for examples of how a Statement of Facts employs the following conventions:

   1.   A Statement of Facts must refer only to facts that are a part of the court record.   For many trial-level briefs, the writer can usually add facts that do not already appear in the record by filing a witness affidavit simultaneously with the brief. When the writer wants to add a document to the record (like a contract, deed, will, or letter), the document can be attached as an exhibit to a witness affidavit. The affidavit sets out the sworn facts necessary to add the document to the record.[5]

   For an appellate brief, facts cannot be added to the record.[6] Since the point of an appeal is to decide whether the lower court's decision on a certain point was supported by the facts and the law *before that court,* the appellate court may consider only the factual record that was before the lower court at the time of the decision from which the appeal has been taken.

   The Statement of Facts must cite the location of the fact in the record.[7] The citation allows the judge to verify that the fact actually appears in the record and to check that the writer's descriptions of the fact and its context are not misleading. Judges *do* check the facts. For an appellate brief, the most common

---

   3.   Later sections in this chapter identify ways to neutralize or de-emphasize unfavorable facts.
   4.   *See* pp. 147-152 and pp. 244-247.
   5.   The facts necessary to allow the court to consider a document differ depending on the nature of the document and the use to which it will be put. You'll learn more about these requirements when you take Evidence.
   6.   There are rare exceptions to this rule, but none that we need worry about here.
   7.   Fed. R. App. P. 28(e).

form for these citations to the record is "R. at [page number]." For a trial-level brief, you should cite according to Practitioners' Note 7 in the Bluebook.[8]

2.   A Statement of Facts is a part of a legal document and retains the formal style of the rest of the brief.   While a Statement of Facts tells the story of the legal dispute, its style is not like a short story. You do not want the style of the fact statement to cause the judge to wonder if she is reading fiction. Therefore, present the facts in an objective style, avoiding obvious appeals to emotion, grand description, dramatic literary devices, and other obvious attempts to manipulate the reader. The style should be dignified and courteous, never sarcastic or angry.

3.   A Statement of Facts does not discuss law.   It sets out all of the facts that the rule makes important, but it does not explain the rule or the rule's relationship to the facts. Rule explanation and application come in the Argument section. The only exception to this convention is that the last paragraph of the fact statement can segue into the legal argument by stating the legal issue the Argument will address.[9]

4.   A Statement of Facts does not contain overt argument, whether legal or factual.   The facts are presented in an objective style, and the writer does not expressly assert factual conclusions. For instance, for a case involving medical malpractice, the Fact Statement might relate the patient's vital signs, the medical test results, the patient's medical history, and the nurse's observations, but the writer would not conclude that the doctor acted carelessly.

Note that this restriction applies to conclusions drawn by the *writer,* but the writer *is* permitted to relate the conclusion of another. For instance, while the writer cannot assert that the doctor acted carelessly, the writer can report the testimony of an expert witness who concluded that the doctor acted carelessly. The testimony of the witness is a *fact* that occurred at a deposition or at trial. Reporting the conclusions of others is sometimes called "masked editorializing."[10] Quotations, used in moderation, are appropriate in a Statement of Facts, and often are effective, as section IV explains.

A Statement of Facts can point out the *absence* of certain facts from the record. The absence of a fact from the record is itself a fact. Thus it is fair game for inclusion in the Statement of Facts.

> At trial, three officers testified that they were stationed at the building's entrance between 5:00 and 6:00. However, no witness testified to seeing the janitor enter or leave the building.

Pointing out a fact's absence can allow the writer to make a point about the evidence while remaining within the legitimate bounds of fact-reporting. One

---

8.   *See* pp. 303-304.
9.   *See* section C, p. 335.
10.   *See* Louis J. Sirico & Nancy Schultz, *Persuasive Writing For Lawyers and the Legal Profession* 42-43 (1995).

of the most common and most unfortunate errors lawyers make is neglecting to notice important *absent* facts.

II ## DEVELOPING A THEORY OF THE CASE AND SELECTING FACTS

While some facts must be included no matter what theory of the case or theme the lawyer selects, other fact-selection decisions are tied directly to the theme the lawyer will develop. This section explores these two interrelated lawyering tasks.

A. DEVELOPING A THEORY OF THE CASE

Lawyers use the term "theory of the case" to refer to the theme they will weave throughout the facts, the theme that will explain the facts from their client's perspective. The theme should be sympathetic to the client. It should help the judge understand why the client acted in the way he did, feels the way he does, needs the things he needs. At the least, a good theory of the case assures the judge that a ruling in favor of your client will not be unjust. At best, the theory convinces the judge that justice requires a ruling for your client.

Of course, a theory of the case must be consistent with the key facts. Creating a theory is easy when the facts are generally favorable and much more difficult when they are not. For troublesome facts, you must work even harder to see and *feel* the story from your client's perspective. Look again at the sample Questions Presented for Carrolton and for Watson on page 320. Can you see what Carrolton's theory of the case will be? How about Watson's?

You have already been working with the facts as you wrote the Argument section of the brief. As you looked at the facts from your client's perspective, you may have found a number of themes playing out. People are complex, after all, and seldom are we motivated by only one need, feeling, or goal. For presentation of the facts in a legal proceeding, however, beware of trying to present several themes at once. The medium of a brief generally is better suited to handle one consistent theme rather than several themes intermixed. Too often, the effort to combine several themes leaves the reader with no coherent theory at all; so pick the theme that is most compelling and best supported by the facts.

The best way to find an effective theory of the case is by talking with your client. However, your client may not be good at communicating the heart of his position and may not even be consciously aware of it himself, so you'll need also to use your imagination. Try to put yourself in his position. Imagine what it must have been like, what it must be like now. Try to understand who this person is and who the other key characters are. Mull it over in the shower, on your morning run, on your way to the grocery store.

If you can do so without breaching client confidentiality, try telling the story orally. Go to lunch with another lawyer from your firm and tell her your client's story. Telling the story and then talking about it with another person often gives you a fresh perspective. After you've developed a clearer sense of your client and the situation, what helps you understand your client's behavior? What moves you about the story? What might move the judge?

Once you have an idea, try articulating it in a few sentences, like so:

> Carrolton bought Watson's company, the only provider of health care products in the area, and immediately began to take advantage of the company's customers by raising prices, limiting product lines, and allowing long delays for special-order items. Since the customers had nowhere else to go for their health care products, they had no choice but to pay the prices and put up with the limited service. Watson, who had continued to work at the business, had to sit by and watch as Carrolton took advantage of her neighbors and long-time customers. Many of them even thought that Watson was intentionally profiting at their expense, since she was still the customer contact person in the office—the only face her old customers saw. Not only was this situation personally distressing to Watson, but she became increasingly convinced that it just wasn't right.

A good theory of the case should be consistent with the facts and with a common sense notion of fairness. It should explain as many of the unfavorable facts as possible, and it should cast your client in a sympathetic light.

B.   SELECTING FACTS

Once you have developed your theory of the case, select the facts you will include in the Statement of Facts. One way to select the facts is to go through the record and make a list that includes facts falling into the following categories:

1.   Facts that fit the theory of the case
2.   All facts mentioned in the Argument section of the brief
3.   All legally significant facts, whether favorable or unfavorable
4.   Significant background facts
5.   Emotionally significant facts

As you make the list, record the location of the fact in the record. At the trial level, the record is the entire court file, which can include the pleadings, discovery responses, motions, briefs, affidavits, exhibits, deposition transcripts, and any oral proceedings that have been transcribed by a court reporter. On appeal, the record is whatever portion of the lower court's file has been certified for inclusion in the record on appeal. Place the citation in parentheses, and use the abbreviations found in Practitioners' Note 7 and Table 8 of the Bluebook for the various kinds of documents to which you refer. Later, when you write out the facts in paragraph form, the citations will appear like so:

> On January 20, 1995, Carrolton filed a complaint in state court alleging that Watson was violating the terms of the covenant-not-to-compete. (Compl. ¶ 27.)

> Carrolton's Vice President, Justin Bakker, stated that the Complaint was filed within one month of Carrolton's discovery of Watson's business activity. (Bakker Aff. ¶ 14.)

Another way to select the facts is by first writing out a draft of the story in a way that will communicate your theory of the case. Starting with the narrative rather than by making a list will use a different thought process; you may find it easier and more effective. Then, go through the record searching for any omitted facts that fall into the categories listed above. Make a note of each missing fact you identify. Insert those whose location in the draft seems obvious, and use the next stage, selecting an organizational plan, to help you decide where to place the others.

If you are writing a trial brief, be sure to ask yourself what additional facts you would like to add to the record to support your argument. For a law school assignment, your instructions may not allow for additional filings; however, in practice, it is common to file affidavits and exhibits along with a motion and the brief supporting it. You will learn more about how to do this in your civil procedure and evidence classes.

Like the process of *legal* analysis, the process of writing the fact statement is recursive. You'll find that your understanding of the possible significance of each fact will develop as you work through each step. This developing understanding will send you back to earlier steps to add, delete, or amend material. Don't resist the need for these revisions; your best work will come from them.

III ORGANIZATION

A. FORMATS

Chapter 13 identified the most common organizational formats for Fact Statements: chronological, topical, and a combination of the two. Take a moment to review the descriptions of these three formats at pages 185-186. This chapter will review these three formats and discuss two more: organizing by *theories of the case* and organizing by *witness and document*.

1. Chronological. For simple facts, a chronological presentation is often best. A set of simple facts does not cover a number of topics with a batch of individual facts pertaining to each topic. For instance, in a simple collection matter, the facts will usually set out the events giving rise to the debt, the default, the plaintiff's demand that the defendant cure the default, and the amount owed. These simple facts are best presented chronologically.

2. Topical or Combination. For more complex facts, the topical or combination formats work best. As you know from Chapter 13, these formats organize facts into topics. For example, in an employment discrimination case, the plaintiff's facts might be organized according to these topics: the nature of the defendant's business; the defendant's usual hiring process; the defendant's usual employee evaluation procedure; the procedures used in selecting employees for layoffs; the hiring process for the plaintiff's position; the hiring decision; the terms of the plaintiff's employment; the plaintiff's employee evaluations; the business conditions that necessitated layoffs; the selection of plaintiff and others for layoff; the defendant's efforts to assist the laid-off employees. The topics should be ordered logically, perhaps chronologically, and the individual facts within each topic should be ordered logically as well.

3.   Theory of the Case.   Occasionally, you may want to consider another organizational format: organizing by theories of the case. This format might be effective when the opposing party has some powerful facts that seem to support her position, but you have some key facts or a compelling theory of the case that will explain away those opposing facts. The format first sets out the powerful facts that seem to support the opposition, and then neutralizes them by setting out the facts that explain or justify the opposition's facts. For instance, in a trial brief,[11] the defendant's lawyer might organize the facts by first setting out the evidence the plaintiff is expected to offer and then setting out the evidence the defendant plans to offer.

Organizing by theory of the case is a more daring choice for several reasons. First, as a general rule, the beginning of a section soaks up far more reader-attention than does later material.[12] Second, there is the risk that a busy judge may not finish reading the Fact Statement. Third, the writer who selects this organization is betting a large stake that the supporting facts will defeat the opposing facts. Since the format sets up such a direct and express juxtaposition of these facts, the writer had better be right.

When this organizational format works, however, it is extraordinarily effective. Having heard the worst facts and having decided that they do not necessarily mean what they seem to mean, the reader is far less likely to be impressed on reading them in the opposing brief, on hearing them at oral argument, or at trial. So, be aware that this organizational format is an option, but choose it only after careful evaluation.

4.   Witness/Document.   One possible format that may occur to you as you work through the record is a witness-by-witness, document-by-document format. You may tend to fall into this format because this is the order in which you are examining the record and gathering facts. However, such a march through the record almost never results in a Fact Statement that is strategically helpful or even particularly understandable to a reader. Rather, devise a format that helps you develop a theme, and relate the particular facts from each

11.   A trial brief is filed shortly before trial. It gives the judge a general description of the evidence expected to be offered. It may alert the judge to expected legal disputes at trial (such as evidentiary disputes or disputes over jury instructions) and argue the writer's position on those disputes. It also may provide the judge with an overview of the elements of the various causes of action and claims for damages.

12.   Other lawyers believe that the position of greater emphasis is the end. But nearly everyone agrees that the position of least emphasis is the middle.

witness and each document in the thematic spot where the particular fact belongs.

B.   SUBHEADINGS

Whatever organizational format you choose, consider using subheadings. For lengthy Fact Statements, subheadings can help the writer organize effectively and help the reader follow the facts. Subheadings are particularly effective for topical or combination formats. Even if your final draft will not need subheadings, consider using working subheadings to help you organize as you write. Then you can delete the working subheadings when you edit the last time.

C.   PROCEDURAL HISTORY

Whichever format you choose, you'll need to decide where to place the procedural history. Court rules or the instructions for your assignment may make this decision for you. Some court rules require the procedural history to appear at the beginning of the Fact Statement.[13] Or the rules or instructions may require a Preliminary Statement (or Introduction), in which case the procedural history goes there, in its own section.

If court rules or your instructions have not identified the location for the procedural history, the two most common places for it are at the beginning or the end of the Fact Statement. At the beginning, it can help to establish the context for the facts that follow. At the end, it can serve as a natural segue into the Argument section. Either way, consider using subheadings to divide the Statement of the Case into at least two subsections—the "Factual History" and the "Procedural History." Since the procedural history will seldom comprise a compelling part of the theory of the case, using subheadings can put the dull procedural facts out of the way of the theme you hope to deliver with the facts.

With this overview of the organizational options in mind, turn your attention to the techniques that should inform your organizational choices.

◇ IV ◇   TECHNIQUES FOR PERSUASION[14]

Before you decide on an organization, keep in mind the following principles for effective persuasion with facts:

---

13.   *See, e.g.,* Fed. R. App. P. 28(a)(4).

14.   Lawyers must not misrepresent facts, so your use of persuasive technique must always remain within the bounds of reasonable and fair argument. All of the techniques described in this section must be used in ways that comport with a lawyer's ethical duties.

A.   General Principles

1. Clarity is more important than using sophisticated techniques for persuasion. Judges won't be persuaded by something they can't understand. If any of the following techniques conflict with the goal of clarity, discard the technique.

2. Don't use a technique that the reader will notice. An effective technique must be invisible, or nearly so. Once a reader recognizes a technique, it has lost its power because the reader's attention is on the technique and not the fact. For instance, assume that you have used the technique of repetition to emphasize a favorable fact. You hoped that it would encourage the reader to realize the significance of the fact, to let it sink in. If, instead, your reader's Commentator[15] observes, "Ah look, the writer is repeating this fact to try to get me to notice it," the reader will be thinking about the technique and the writer's goals rather than the fact. Your Fact Statement would have been more persuasive if you had not used the technique at all.

3. Don't overuse any technique. Overuse creates monotony, decreases the technique's power, and increases the chances that the reader will notice the technique rather than the facts.

4. Any technique for emphasizing one fact or group of facts de-emphasizes the remaining facts. To the extent you try to use techniques of emphasis for nearly all of the facts, your strategy will fail. You have to pick the few facts you want most to emphasize and allow the others to serve as the background.

5. Some of the techniques described below are inconsistent with each other. The inconsistency does not mean that one is right and the other wrong, but only that each has its advantages and disadvantages. The writer's job is to select the technique that will work best for the needs of a particular fact statement.

B.   Large-Scale Organization

The Beginning

6. Unless you know differently, assume that the judge is not already familiar with the case. The beginning of the Statement of Facts should establish the context for the facts that follow. Otherwise, the judge may find herself reading a chronological account of a series of events without knowing why these events are important. Context can be provided by a procedural history or by a short summary of what the case is about, written consistently with your theory of the case. Here is an example written on behalf of Carrolton:

> This is an action to enforce the terms of a covenant-not-to-compete. As part of the sale of her business to Carrolton Company, the defendant promised that for the three years immediately following the sale she would not compete with Carrolton in the three counties closest to Carrolton's headquarters.
>
> Eighteen months after the sale was completed, the defendant opened a competing business just one mile from Carrolton's office. She has been competing

15. *See* Chapter 11, p. 151.

directly with Carrolton in the three prohibited counties ever since. This action seeks to enjoin her continued breach of the covenant-not-to-compete.

7. The reader's attention level is greatest in the first few paragraphs. When you can find a way to do so logically, capitalize on the increased attention level by selecting an organization that allows you to place there material you want to emphasize. This strategy can be consistent with a summary of the case drafted from your client's perspective, like the one above.

8. Aim for a beginning that will spark the reader's interest. Journalists call this "the lead." The conventions of a legal document do not allow for some of the more dramatic forms of grabbing attention, but you do want the reader to be drawn into the story and want to read on. For example, a prosecutor's brief might begin with the facts of the crime rather than with the procedural history of the appeal.

The Middle

9. Here is the place for the facts you want to de-emphasize. Normally a reader's attention level is at its lowest about three-fourths of the way through the section.[16]

The End

10. Readers pay more attention to the material at the beginning, but they remember longest the material at the end. Readers tend to take a mental break to let the story sink in, and when they do, the last sentence still lingers in their mind. Try to select an organization that allows you to place at the end material you most want the reader to remember.

11. The last paragraph should have the "feel" of a concluding paragraph. One way to accomplish this is to close with a transition into the legal argument to follow by identifying the legal positions staked out by the parties. Be careful not to include overt legal argument. Limit yourself to identifying the positions each side will take on the legal dispute. Avoid stating the opposing position any more favorably than you have to. Keeping in mind that the last sentence lingers in the reader's mind, end with your legal position rather than your opponent's. Here is an example of such a transition:

> The bank has admitted that it did not disclose the effective interest rate to the Turners. However, it claims that disclosure was not required, arguing that the transaction was not a "consumer loan" under the Consumer Protection Act. This brief will show that the transaction was, indeed, a "consumer loan" and that the bank's failure to disclose to the Turners the effective interest rate was a violation of the Act.

16.   Mary Barnard Ray & Barbara J. Cox, *Beyond the Basics: A Text for Advanced Legal Writing* 166-167 (1991).

C.   PARAGRAPH ORGANIZATION

12. A reader devotes more attention to the beginning and the end of a paragraph than to the middle. Put facts you want to emphasize in the first sentence or in the last clause or phrase of the last sentence. De-emphasize unfavorable facts by placing them in the middle.

13. Be conscious of paragraph length. In sections where you want to emphasize the facts, keep paragraphs relatively short. Where you want to de-emphasize facts, let the paragraphs get longer and put the facts you particularly want to de-emphasize deep in the paragraph.

D.   TECHNIQUES WITH SENTENCES

14. As a general rule, reduce clutter by using the techniques in Chapter 15 to eliminate surplusage. Clutter reduces clarity, irritates the reader, and de-emphasizes the important facts. Occasionally, you can allow just a bit of clutter to surround an unfavorable fact. The clutter will reduce emphasis by lengthening the sentence and by making it less striking. Use this technique sparingly.

15. Use active verbs for emphasis and passive verbs for de-emphasis or to avoid focus on the identity of the person who took the action.

   a.   *To encourage focus on the person taking the action:*

   Shaffer kicked in the front door of the house and attacked his estranged wife, breaking her forearm.
   [Here the prosecutor wants all attention on Shaffer as he takes these violent actions.]

   b.   *To avoid focus on the person taking the action:*

   Acme Health Equipment was formed and began operation on April 22, 1995.
   [Here the writer seeks to deflect attention away from the person who formed and ran Acme—Watson.]

   c.   *To focus on a person other than the one taking the action:*

   In the early morning of January 1, 1995, after attending several New Year's Eve parties, the defendant was stopped for a routine sobriety test.
   [Here the writer is not so much trying to keep attention *away from* the police officer who stopped the defendant as to keep the focus *on* the defendant who was stopped.]

16. Place favorable facts in main clauses and unfavorable facts in dependent clauses. Consider this sentence in a brief for Watson:

   Although Acme's business does compete with Carrolton [dependent clause], the competition only extends to three small product lines and could only impact, at the most, four percent of Carrolton's profits [main clause].

If an unfavorable fact *must* go in the first or last sentence of a paragraph, place the dependent clause carrying the unfavorable fact toward the interior of the paragraph. Thus, for the first sentence of the paragraph, a dependent clause carrying an unfavorable fact should go at the end of the sentence. Which party's brief would contain this sentence?

> Acme competes directly with Carrolton in the three prohibited counties [main clause], although the competition presently extends only to three product lines [dependent clause] . . . [paragraph continues by setting out the facts of the competition].

For the last sentence of the paragraph, try putting the dependent clause at the beginning:

> [paragraph has set out the facts establishing the competition] Thus, while the competition extends only to three product lines [dependent clause], Acme directly and openly competes presently with Carrolton in the three prohibited counties [main clause].

17. Occasionally, when you want the reader to slow down and take in the significance of the material in all parts of the sentence, place a phrase or dependent clause in the middle of the sentence, interrupting the reader's usual path from the subject directly to the verb.

> Watson, who admits that she is intentionally violating the terms of her covenant, asks this Court to use its equitable powers to relieve her of the consequences of her own actions.

Use this technique sparingly because it makes sentences less readable.

18. Use shorter sentences for material you want to emphasize and longer sentences for material you want to de-emphasize.

Longer Sentences for Less Emphasis

> On July 1, while Mr. and Mrs. Emilio and their daughter Ashley were driving south on Interstate 75 toward Valdosta, a car swerved across the median and hit the Emilio car. Mr. and Mrs. Emilio survived, although they were seriously injured. Their daughter, who had been riding in the back seat, died as a result of the injuries she sustained in the accident.

Shorter Sentences for Greater Emphasis

> On July 1, Mr. and Mrs. Emilio were driving south on Interstate 75 toward Valdosta. Their daughter Ashley was riding in the back seat. A car swerved across the median and hit the Emilio car. Mr. and Mrs. Emilio survived, though seriously injured. Ashley, however, died.

E. OTHER SMALL-SCALE TECHNIQUES

19. Compress the space you devote to unfavorable facts and expand the space you devote to favorable facts. The more material you provide about the favorable facts, the more emphasis they soak up.

20. Use detail to describe the material you want to emphasize. Conversely, limit the detail of your discussion of the unfavorable facts, though of course you cannot omit any significant facts.

21. Use *visual* facts and images to describe favorable facts; avoid them for unfavorable facts. Visual images carry particular power for placing the reader, mentally, at the scene.

> On July 1, Mr. and Mrs. Emilio were driving south on Interstate 75 toward Valdosta. Their daughter Ashley was riding in the back seat. A car swerved across the median and slammed into the Emilios. The front of the other car hit the Emilio car at the left rear door, precisely where Ashley was sitting, strapped in by her seat belt.
>
> The force of the impact carried the other car's engine well into the passenger cabin of the Emilio car. It ripped Ashley from her seat belt, pinned her against the opposite door, and crushed her thoracic cavity.
>
> Mr. and Mrs. Emilio survived, though seriously injured. Ashley, however, died at the scene.

22. Short quotations (a sentence or two) or snippet quotations (just a word or a phrase) can be powerful facts. If the words of the witness or document are particularly helpful, quote them.

> Shaffer left the bar, declaring "I'm going to go talk to my wife, and she'll need a doctor before I'm through."

Avoid overquoting, however. Overquoting will result in a disjointed story and will cause the most effective quotes to fade into the pack with the rest of the quotes.

23. When you can repeat key facts *unobtrusively*, the repetition serves to emphasize those facts or concepts. For instance, the first sentence of the paragraph might summarize the facts and the remaining sentences could set out the facts in more detail. Or the beginning of a sentence might refer to the facts of the prior sentence as a transition.

> Marie Claxton, the expert witness who testified on behalf of Pyle, concluded that a reasonable and prudent lawyer would have checked the deed for easements. Claxton explained that deeds often contain restrictions that significantly affect the use of the property. She testified that any prudent lawyer would know that such restrictions are common. According to Claxton, Gavin's failure to check the deed fell below the standard of professional skill and diligence of a reasonable and prudent lawyer.

Don't just repeat particular facts, seemingly for no reason, however. It will bore and irritate your reader. Remember that the Argument section gives you a natural opportunity to repeat the key facts.

24. Place unfavorable facts in a favorable or mitigating context. You can juxtapose the unfavorable fact with favorable facts or you can place the unfavorable fact in a context that negates some of the unfavorable inferences the fact might otherwise invite.

Juxtaposing an Unfavorable Fact with Favorable Facts

Although Acme's business does compete with Carrolton, the competition only extends to three small product lines and could only impact, at the most, four percent of Carrolton's profits.

Placing the Unfavorable Fact in a More Favorable Context

While the demonstrations against the abortion clinic are disruptive to the family practice office, the McSwains cannot prevent the demonstrations; nor can they force the clinic to move until the clinic's lease term expires.

25. Humanize your client. The most important way to do this is by telling the story from the client's perspective, as your theory of the case will already accomplish. Include, where possible, a description of the client's feelings, responses, and motivations. Also helpful is referring to your client by name and using honorary titles that communicate respect, like "Mr.," "Ms.," "Dr.," or "Officer."

It is especially important to humanize corporate clients. Remember that every story involving a corporation is really a story about people. Identify the people who took the actions, and humanize those people. Portray them in a sympathetic light by setting out the context for their actions.

26. Don't go out of your way to humanize opposing parties. Where there is no need to use the names of opposing individuals, consider using generic descriptions instead ("the officer," "the insurance agent," "the electrician"). Generic descriptions can be especially helpful where the description has unsympathetic connotations, such as "the finance company," "the insurance company," or "the corporation."

While it is generally best to avoid unnecessarily humanizing opposing parties, an exception occurs where your theory of the case depends on showing the judge not only the sympathetic facts about your client but also the outrageously bad behavior of one or more of the opposing parties. In such a case, your strategy may require you to humanize the opposing party so you can show the outrageousness of his or her behavior.

27. Use graphic words, especially verbs, for facts you want to emphasize.

The van *crashed into* [instead of "hit"] the taxi, and the force of the impact *splintered* [instead of "broke"] the driver's spine.

28. Refrain from name-calling. Name-calling tells your reader that you don't have good facts, so you are compelled to resort to derogatory characterizations.

29. Where possible, delete adverbs in favor of additional facts and more vivid verbs. Vivid verbs, alone, are much more powerful than a ho-hum verb with an adverb. Avoid such artificial intensifiers as "very" or "extremely."[17]

30. Pay careful attention to common connotations of words. Choose words with helpful connotations and avoid those with unhelpful connotations.

17. *See* Chapter 15, p. 232.

A Word with Potentially Troubling Connotations

Mr. and Mrs. McMann were *anxiously* awaiting the birth of their first child.

["Anxiously" carries the connotation of worry. Use it if the connotation helps your theory, but avoid it if the connotation either impedes the theory or may distract the reader into wondering what they were worried about.]

An Option with a Better Connotation

Mr. and Mrs. McMann were *anticipating* the birth of their first child.

Finally, put the draft aside for a day or at least a few hours and then read it afresh. Try not to look for the techniques you used, but rather read openly, as you hope your reader will. Notice your reactions and fix anything that troubles you.

Checklist for Statement of Facts

LARGE-SCALE ORGANIZATION

1.   Does the organization present the facts clearly? Is it easy to follow?
2.   Does the organizational format allow you to put most of the unfavorable facts in the middle and put some of the favorable facts at the beginning and the end? (The "theory of the case" format is an intentional exception to this principle.)
3.   Does the material placed at the beginning catch the reader's interest?
4.   If your reader needs context, does the material at the beginning provide it?
5.   Does the draft communicate your theory of the case?
6.   Does the draft include all significant facts and all facts mentioned in your Argument?
7.   Does the draft include enough context to allow the reader to understand the dispute and your theory of the case, but no more?
8.   Does the draft place the procedural history at an appropriate location?
9.   Does the last paragraph have the "feel" of an ending?
10. Does the draft end with a sentence that you want the reader to remember?

PARAGRAPH ORGANIZATION

11. Are your best facts on the outside ends of the paragraph while your least favorable facts are in the middle?
12. Does the last phrase or clause of the paragraph contain favorable information?
13. Are the paragraphs with facts you want to emphasize relatively short? Are those with facts you want to neutralize longer?

TECHNIQUES WITH SENTENCES

14. Are the sentences (except one or two carrying unfavorable facts) free of clutter?
15. Do the passive-voiced verbs serve a purpose? Are there any actions you'd like to de-emphasize by changing to passive?
16. Where appropriate, are unfavorable facts in dependent clauses, juxtaposed with more favorable facts or explanatory context?
17. Do the shorter sentences carry favorable facts? Where appropriate, are the unfavorable facts in longer sentences?
18. Using brackets in the margins of the draft, identify the text that deals with favorable topics and the text that deals with unfavorable topics. How does the total allocation of space to each compare?
19. Notice where you have used detail and visual images. Notice where you have not.
20. Do the quotations really help?
21. If you have used the technique of repetition, is it too obvious?
22. How have you referred to your client? To the opposing parties?
23. At spots where you are presenting favorable material, are there any verbs you can switch for more powerful or graphic synonyms?

EXERCISE 1.   Critiquing the Statement of Facts

Here are two basic Statements of Facts on the Watson covenant-not-to-compete issue. Each fact statement has strengths. Neither is perfect. Evaluate each, identifying what works well and what could be improved.

Recall from Chapter 17 that one formulation of the governing rule of law is:

> A covenant-not-to-compete is enforceable if all of the following elements are reasonable:
>
> A. the kind of activity that is restrained;
> B. the geographic area where it is restrained; and
> C. the time period of the restraint.

Another formulation of the rule is:

> To be enforceable, a covenant-not-to-compete must be reasonable. Factors for deciding reasonableness are:
>
> A. the needs of the restraining party
> B. the needs of the public
> C. the needs of the restrained party
> D. any other relevant circumstances

Which rule formulation does the drafter of each Statement of Facts seem to have in mind?

Statement of Facts on behalf of Carrolton

STATEMENT OF FACTS

This is an action to enforce the terms of a covenant-not-to-compete. On Dec. 1, 1994, the Defendant sold Carrolton Company to Richard Meyers, Andrea McPhane, and James Rey ("Purchasers") for $220,000. (Compl. ¶ 10.) The sale included not only Carrolton's inventory and accounts receivable, but also the company's good will in the community. (Compl. ¶ 11.) As part of the contract of sale, the Defendant promised that she would not compete with Carrolton for the three years immediately following the sale. (Compl. ¶ 13.) The covenant covers only Quincy, Herring, and Gawin Counties, the three counties closest to Carrolton's office. (Compl. ¶ 13.)

The covenant-not-to-compete was an integral part of the Defendant's sale of Carrolton to the Purchasers. (McPhane Aff. ¶ 8.) Carrolton retails in-home health care products in the Kinston, Georgia area. (Compl. ¶ 13.) Through her ownership of Carrolton, the Defendant had been engaged in the retail sales of health care products in the Kinston area for fifteen years. (McPhane Aff. ¶ 8.) On behalf of Carrolton, she had made and maintained the sales contacts necessary to a successful retailer of those products. (McPhane Aff. ¶ 9.) Her contacts and on-going relationships with physicians and customers were part of the good will for which the Purchasers paid. (McPhane Aff. ¶ 10.) Thus, these contacts and relationships were a critical part of the sale of the business. (Compl. ¶ 14.) The covenant prohibits the defendant from making sales contacts for in-home health care products in the three counties that comprise the heart of Carrolton's marketing area. (Compl. ¶ 15.)

After the Defendant sold Carrolton to the Purchasers, the Defendant remained with the company, employed as Carrolton's General Manager. She held that position of trust for fourteen months after the sale. (Compl. ¶ 16.) On February 21, 1996, the Defendant left her position as Carrolton's General Manager and immediately opened a competing business one mile from Carrolton's office. (Compl. ¶ 17.) Since that date, the Defendant has been making sales contacts for health care products in the three prohibited counties, in direct competition with Carrolton. (Compl. ¶ 18.) The Purchasers have filed this action seeking to enjoin the Defendant's continued breach of the covenant not to compete.

Statement of Facts on behalf of Watson

STATEMENT OF FACTS

In 1979, Sharon Watson founded Carrolton Company, a retailer of in-home health care equipment in Kinston, Georgia. (Watson Aff. ¶ 3.) Before Carrolton opened, residents of Kinston and the surrounding area had to travel seventy-five miles to the nearest retailer of health care equipment. (Williams Aff. ¶ 2.) The lack of a nearby health care equipment retailer was particularly problematic for the Kinston community because people needing in-home health care equipment are among those least able to make a seventy-five mile trip to purchase that equipment. (Williams Aff. ¶ 3-6.) With Carrolton's opening, area residents had local access to the health care equipment they needed. (Williams Aff. ¶ 8.)

As the only retailer of in-home health care equipment in the area, Carrolton did a large volume of business. (Watson Aff. ¶ 7.) Ms. Watson believed that Carrolton's virtual monopoly brought with it an obligation not to take advantage of her customers. (Watson Aff. ¶ 9.) Thus, she used a mark-up of only 35 percent to insure that her customers paid fair prices. (Watson Aff. ¶ 10.) She kept the business responsive to customer needs, making diligent efforts to fill special orders and maintaining close communication with local physicians. (Williams Aff. ¶ 8; Watson Aff. ¶ 11.) She made certain that Carrolton was a concerned and responsible commercial citizen of the community. (Tharpe Aff. ¶ 6; William Aff. ¶ 9.)

In early 1994, a group of Atlanta investors approached Ms. Watson about the possibility of buying Carrolton. (Compl. ¶ 5.) Over the next few months the parties discussed the terms of a possible sale. (Compl. ¶ 7.) During these conversations, Ms. Watson expressed concern about how the business, still a virtual monopoly, would be run. (Watson Aff. ¶ 12.)

In response to these concerns, the investors suggested that Ms. Watson remain with the company as General Manager and continue to manage the operation. (Watson Aff. ¶ 14.) The investors explained that they would not want Carrolton's fundamental operating policies to change, and Ms. Watson's continued management would be a way to continue the company's successful marketing approach. (Watson Aff. ¶ 15.) They explained that Ms. Watson's approach was so important to them that they would like the transaction to include the covenant that Ms. Watson would not leave Carrolton to compete in the local market for at least three years. (Watson Aff. ¶ 15.) Ms. Watson agreed, and on Dec. 1, 1994, after fifteen years of building the business, Ms. Watson sold Carrolton to its present owners. (Compl. ¶ 10.)

The terms of the sale placed Ms. Watson in the position of General Manager. (Compl. ¶ 12.) While the contract did not expressly state the reason for the terms, the parties had always discussed Ms. Watson's continued service and noncompetition covenant as a method to maintain continuity of management philosophy. (Watson Aff. ¶ 14.) The covenant prohibited Ms. Watson from competing with Carrolton's new owners in the three counties that make up Carrolton's virtual monopoly. (Compl. ¶ 11.)

Within a month after the sale, Carrolton's new owners began implementing management changes. (Williams Aff. ¶ 11; Watson Aff. ¶ 16; Tharpe Aff. ¶ 8.) They issued new pricing policies, raising the company's mark-up on its product lines. (Watson Aff. ¶ 16.) They ordered Ms. Watson to lay off one of Carrolton's only two other employees, and they eliminated most special orders. (Watson Aff. ¶ 17.) Eliminating these special orders effectively blocked the access of area customers to any health care products not a part of Carrolton's regular inventory. (Tharpe Aff. ¶ 9.)

In response to Ms. Watson's protests, the owners argued that these new policies maximized efficiency and company profits. (Watson Aff. ¶ 19.) They maintained that customer complaints were not important since without Carrolton, customers would have no local access to health care equipment at all. (Watson Aff. ¶ 20.)

On Feb. 21, 1996, after repeated attempts to persuade Carrolton's new owners to rescind their new policies, Ms. Watson left her position at Carrolton. (Watson Aff. ¶ 22.) Believing that Carrolton's owners had breached their assurances that Carrolton would continue being responsive to its customer's needs, Ms. Watson formed Acme Health Care. (Watson Aff. ¶ 22.) Ms. Watson incurred $75,000 in personal debt to open Acme, mortgaging her home to secure the loan. (Watson Aff. ¶ 23.) In the first two years of business Acme will do well to break even. During that time, Ms. Watson will have to make loan payments from her personal savings. (Watson Aff. ¶ 24.)

Although Ms. Watson hopes that one day Acme will represent a viable customer alternative to Carrolton, (Watson Aff. ¶ 27.), presently Acme competes with Carrolton in only three product lines: respiratory equipment, diabetic monitoring equipment, and wheelchairs. (Watson Aff. ¶ 25.) Even in these lines, Acme's business is just beginning. Presently, Acme carries only the products of the two leading manufacturers in these product lines. (Watson Aff. ¶ 26.) During the next nineteen months (the remaining term of the covenant-not-to-compete), Acme cannot expect to attract more than 30 percent of Carrolton's business in these product lines. Acme will have no impact on Carrolton's virtual monopoly over the twenty-two other product lines Carrolton sells. (Watson Aff. ¶ 29.)

Even if Acme meets with phenomenal success during the next nineteen months, Carrolton will still make healthy profits. (Watson Aff. ¶ 32.) During the remaining covenant term, Acme poses no realistic threat to Carrolton's business. (Watson Aff. ¶ 34.) Acme's potential threat to Carrolton is the potential end to Carrolton's virtual monopoly over the in-home health care market in the Kinston area. (Watson Aff. ¶ 35; Williams Aff. ¶ 17; Tharpe Aff. ¶ 15.) That threat to Carrolton's market position would arise, if at all, long after the covenant has expired. (Watson Aff. ¶ 36.)

EXERCISE 2.   Drafting a Statement of Facts

You represent the Plaintiff, Shakira Turner, in the following litigation. Using the following excerpts from a trial court record, draft a Statement of Facts for a brief opposing Defendant's Motion for Summary Judgment.

Verified[18] *Complaint*
[simplified version]

1.   The Plaintiff, Shakira Turner, is an American citizen of African descent.
2.   The Defendant, Grisham Employment Services, is regularly engaged in the business of procuring employees for employers and in procuring for employees opportunities to work for an employer.
3.   On May 20, 1995, Turner successfully completed the course of study in computer repair at Kelly Technical College.

18.   A complaint is "verified" when the plaintiff has signed an attached statement swearing to the truth of the matters asserted in the complaint.

4. Turner contracted with the Defendant for the purpose of obtaining employment as a computer repair specialist.
5. During the time of Turner's contract with the Defendant, the Defendant never referred Turner to an employer seeking a computer repair specialist.
6. The Defendant referred Turner to only one potential employer, and that employer was seeking to fill a position sorting and delivering incoming mail.
7. During the time of Turner's contract with the Defendant, the Defendant has referred a white graduate of Kelly Technical College's computer repair course to three employers seeking to fill positions for computer repair specialists.
8. Turner and the white graduate have equivalent training and job qualifications.
9. The Defendant's failure to refer Turner for employment was based on her race and constitutes a violation of 42 U.S.C. § 2000e-2(b).

Dated: January 6, 1996   _____

                                           Attorney for Plaintiff

Excerpts from Interrogatory Responses by Defendant

12. List the names, contract dates, and EEOC racial classification of each applicant for a position as a computer repair specialist you have served in the past five years.

Answer:

Name:	Dates:	Race:
Jay Griffith	4/9/92-6/18/92	white
Alice Harris	4/21/92-6/18/92	white
Ian Sothby	4/17/93-7/1/93	white
Scott Metz	4/29/94-6/6/94	white
Carlos Vinueza	4/7/94-7/18/94	hispanic
Teresa McMullan	4/1/95-8/21/95	white
Shakira Turner	4/29/95-1/2/96	black

13. For each person listed in your answer to Interrogatory 12, state the number of referrals you provided to that applicant and state whether the applicant was placed as a computer repair specialist as a result of your referral. For each applicant not placed, explain the circumstances that terminated your contract with that applicant.

Answer:

Name:	Referrals:	Placed:	Termination Circs:
Griffith	2	yes	N/A
Harris	3	yes	N/A
Sothby	2	yes	N/A

Name:	Referrals:	Placed:	Termination Circs:
Metz	4	yes	N/A
Vinueza	3	yes	N/A
McMullan	3	no	moved out of state
Turner	2	no	applicant withdrew

Page 25 from Deposition of Joseph Grisham
[owner of Grisham Employment Services]

Line No.:		
1	Q:	So your records indicate that you gave the Plaintiff two referrals
2		for positions as a computer repair technician?
3	A:	That's right.
4	Q:	How did you communicate those referrals to her?
5	A:	By telephone and by confirming letter.
6	Q:	Do your records indicate the dates of the calls and letters?
7	A:	Yes, the first call and letter were on June 10 and the second call
8		and letter were on July 6.
9	Q:	Do your records contain copies of the letters?
10	A:	No, we don't keep copies of those letters. We don't have the space.
11	Q:	Do your records indicate whether you actually talked to Ms.
12		Turner?
13	A:	No. If the applicant isn't home, we leave messages on an answering
14		machine or with another person. But the confirming letter should
15		cover any times when the applicant doesn't get the message.
16	Q:	Do your records indicate whether Ms. Turner ever responded to
17		these referrals?
18	A:	I see no indication of a response in the file.
19	Q:	What were the dates of the referrals to Teresa McMullan?
20	A:	April 25, June 10, and July 6.
21	Q:	Did she go for interviews for all three of those positions?
22	A:	Yes.

Defendant's Motion for Summary Judgment

The Defendant moves the Court for an order entering summary judgment on the grounds that the record shows no genuine issue as to any material fact and that the Defendant is entitled to judgment as a matter of law. The undisputed facts in the record do not support the allegations of the Plaintiff's Complaint.

Dated: April 2, 1996   _____

                                          Attorney for Defendant

Excerpt from Turner's Affidavit

5. Shortly before my graduation from Kelly Technical College, I contracted with Grisham Employment Services for the purpose of securing a position as a computer repair technician.

6. During the time of my contract with the Defendant, I never traveled out of town, and my telephone answering machine was never out of order. Each Tuesday and Friday I would visit the Defendant's office to inquire about any possible referrals.

7. In the approximately seven months of my contract with the Defendant, I never received a referral for a computer repair technician's position.

8. In September 1995, the Defendant gave me a referral for a position as a mail clerk, sorting and delivering incoming mail. I declined to be interviewed for that position.

9. In December 1995, I had a telephone conversation with my former classmate, Teresa McMullan. During that conversation Ms. McMullan told me that during the spring and summer of that year she had received three referrals from the Defendant for positions as a computer repair technician.

10. In early January 1996, I terminated my contract with the Defendant and contracted with Employment Plus, Inc. Within two weeks I had received a referral and accepted employment as a computer repair technician.

Dated: April 17, 1996   _____

                                        Shakira Turner

Excerpts from Decembrino's Affidavit

1. I am the Placement Officer at Kelly Technical College. My duties include working with our graduates to help them locate employment. My job requires that I remain informed about the local job market for our graduates and that I become familiar with the qualifications of our individual graduates.

2. During 1996 the local job market for computer repair technicians was adequate. All ten of Kelly's graduates in computer repair were employed with positions in their field within two months of graduation except Teresa McMullan and Shakira Turner. Ms. McMullan moved out of state and did not pursue a computer repair position. Ms. Turner did not locate a position until early 1996.

3. Both Ms. McMullan and Ms. Turner were fully qualified computer repair technicians. Ms. McMullan graduated fifth in her class of ten. Ms. Turner graduated third in that same class.

Dated: April 17, 1996   _____

                                        Antonio Decembrino

stage
four

REVISING TO ACHIEVE A FINAL DRAFT

Editing the Brief

Now that you have a complete draft of the brief, turn your attention to editing. Put the document aside for a day or two, if you can, and try to read the document with fresh eyes. Seek feedback from a colleague if collaboration is permitted by your assignment. Before you go further in this chapter, return to Chapters 14 and 15. Use those chapters as checklists to edit your usage, style, citation form, and quotations. Once you have completed those tasks, edit the following aspects of your brief.

 **PERSUASIVE STYLE**

A. DEGREE OF FORMALITY

While the degree of formality of an office memo will vary depending on the particular firm's custom and the preference of the requesting attorney, the degree of formality of a brief does not vary. Any document filed with a court should use traditional professional formality. This means, for instance, that the document should not contain contractions, slang, or humor.[1] It should not contain references to the writer, the judge, or opposing counsel unless the references are necessary for the legal discussion of the issues. For an

---

1. Unless, of course, the document is quoting another speaker or writer and the substance of the quotation is legally relevant.

example of traditional professional formality, review the level of formality used in the sample briefs in Appendices B and C.

B. COMPETENCE AND CLARITY

Communicating clearly and convincing the reader of your competence are two of an advocate's most important techniques. Here are four editing strategies to increase clarity and send the message of competence:

1. Tabulate. When your document deals with several items (such as elements of a rule, factors, guidelines, categories of facts), consider tabulating the items.

> A lawyer has a responsibility to undertake legal service in the public interest. Among the possible avenues of service are: (1) free or reduced-fee representation of the poor; (2) free or reduced-fee representation of public service organizations; (3) participating in activities designed to improve the legal system; or (4) financially supporting legal services programs.

Tabulating not only helps your reader navigate through the substance of your text; it also demonstrates to your reader that you are controlling the substance rather than the other way around. Your reader will be more willing to follow you along your line of reasoning if the reader finds you an effective leader.

2. Where helpful, create shortened forms of reference for people and things your text refers to often. This is another technique for sending the message that you are in control of the material. Introduce the shortened reference at the earliest feasible occasion, and maintain consistency of reference from then on. If you will use several shortened references, consider a paragraph or footnote early in the text introducing all of them.

> This brief will refer to Defendants Carter, Colham, Tellerhoff, and Winston, in combination, as "the employers," and to Defendants Allen, Rakestraw, and Vernon, in combination, as "the employees." The brief also refers to 42 U.S.C. § 2000e-17 by its popular name "Title VII," and to 42 U.S.C. § 1983 by its popular reference "Section 1983."

Where possible, select a shortened reference that will facilitate your theory of the case. Avoid references that will work at odds with your theory of the case.

3. Add explanatory parentheticals to citations. Go back through your citations to find any authorities that could use an explanatory parenthetical.[2] A citation might profit from a parenthetical if you are not discussing its facts and reasoning in the text, such as when: (a) you are citing it simply as additional authority for a proposition principally supported in some other way; or (b) you are citing it cursorily as support for a minor and uncontested

---

2. *See* Bluebook Rule 10.6

proposition. You can use the parenthetical to quote a nugget of language or to highlight examples of relevant facts from the cited case. Here are two examples:

1. Following a discussion of several cases dealing with the evidentiary significance of racial statements by supervisors:

   See also Slack v. Havens, 7 F.E.P. 885, 885 (S.D. Cal. 1973) *aff'd as modified,* 522 F.2d 1091 (9th Cir. 1975) ("Colored folks are hired to clean because they clean better.")

2. Where the ineffectuality of serving process by trickery is a minor and uncontested point:

   Courts have held that a defendant who resides out-of-state cannot be lured into the state by fraud or trickery and then served with process. *McClellan v. Rowell,* 99 So. 2d 653 (Miss. 1958) (petitioner told his ex-wife that his mother was dying and wanted to see the couple's child one last time); *Zenker v. Zenker,* 72 N.W.2d. 809 (Neb. 1955) (plaintiff told defendant that his presence was needed to convey certain real estate).

4. Purge your document of vague references like these:

this matter	with regard to
it involves	it deals with
it pertains to	it concerns

Writing peppered with these phrases forces the reader to struggle to understand the reference and to wonder whether the writer is in control of the material.

C. TACT AND GOOD JUDGMENT

Here are four "attitude" problems to watch for and edit out.

1. Don't tell a court what it "must" do or what it "cannot" do. Use less confrontational language when referring to limits on the court's authority or power. For instance, avoid:

The Court must reverse the trial court's order . . .
The Court cannot grant the defendant's motion . . .
The Court is not permitted to consider subsequent negotiations . . .

Here are some better options:

a. Shift the focus to a tactful statement of another court's error.

   The lower court erred in ordering that . . .

b. Use a passive-voiced verb (to avoid identifying the court as the actor); substitute "should" for "cannot"; and switch to a permissive statement (what the court *should* do) rather than a prohibitory statement (what the court *shouldn't* do).

The defendant's motion should be denied . . .

c. Focus on the rule that governs the issue rather than on the entity that must follow the rule.

The rule allows consideration of subsequent negotiations only where . . .

2.   Edit out signs of negative emotion.   Cool reason is much more persuasive than sarcasm or anger. Cool reason says to your reader, "The law and the facts are on my side, so I don't have to be disturbed by the opposing side's position."

3.   Focus on the judge rather than on the opposing party or the opposing lawyer.   A brief-writer's focus can be distracted by becoming caught up in seeing the litigation as a battle with opposing parties or their lawyers. Don't let your day-to-day contact with the parties and their lawyers cause you to forget that the primary focus of your brief must be the *reader* (the judge). Professors Ray and Cox counsel brief-writers to think of themselves as advisors helping the judge resolve the parties' dispute.[3]

AN ARGUMENT PHRASED AS AN ADVISOR TO THE COURT

The test for determining whether a document is subject to the qualified immunity from discovery under the work product rule is whether . . .
This document meets this test. The litigation to protect Hammond's interest . . . Thus, . . .
To compel production of material subject to qualified immunity, defendant debtors must at least make a showing of . . .
They have not done so . . . Moreover, . . .

AN ARGUMENT FOCUSING ON THE ATTORNEYS' DEBATE

Despite their extensive arguments, the defendant's attorneys have failed to show the necessity of obtaining the requested documents, which were . . .
The defendant has not shown that the documents requested do not meet the test for determining qualified immunity, so the documents should not be discoverable. Documents are subject to qualified immunity when . . .[4]

As Professors Ray and Cox point out, the second writer "has yielded the stage to the defendant."[5] While the second writer ostensibly is writing to the judge, the real intended recipients of the second writer's message are the opposing party and the opposing lawyers. The second writer needs to turn her mental attention from the noisy debate with the opposition and return to a calm, focused "consultation" with the judge.

3.   Mary Barnard Ray & Barbara J. Cox, *Beyond the Basics: A Text for Advanced Legal Writing* 221-223 (1991).
4.   *Id.*
5.   *Id.* at 222.

4. Make a final check on your perspective; moderate any exaggerations of the law, the facts, or the inferences. A necessary part of the advocacy process is the shift from an objective perspective to a partisan perspective. But a brief-writer still must evaluate the final draft of the brief with an objective eye, being careful not to overstate the law or the facts. Remember that a reader who suspects that the advocate has exaggerated one point will doubt all of the writer's other points as well.

D. THE RHETORIC OF PERSUASION

Rhetoric is the art of speaking or writing effectively. Rhetorical techniques govern every aspect of the advocate's writing process. These techniques have been the object of academic study for thousands of years, and this text cannot begin to do them justice. However, here are three small editing suggestions to increase the persuasive power of a brief. You won't have time to examine each sentence of the brief with these techniques in mind, but take a few minutes to polish the key sentences.

1. The artful use of passive-voiced verbs. Remember that an occasional passive verb can help solve a writing awkwardness or serve a rhetorical goal. We have already seen two examples of the artful use of passive verbs: A passive verb can help a writer avoid telling a court what it can and cannot do[6] and it can help a writer achieve gender-neutral writing.[7]

The passive voice has other uses as well. Sometimes a writer wants to focus attention on the *object* of the action rather than on the *actor* doing the action. The actor may be unknown or irrelevant. Perhaps the writer wants to downplay the client's unfavorable conduct. Or perhaps the writer's topic for the discussion is the object of the action rather than the actor. Here are examples of such occasions:

a. *Identity of actor unknown and irrelevant:*

   The notice of termination *was placed* in Mr. Alexander's box.

b. *Downplaying the client's unfavorable conduct:*

   In his anger, Mr. Shaffer pushed Mrs. Shaffer. She fell against the table and her arm *was broken* in the fall.

c. *Writer's topic is the object rather than the actor:*

   The Fun Run was a major success. It *was scheduled* for Labor Day weekend, and it attracted a record field of runners.

---

6. *See* section C(1) above.
7. *See* p. 224.

2.   The rhetoric of counter-argument.   As you recall from Chapter 17 and from section C(3) above, affirmatively presenting your own argument first is far more effective than beginning your presentation by focusing on your opponent's argument. Your draft should already reflect this emphasis and order of discussion. Now consider downplaying your opponent's argument even further by shortening or removing entirely any *statement of the opponent's argument*. Where possible, replace the introductory statement of the position with an immediate assertion that the position is flawed (going on, of course, to explain why). For example, replace the first version with the second:

FIRST VERSION

The defendant argues that the artificial condition must have drawn the child onto the property, citing to *Andersonville v. Goodden* [citation omitted]. However, recent cases have discarded this requirement. . . . [Discussion goes on to support the assertion that the requirement has been discarded.]

[This version states the opponent's argument first, before pointing out its fallacy, and labels it as the opponent's position. The label draws subtle attention to the argument and the initially unquestioned statement of the argument has the momentary effect of asserting it.]

SECOND VERSION

Nor does the attractive nuisance doctrine require that the artificial condition must have actually drawn the child onto the property, as the defendant argues. Though the early case of *Andersonville v. Goodden* set out this element, the court implicitly rejected this requirement in the more recent case of *Newcomb v. Roberts* [citation omitted]. In *Newcomb,* the swimming pool did not draw the child into the yard, but the court allowed recovery nonetheless. [further discussion of the facts and holding of *Newcomb*].

[This version subtly de-emphasizes the opponent's argument by downplaying the attention-drawing label (it can even be removed entirely) and by stating the opponent's argument only in the sentence asserting its fallacy.]

3.   Defusing your opponent's rhetoric.   If your opponent has used rhetoric that is either excessive or particularly effective, consider ways to defuse that opposing rhetoric. Confront excessive rhetoric if you think that, left unconfronted, it may influence the judge. Confront particularly effective rhetoric if you can devise a way to remove the rhetoric's power. By far the best way to remove the power of rhetoric is by using the law or the facts or both. For example:

Defendant's brief contains broad general conclusions such as "preemptive effect . . . is firmly established in the case law," a "comprehensive network of agency regulations," "pervasive nature of the regulations," and the agency's "specifically stated intent." Def. brief 4. The support and analysis of these grandiose phrases and broad-brush conclusions consists simply of three agency source materials, plus an extensive reliance on one district court opinion, *Simon.* We now show these authorities do not support these statements.[8]

8.   Irwin Alterman, *Plain and Accurate Style in Court Papers* 125-126 (Student ed. 1994).

4. Sentence structure. Notice where you put your modifying phrases and how those placements affect your sentences. Do you tend to place these phrases somewhere in the middle of the main clause, where they interrupt the main clause's movement from the subject to the verb to the object?

> The plaintiff, instead of dismissing the complaint and admitting the fallacy of the unsupported allegations, filed a motion for a preliminary injunction.

Do you tend to "front-load" the sentence by placing the phrase at the beginning of the sentence, where it postpones the main clause?

> Instead of dismissing the complaint and admitting the fallacy of the unsupported allegations, the plaintiff filed a motion for a preliminary injunction.

Do you tend to place the phrase at the end of the sentence, after the main subject and verb?

> The plaintiff filed a motion for a preliminary injunction instead of dismissing the complaint and admitting the fallacy of the unsupported allegations.

Each of these placements has a useful rhetorical function.[9] Placement in the middle of the sentence slows down the reader's pace and emphasizes the content of the dependent clause. Placement at the beginning can build suspense but sometimes reduces clarity or readability. Placement at the end speeds the reader on through the sentence, increases readability, and emphasizes the main clause. All three placements help determine which words will be placed at the end of the sentence, to linger longer in the reader's mind.

Good writing uses all three placements, but selects wisely, based on the rhetorical goal of the writer. Most sentences should carry the dependent clause or phrase at either the beginning or end. Decide which based on what material you want to emphasize and what words you want to place last. If you want to slow the reader down and distribute some emphasis to the beginning, middle, and end of the sentence, place the phrase in the middle. Overuse of this sentence structure is not effective, though, so select carefully the occasions for its use. Experimenting with several versions of the sentence will give you a better sense of the options.

---

9. *See* Chapter 20.

FINAL CHECKLIST

1. Look one last time at the court rules governing briefs. Does your brief comply with all of them?
2. Check the listings and page numbers in the Table of Contents. Are they still complete and accurate after the final edit?
3. Check the listings and page numbers in the Table of Authorities. Are they still complete, accurate, and in proper alphabetical order after the final edit?
4. Check the citations to the record in the Statement of Facts and in the rule application sections of the Argument. Confirm that any necessary additions to the record (such as affidavits to be filed simultaneously with the brief) are prepared and ready.
5. Confirm that any appendices are complete and attached to the brief.
6. Confirm that a proper Certificate of Service is appended.
7. Do a final check for spelling and typographical errors.
8. Sign the signature line, remembering that your signature constitutes your representation that the brief is not being submitted for any improper purpose; that the contentions are not frivolous; and that the facts alleged are consistent with the evidence.[10]

---

10.   Fed. R. Civ. P. 11.

Epilogue

You have come a long way. You have used the writing process to improve your analytical skills, and you have learned how to communicate your analysis both in a predictive office memo and in a persuasive brief. Along the way you have learned about the legal system, about lawyers' professional responsibilities, about judges and other law-trained readers, about strategy and legal storytelling, and perhaps even some things about yourself.

You should now have a deeper understanding of some important concepts. You can better see the connection between writing and thinking. You know how the goals of the writer differ from one stage to the next in the writing process, and that a conscious recognition of these differences frees the writer to use the opportunities of each stage fully. You may have been surprised to see how complicated and difficult the thinking and writing process is. At times you may have been frustrated to see how long the process takes. Don't worry. Experience will enable you to combine some of the steps and speed things along.

Your practice in both predictive and persuasive analysis have probably given you a clearer sense of how important each skill is to the other. When you wrote the brief, you used the authorities to formulate and structure the most favorable rule you could. You saw examples of using the same authorities to formulate different rules—rules whose differences could win or lose the case. Now that you have seen how the same authorities can support critically different rules, you can see why an accurate *prediction* must recognize and evaluate the different rules an advocate could formulate.

Likewise, when you wrote the brief, you saw how you had to use your skills of objective analysis to gauge how *persuasive* a neutral decision-maker might find the arguments you were considering. Neither perspective can yield a thorough and effective analysis without the other. And the more practice you have with the one, the more your skills with the other will improve.

Finally, you have begun to develop your sense of a lawyer's professional responsibilities—both the "negative" responsibilities (to refrain from false statement, concealment of authority, maintenance of frivolous claims, ex parte communications with the judge, misrepresentation even by inference) and the "affirmative" responsibilities (competence, diligence, loyalty, candor, and promptness). Your law practice will present you with challenges to these responsibilities on a daily basis. If you begin to develop a solid professional ethos now, while you are in law school, you'll be far more ready to meet those challenges in a couple of years.

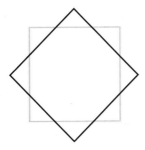

APPENDICES

APPENDIX

A

Sample Office Memorandum

To: Requesting Attorney
From: Summer Clerk
Date: November 9, 1995
Re: Beth Buckley; file # 756385; stolen car; whether Buckley can disaffirm purchase of car based on her minority

QUESTION PRESENTED

Can Buckley, a minor, disaffirm the purchase of a car when she misunderstood the sales agent's question and therefore accidentally misrepresented her age as eighteen?

BRIEF ANSWER

Probably yes. A minor can disaffirm a contract unless the minor's fraudulent misrepresentation induced the other party to enter into the contract. On Buckley's facts, a court would probably rule that an innocent misrepresentation such as Buckley's is not fraudulent and therefore would not prevent a minor from disaffirming a contract. Though less likely, a court might also rule that the seller did not justifiably rely on Buckley's representation.

FACTS

Our client, Beth Buckley, is seventeen and a high school senior. She will turn eighteen on December 15. Two months ago she bought a used

-1-

car for $3,000 from Willis Chevrolet. She paid cash, using the money she had saved from her summer job. Buckley purchased collision insurance for the car, but she did not insure against theft. Last week the car was stolen, and Buckley has asked what she can do about her loss.

When Buckley first looked at cars on the lot, the sales agent asked if she was old enough to buy a car. Buckley did not realize that she had to be eighteen to enter into a contract, even when paying cash. She thought the sales agent was asking whether she was old enough to drive, so she said "yes." The agent did not ask to see any identification and did not raise the subject of age again.

The next day Buckley returned to the lot, selected the car she wanted to purchase, and completed the transaction. She recalls "signing a bunch of papers," but she did not read them and does not know what they said. She says that the sales agent did not attempt to explain the documents. He simply showed her where to sign, and she signed on those lines. She does not know if she still has copies of the documents, but she will look among her papers and let us know.

<u>DISCUSSION</u>

I.   Can Beth Buckley disaffirm the contract?

A minor does not have the capacity to make a binding contract, but a contract made by a minor is not automatically void. *Hood v. Duren,* 125 S.E. 787 (Ga. Ct. App. 1924). Generally, one who is a minor at the time of making a contract can disaffirm the contract within a reasonable time after reaching the age of majority. O.C.G.A. § 13-3-20 (1982);[1] *Merritt v. Jowers,* 193 S.E. 238 (Ga. 1937). The rationale for the rule is the recognition that minors have not yet attained sufficient maturity to be responsible for the decisions they make, so the rule protects them from at least some of the consequences of bad decisions. *See generally White v. Sikes,* 59 S.E. 228 (Ga. 1907).

However, a minor is estopped from disaffirming a contract if (a) the minor made a false and fraudulent representation of his or her age; (b) the contracting party justifiably relied on the minor's representation; and (c) the minor has reached the age of discretion. *Carney v. Southland Loan Co.,* 88 S.E.2d 805 (Ga. 1955). Because the first element is most likely to be dispositive in Buckley's case, the memo will discuss it first.

A.   Buckley's unintentional misrepresentation of her age probably is insufficient to establish fraudulent misrepresentation.

The first element necessary for estoppel is a false and fraudulent representation. A minor makes a false and fraudulent representation when

---

1.   The Bluebook format for citation to the Georgia Code is "Ga. Code Ann." However, Georgia practitioners overwhelmingly use the format "O.C.G.A." standing for "Official Code of Georgia Annotated." When you are writing for a practitioner, use the format the practitioner prefers.

the minor affirmatively and intentionally states a false age, intending that the seller rely on the information. For instance, in *Carney* the minor told the car sales agent that he was twenty-two, the agent recorded that information on the loan application, and the minor signed the application and purchased the car. The court affirmed the trial court's holding that the minor had fraudulently misrepresented his age and was estopped from disaffirming the contract. *Id.* at 807-808.

Similarly, in *Clemons v. Olshine,* 187 S.E. 711 (Ga. Ct. App. 1936), the minor told the clothing sales agent that he was twenty-one and signed a contract confirming the representation. The court held that his fraudulent misrepresentation estopped him from disaffirming. In *Watters v. Arrington,* 146 S.E. 773 (Ga. Ct. App. 1929), another car purchase case, several agents of the seller testified that the minor had twice affirmatively stated his age to be twenty-one. The court affirmed the jury's verdict for the seller, holding that a minor's fraudulent misrepresentation of age estops the minor from disaffirming the contract.

The courts distinguish this kind of intentional, knowing misrepresentation from unintentional, even negligent misrepresentations of age. For instance, in *Woodall v. Grant & Co.,* 9 S.E.2d 95 (Ga. Ct. App. 1940), the minor had simply signed without reading a form contract that contained a representation that he was of age. There the court held that the representation in the contract did not estop the minor because the minor had not read the contract. The court reasoned that minors are not required to read contracts. *Id.* at 95. The *Carney* decision distinguished *Woodall* by pointing out that in *Woodall* "the minor's only sin, if any, was his failure to read a contract which . . . stated that he was of age, while in [*Carney*] the minor falsely gave the information put into the contract." *Carney,* 88 S.E.2d at 808.

The most recent relevant case, *Siegelstein v. Fenner & Beane,* 17 S.E.2d 907 (Ga. Ct. App. 1941), reaffirmed the *Carney/Woodall* distinction. In *Siegelstein,* the jury returned a verdict for the defendant, and the appellate court reversed on other grounds. However, the appellate court affirmed the trial court's jury instruction, stating that a minor's false representation of age "will not affect his power to disaffirm a contract unless [the representation] was made *fraudulently.*" *Id.* at 910 (emphasis supplied).

The rule holding minors responsible only for intentional affirmative misrepresentations is consistent with the policy behind allowing minors to disaffirm their contracts. Minors, by definition, are more likely than adults to make errors and other innocent misrepresentations. Given this symmetry of rationale, the courts are likely to continue allowing minors to disaffirm despite innocent, even negligent, misrepresentations.

Here, the sales agent simply asked Buckley whether she was old enough to buy a car. Buckley misunderstood the question, thinking that the agent was asking whether she was old enough to drive. Thus she innocently answered "yes." She did not affirmatively state an age at all. This kind of misunderstanding is exactly the sort of confusion a minor is likely to experience. Since Buckley did not intend to deceive Willis Chevrolet, a court would probably allow her to disaffirm the contract.

However, Buckley must realize that the sales agent's testimony describing their conversation may differ from hers. The agent may remember the conversation differently or may testify falsely. Others may claim to have overheard the conversation. One way or another, Buckley's testimony may be controverted. Further, the documents Buckley signed may have contained representations of age, and other witnesses may testify that Buckley read them. If we decide to proceed with Buckley's case, we will need to learn what testimony Willis Chevrolet will offer and what the documents contain. On the facts we now have, however, a court would probably conclude that Buckley did not fraudulently misrepresent her age.

> B.   Willis Chevrolet's reliance on Buckley's representation was probably reasonable.

The next element requires the injured party to have justifiably relied on the representation. *Carney,* 88 S.E.2d at 808. The cases that describe this element allude to the minor's physical appearance, the minor's life circumstances known to the injured party, the lack of any reason to cause the party to suspect the representation, and the lack of a ready means of confirming the representation. *Clemons,* 187 S.E. at 712-713; *Hood,* 125 S.E. at 788; *Carney,* 88 S.E.2d at 808; *Watters,* 146 S.E. at 773-774.

For instance, in *Carney,* the court points out that the minor was married, was a father, and appeared to be of the age of majority. 88 S.E.2d at 808. In *Hood,* the court points to the minor's physical appearance and to the seller's knowledge that the minor had been married and living independently with his wife for about four years. 125 S.E. at 788. While the decisions sometimes articulate the standard as whether the defendant "failed to use all ready means" to ascertain the truth, *see, e.g., Carney,* 88 S.E.2d at 808, none of the reported decisions have found circumstances requiring the defendant to go further than the minor's representation. In fact, *Clemons* specifically held that a contracting party need not undertake an affirmative investigation beyond the representation of age when the contracting party has no reason to doubt the assertion. 187 S.E. at 713-714.

Buckley's facts do not indicate whether the sales agent knew anything about Buckley's life circumstances that would lead the agent to suspect that Buckley might not be eighteen. The facts also do not include a physical description of Buckley, although we can infer that she looks young, since the agent questioned her about her age. Although this issue would be a question of fact at trial, the facts seem similar to the facts in the reported cases; therefore, the facts may not be sufficient to require the agent to go further than questioning Buckley.

However, one might argue that the agent had at least one "ready means" to verify Buckley's answer, namely asking to see her driver's license. Not only would this solution have been simple, but requiring it would facilitate an important policy rationale for the rule. The rule is designed to discourage sellers from being too ready to contract with minors, despite the inherent pressure to make sales. Requiring sellers to verify the ages of buyers who appear young would counteract the possible tendency of sellers to be too easily convinced of a buyer's majority.

The court's ruling on the second element would depend primarily on the facts elicited at trial. On the facts as we now know them, a court reasonably could rule either way on this element.

C. Buckley had almost certainly reached the age of discretion when she made the representation of her age.

A minor cannot be held responsible for a misrepresentation unless the minor had reached the age of discretion when he or she made the misrepresentation. *Carney,* 88 S.E.2d at 808; *Clemons,* 187 S.E. at 713. A minor reaches the age of discretion when the minor has developed the capacity to conceive a fraudulent intent. *Clemons* points out that most minors have reached the age of discretion for criminal prosecution for fraud at least by the age of fourteen, though probably not by the age of ten. *Clemons* concludes that the eighteen-year-old minor in that case was well within the age of discretion. *Id.* at 713.

Buckley was seventeen when she bought the car, just a few months away from the age of majority. She is three years older than the presumptive age of discretion for criminal prosecution, and criminal prosecution probably requires more assurance of sufficient age than simple estoppel in a contract action. A court almost certainly would conclude that Buckley had reached the age of discretion.

CONCLUSION

Buckley can disaffirm unless (1) she fraudulently misrepresented her age, (2) Willis Chevrolet justifiably relied upon the misrepresentation, and (3) Buckley had reached the age of discretion. On the facts as we presently understand them, a court would probably rule that Buckley did not misrepresent her age. A court might also rule that Willis Chevrolet was not justified in relying on Buckley's representation. Given the probable absence of one required element and the possible absence of another, Buckley can probably disaffirm the contract.

APPENDIX B

Sample Trial-Level Brief

IN THE UNITED STATES DISTRICT COURT
FOR THE DISTRICT OF COLORADO

RANDALL BROWNLEY,
      Plaintiff

    v.

SCOTT DUNN, d/b/a DUNN CREDIT
BUREAU,
      Defendant

Civ. No. 95-14867

BRIEF IN SUPPORT OF DEFENDANT'S MOTION
TO SET ASIDE DEFAULT JUDGMENT

INTRODUCTION

This is an action alleging a violation of Section 607(b) of the Fair Credit Reporting Act (FCRA), 15 U.S.C.A. § 1681e(b). The Complaint was filed and served upon Scott Dunn on October 27, 1995. Default judgment was entered six days ago on November 17, 1995, just one day after the expiration of Mr. Dunn's time to answer the Complaint. Mr. Dunn now files a Motion to Set Aside this Default Judgment, along with a supporting affidavit and a proposed Answer to the Complaint. This brief is filed in support of Mr. Dunn's Motion.

STATEMENT OF FACTS

In September 1995, a potential lender contacted Dunn Credit Bureau requesting a credit report on the Plaintiff. (Dunn Aff. ¶ 10.) The Credit Bureau prepared the report, and it contained a reference to an unpaid department store account. (Dunn Aff. ¶ 11.) Upon the discovery of this item on his credit report, the Plaintiff contacted Mr. Dunn to demand that the item be removed, arguing that the charged merchandise had been defective and that the defect was the reason for his nonpayment. (Dunn Aff. ¶ 12.) Mr. Dunn asked the Plaintiff to provide this explanation in writing and promised to include it along with the store's version of the account. (Dunn Aff. ¶ 13.)

The Plaintiff refused to provide the written explanation, but again demanded that the item be entirely removed. (Dunn Aff. ¶ 14.) Mr. Dunn replied by letter, declining to delete the item entirely but repeating the offer to include the Plaintiff's defense to the item. (Dunn Aff. ¶ 14.) The Plaintiff did not respond to Mr. Dunn's letter, and Mr. Dunn did not hear from the Plaintiff again. (Dunn Aff. ¶ 15.)

On October 27, 1995, copies of the Summons and Complaint in this action were served at Mr. Dunn's home by leaving them with Mr. Dunn's sixteen-year-old son, Gregory. (Ret. of Serv. filed 10/30/95.) On that day, Mr. Dunn and his wife had traveled to Denver, planning to return the next day. (Dunn Aff. ¶ 3.)

However, on the evening of October 27, Mrs. Dunn suffered a serious heart attack and was hospitalized. (Dunn Aff. ¶ 4.) Gregory left immediately for Denver. In the midst of the crisis surrounding his mother's heart attack, Gregory did not think to tell his father about the delivery of an envelope to the family home. (Dunn Aff. ¶ 6.)

Mr. Dunn remained in Denver with his wife for two weeks until Mrs. Dunn was released from the hospital to return home. (Dunn Aff. ¶ 5.) Upon his return, Mr. Dunn began going in to his office part-time, while continuing to care for his wife. (Dunn Aff. ¶ 7.) Mr. Dunn did not find the envelope until November 20, 1995. On that day, Mr. Dunn moved a stack of papers on the table in the family room and found the envelope there. (Dunn Aff. ¶ 8.)

Mr. Dunn immediately called his attorney and began the preparations to file an Answer to the Complaint. (Dunn Aff. ¶ 9.) Shortly after the initial telephone conversation with his attorney, Mr. Dunn learned that a default judgment had been entered three days earlier. (Dunn Aff. ¶ 9.) Mr. Dunn now seeks an order, pursuant to Fed. R. Civ. P. 60(b), setting aside this default judgment.

<u>ARGUMENT</u>

I.   THE DEFAULT JUDGMENT SHOULD BE SET ASIDE BECAUSE IT WAS ENTERED AS A RESULT OF INADVERTENCE OR EXCUS-ABLE NEGLECT AND BECAUSE THE DEFENDANT HAS A MERI-TORIOUS DEFENSE TO THE PLAINTIFF'S ALLEGATIONS.

Rule 60(b) grants the Court the discretion to relieve a party from a final judgment entered as a result of inadvertence or excusable neglect. When the judgment was entered upon the moving party's default, the moving party must also demonstrate the existence of a potentially merito-rious defense. *In re Stone,* 588 F.2d 1316, 1319 (10th Cir. 1978). Rule 60(b) is to be liberally construed, *Pierce v. Cook & Co.,* 518 F.2d 720, 722 (10th Cir. 1975), with doubts resolved in favor of adjudication on the merits, *In re Roxford Foods, Inc.,* 12 F.3d 875, 879 (9th Cir. 1993); *Tolson v. Hodge,* 411 F.2d 123, 130 (4th Cir. 1969).

A.   <u>The Defendant's default resulted from excusable neglect because service was effected upon Defendant's minor son and the crisis of his mother's heart attack caused the son to forget to inform Defendant of the service.</u>

The United States Supreme Court has defined the term "excusable neglect," in the context of bankruptcy filings, to include giving "little attention or respect" or "leav[ing] undone or unattended . . esp[ecially] through carelessness." *Pioneer Inv. Servs. Co. v. Brunswick Assocs. Ltd. Partner-ship,*—U.S.—,113 S. Ct. 1489, 123 L. Ed. 2d 74 (1993). Last year the Tenth Circuit adopted this definition of excusable neglect in the context of a Rule 60(b) motion. *City of Chanute, Kansas v. Williams Nat. Gas Co.,* 31 F.3d 1041 (10th Cir. 1994). The Tenth Circuit specifically held that Rule 60(b) relief is not limited to circumstances beyond the moving party's control. *Id.* at 1046.

The Tenth Circuit analysis of excusable neglect considers four factors: (1) the potential prejudice to the nonmoving party; (2) the length of delay; (3) the reason for the delay; and (4) the degree of good faith of the moving party. *Id.* at 1046-1047.

The first factor, the prejudice to the nonmoving party, must amount to more than simply delaying enforcement of the judgment. *Feliciano v. Reliant Tooking Co.,* 691 F.2d 653, 656-657 (3d Cir. 1982). Usually cogniza-ble prejudice involves some change of position in reliance on the judg-ment. The second factor, the length of delay, measures both the time since the entry of judgment and the time since the party because aware of the judgment. *Lasky v. International Union,* 27 Fed. R. Serv. 2d (Cal-laghan), 473, 477 (E.D. Mich. 1978).

The third factor examines the validity of the reason for the delay and whether the delay was willful. The Tenth Circuit has consistently affirmed orders setting aside default judgments entered as a result of understandable error or inadvertence as opposed to willful action by the defendant. For example, the court affirmed a decision to set aside a default judgment entered while the plaintiff believed that his new attorney was negotiating a settlement that would resolve the litigation. *Thompson v. Kerr-McGee Ref. Corp.*, 660 F.2d 1380 (10th Cir. 1981). The Tenth Circuit also affirmed an order granting Rule 60(b) relief from a judgment caused by confusion about filing a notice of appeal. *Romero v. Peterson*, 930 F.2d 1502 (10th Cir. 1991).

The excusable reasons for delay in these cases contrast with cases in which the default resulted from a willful decision by the defendant. For example, in *Cessna Fin. Corp. v. Bielenberg Masonry Contracting, Inc.*, 715 F.2d 1442 (10th Cir. 1983), the court affirmed the trial court's decision denying relief to a corporate defendant whose representatives had decided not to answer the complaint because they believed that the corporate defendant would escape liability in bankruptcy. In *United States v. Theodorovich*, 102 F.R.D. 587 (D.D.C. 1984), the court denied relief because the default judgment had resulted from defendant's willful decisions not to attend his own properly scheduled depositions.

The final factor asks whether the defendant has acted in good faith. This factor invites the court to consider the broad equitable question of whether the moving party has dealt in good faith with the court and with the other parties to the litigation.

Applying these four factors to the present case demonstrates that Rule (60)b relief is more than appropriate here. First, granting the Defendant's Motion would not cause the Plaintiff to suffer any cognizable prejudice. The default judgment was entered less than one week ago. The only cognizable prejudice that would result from setting aside the judgment stems from the costs the Plaintiff incurred in seeking the entry of the judgment. The Defendant has offered to pay those reasonable costs (Dunn Aff. ¶ 16), and an order to that effect would sufficiently relieve the Plaintiff of even this small prejudice. *Littlefield v. Walt Flanagan and Co.*, 498 F.2d 1133 (10th Cir. 1974).

The "length of delay" factor also weighs in favor of granting the motion. Only three days elapsed between the entry of the default judgment and the Defendant's discovery of the litigation. Only three days elapsed between the Defendant's discovery and the filing of the Motion and supporting documents. By comparison, the Tenth Circuit found a delay of thirty-one days "short." *City of Chanute*, 31 F.3d at 1047. A six-day delay is well within permissible bounds.

The third factor, the validity of the reason for delay, is often the most important factor. In the present case, this critical factor is the most compelling of all. Here, the delay was caused by the sudden and serious heart attack of Mr. Dunn's wife and Gregory's mother (Dunn Aff. ¶¶ 4-9). That a teenager should forget to tell his father about the Summons and Complaint under such circumstances is certainly understandable. This is precisely the sort of omission that Rule 60(b) is designed to forgive.

Mr. Dunn's good faith also argues for relieving the Defendant from judgment. Mr. Dunn has dealt with both the Court and the Plaintiff entirely in good faith. The delay was not caused by any stratagem or artifice. Mr. Dunn was entirely unaware of the litigation. Immediately upon learning of the Complaint, Mr. Dunn hurriedly contacted his attorney and began the process of responding to the litigation (Dunn Aff. ¶ 9). Mr. Dunn's offer to bear the Plaintiff's costs is further evidence of his good faith.

Thus all four factors of the Rule 60(b) analysis place the Defendant's situation squarely within the parameters for Rule 60(b) relief.

> B. The Defendant has a meritorious defense to the complaint because the credit report accurately reflects the Plaintiff's admitted failure to pay the account.

Mr. Dunn also meets the second requirement for Rule 60(b) relief, the existence of a meritorious defense. A plaintiff alleging a violation of 15 U.S.C. § 1681e(b) must establish two elements: (1) whether the credit report is inaccurate; and if so, (2) whether the inaccuracy flows from a failure by the reporting agency to follow reasonable procedures. *Cahlin v. General Motors Corp.,* 936 F.2d 1151, 1156 (11th Cir. 1991). Establishing inaccuracy is a threshold requirement for a Section 1681e(b) claim. *Id.* at 1156. In the present case, the Plaintiff's credit report is accurate, and therefore Mr. Dunn has a meritorious defense to the complaint.

The accuracy requirement of the FCRA does not require the credit reporting agency to delete all reference to an unpaid account merely because it is disputed. This is true even if the consumer ultimately pays the account. *Id.* In *Cahlin,* the plaintiff's credit report included reference to a disputed account. Initially the account was unpaid, but after it appeared on the credit report, the consumer settled the account for partial payment. The consumer then demanded that the credit agency delete all reference to the account. *Id.* at 1155.

The Eleventh Circuit held that Section 607(b) does not require a credit reporting agency to report only favorable information. The court specifically held that the agency did not have to delete the reference to the disputed account even though the dispute was settled, explaining that such an interpretation would gut the very purpose of a credit report. *Id.* at 1158.

Here the Plaintiff's credit report accurately reflects his failure to pay the balance owed on a department store charge account (Dunn Aff. ¶ 11). Further, unlike the account in *Cahlin,* the Plaintiff's account remains unpaid. The Credit Bureau offered to include the consumer's written statement describing the dispute, as required by 15 U.S.C.A. § 1681i(b). The Plaintiff refused. This refusal is the only impediment to a more complete description of the Plaintiff's dispute with the account holder. The Plaintiff's demand that the item be removed entirely would have decreased rather than increased the report's accuracy because it would have omitted all reference to an admittedly unpaid, though disputed, debt. The Act simply does not require this sort of concealment of a consumer's true credit history.

Thus, the Plaintiff's credit report is accurate, and the Credit Bureau did not violate FCRA. Mr. Dunn has a meritorious defense to the Plaintiff's Complaint.

CONCLUSION

Mr. Dunn meets both requirements for Rule 60(b) relief. All four factors for evaluating inadvertence or excusable neglect strongly argue in favor of granting Mr. Dunn relief under Rule 60(b). Further, the Plaintiff's credit report met the accuracy requirement under the FCRA, and thus Mr. Dunn has a meritorious defense to the complaint. Mr. Dunn respectfully requests the Court to enter an order setting aside the judgment and allowing him to file his Answer and to otherwise defend this action.

DATED: _____   _____
                                        Attorney for the Defendant

CERTIFICATE OF SERVICE

I, _____, attorney for the Defendant, do hereby certify that I have served upon the Plaintiff a complete and accurate copy of this Brief in Support of the Defendant's Motion to Set Aside Default Judgment, by placing the copy in the United States Mail, sufficient postage affixed, and addressed as follows:

[name and address of Plaintiff's attorney]

DATED: _____   _____
                                        Attorney for the Defendant

Sample Appellate Brief

APPENDIX C

1. This is a hypothetical circuit.
2. This brief is adapted from a student brief written by Phillip C. Griffeth, Donna G. Hedgepeth, and Angela D. Medders.

Table of Contents

TABLE OF AUTHORITIES

QUESTIONS PRESENTED

1. Can a plaintiff enforce an offer of judgment made pursuant to Fed. R. Civ. P. 68 when the plaintiff responded to the offer with a counter-offer rather than an acceptance and when the plaintiff did not specify an intention to take the offer under advisement?
2. Can a plaintiff enforce a Rule 68 offer of judgment when the plaintiff did not accept the offer until after the court adjudicated the plaintiff's claims by granting summary judgment?

STATUTE INVOLVED

Rule 68 of the Federal Rules of Civil Procedure provides as follows:

At any time more than 10 days before the trial begins, a party defending against a claim may serve upon the adverse party an offer to allow judgment to be taken against the defending party for the money or property or to the effect specified in the offer, with costs then accrued. If within 10 days after the service of the offer the adverse party serves written notice that the offer is accepted, either party may then file the offer and notice of acceptance together with proof of service thereof and thereupon the clerk shall enter judgment. An offer not accepted shall be deemed withdrawn and evidence thereof is not admissible except in a proceeding to determine costs. If the judgment finally obtained by the offeree is not more favorable than the offer, the offeree must pay the costs incurred after the making of the offer. The fact that an offer is made but not accepted does not preclude a subsequent offer. When the liability of one party to another has been determined by verdict or order or judgment, but the amount or extent of the liability remains to be determined by further proceedings, the party adjudged liable may make an offer of judgment, which shall have the same effect as an offer made before trial if it is served within a reasonable time not less than 10 days prior to the commencement of hearings to determine the amount or extent of liability.

JURISDICTION

The jurisdiction of this Court is invoked pursuant to 28 U.S.C. §1291 (1988).

STATEMENT OF THE CASE

On August 3, 1991, the Plaintiff filed this diversity action alleging medical malpractice against Dr. June Temple and the Northpark Family Clinic. (R. 1)   On January 17, 1992, after extensive discovery, the Defendants moved for summary judgment. (R. 11)   The District Court took the motion under advisement.

On June 1, 1992, while the motion was pending, the Defendants made an Offer of Judgment in the amount of $100,000, pursuant to Fed. R. Civ. P. 68. (R. 24)   The Plaintiff did not accept the offer but rather, on June 4, he served a document entitled "Plaintiff's Offer of Judgment." (R. 27)   The document purported to be a Rule 68 offer to accept the entry of judgment in the amount of $225,000. The Plaintiff never specified that he was still considering the Defendants' initial Offer. (R. 27)

On June 7, the District Court granted the Defendants' Motion for Summary Judgment. (R. 18-23) After learning of the Order granting summary judgment against him, the Plaintiff attempted to accept the Defendants' initial Offer of Judgment by serving an Acceptance of Offer of Judgment on June 8, 1992. (R. 25) The Defendants moved for an order striking the Plaintiff's Acceptance. (R. 26) After hearing argument, the District Court denied the motion to strike and entered judgment in favor of the Plaintiff for $100,000 plus costs. (R. 34) The Defendants have filed this appeal seeking reversal of the District Court's order enforcing the Offer of Judgment.

SUMMARY OF ARGUMENT

The Plaintiff's counter-offer constituted a rejection of the Defendants' Offer of Judgment and thus extinguished it. This interpretation is consistent with the policies and purposes behind the Rule and with existing case law and commentary upon it. Further, it is consistent with long-standing contract principles, which establish that a counter-offer terminates the offeree's power to accept the original offer. In addition, interpreting Rule 68 to permit an absolute ten-day period within which a plaintiff can consider acceptance would exceed the Court's judicial authority under the Rules Enabling Act.

Even if the counter-offer had not extinguished the initial Offer, the District Court's order granting summary judgment would have extinguished it. The order was an adjudication on the merits and terminated any rights the Plaintiff may have had to enforce the original Offer. Interpreting the Rule to allow acceptance after an order granting summary judgment would do nothing to further the Rule's purpose of encouraging settlement of pending litigation. Further, such an interpretation would create unfair tactical advantages for plaintiffs at the expense of defendants.

ARGUMENT

The Defendants' Offer of Judgment was extinguished either by the Plaintiff's counter-offer or by the District Court's Summary Judgment Order. The facts surrounding these two events are undisputed, and the determination of the issues raised by this appeal will not require the application of these facts to a particular legal standard. Therefore, both issues are pure questions of law, to which a de novo standard of review applies, *Traywick v. Juhola*, 922 F.2d 786, 787 (11th Cir. 1991).

I. THE PLAINTIFF'S COUNTER-OFFER EXTINGUISHED THE DEFENDANTS' OFFER OF JUDGMENT AND THEREFORE THE JUDGMENT SHOULD BE REVERSED.

Federal Rule 68 provides that a defendant may serve upon the plaintiff an offer to allow judgment to be taken against the defendant upon the terms specified in the offer. If the plaintiff accepts the offer within ten days, the agreement becomes binding, and the court enters judgment. Fed. R. Civ. P. 68. An offer that is not accepted is deemed withdrawn. *Id.* If the judgment ultimately entered is not more favorable than the offer, the plaintiff must pay the litigation costs incurred after the offer was made. *Id.* The Rule's purpose is to encourage parties to settle litigation. *Marek v. Chesney,* 473 U.S. 1, 5 (1985); *accord Delta Air Lines, Inc. v. August,* 450 U.S. 346, 352 (1981).

Any response to a Rule 68 offer other than an unqualified acceptance operates as a rejection. For example, in *Rateree v. Rockett,* 668 F. Supp. 1155 (N.D. Ill. 1987), the court noted that, consistent with the guidelines of *Marek,* "a plaintiff *cannot* do anything except simply say 'I accept' if he or she expects to enforce the offer under Rule 68." *Id.* at 1158.

The Rules Advisory Committee also understands the present language of Rule 68 to mean that an attempted counter-offer operates as a rejection of the initial offer. In 1984, the Committee proposed amendments to Rule 68. In a note explaining the proposed changes, the Committee explained that under the proposed Rule "a written counter-offer would not constitute a rejection unless it expressly so stated." Committee on Rules of Practice and Procedure of the Judicial Conference of the United States, Preliminary Draft of Proposed Amendments to the Federal Rules of Civil Procedure (Sept. 1984), *reprinted in* 102 F.R.D. 407, 435 (1985). The Committee's explanation of the proposed amendment (never adopted) demonstrates that under the present Rule, a counter-offer *does* constitute a rejection. Further, the fact that the proposed amendment was not adopted demonstrates that such a construction of the Rule has been specifically considered and rejected.

Rudimentary contract principles support this interpretation of the Rule. To whatever extent the language of the Rule does not specifically address the effect of a counter-offer, the court's interpretation creates a common law construction that is essentially federal in character. *See generally Kamen v. Kemper Fin. Servs., Inc.,* 111 S. Ct. 1711, 1717 (1991). In *Kamen,* the Supreme Court observed that such constructions of federal law should not be "wholly the product of a federal court's devising." Rather, the Supreme Court cautioned that the federal court should "fill the interstices of a federal . . . scheme" by incorporating state law. *Id.* This presumption is especially strong when the parties have reason to believe that state law will apply to their rights and obligations. *Id.*

Rule 68 is a process by which the parties can achieve a private contractual agreement. *Greenwood v. Stevenson,* 88 F.R.D. 225, 229 (D.R.I. 1980). Therefore, courts have consistently held that general contract principles apply to determine whether an offer or acceptance complies with the Rule's requirements. *Radecki v. Amoco Oil Co.,* 858 F.2d 397, 400 (8th Cir. 1988). *See also Johnson v. University College of the Univ. of Ala.,* 706 F.2d 1205, 1209 (11th Cir.), *cert. denied,* 464 U.S. 994 (1983); *Adams v. Wolff,* 110 F.R.D. 291, 293 (D. Nev. 1986); *Bentley v. Bolger,* 110 F.R.D. 108, 113-114 (C.D. Ill. 1986); *Boorstein v. City of New York,* 107 F.R.D. 31, 33-34 (S.D.N.Y. 1985).

Thus, parties utilizing Rule 68 have long had reason to believe that general contract principles will apply to their Rule 68 filings. Since the presumption to incorporate state law is especially strong in such cases, a federal court should "fill the interstices" of Rule 68 by incorporating the substantive law of contracts.

It is a rudimentary contract principle that a counter-offer terminates the power to accept the previously made offer. Restatement (Second) of Contracts, §§ 36(1) & 39(2) (1981); 1 Arthur L. Corbin, *Corbin on Contracts* § 90 (1963). *See also* 1 Walter H.E. Jaeger, *Williston on Contracts* § 51 (3d ed. 1959). Only a counter-offer that specifies an intention to take the original offer under advisement would not have the effect of extinguishing the original offer. Restatement (Second) of Contracts § 39(2) (1981). *See also* 1 Corbin, *Contracts* § 92.

For instance, in *Collins v. Thompson,* 679 F.2d 168 (9th Cir. 1982), a suit by prison inmates, the parties reached a settlement and the State filed the terms in a proposed consent decree. Subsequently the State submitted a revised proposal with a later compliance date. The prisoners moved to enforce the first proposed decree or, in the alternative, for amended notice to class members of the later date. *Id.* at 169. The court observed that, by their alternative motion, the prisoners had indicated their continued interest in accepting the later date should the earlier date not be enforceable. *Id.* at 172.

The argument that the Rule gives the plaintiff an absolute ten-day period during which to consider acceptance is without merit. A plaintiff cannot enforce an offer unless the plaintiff's response is an unqualified acceptance. *Rateree v. Rockett,* 668 F. Supp. 1155 (N.D. Ill. 1987); Roy D. Simon, Jr., *Rule 68 at the Crossroads: The Relationship Between Offers of Judgment and Statutory Attorney's Fees,* 53 U. Cin. L. Rev. 889, 921 (1984). Once a plaintiff responds with something other than an acceptance, the original offer is deemed withdrawn. The Rule allows a plaintiff a ten-day *maximum* period during which the plaintiff can consider the offer. However, the Rule does not *require* a plaintiff to use the entire ten days allotted by the Rule.

If Rule 68 created an absolute ten-day period, the Rule would exceed the Court's authority under the Rules Enabling Act, 28 U.S.C. § 2072 (1988). The Act gives the Supreme Court the power to prescribe general rules of procedure for the federal courts. However, the Act specifically cautions that "[s]uch rules shall not abridge, enlarge or modify any substantive right." 28 U.S.C. § 2072(a)-(b).

The Supreme Court defined "substantive rights" as used in the Act to mean those "rights conferred by law to be protected and enforced in accordance with the adjective law of judicial procedure." *Sibbach v. Wilson & Co., Inc.,* 312 U.S. 1, 13 (1941). According to the Supreme Court, the test is whether the rule regulates "the judicial process for enforcing rights and duties" or whether the rule regulates the substantive law that grants those rights and duties. *Id.* at 14.

A construction of Rule 68 that caused an offer to survive a counter-offer would "abridge, enlarge, or modify" substantive rights. Under the Rule, the district court plays a minor role in the actual settlement negotiations. A defending party does not file the Offer with the court, but rather serves it upon the adverse party. Fed. R. Civ. P. 68. The court does not even become aware of the Offer unless the parties reach an agreement. *Id.* The district court only "formaliz[es] the agreement hammered out by the parties." *Greenwood*, 88 F.R.D. at 229. Thus, a defendant's right to contract for settlement is a substantive right, and a construction of Rule 68 that caused a settlement offer to survive a counter-offer would abridge those substantive rights.

Here, the Plaintiff's counter-offer operated as a rejection of the Defendants' Offer and thus extinguished it. Defendants' Offer of Judgment under Rule 68 created a power of acceptance in the Plaintiff. If the Plaintiff had any interest in keeping the Offer alive, he had several options: He could have chosen to accept the Offer on its terms; he could have filed no formal response to the Offer but negotiated with the Defendants outside the constraints of Rule 68; or he could have filed a "counter-offer" specifically indicating his intention to consider the original Offer.

Instead, three days after receiving the Offer, he served a counter-offer (R. 27). His counter-offer made no mention of the original Offer and did not specify any intention of taking that Offer under advisement. Further, the counter-offer specified an amount more than twice the amount of the initial Offer (R. 27). His action can only be construed as a rejection of the original Offer, thus terminating his power of acceptance.

The Plaintiff did not have to respond to the Offer at all; however, he chose to do so. He cannot later change his mind, after learning that the District Court had granted summary judgment against him, and attempt to accept the Offer he had already rejected.

II. EVEN IF THE COUNTER-OFFER HAD NOT DONE SO, THE ORDER GRANTING SUMMARY JUDGMENT EXTINGUISHED THE OFFER OF JUDGMENT; THEREFORE, THE JUDGMENT SHOULD BE REVERSED.

The District Court's order granting summary judgment was an adjudication on the merits of the case and a final decision of the rights and liabilities of the parties. Therefore, it terminated any remaining right the Plaintiff may have had to enforce the original Offer.

Rule 68 encourages settlement of pending controversies by allowing litigants to balance the risks and costs of litigation with the chances for success. *Marek v. Chesney*, 473 U.S. 1, 5 (1985). The Rule is not intended to permit acceptance after the court has resolved the case. At this point, settlement of the dispute is no longer an option for the loser, because a legal dispute no longer exists.

Further, allowing a plaintiff to accept an offer after the court has decided the case would unfairly advantage the plaintiff over the defendant. The Supreme Court has held that the Rule's "policy of encouraging settlements is neutral, favoring neither plaintiffs nor defendants." *Marek,* 473 U.S. at 10. Permitting acceptance of the original offer of judgment after the granting of summary judgment would frustrate this policy by giving significant tactical advantages to the plaintiff.

These tactical advantages are demonstrated by the policy rationale behind another provision of Rule 68—the provision that prohibits offers made within ten days of trial. This prohibition dovetails with the allowance of ten days in which to respond to an offer. *Greenwood,* 88 F.R.D. at 228 (citing 12 Charles A. Wright & Arthur R. Miller, *Federal Practice and Procedure* § 3003 (1973)). The purpose of the ten-day prohibition is to insure that the Rule 68 process is completed while the parties have an equal opportunity to assess the risks of continuing the litigation. One judge aptly illustrated the result the ten-day prohibition is intended to avoid:

> [Otherwise an offeree could] watch how the case is unfolding and weigh the probabilities. If the trial is going well, the offer can simply be ignored; if things begin to look grim, the offeree can decide to go with the sure thing . . . . [L]ocking one side into a settlement offer while the other side assesses the ongoing trial is, purely and simply, stacking the deck.

Greenwood, 88 F.R.D. 225, 228-229 (D.R.I. 1980).

The "deck stacking" that would result from allowing a plaintiff to accept an offer after a final adjudication would be far worse than the "deck stacking" described in *Greenwood.* The ten-day prohibition is intended to prevent the plaintiff from having a better opportunity to assess the probabilities of losing; however, at least under the *Greenwood* scenario, both parties would still be assessing *probabilities.*

Here, the Plaintiff asks the Court to allow a procedural favoritism far worse than that prevented by the ten-day prohibition. He asks the Court to allow him to wait until the litigation probabilities have become *certainties.* As the Supreme Court has cautioned, it is "inappropriate for the Judiciary, without legislative guidance, to reallocate the burdens of litigation." *Alyeska Pipeline Serv. Co. v. Wilderness Soc'y,* 421 U.S. 240, 247 (1975). Allowing a plaintiff to wait until *after* the case is resolved before accepting an offer the defendant made *before* the case was resolved would do just that.

This Court should not condone manipulations of Rule 68 that would so distort the Rule's fundamental policy of neutrality. The Rule was never intended to allow the result the Plaintiff urges. Rather, the Rule was intended to allow the parties to traverse Rule 68 terrain on equal footing. Therefore, once the rights and liabilities of the parties have been adjudicated by the court, any pending Rule 68 offer is extinguished.

CONCLUSION

For the foregoing reasons, Respondents request that the Judgment of the District Court be reversed and that the case be remanded with instructions to the District Court to enter judgment in favor of the Defendants.

Respectfully submitted,

DATED: _____

_____
Attorney for the Appellants

CERTIFICATE OF SERVICE

I, _____, do hereby certify that I have this date served a true and correct copy of the Appellants' Brief upon the Appellee's counsel by placing a true copy of the Appellants' Brief in the United States mail, with sufficient postage affixed, and addressed as follows:

William J. Beck
P.O. Box 1670
Hutchfield, [state]

DATED: _____

_____
Attorney for the Appellants

APPENDIX D

Cases Used in the Text's Examples and Exercise[1]

COFFEE SYSTEM OF ATLANTA V. FOX
226 Ga. 593, 176 S.E.2d 71 (1970)

Supreme Court of Georgia

HAWES, Justice.

The appeal here is from the final judgment and order dismissing the complaint for failure to state a claim upon which relief can be granted. Coffee System of Atlanta sued Fox and Intercontinental Coffee Service Plan seeking damages and a temporary and permanent injunction against the continued violation of a restrictive covenant entered into between Fox and the plaintiff as a part of an employment contract. Under the contract, Fox was employed by Coffee System, Inc., as a senior sales representative "to offer, on its behalf, its 'Coffee System' service, and to sell its replacement kits, within" the territory of Fulton, DeKalb, Cobb and ten other named counties in the State of Georgia. The trial court issued a temporary ex parte restraining order on the 7th day of January, 1970. On January 26, 1970, the matter came on for a hearing on the question of whether the temporary injunction should be granted, and at that time the defendant Fox filed a written motion to dismiss the complaint for failure to state a claim. The judge, before whom the matter was heard, passed an order, which, insofar as is pertinent, reads: "After hearing argument of counsel for defendant and plaintiff, . . . it appearing that the restrictions in the contract under consideration . . . are uncertain, indefinite, unreason-

---

1. [Citations and footnotes within the cases quoted in this Appendix have been deleted without indication. Where footnotes are included, the original footnote numbers have been retained.]

387

able, and impose upon the employee greater limitations than are necessary for the protection of the employer, they are therefore illegal, unenforceable, null and void. . . . Therefore, it is hereby ordered, adjudged and decreed that the complaint be, and it is hereby, dismissed for failure to state a claim upon which relief can be granted."

The material and relevant parts of the contract sued on provide that Fox "agrees to use his best efforts to the exclusion of all other employment, in order to promote and solicit sales of the company's coffee system service in the aforesaid territory, and to perform any and all other services reasonably required by company in connection with the merchandising of such service . . . [He] agrees that, for the term of this agreement and for one (1) year following the termination hereof, he will not, directly or indirectly in any capacity, solicit or accept orders of business located within the area assigned to [him] during any part of the two (2) year period immediately preceding the termination of his employment for any program, service, equipment or product similar to or competitive with the business of the company from any organization or individual which or who has been a customer of the company during any part of the two (2) year period immediately preceding termination of his employment, or who or which was actively solicited as a customer by company during the period of this agreement. . . . That he will not, during the term of his employment, and for a period of one year thereafter divulge to anyone other than an authorized employee of employer, and after the term of his employment will not use any information or knowledge relating to sales prospects, business methods and/or techniques which were acquired by him during the term of his employment."

1. Among those contracts which are against public policy and which cannot be enforced are contracts in general restraint of trade. Code § 20-504. However, "a contract only in partial restraint may be upheld, 'provided the restraint be reasonable,' and the contract be valid in other essentials. A contract concerning a lawful and useful business in partial restraint of trade and reasonably limited as to time and territory, and otherwise reasonable, is not void."

2. An examination of the decided cases on restrictive covenants reveals that this court has customarily considered three separate elements of such contracts in determining whether they are reasonable or not. These three elements may be categorized as (1) the restraint in the activity of the employee, or former employee, imposed by the contract; (2) the territorial or geographic restraint; and (3) the length of time during which the covenant seeks to impose the restraint. It has been said that no better test can be applied to the question of whether a restrictive covenant is reasonable or not than by considering whether the restraint "is such only as to afford a fair protection to the interest of the party in favor of whom it is given, and not so large as to interfere with the interest of the public. Whatever restraint is larger than the necessary protection of the party can be of no benefit to either; it can only be oppressive, and if oppressive, it is in the eye of the law unreasonable. . . . There can be no doubt that an agreement that during the term of the service, and for a reasonable period thereafter, the employee shall not become interested in or engage in a rival business, is reasonable and valid, the contract being otherwise legal and not in general restraint of trade. This is the rule followed by a majority of the American Courts and is supported

by reason. . . . This court seems to be committed to the rule that the contract must be limited both as to time and territory, and not otherwise unreasonable. If limited as to both time and territory, the contract is illegal if it be unreasonable in other respects. And, with respect to restrictive agreements ancillary to a contract of employment, the mere fact that the contract is unlimited as to either time or territory is sufficient to condemn it as unreasonable." Shirk v. Loftis Bros. & Co., 148 Ga. 500, 504, 97 S.E. 66.

3. Two of the elements referred to in the preceding division lend themselves to more or less exact comparison with the yardstick laid down by previous cases. The proscription against competition by the defendant embodied in the restrictive covenant in this case extends to 13 named counties in the State of Georgia. Insofar as geographic area is concerned, this is undoubtedly a reasonable restriction to be upheld by the courts if the contract is otherwise reasonable and not oppressive. The limitation as to the time within which the defendant may not engage in a competitive employment or enterprise, being one year from the termination of his employment with the plaintiff, is reasonable and not such a restriction as would render the contract void.

4. We now turn to the question of the reasonableness of the restriction against the activities of the defendant as contained in the covenant. The defendant Fox was employed by the defendant as a sales representative to offer on behalf of the plaintiff its " 'Coffee System' service, and to sell its replacement kits." He agreed that he would not, directly or indirectly, in any capacity, solicit or accept orders of business located within the area assigned to him (that is, the 13 named counties) during his employment with the plaintiff and for one year thereafter "for any program, service, equipment or product similar to or competitive with the business of" the plaintiff, and that he would refrain from doing this with respect to any organization which, or individual who, had been a customer or had been solicited as a customer of plaintiff during that term. It must be noted that the contract does not restrict the plaintiff from accepting *employment* with a competitor, so long as such employment does not involve the direct or indirect solicitation and acceptance of orders from customers or those solicited as customers of the plaintiff. Even if the enforcement of the broad language forbidding the use by the defendant of business methods and techniques acquired during his employment with the plaintiff should, if enforced, effectively prevent the defendant from accepting employment with any other competitor of the plaintiff within the limited area and time of the operation of the contract, it would not render the contract void as a matter of law. See Shirk v. Loftis Bros. & Co., supra, where a contract in which the employee covenanted that he would "not directly or indirectly, under any circumstances or conditions whatsoever, for himself [or] for any other person, firm, or corporation, engage in or be or become interested or be employed, directly or indirectly . . . as an individual, partner, stockholder, director, officer, clerk, salesman, buyer, principal, agent, employee, trustee, or in any relation or capacity whatsoever, in the line of business carried on by" the plaintiff. That contract was upheld by this court as not imposing too broad a restriction on the defendant since the proscription of the contract only related to Fulton County and was limited as to time to four years. As a general rule, this court seems to have established the principle in cases of this kind that, where the restraint as to time and territory is reasonably limited,

a general prohibition against soliciting customers and accounts of the employer will be upheld. We need hold no more than that in this case.

With respect to the definition or description of the business engaged in by the plaintiff and which the defendant was employed by the plaintiff to conduct, the contract only refers to it as a "Coffee System Service," but we think this is enough. This court has upheld restrictive covenants where the description of the business was no more specific. The restraint imposed by the contract in this case is no more than is reasonably necessary to afford fair protection to the interests of the employer and is not unduly oppressive of the employee. It is not void for any reason urged by the appellee.

5. It follows that the trial court erred in sustaining the motion to dismiss and in dismissing the complaint. It should be kept in mind that this case was brought under the Civil Practice Act, and that the former rules of strict pleading no longer apply. We have looked only to the contract, as it is apparent the trial court did, in reaching the conclusion we have reached. The complaint, itself, sufficiently sets forth the existence of the contract and a breach thereof and it was not subject to being dismissed for failure to state a claim. From the language of the order appealed from, it is clear that the trial judge did not reach the question of whether to grant or deny a temporary injunction. Therefore, no question in that regard is presented for our decision on this appeal.

Judgment reversed.

All the Justices concur.

GOLDMAN V. KANE
3 Mass. App. Ct. 336, 329 N.E.2d 770 (1975)
Massachusetts Appeals Court

HALE, Chief Justice.

[Barry Kane represented Lawrence Hill, a law school graduate but not a lawyer. Kane had represented Hill for several years on various matters. In April 1971, Hill signed an agreement to purchase a boat for $31,500 and paid a deposit of $3,150. Hill agreed to pay the balance on May 17. Kane advised Hill about miscellaneous legal matters pertaining to the purchase and registration of the boat. Hill also asked Kane to arrange for the financing of the balance of the purchase price. When Kane could not arrange a loan through a bank, Hill told Kane to sell a piece of real property Hill owned. Kane put the property on the market, but the property did not sell. With one day to go before losing the deposit, Hill told Kane that he was in dire need of the money to complete the sale. Kane told Hill that the timing and Hill's financial circumstances made it "virtually impossible" to get a loan. After several telephone conversations, Kane offered to arrange for Kane's corporation to lend Hill $30,000. However, Hill would have to transfer to Kane's corporation absolute title to the unsold real property, to all of the personal property located on the real property, and to a smaller boat Hill owned. In addition, Hill would have to secure the loan with a mortgage on the new boat. Kane urged Hill not to accept these terms, but Hill insisted. In July 1971, Kane's corporation sold the real property and the personal property located on it for $86,000. Subsequently, Hill defaulted on the loan. Kane seized the boat and sold it. Hill's estate thereafter sued Kane and his corporation, alleging that Kane had breached his fiduciary duty as Hill's attorney. Judgment for the plaintiff; defendants appealed.]

The defendants argue that even if an attorney-client relationship existed the record does not support the conclusion that there was a breach of that relationship. We disagree. The relationship of attorney and client is highly fiduciary in nature. "Unflinching fidelity to their genuine interests is the duty of every attorney to his clients. Public policy hardly can touch matters of more general concern than the maintenance of an untarnished standard of conduct by the attorney at law toward his client."

The law looks with great disfavor upon an attorney who has business dealings with his client which result in gains to the attorney at the expense of the client. "The attorney is not permitted by the law to take any advantage of his client. The principles holding the attorney to a conspicuous degree of faithfulness and forbidding him to take personal advantage of his client are thoroughly established." When an attorney bargains with his client in a business transaction in a manner which is advantageous to himself, and if that transaction is later called into question, the court will subject it to close scrutiny. In such a case, the attorney has the burden of showing that the transaction "was in all respects fairly and equitably conducted; that he fully and faithfully discharged all his duties to his client, not only by refraining from any misrepresentation of concealment of any material fact, but by active diligence to see that his client was fully informed of the nature and effect of the transaction proposed and of his own rights and interests in the subject matter involved, and by seeing to it that his client either has independent advice in the matter or else receives from the attorney such advice as the latter would have been expected to give had the transaction been one between his client and a stranger."

Applying these principles to the case at bar, it is clear that the judge was correct in concluding that Kane, by entering into the transaction, breached his fiduciary duty to Hill. While the defendants contend that Kane's conduct did not constitute a breach of his fiduciary duty because Hill fully understood the nature and effect of the transaction and because Kane advised Hill against it, in the circumstances of this case, Kane's full disclosure and his advice were not sufficient to immunize him from liability. The fundamental unfairness of the transaction and the egregious overreaching by Kane in his dealings with Hill are self-evident. In light of the nature of the transaction, Kane, at a bare minimum, was under a duty not to proceed with the loan until he was satisfied that Hill had obtained independent advice on the matter. The purpose of such requirement is to be certain that in a situation where an attorney deals with a client in a business relationship to the attorney's advantage, the "presumed influence resulting from the relationship has been neutralized." . . .

Judgment affirmed.

CLEIN V. KAPILOFF

213 Ga. 369, 98 S.E.2d 897 (1957)

Supreme Court of Georgia

ALMAND, Justice.

The bill of exceptions assigns error on orders overruling general demurrers to an equitable petition, and granting an interlocutory injunction.

The petition of Harry Kapiloff and Sam Turetsky sought to restrain the defendant Sidney A. Clein from engaging in the retail clothing business in violation of a restrictive covenant entered into by the defendant Clein and other named defendants with the plaintiffs. In substance, the petition alleged: that the plaintiffs, prior to August 28, 1950, owned and controlled Macey's, Inc., a corporation engaged in the retail jewelry business at 110 Whitehall Street in the City of Atlanta; that the plaintiffs sold said business to Sterling Jewelry Company, a corporation owned and controlled by the named defendants; that the written contract of sale, signed by both corporations through the plaintiff Kapiloff as president of Macey's, Inc., and the defendant Clein as vice-president of Sterling Jewelry Company, Inc., contained the following covenant: "4. *Restrictive covenants.* Seller covenants and agrees that it will not, throughout the term of the lease assigned hereunder [July 31, 1959], engage in the retail jewelry business, or in the sale of any items normally sold by a retail jewelry company, other than television sets, within a radius of one mile from the premises herein described, and *buyer covenants that it will not engage in the operation of a retail clothing business on the premises, nor will it engage in the sale of items normally sold in a retail clothing store on the premises or within a radius of one-half mile of the premises, throughout the term of the lease* [July 31, 1959] *herein assigned."* (Italics and brackets supplied.) Following the corporate signatures in the contract of sale, all of the named plaintiffs and defendants agreed in writing that the "restrictive covenants mentioned in paragraph 4 of the within agreement are hereby adopted and agreed to by us individually, and any one acting for us, or any firm, corporation, or partnership in which any of us may have an interest." The seller conveyed to the buyer all of his accounts receivable, the plaintiff Kapiloff agreed to assign the lease in 110 Whitehall Street to the buyer, and the defendant Clein agreed to endorse the purchase money notes. At the time of the sale, the plaintiffs were engaged in the retail clothing business at 114 Whitehall Street under the name of Hollywood Credit Clothiers. It was alleged that, at the time of the sale, the defendants "knew that the accounts of customers of said jewelry business were in a great part the same as the accounts of the petitioners' retail credit clothing business and petitions as a consideration of said sale and agreement insisted that defendants covenant not to engage in the clothing business because a great number of the accounts of the two said stores were of the same customers. Petitioners show that defendants knew that if they were allowed to sell clothing to petitioners' jewelry accounts after said jewelry business was sold to them, that they would be dealing with many of the customers of petitioners' said credit clothing business, as aforesaid, and they knew that petitioners insisted upon said covenant to protect themselves from that situation." It was further alleged that the defendant Clein is now engaged in the business of selling clothing at retail at 132 Whitehall Street, which is within one-half mile of the premises at 110 Whitehall Street, in violation of this covenant, and that the defendant Clein, by engaging in the retail clothing business in competition with the plaintiffs, will cause them irreparable damage and injury.

1. As a general rule, a contract in general restraint of trade is void, but a contract only in partial restraint may be upheld provided the restraint is reasonable and the contract is valid in the other essentials. In determining the reasonableness of a restrictive covenant, a greater latitude is allowed when the covenant relates to the sale of a business than in cases where the covenant is ancillary to a contract of employment. The agreement must be considered with reference to the situation, business and objects of the parties in light of all of the surrounding circumstances. The restrictive covenant in the instant case is reasonable as to time and territory, its area of operation being within a radius of one-half mile, and its time being limited to July 31, 1959. The true test of the validity of the contract is whether it is supported by a sufficient consideration and whether the restraint is reasonable. In determining whether the covenant is "otherwise reasonable," the covenant must be reasonably necessary to protect the interests of the party is whose favor it is imposed, and must not unduly prejudice the interests of the public, and must not impose greater restrictions than are necessary for the protection of the promisee.

In this case, the plaintiffs bound themselves not to compete with the defendants in the retail jewelry business within one mile of 110 Whitehall Street during a period ending July 31, 1959, and the defendants, knowing that the plaintiffs were then engaged in the retail clothing business at 114 Whitehall Street, agreed that, within a like period of time, they would not engage in the retail clothing business within one-half mile of 110 Whitehall Street. The covenant is reasonable in all respects, and there are no allegations in the petition which indicate that the public would suffer in having one less retail clothing store in this limited area for the time specified. We have here simply a case where the sellers and the buyers of a business have entered into a valid contract containing mutual obligations, and one party has chosen to ignore his obligation. In such a case, equity will exercise its restraining arm and require him to abide by his promise.

The petition sets forth a cause of action for the relief prayed, and the court did not err in overruling the general demurrers of Clein.

2. On the interlocutory hearing, the case was submitted upon an agreed stipulation of facts. Under the evidence submitted, the court did not err in granting an interlocutory injunction.

Judgment affirmed.

All the Justices concur.

WHEELER V. WHITE
398 S.W.2d 93 (Tex. 1965)

Supreme Court of Texas

SMITH, Justice.

This is a suit for damages brought by petitioner, Ellis D. Wheeler, against respondent, S.E. White. Wheeler alleged that White had breached a contract to secure a loan or furnish the money to finance the construction of improvements upon land owned by Wheeler. Wheeler further pleaded, in the alternative, that if the contract itself was not sufficiently definite, then nevertheless White was estopped from asserting such insufficiency. White filed special exceptions to all of Wheeler's Third Amended Original Petition. The special exceptions asserted that the pleaded contract did not contain essential elements to its enforceability in that it failed to provide the amount of monthly installments, the amount of interest due upon the obligation, how such interest would be computed, when such interest would be paid, and that the alternative plea of estoppel was, as a matter of law, insufficient to establish any ground of recovery. All special exceptions were sustained, and upon Wheeler's declination to amend his pleadings, the trial court entered its judgment dismissing the case and ordered that Wheeler take nothing from White by reason of his suit. The Court of Civil Appeals has affirmed the judgment of the trial court. 385 S.W.2d 619. We have concluded that the trial court did not err in sustaining the special exceptions directed at the sufficiency of the contract itself, but that Wheeler's pleadings on the theory of estoppel state a cause of action. Accordingly, we reverse the judgments of the trial court and the Court of Civil Appeals and remand the cause for trial.

Since the trial court sustained White's special exceptions to Wheeler's petition, we necessarily must assume that all the alleged material facts are true. Wheeler alleged that as the owner of a three-lot tract of land in Port Arthur, Texas, he desired to construct a commercial building or shopping center thereon. He and White entered into an agreement, embodied in the written contract involved here, whereby White was to obtain the necessary loan for Wheeler from a third party or provide it himself on or before six months from the date of the contract. The loan as described in the contract, was to be " . . . in the sum of SEVENTY THOUSAND AND 00/100 ($70,000.00) DOLLARS and to be payable in monthly installments over a term of fifteen (15) years and bear interest at a rate of not more than six (6%) per cent per annum." Additionally, under the contract White was to be paid $5,000.00 for obtaining the loan and a five per cent commission on all rentals received from any tenants procured by White for the building. Wheeler alleged that he has been ready and willing to comply with his part of the agreement at all times since the contract was made.

After the contract had been signed by both parties, White assured Wheeler that the money would be available and urged him to proceed with the necessary task of demolishing the buildings presently on the site so as to make way for construction of the new building. The buildings on the site had a reasonable value of $58,500.00 and a rental value of $400.00 per month. By way of reassurance, White stressed the fact that in the event the money was unobtainable elsewhere, he would make the loan himself. Pursuant to such promises Wheeler proceeded to raze the old building and otherwise prepare the land for the new structure; thereafter, he was told by White that there would be no loan. After White's refusal to perform, Wheeler made reasonable efforts to obtain the loan himself but was unsuccessful. In the pleadings Wheeler pleaded the necessary elements of inducement and reliance which entitle him to recover if he can prove the facts alleged.

Where a promisee acts to his detriment in reasonable reliance upon an otherwise unenforceable promise, courts in other jurisdictions have recognized that the disappointed party may have a substantial and compelling claim for relief. The Restatement, Contracts, § 90, says:

> A promise which the promisor should reasonably expect to induce action or forbearance of a definite and substantial character on the part of the promisee and which does induce such action or forbearance is binding if injustice can be avoided only by enforcement of the promise.

According to Dean Hildebrand's Texas Annotation to the Restatement, Texas follows Section 90, supra. See Ferguson v. Getzendaner, 98 Tex. 310, 83 S.W. 375 (1904); Morris v. Gaines, 82 Tex. 255, 17 S.W. 538 (1891); and others. These early cases do not speak of the doctrine of promissory estoppel in specific terms since those cases were written before the compilation of the Restatement, but, while many of them dealt with subscription transactions or transactions within the statute of frauds, it is readily apparent that the equities involved in those cases are applicable to the instant case. . . .

. . . As to the argument that no new cause of action may be created by such a promise regardless of its established applicability as a defense, it has been answered that where one party has by his words or conduct made to the other a promise or assurance which was intended to affect the legal relations between them and to be acted on accordingly, then, once the other party has taken him at his word and acted on it, the party who gave the promise cannot afterward be allowed to revert to the previous relationship as if no such promise had been made. This does not create a contract where none existed before, but only prevents a party from insisting upon his strict legal rights when it would be unjust to allow him to enforce them.

. . . In the case of Goodman v. Dicker, 83 U.S. App. D.C. 353, 169 F.2d 684 (1948), the trial court held that a contract had not been proven but that ". . . appellants were estopped from denying the same by reason of their statements and conduct upon which appellees relied to their detriment." In that case, Dicker relied upon a promise by Goodman that a franchise to sell radios would be granted and radios would be supplied. In reliance upon the promise, Dicker incurred expenses in making preparations to engage in the business of selling radios. The franchise was not granted and Goodman failed to deliver the radios. The appellate court in holding that Dicker was entitled to damages for moneys expended in preparing to do business, said:

> We are dealing with a promise by appellants that a franchise would be granted and radios supplied, on the faith of which appellees with the knowledge and encouragement of appellants incurred expenses in making preparations to do

business. Under these circumstances we think that appellants cannot now advance any defense inconsistent with their assurance that the franchise would be granted. Justice and fair dealing require that one who acts to his detriment on the faith of conduct of the kind revealed here should be protected by estopping the party who has brought about the situation from alleging anything in opposition to the natural consequences of his own course of conduct. . . .

The Court, having so held, rendered its judgment that Goodman was liable for moneys expended in preparing to do business under the promised dealer franchise, but was not liable for loss of profits on the radios which were never delivered. . . .

The judgments of the trial court and the Court of Civil Appeals are both reversed and judgment is here entered remanding the cause to the trial court for trial on its merits in accordance with this opinion.

JACOBSON V. KAMERINSKY[1]

Karen Jacobson had gallbladder surgery on June 30, 1984. Her doctor negligently left a surgical sponge in the surgery site when he closed the incision. The sponge caused Jacobson considerable physical difficulty and subsequently resulted in a second surgery to remove it. After the second surgery Jacobson decided to seek legal representation for a medical malpractice claim against her first surgeon. She saw Kamerinsky's office sign, sought his advice, and agreed to retain him to bring her claim. Kamerinsky had been admitted to practice law only ten weeks when he accepted Jacobson's case.

Kamerinsky correctly realized that the surgeon was clearly liable for Jacobson's damages. He tried to negotiate a settlement of the claim with the surgeon and the surgeon's insurance carrier so that litigation would not be necessary. As the weeks and months went by, Jacobson contacted Kamerinsky periodically to learn whether there was any progress on her claim. He would tell her that negotiations were proceeding well and that he should have a settlement for her soon. Several times he told her that he had obtained an expert opinion that leaving a surgical sponge inside the body was clearly medical malpractice. He explained that he had not yet filed suit because, since liability was so clear, he hoped to negotiate a settlement without the necessity of filing suit.

Shortly before the statute of limitations expired, when negotiations had not been successful, Kamerinsky filed suit in the appropriate state trial court. However, he had failed to research the requirements for bringing a medical malpractice action. State law requires that prior to filing suit a medical malpractice plaintiff must first file a charge before the medical Malpractice Screening Panel, complete the Panel's discovery and hearing process, and obtain a decision from the Panel. [citation omitted] Failure to go through these steps results in the dismissal of the plaintiff's court action. [citation omitted] The lawyer for the doctor successfully moved for the dismissal of the plaintiff's claim, and the plaintiff was precluded from completing the Screening Panel process and refiling the suit because by then the statute of limitations had expired and the medical malpractice claim was barred.

Ms. Jacobson brought this legal malpractice claim against Kamerinsky, arguing that Kamerinsky's failure to file a charge before the Screening Panel constituted legal malpractice and resulted in $500,000 damage to Jacobson. A jury found in favor of Jacobson and awarded her $425,000 in damages. Kamerinsky appeals, arguing that his error did not constitute malpractice.

A lawyer is held to a standard of competency that meets or exceeds the professional skill and diligence commonly exercised by reasonable and prudent lawyers in this state [citation to state's highest court]. Lawyers are not guarantors of a successful result; nor are they required to surpass human limitations. Lawyers are often called upon to exercise professional judgment in representing and advising clients. A good faith error in judgment is not legal malpractice as long as the lawyer's judgment was reasonable under the circumstances.

Kamerinsky's failure was more than an error in judgment, however. The failure to comply with the filing requirements was readily preventable by proper legal research. The Medical Malpractice Act creates the Screening Panel

---

1. [This is a hypothetical case based on several real cases.]

and the requirement of completing the Panel's hearing process before suit is filed. The debate and ultimate passage of the Act had been covered by the press extensively, the Screening Panel requirement being the most controversial provision of the Act. Even if Kamerinsky was not aware of the Act from the public press coverage, he certainly should have been aware of the Act and its requirements as a result of the prominent coverage of the new requirements by the State Bar Journal and the several Continuing Legal Education programs that explained the Act's provisions.

However, no lawyer should rely on press or state bar journalists to keep apace with statutory changes. Kamerinsky had a duty to conduct thorough legal research concerning statutory requirements for filing a lawsuit. Filing lawsuits is something general practitioners are familiar with doing, and it is well within the area of competence required of all lawyers.

Kamerinsky argues that medical malpractice litigation is a complex and difficult area of the law and that he, as a novice lawyer, should not be held to the standard of an experienced litigator. As we established above, researching and complying with statutory requirements for filing a lawsuit are tasks well within the standard of practice expected of all lawyers. However, even if they were not, Kamerinsky cannot undertake representation on a case without being held to the standard expected of all lawyers practicing in this state. A lawyer must either decline the representation or meet the appropriate standard of competence required for the representation. If bringing a medical malpractice claim requires knowledge or experience that Kamerinsky did not already have or could not obtain, he had no business accepting the case. All clients are entitled to at least the minimum standard of knowledge, skill, and diligence. Further, allowing lawyers to meet a lower standard if they can demonstrate a lower level of skill or knowledge would not encourage lawyers to develop their levels of skill, knowledge, and experience.

Judgment affirmed.

Lucy v. Zehmer
196 Va. 493, 84 S.E.2d 516 (1954)

Supreme Court of Appeals of Virginia

BUCHANAN, Justice.

This suit was instituted by W.O. Lucy and J.C. Lucy, complainants, against A.H. Zehmer and Ida S. Zehmer, his wife, defendants, to have specific performance of a contract by which it was alleged the Zehmers had sold to W.O. Lucy a tract of land owned by A.H. Zehmer in Dinwiddie county containing 471.6 acres, more or less, known as the Ferguson farm, for $50,000. J.C. Lucy, the other complainant, is a brother of W.O. Lucy, to whom W.O. Lucy transferred a half interest in his alleged purchase.

The instrument sought to be enforced was written by A.H. Zehmer on [Saturday,] December 20, 1952, in these words: "We hereby agree to sell to W.O. Lucy the Ferguson Farm complete for $50,000.00, title satisfactory to buyer," and signed by the defendants, A.H. Zehmer and Ida S. Zehmer.

The answer of A.H. Zehmer admitted that at the time mentioned W.O. Lucy offered him $50,000 cash for the farm, but that he, Zehmer, considered that the offer was made in jest; that so thinking, and both he and Lucy having had several drinks, he wrote out "the memorandum" quoted above and induced his wife to sign it; that he did not deliver the memorandum to Lucy, but that Lucy picked it up, read it, put it in his pocket, attempted to offer Zehmer $5 to bind the bargain, which Zehmer refused to accept, and realizing for the first time that Lucy was serious, Zehmer assured him that he had no intention of selling the farm and that the whole matter was a joke. Lucy left the premises insisting that he had purchased the farm.

Depositions were taken and the decree appealed from was entered holding that the complainants had failed to establish their right to specific performance, and dismissing their bill. The assignment of error is to this action of the court. . . .

The defendants insist that the evidence was ample to support their contention that the writing sought to be enforced was prepared as a bluff or dare to force Lucy to admit that he did not have $50,000; that the whole matter was a joke; that the writing was not delivered to Lucy and no binding contract was ever made between the parties.

It is an unusual, if not bizarre, defense. When made to the writing admittedly prepared by one of the defendants and signed by both, clear evidence is required to sustain it.

In his testimony Zehmer claimed that he "was high as a Georgia pine," and that the transaction "was just a bunch of two doggoned drunks bluffing to see who could talk the biggest and say the most." That claim is inconsistent with his attempt to testify in great detail as to what was said and what was done. It is contradicted by other evidence as to the condition of both parties, and rendered of no weight by the testimony of his wife that when Lucy left the restaurant she suggested that Zehmer drive him home. The record is convincing that Zehmer was not intoxicated to the extent of being unable to comprehend the nature and consequences of the instrument he executed, and hence that instrument is not to be invalidated on that ground. It was in fact conceded by defendants' counsel in oral argument that under the evidence Zehmer was not too drunk to make a valid contact.

The evidence is convincing also that Zehmer wrote two agreements, the first one beginning "I hereby agree to sell." Zehmer first said he could not remember about that, then that "I don't think I wrote but one out." Mrs. Zehmer said that what he wrote was "I hereby agree," but that "I" was changed to "We" after that night. The agreement that was written and signed is in the record and indicates no such change. Neither are the mistakes in spelling that Zehmer sought to point out readily apparent.

The appearance of the contract, the fact that it was under discussion for forty minutes or more before it was signed; Lucy's objection to the first draft because it was written in the singular, and he wanted Mrs. Zehmer to sign it also; the rewriting to meet that objection and the signing by Mrs. Zehmer; the discussion of what was to be included in the sale, the provision for the examination of the title, the completeness of the instrument that was executed, the taking possession of it by Lucy with no request or suggestion by either of the defendants that he give it back, are facts which furnish persuasive evidence that the execution of the contract was a serious business transaction rather than a casual, jesting matter as defendants now contend. . . .

If it be assumed, contrary to what we think the evidence shows, that Zehmer was jesting about selling his farm to Lucy and that the transaction was intended by him to be a joke, nevertheless the evidence shows that Lucy did not so understand it but considered it to be a serious business transaction and the contract to be binding on the Zehmers as well as on himself. The very next day he arranged with his brother to put up half the money and take a half interest in the land. The day after that he employed an attorney to examine the title. The next night, Tuesday, he was back at Zehmer's place and there Zehmer told him for the first time, Lucy said, that he wasn't going to sell and he told Zehmer, "You know you sold that place fair and square." After receiving the report from his attorney that the title was good he wrote to Zehmer that he was ready to close the deal.

Not only did Lucy actually believe, but the evidence shows he was warranted in believing that the contract represented a serious business transaction and a good faith sale and purchase of the farm.

In the field of contracts, as generally elsewhere, "We must look to the outward expression of a person as manifesting his intention rather than to his secret and unexpressed intention. 'The law imputes to a person an intention corresponding to the reasonable meaning of his words and acts.' "

At no time prior to the execution of the contract had Zehmer indicated to Lucy by word or act that he was not in earnest about selling the farm. They had argued about it and discussed its terms, as Zehmer admitted, for a long time. Lucy testified that if there was any jesting it was about paying $50,000 that night. The contract and the evidence show that he was not expected to pay the money that night. Zehmer said that after the writing was signed he laid it down on the counter in front of Lucy. Lucy said Zehmer handed it to him. In any event there had been what appeared to be a good faith offer and a good faith acceptance, followed by the execution and apparent delivery of a written contract. Both said that Lucy put the writing in his pocket and then offered Zehmer $5 to seal the bargain. Not until then, even under the defendants' evidence, was anything said or done to indicate that the matter was a joke. Both of the Zehmers testified that when Zehmer asked his wife to sign he whispered that it was a joke so Lucy wouldn't hear and that it was not intended that he should hear.

The mental assent of the parties is not requisite for the formation of a contract. If the words or other acts of one of the parties have but one reasonable meaning, his undisclosed intention is immaterial except when an unreasonable meaning which he attaches to his manifestations is known to the other party. ". . . The law, therefore, judges of an agreement between two persons exclusively from those expressions of their intentions which are communicated between them. . . ."

An agreement or mutual assent is of course essential to a valid contract, but the law imputes to a person an intention corresponding to the reasonable meaning of his words and acts. If his words and acts, judged by a reasonable standard, manifest an intention to agree, it is immaterial what may be the real but unexpressed state of his mind.

So a person cannot set up that he was merely jesting when his conduct and words would warrant a reasonable person in believing that he intended a real agreement.

Whether the writing signed by the defendants and now sought to be enforced by the complainants was the result of a serious offer by Lucy and a serious acceptance by the defendants, or was a serious offer by Lucy and an acceptance in secret jest by the defendants, in either event it constituted a binding contract of sale between the parties. . .

The complainants are entitled to have specific performance of the contract sued on. The decree appealed from is therefore reversed and the cause is remanded for the entry of a proper decree requiring the defendants to perform the contract in accordance with the prayer of the bill.

Reversed and remanded.

BARTON V. MITCHELL COMPANY
507 So. 2d 148 (Fla. Dist. Ct. App. 1987)

Fourth District Court of Appeal of Florida

WALDEN, Judge.

This is a landlord tenant action. Ms. Barton leased [the] premises for five years from the Mitchell Company for the purpose of operating a retail store selling patio furniture. The lease began on November 1, 1982. On August 3, 1985, Ms. Barton vacated the property. The landlord sued Ms. Barton, and following the non-jury trial, received judgment for $18,929.57, plus interest, basically representing rent to the date of the judgment and rent thereafter for the unexpired term. Ms. Barton appeals. We reverse based upon our view that the landlord breached a material provision of the lease to the end that Ms. Barton was constructively evicted from the premises.

The pertinent facts are not disputed.

In October or November of 1984, the landlord leased an adjacent space to Body Electric, which space adjoined Ms. Barton's space on two sides. Body Electric operated an exercise studio. Loud music, screams, shouts and yells accompanied the operation of Body Electric during business hours. The intensity and volume of such noise manifestly impacted upon the operation of Ms. Barton's business. It caused the walls to vibrate, and a painting to fall off the wall. It made it difficult, if not impossible, for Ms. Barton to conduct her business. She lost customers and salespersons because of the noise.

Ms. Barton complained over and over to the landlord. The landlord promised repeatedly to remedy the problem to include insulating the uninsulated party walls. The landlord did nothing in the period from October or November 1984 till August 3, 1985 when Ms. Barton vacated. On the same day and immediately following Ms. Barton's departure, the landlord undertook some measures to alleviate the noise problem. . . .

As we view it, the dispositive lease proviso is paragraph 40 entitled Quiet Enjoyment:

> Tenant, upon paying the rents and performing all of the terms on its part to be performed, shall peaceably and quietly enjoy the Demised Premises subject nevertheless, to the terms of this lease and to any mortgage, ground lease or agreements to which this lease is subordinated or specifically not subordinated as provided in Article 29(b) hereof.

When there is a constructive eviction such constitutes a breach of the covenant of quiet enjoyment. *Richards v. Dodge,* 150 So.2d 477 (Fla. 2d DCA 1963). A constructive eviction occurs when a tenant is essentially *deprived of the beneficial enjoyment of the leased premises where they are rendered unsuitable for occupancy for the purposes for which they are leased* (emphasis added). Hankins v. Smith, 103 Fla. 892, 138 So. 494 (1931).

Since this was a large shopping center, we assume, we hope correctly, that all leases were similar. In paragraph 11 of the printed lease, it was stated that, "nor shall tenant maintain any loud speaker device or any noise making device in such manner as to be audible to anyone not within the premises."

Thus, from our overview, we hold, according to the mentioned authorities, that Ms. Barton was constructively evicted from the premises at the time of her departure and, therefore, has no responsibility for rent thereafter. Here, the landlord was advised of the difficulty. The landlord acknowledged responsibility and agreed to remedy the situation and had the means to do so. The terms of the lease with reference to noise could have been enforced against Body Electric. The walls could have been insulated. Yet the landlord did nothing. Despite the damage to her business, Ms. Barton waited a reasonable time for the landlord to act.

The judgment on appeal is REVERSED.

ANSTEAD and DELL, JJ., concur.

BOULEVARD SHOPPES V. PRO-1 REALTY, INC.
605 So. 2d 1317 (Fla. Dist. Ct. App. 1992)

Fourth District Court of Appeal of Florida

PER CURIAM.

Boulevard Shoppes, the landlord, appeals a final order granting only partial relief in its suit against Pro-1 for breach of a lease agreement. We reverse.

The parties have agreed to a statement of the facts. On March 1, 1990, tenant moved into the premises. The tenant did not pay rent for the months of February, March and April of 1991 because of its dissatisfaction with the maintenance of the premises. The landlord gave the tenant notice to pay the rent or deliver possession of the property and the tenant moved.

The landlord sued to recover past due rent and common area maintenance. The landlord also sought acceleration of the remaining lease payments through the date the premises were re-rented, as permitted by the lease.

The tenant was ordered to pay rent only for the time it was in the premises and the time in which it failed to notify the landlord that it had left, February through June. The trial court did not assess attorney's fees and costs, although the lease required such payment to the prevailing landlord.

The tenant admits that it failed to pay rent and abandoned the premises, but asserts that it was entitled to do so because of its dissatisfaction with the manner in which the premises were maintained. However, we conclude that no constructive eviction is demonstrated on this record. An essential element of constructive eviction is an interference with the tenant's use and enjoyment of the premises. Therefore, the tenant is not relieved of further liability for the payment of rent for the unexpired term prior to re-renting.

Where a claim of constructive eviction is based on the landlord's need to make repairs, the tenant must give the landlord notice and opportunity to make repairs. If a needed repair does not render the premises untenantable, the tenant's abandonment of the premises is not warranted and the tenant is not relieved of further liability for rent.

The trial court determined that the tenant was excused from further rental payments due to its "dissatisfaction" with the premises. However, mere dissatisfaction which falls short of a constructive eviction does not relieve a tenant from its obligation to pay rent.

The record evidence of the tenant's dissatisfaction did not support a finding that a constructive eviction occurred. The tenant had complained that the roof leaked, but in the agreed statement of the case the tenant admitted that the leak was fixed and did not cause any damage. Therefore, the landlord did not fail to repair the roof and no constrictive [sic] eviction resulted. The tenant complained that the landlord did not hold a grand opening, but the tenant admitted in the agreed statement of the case that the lease did not require the landlord to have such an opening and that the landlord's oral offer to have the opening was conditioned on the tenant's payment for half of the costs. The tenant did not agree to pay for half the costs, and the landlord was never obligated to have the opening. Therefore, the failure to have the opening did not result in the tenant's constructive eviction. Lastly, the tenant complained that the landlord did not clean up beer cans and dog "deposits" in front of its door for several days. In another incident, ice cream was dropped near its door. These events did not render the premises untenantable or amount to a constructive eviction of the tenant. The landlord was entitled to, and did, correct the problems as they occurred. . . .

The final order is reversed and remanded for further proceedings.

GLICKSTEIN, C.J., and LETTS and STONE, JJ., concur.

HANKINS V. SMITH
103 Fla. 892, 138 So. 494 (1931)

Supreme Court of Florida

ANDREWS, C.

This is an action at law based upon a contract of lease in which action the lessee seeks to recover damages sustained as a result of fifteen months' eviction from premises on which he had a ten-year lease, . . .

The nearest approach to such a charge in the declaration against Smith is that it is alleged in substance that he conveyed the fee-simple title to the property to Roth, a "straw man," and placed him in possession and control, and said Roth was then and now insolvent and judgment proof, and shortly after being in control Roth tore the roof and two upper stories from over the leased drug store and caused the damages alleged, and that the defendant, Smith, by and through the said Alan Roth, thus evicted the plaintiff, etc.

Under proper allegations a lessee in possession may show that a conveyance of the leased premises was a mere "colorable sale," or formal transfer with no bona fide intent to permanently deed away the property, but was made merely for the purpose of ousting the lessee; . . .

In substance plaintiff argues that, the lease having been made in 1924, the great increase in value of the leased premises by 1925 caused a colorable sale of the fee title to a judgment proof grantee who by tearing down the upper two stories of the building tried to evict permanently the plaintiff lessee.

It could hardly be maintained that there is alleged an "actual" eviction. In fact it is noted from the declaration that the cause of action is apparently based upon a "constructive," rather than actual, eviction. A "constructive eviction" is an act which, although not amounting to an actual eviction, is done with the express or implied intention, and has the effect, of essentially interfering with the tenant's beneficial enjoyment of the leased premises. It may constitute a constructive eviction if the landlord does any wrongful act or is guilty of any default or neglect whereby the leased premises are rendered unsafe, unfit, or unsuitable for occupancy in while, or in substantial part, for the purposes for which they were leased. . . .

We find that the following principle as to implied covenants for quiet enjoyment are established in most of the other states: "While there was some difference of judicial opinion regarding the rule at an early time, it seems now to be established that, in the absence of an express covenant inconsistent therewith, the ordinary lease of realty raises an implied covenant that the lessee shall have the quiet and peaceable possession and enjoyment of the leased premises, so far as regards the lessor, . . . or anyone asserting a title to the leased premises superior and paramount to that of the lessor."

It can hardly be questioned that one of the most valid and indispensable elements of a lease for a term of years is the peaceful uninterrupted enjoyment of the premises leased; otherwise a lease, in most instances, might be of little or no value. However, there is not direct allegation in the declaration, nor can it be gathered from the declaration as a whole, except possibly by inference, that the acts complained of were instigated or sanctioned by the lessor, and unless it does so appear, the lessor cannot be held liable for the acts of his grantee after lessor had parted with his title and ownership, especially if the lessee continued to attorn thereafter to the new landlord; therefore it was not error to sustain defendant's demurrer. It appearing that error was not committed by the trial court in sustaining the demurrer, said judgment ought to be affirmed.

Judgment affirmed.

RICHARDS V. DODGE

150 So. 2d 477 (Fla. Dist. Ct. App. 1963)

Second District Court of Appeal of Florida

ALLEN, Judge. . . .

Plaintiff sued the defendants for nonpayment of rent pursuant to a written lease entered into between them for the period September 1, 1960, to August 1, 1961. The leased premises, an apartment house, were to be used as living quarters for girls attending the school owned by defendants. A two bedroom apartment, occupied by plaintiff at the time the lease was executed, was expressly excepted from the lease and reserved to plaintiff.

It was stipulated in advance of trial that rental payments for the months of May, June and July, 1961, totaling $3,270.00 were unpaid. Execution of the lease was also stipulated. . . .

It is undisputed that defendants executed the lease, went into possession of the premises and continued in possession until May 1, 1961. On that date they vacated the premises, although three months remained during which they were obligated under the lease. In answering the complaint for the unpaid rent for these three months, defendants alleged and attempted to prove that plaintiff, in vacating her apartment in January, 1961, violated a parol agreement to act as a "housemother" and, in leasing her apartment to a male tenant, constructively evicted defendants and breached the implied covenant of quiet enjoyment.

Plaintiff denied the existence of a parol agreement and contended that there had been no breach of covenant, or, if there was, that defendants were estopped to complain by virtue of the fact that the male tenant went into possession in early February, 1961, but that defendants, continued to pay rent through April and did not complain that the male tenant was offensive or give any notice of dissatisfaction until April 13, 1961—a little more than two weeks before vacating. Even this notice, a letter from defendants' attorney, merely announced defendants' unilateral rescission of the lease and did not state with any particularity the facts constituting the supposed breach of covenant. Apparently, after receiving the letter, plaintiff did ascertain by phone that the male tenant's presence was the cause of rescission.

On complaint, answer and counterclaim, the case went to trial before the judge without a jury. Judgment was entered for defendants on plaintiff's complaint. Plaintiff's motion for new trial, or amended judgment, was denied and this appeal taken. . . .

Turning to the merits of the appeal, it appears that two real issues are presented, the validity of the finding of a constructive eviction and the validity of the finding that defendants had not waived their rights arising from the breach of covenant occasioned by the constructive eviction. . . .

As indicated earlier, the lower court apparently found that plaintiff-appellant, in vacating her apartment and/or leasing it to a male tenant, constructively evicted defendant-appellees. A "constructive eviction," as distinct from actual eviction, is an act, which, though not amounting to actual eviction, is done with the express or implied intent of essentially interfering with the tenant's use and enjoyment of the premises. The requisite intent can be implied or presumed from the act's effect. Hankins v. Smith, 1931, 103 Fla. 892, 138 So. 494. Generally, abandonment of the premises within a reasonable time after the landlord's wrongful act is a necessary element of constructive eviction. Constructive eviction can constitute a breach of the covenant of quiet enjoyment implied in a lease.

Insofar as plaintiff's alleged violation of a parol agreement to act as housemother is concerned, it seems clear that this, as a matter of fact or law, could not constitute a constructive eviction as heretofore defined—and that such rights as may have accrued to defendants by virtue of the alleged violation were unquestionably waived.

The record reveals that defendants were dissatisfied with plaintiff's activities as housemother, felt her incompetent in this respect and secured a replacement even before plaintiff vacated her apartment. This replacement continued in the capacity of housemother after the premises were vacated and new quarters secured. Accordingly, it would seem clear that plaintiff's alleged failure did not so impair the use of the premises as to constitute constructive eviction. The record further reveals that at some time after the replacement was secured, defendants and plaintiff reached an agreement whereby the monthly rent was reduced to offset defendants' expenses in securing maid and cleaning service. The record does not indicate that defendants objected to plaintiff's vacating her apartment or complained of this until this suit was filed. . . .

Defendant-appellees having so failed, the trial judge's entry of judgment for them was error, and is reversed for entry of judgment in favor of the plaintiff-appellant.

Reversed.

KAPLAN v. McCABE
532 So. 2d 1354 (Fla. Dist. Ct. App. 1988)

Fifth District Court of Appeal of Florida

COBB, Judge.

This appeal involves the question of whether a three-day notice to pay rent or quit can constitute a constructive eviction.

Appellant (Kaplan) and appellee (McCabe) agreed to be equal owners of a bingo hall to be located in warehouse owned by Kaplan.[1] The business was designated Marto Enterprises, Inc. A lease agreement was executed between the parties[2] on September 26, 1985, and was to commence on October 1, 1985, continuing for a period of five years. . . .

On December 2, 1985, a letter was mailed to McCabe explaining that the rent for the months of November and December was past due and that pursuant to the lease, if the rent was not paid within five days, a ten percent penalty would be assessed.[3]

The bingo hall opened for business on December 7, 1985, but apparently did not do well during the first two weeks of operation. Subsequently, Kaplan and McCabe discussed the rent, and McCabe stated he did not have the money. On December 20, 1985, a "3-DAY NOTICE TO PAY RENT OR QUIT" was delivered to Marto Enterprises demanding Marto Enterprises pay the November and December rent or surrender possession. On December 25, 1985, a letter was sent from McCabe stating that his records revealed that rent was not past due for the bingo hall. By January 6, 1986, McCabe had vacated the leased premises.

Kaplan filed a complaint against Marto Enterprises and Mr. and Mrs. McCabe individually, alleging among other things a breach of the lease. McCabe filed a counterclaim alleging breach of contract and unjust enrichment. . . .

The Florida Supreme Court has recognized and defined the constructive eviction defense in *Hankins v. Smith*, 103 Fla. 892, 138 So. 494, 495 (1931).

> A "constructive eviction" is an act which although not amounting to an actual eviction, is done with the express or implied intention, and has the effect, of essentially interfering with the tenant's beneficial enjoyment of the leased premises.

1. As trustee for Northpark Commerce Center.
2. Marto Enterprises, Inc. was the designated tenant.
3. Apparently, a letter requesting November's rent had been sent but was never received by McCabe.

Under *Hankins,* constructive eviction arises out of a wrongful act by the land-lord "whereby the leased premises are rendered unsafe, unfit, or unsuitable for occupancy in whole, or in substantial part, for the purposes for which they were leased." 138 So. at 496.

In *McCready v. Booth,* 398 So. 2d 1000, 1001 (Fla. 5th DCA 1981) this court cited with approval *Sentry Water Systems, Inc. v. Adca Corp.,* 355 So. 2d 1255, 1257 (Fla. 2d DCA 1978):

> Underlying or implicit in all decisions is that the act of the landlord constituting the constructive eviction be wrongful, unwarranted, or unlawful. Eviction, whether actual or constructive, to be actionable must be wrongful.

. . . The majority view among the various jurisdictions in regard to a notice to quit is stated in 14 A.L.R.2d 1450, 1451 (1950):

> There is some authority to the contrary, but the prevailing view would seem to be that a mere notice to the tenant to quit, followed by his vacation of the premises, is not of itself sufficient to constitute an eviction and give the tenant a right to damages. The theory being that to constitute a constructive eviction there must be some substantial interference which is injurious to the tenant's beneficial use and enjoyment of the premises.

In the instant action, Kaplan presented McCabe with a "NOTICE TO PAY RENT OR QUIT" pursuant to section 83.20(2), Florida Statutes (1985). . . .

The notice to pay rent or quit was not proper or legally sufficient, because the rent became due when the lease commenced on November 15, 1985. This first month's rent was prepaid by McCabe. A demand for rent due must be made by the landlord or his agent, of the exact amount due, on the date it is due. While mistaken information contained in a "notice" made in the good faith belief that it is true information may, in some instances, make the notice legally insufficient, the notice should not take on greater importance than the "technical defect" which it represents.

In *Hankins,* it was stated that the wrongful conduct on the part of the landlord must be done with the express or implied intention of interfering with a tenant's beneficial enjoyment of the leased premises. The facts of this action make it clear that a notice to pay rent or quit, standing alone and without other coercive or abusive-type conduct on the part of the landlord, cannot serve as a basis for constructive eviction.

A notice to pay rent or quit does not give rise to a presumption that the landlord *intends* that the tenant should no longer enjoy the premises. When a landlord requests that a tenant *pay rent,* just the opposite is true. The presumption is that the landlord wishes the tenant to continue to enjoy and occupy the premises. Any other interpretation would permit a tenant who desires to avoid a lease obligation to do so when a demand for rent contains any technical defect such as the wrong date or an incorrect amount of money. . . .

Reversed and remanded for further proceedings.

BERMUDA AVENUE SHOPPING CENTER ASSOCIATES V. RAPPAPORT
565 So. 2d 805 (Fla. Dist. Ct. App. 1990)

Fifth District Court of Appeal of Florida

DANIEL, Chief Judge.

Bermuda Avenue Shopping Center Associates, L.P. (landlord) appeals a final judgment in favor of Moe and Joe Rappaport (tenants) in an action for breach of a lease agreement. The landlord contends that the trial court erred in finding that the tenants had been constructively evicted. The landlord also argues that the evidence does not support the award of $15,000 in damages to the tenants. We find no error and affirm.

The tenants leased space in a shopping mall from the landlord to use as an indoor golf arcade. The lease was signed in May, 1987. The lease term was to commence 45 days later as the tenants wanted to be open for business by the July 4th weekend. The tenants were aware that the landlord intended to do away with an exterior wall in the mall but were not told about any other plans for renovations.

According to the tenants, the premises were not ready for occupancy until July 22, 1987, and even then the landlord had failed to properly finish the floors and to provide electrical outlets and a sprinkler system. In any event, from July 23 until August 18, the arcade was busy. On August 18, the renovation of the mall began in front of the arcade. According to the tenants, their store sign was taken down, there were debris and dust in front of the store, the sidewalks and parking spaces in front of the store were taken away and their business "died." The tenants closed their arcade on September 30 and testified that they would never have signed the lease had they been informed that the mall was about to undergo a complete renovation.

The following month, the tenants filed suit against the landlord, alleging in part that they had been constructively evicted. The landlord counterclaimed for breach of the lease, seeking lost rental income as part of its damages. The trial court found in favor of the tenants on their claim and against the landlord on its counterclaim.

A "constructive eviction" is an act which, although not amounting to an actual eviction, is done with the expressed or implied intention and has the effect of essentially interfering with the tenant's beneficial enjoyment of the leased premises. *Hankins v. Smith*, 103 Fla. 892, 138 So. 494 (1931); *Kaplan v. McCabe*, 532 So. 2d 1354 (Fla. 5th DCA 1988). Under *Hankins*, constructive eviction arises out of a wrongful act by the landlord "whereby the leased premises are rendered unsafe, unfit, or unsuitable for occupancy in whole or in substantial part, for the purposes for which they are leased." *Kaplan*, 532 So. 2d at 1356, *quoting Hankins*, 138 So. at 496.

The evidence in the present case supports the determination that the tenants were constructively evicted. The tenants' accountant testified that their business made a net profit from its opening until renovation of the mall began, and that a net profit was unusual for a new business. After the renovation, however, the business suffered a net loss. The tenants' employee testified that the business went from 200 customers per day to 20 to 15 customers per day. Other witnesses testified that the stores near the construction appeared as though they were closed and that the parking spaces and sidewalks near the stores had been eliminated. There was also evidence of dirt, dust, and debris from the construction which affected the stores. The tenants testified that they complained about the situation without relief and then finally closed their business. Since the evidence supports a determination that renovation of the mall rendered the premises unsafe, unfit, and unsuitable for the tenants' occupancy, the trial court was correct in entering judgment for the tenants and against the landlord. . . .

AFFIRMED.

STINSON, LYONS, GERLIN & BUSTAMANTE V. BRICKELL BUILDING 1 HOLDING COMPANY
923 F.2d 810 (11th Cir. 1991)

United States Court of Appeals, Eleventh Circuit

JOHNSON, Circuit Judge:

This case arises on an expedited appeal of the district court's finding that the plaintiff Stinson, Lyons, Gerlin & Bustamante ("the Tenant") had not been constructively evicted from its leasehold by its landlord.

I. STATEMENT OF THE CASE

A. Background Facts

The Tenant is a general practice law firm with sixteen attorneys and approximately fifty-five total employees. Its offices are located in a fourteen-story professional office tower at 1401 Brickell Avenue in Miami, Florida. In March of 1973, the tenant entered into the Lease at issue for a period of ten years. The Lease granted the Tenant two successive five-year options to renew. On June 1, 1988, the Tenant exercised its final option, renewing the Lease until May 31, 1993. At the time the Tenant exercised this option, it had leased all of the ninth floor and part of the eighth floor.

When the Lease was originally negotiated, the building provided its tenants with first-class amenities in a prestigious location. In the ensuing eighteen years, however, the building and its support systems gradually deteriorated. Because of advances in technology and revisions in the applicable codes, the building did not contain the state-of-the-art health, safety, and amenity features offered by newer buildings in the area. The Landlord found itself losing tenants to competitors. At the time of the trial, the building contained only four tenants and only twenty percent of its space was occupied. Faced with this situation, the Landlord decided to renovate the building and upgrade both its appearance and its mechanical systems in an effort to attract additional tenants.

In late March or early April of 1989, the Landlord informed the Tenant of its renovation plan. The following renovations and repairs had the greatest impact on the Tenant's demised premises:[2] (1) installation of a fire sprinkler system on each floor, except the Tenant's, and pressurization of the fire stairs; (2) removal of asbestos on each floor, except the Tenant's; (3) replacement of the existing plaza; (4) enclosure of a walkway connecting the building to the garage; (5) replacement of the exterior curtain wall with a new curtain wall; (6) replacement of the air-conditioning cooling towers and chillers; and (7) installation of high pressure air-conditioning ducts on each floor, except the Tenant's.[3]

Without question the most controversial renovation was the Landlord's plan to replace the existing pre-cast concrete exterior curtain walls and windows with new curtain walls and windows. This replacement necessitated exposing the Tenant's exterior offices to the open environment. According to the plan, each wall was to be replaced over a single week-end. The removal of the pre-cast concrete panels would require the removal of two feet of the Tenant's ceiling at the perimeter of the building. All partition walls separating the Tenant's offices were to be cut back either one or two feet from the perimeter as well. The carpet in each perimeter office was to be rolled back at least two feet. At least four feet of clear working space was to be needed in each office, necessitating the removal or relocation of the Tenant's furniture and files in order to accomplish the wall replacement. The Tenant's walls and ceilings were to be restored no later than the conclusion of the following weekend. The offices were to be fully useable, however, during the intervening week.

The Landlord proposed various options to accommodate the Tenant during the renovation including: (1) building out renovated space above the Tenant's floors and moving the Tenant to that new space, all at the Landlord's expense, with the Tenant free to depart at the end of the lease term or to negotiate a new lease; (2) paying the Tenant's moving expenses to a comparable office building nearby and paying any rental increase for the duration of the Tenant's lease term;[4] or, (3) allowing the Tenant to terminate the Lease with a cash payment from the Landlord of $350,000. The Tenant rejected all of these options and decided to move into a new building on its own by December 1, 1990.[5] . . .

The following issues are raised in this appeal: (1) whether the lease authorized the Landlord to undertake the challenged renovations and repairs without liability to the Tenant; (2) whether the Landlord has constructively evicted the Tenant from the premises; and (3) whether the district court erred in refusing to admit additional testimonial and videotape evidence after the close of evidence.

---

2.   The renovation also included gutting and renovating each floor, other than the Tenant's. The Landlord also planned to renovate the elevators, reconstruct and expand the penthouse floors, and pour new footings for the building. It is undisputed that the renovations planned will result in the virtual reconstruction of the building from its skeleton.

3.   To accommodate the Tenant, the Landlord agreed to forgo installing fire sprinklers and air conditioning ducts and removing asbestos from the Tenant's floor.

4.   The Landlord provided the Tenant with a list of five buildings from which to select new office space.

5.   At oral argument on December 19, 1990, however, the Tenant informed the Court that it continued to occupy the premises at issue in this litigation.

II. ANALYSIS . . .

B. Constructive Eviction

The district court held that the Tenant failed to prove constructive eviction. The Tenant argues, however, that because of their scope and intrusiveness, the renovations rise to the level of a constructive eviction as a matter of law.

In *Hankins,* 138 So. at 496, the Florida Supreme Court defined a constructive eviction as a wrongful act by the landlord which, though not amounting to an actual eviction, is done with the express or implied intention of interfering with the tenant's beneficial enjoyment of the leased property. For the landlord to be liable for the act allegedly causing the constructive eviction, the act must be "wrongful, unwarranted, or unlawful." *Sentry Water Systems, Inc. v. Adca Corp.,* 355 So. 2d 1255, 1257 (Fla. Dist. Ct. App. 1978); *accord McCready v. Booth,* 398 So. 2d 1000, 1001 (Fla. Dist. Ct. App. 1981). To establish a claim for constructive eviction, Florida law generally requires a tenant to abandon the premises within a reasonable time after the landlord's wrongful act. *Richards v. Dodge,* 150 So. 2d 477, 481 (Fla. Dist. Ct. App. 1963). Whether constructive eviction has occurred is a question of fact. *Sentry,* 355 So. 2d at 480.

In the instant case, the Landlord has committed no wrongful act. The Lease authorizes the renovations, and the district court specifically found that the Landlord undertook the renovations for economic reasons and not to evict the Tenant. Moreover, the Tenant has continued to occupy the premises despite the renovations which have occurred to this point. The Tenant also testified that it had been able to operate its law firm at more than ninety percent capacity. Accordingly, the district court's finding that there was no constructive eviction is not clearly erroneous. *See Hardwick,* 363 S.E. 2d at 34 (holding that renovations contractually authorized by the lease do not amount to a constructive eviction). . . .

III. CONCLUSION

Upon close scrutiny of the record, we are left with the impression that the Tenant, by this litigation, is attempting to take advantage of the Landlord's economic need to renovate its building in order to obtain premises superior to those it currently enjoys.[8] Apparently dissatisfied with the options offered to it by the Landlord, the Tenant chose to litigate in hopes of securing a better deal. Commercial tenants are frequently confronted with their landlord's need to renovate the property of which the demised premises are a part in order to maintain its economic viability. Such tenants cannot expect to hold hostage contractually authorized renovations as a means of securing superior premises.

In closing, we concur with the district court that the Lease authorizes all the work covered by the renovations and that the Landlord has done its best to minimize the noise, inconvenience, and disruption to the Tenant's law business. Accordingly, this Court AFFIRMS the decision of the district court.

---

8.   As an item of damages, the Tenant sought payment from the Landlord for the differences in rent between its current premises and its proposed premises which are located in a recently constructed office building with state-of-the-art facilities and mechanical systems.

Index

Index